Date Due

FEB 4			
FEB 25			
JAN 5			
JAN 20			
APR 24			
JAN 18			
APR 13			
APR 26			
FEB 27			
DEC 15			
MAR 30			
APR 27			
JAN 10			
DEC 27 2006			
FEB 19 2010			
®	PRINTED	IN U. S. A.	

MAN
AND
HIS HAPPINESS

THE THEOLOGY LIBRARY

The translation of the entire library
is under the direction of the Rev.
Louis J. Putz, C.S.C., University
of Notre Dame

THEOLOGY LIBRARY—VOLUME III

MAN
AND
HIS HAPPINESS

By a group of theologians
under the editorship of
A. M. Henry, O.P.

Translated by Charles Miltner, C.S.C.

Fides Publishers Association
Chicago, Illinois

Library of Congress Catalog Card Number: 56-11631

NIHIL OBSTAT:
Albert L. Schlitzer, C.S.C., S.T.D.
University of Notre Dame

IMPRIMATUR:
✠ Leo A. Pursley, D.D., Apostolic
Administrator of the Diocese of
Fort Wayne, Indiana

NIHIL OBSTAT:
Parisiis, die 19a *dec.* 1952
Th. Camelot, O.P.
Stud. reg. in Fac. "Le Saulchoir"
J. Tonneau, O.P.
Mag. in S. Theol.

IMPRIMI POTEST:
Parisiis, die 19a *dec.* 1952
A.-M. Avril, O.P.
Prior prov.

IMPRIMATUR:
Parisiis, die 19a *dec.* 1952
M. Potevin
Vic. gen.

Published originally by Les Editions du Cerf, 29,
Boulevard Latour-Maubourg, Paris 7, France

COPYRIGHT: Fides Publishers Association
Chicago, Illinois, 1956

Manufactured by American Book–Stratford Press, Inc., New York
55

Faithfully Dedicated

to

Our Lady Immaculate

PLAN OF THE THEOLOGY LIBRARY

VOLUME THREE

Man and His Happiness

CONTENTS

ORIGINALITY OF ST. THOMAS

by M. D. Chenu, O.P.

Morality and the Gospels

The arrangement of the contents of the Word of God into an organic science is an undertaking as difficult as it is rewarding. But if it is a question of thus converting to the sacred "science" of theology, not only the truths to be believed in this revelation, but the moral behaviors which this revelation inspires in the grace of the Spirit, then the undertaking seems paradoxical. Even more than in a realm of human values, it appears in the spontaneous personal relations of God with the soul, at the point where life and action are dependent, that rational concepts and laws cannot contain the irreducible originality of action and of life.

Anyone can prove this paradox by making a comparison of the Gospels and the *II^a Pars,* called the moral part of St. Thomas' *Summa Theologiae.* How can the one come from the other? Vocabulary, literary form, repeated quotations from pagan moralists rather than from Christian spiritual writers, absence of reference to the experiences of the saints, strict arrangement of definitions and proofs, continual rationalization, reduction of evangelic inspirations to objective rules, almost complete absence of a Christian economy developed into a sacred history: all this leads to a spiritual uprooting which our fervor, curious about its faith, overcomes with difficulty.

As a matter of fact, the history of moral theology seems to reveal the continual defeat of such an effort. Suggestive and prolific as the history of spiritualities is, so the history of speculative morality is chaotic and distressing. True, the great centuries of the early Church, with dogmatic definitions of truths of faith defined in the Councils, show an admirable flowering of catechetical instruction and development but show nothing in moral "science" because that would have appeared as a remnant of pagan wisdom. Was St. Thomas, the great master of theology, able to manage in the homogeneous scientific

fabric of the *Summa* a science of morality which respects the originality of its object without disrupting either the doctrinal or the
sacred character of the *doctrina sacra*, as he called theology?

We believe that St. Thomas succeeded in this task, and that in it
he surpassed his masters (Albert the Great and, among the Fathers,
Augustine) and his contemporaries (Bonaventure), for it is in this
sphere particularly that he is original. The originality of this success
appears, alas, even in the distressing failure of most of the moralists
who succeeded him. His moral theology has scarcely survived except in fragments.

The originality of St. Thomas' moral theological structure first
appears in the structure of his *Summa*. Most of his contemporaries
find a place for the moral topic of Christian doctrine only by means
of a rather brief incident; while reading the Treatise on the Incarnation they ask this question: "Did Christ possess the virtues of faith,
hope and charity, besides the cardinal virtues of justice, fortitude,
prudence and temperance?"—and thereupon enters the study of the
mechanics of virtue.

Such was the arrangement of topics in the outline of Peter Lombard's *Liber Sententiarum*, the universal plan of instruction in the
13th century, and even well into the 14th century. It was a very significant arrangement for this collector of tradition, when we remember that, for the early Doctors of the Church, morality did not
figure in their doctrinal (even conciliar) teaching, but stimulated
only exhortatory writings. The burden of that cumbersome arrangement, even in Peter Lombard, still lay heavy on the theology of
the 13th century. Unquestionably (and this was the great advantage
of the arrangement), virtues and faults appeared in strict connection
with the Christian economy and with the person of Christ; but
objective analysis of their structures, of their profundities, of their
techniques, could not at that time realize all rational demands. St.
Thomas is still a prisoner of this arrangement in his youthful work,
Commentary on the Sentences, which does not group the part of
morality in its proper place.

If, on the strength of this fact, we observe that in this same
period the high doctrinal value of the masters of sanctity (such as
St. Bernard) was expressed in works placed outside theological
teaching, framework and attitudes, we see how deep is the schism
now centuries old between morality and spirituality, between sacred
moral science objectively structured and empirical induction from

personal experience. The division of the subject matter alone into the three parts of the *Summa* unified under the great theme of descent from and return to God—a philosophic and religious classic —demonstrates by itself the interior dynamic of the moral science in the understanding and development of the economy of salvation.

From the very beginning of his masterpiece, the *Summa,* St. Thomas establishes this unity: theology is the most synthesized of the sciences; it is the only one which rises above the dichotomy so natural and painful for man between knowing and doing. This is why it is a "wisdom," rather than a science. But being a "wisdom" does not make it veer toward a divine experimentalism, which would be neither speculative nor practical in the manner in which moral philosophy is itself practical. This solution, current under various forms (in such contemporaries as Albert the Great and Bonaventure), and still surviving in a larval state in present-day teaching, is rejected by St. Thomas. Imitating poorly, perhaps, but truly the behavior of God, sacred doctrine is for St. Thomas consummated in a supreme unity where contemplation and action, contrary to our earthly tensions, complement one another in a coherent whole. It gives thus an impression of one divine science according to which God knows Himself and all that He effects. It is the science of salvation, therefore, with the tension which salvation implies in Christ and in us, but a science nevertheless. Cf. Ia, q. 1, a. 3-6.

The gap between dogmatic and moral theology—terms unknown to St. Thomas—which is currently stretched into the false autonomies of asceticism and mysticism, of spiritual, pastoral, casuistic, and charismatic theology, testifies to the collapse of this supremacy.

The efficacy of this lofty concept is revealed from the first page of the Thomistic undertaking which begins with the Treatise on Happiness. At that time the Christian doctrine of beatitude appeared in previous works only as a special chapter on "last ends" (*De Novissimis*). Now it becomes the key and the keystone of the whole structure. We shall see presently, in this work, the tremendous bearing of this innovation on the spiritual architecture of a theology of human action: of human action in general and all human actions in particular.

The strength of this architecture appears in a curious way in the unexpected meeting, for the purpose of defining this happiness, of the great evangelic theme of the beatific vision and of the rational principle of man's last end, by which Aristotle begins his *Ethics*. From now on, from start to finish, the principal reason and rule of Christian morality is fixed and exercised under the light of faith and within theological discipline.

Just as in the speculative elaboration of the Word of God faith engenders theology according to the same structures of reason which it assumes, and thus, with the necessary discretion according to all the techniques which it approximates—such as conceptual partition, multiplicity of analyses, definitions and divisions, classifications, inferences, reasonings—, so also in the theological science of human action faith engenders practical judgments and effective behaviors according to the same structures of reason, and, therefore, with the discretion which freedom of the Spirit imposes and according to all the techniques which it involves. The balance of this morality, at once wholly religious and wholly rational, is the ideal characteristic of this kind of science. The analytic apparatus in which the proceedings of St. Thomas develop, especially in proportion as it reaches to the least detail of the virtues, is at first confusing. We perceive however that it eventually serves the synthetic and concrete unity of action, and, in action, unity of nature and of grace.

At the heart of this original analysis of "virtues," which the precepts apply, and not vice-versa, contrary to the ever menacing legalisms,[1] there is, as a characteristic example, the virtue of prudence. How St. Thomas conceives this masterpiece of morality, so delicate yet so powerful, will be told in the course of the *Theology Library*. Henceforth, according to the purpose of this preface, let us point out its originality while stating that it has almost completely disappeared, at least in architectonic value, from manuals of modern theology as well as from the summary voluntarism of ascetic treatises.

But are we not decidedly far from the Gospels, even in the meaning of the words? Does not evolution, even of the word prudence, in the language of man and in its mediocre significance, underline a kind of belittling in connection with the heroism of sanctity? Does not this originality of the theology of action in St. Thomas place him by this exaggerated intellectualism outside the spiritual giants?

Words have their destiny, a destined fate which, perhaps irreversi-

[1] How different this is from theology texts and catechisms that are built on the enumeration of precepts! In St. Thomas, precepts are taken into consideration at the end of each treatise on virtue.

ble, denounces in any case the change which has been wrought on a theology where the treatise on "conscience," with its famous "systems of morality," has become the bone of contention. Even if not fruitless and unreasonable, this inversion has at the very least jeopardized the major role of prudence, which is the instrument of Divine Reason in us. It is a role truly filled with Biblical strength and Christian experiences, from Cassian to St. Francis de Sales, thanks to which the virtuous man is the living example of his deeds and the Christian is free in the freedom of the Spirit. The *II^a Pars* of the *Summa Theologiae* gives us a definition of this sanctity.[2]

[2] Without other bibliography, inopportune for this simple preface, mention should be made of the work of Fr. Th. Deman, *Aux origines de la théologie morale* (Montréal-Paris, 1951), whose aim is precisely that of placing the morality of St. Thomas in the history of Christian thought.

Introduction

AT THE THRESHOLD OF THE *SECUNDA PARS:* [1]
MORALITY AND THEOLOGY

by J. Tonneau, O.P.

Admission into the Church will never come without a change of moral habits. While the catechumens were being taught the mysteries of faith, set forth in symbolic form, certain rules of conduct were prescribed for them and they were warned against the dissoluteness of pagan society. In this respect, the catechist found his sources in Holy Scripture, where numerous moral precepts are to be found, joined to pedagogic exhortations and to examples capable of inciting imitation from the faithful.

The letters of the Apostles and bishops to the various churches and the sermons and homilies readily discussed moral problems when the occasion arose. Certain documents like the *Didache,* The *Pastor* of Hermas, letters from Clement of Rome, show a special liking for this kind of exhortation. For we must agree that these texts, strictly dependent on circumstances, did not claim to outline a moral science; they answered concrete difficulties, they aimed at touching and winning over men of good will. It also is a fact that the first Christian pastors, undeceived about the artful and inefficacious considerations which delighted the pagan moralists, were not inclined to scientific speculations in the field of morals. Before the overwhelming transformations wrought in souls by the grace of the Holy Spirit, they did not avoid a certain pragmatism, a touch of anticlericalism. The Fathers of the Church ridiculed for a long time, as spiritual men will always attempt to do, those who discuss, define, analyze, and who exhaust themselves pondering over laws and the Christian life, perhaps without leading Christian lives.

It is not astonishing to see the scientific effort of Christian thought, applying itself first to the truths of faith, leave moral considerations to the fate of an immediately practical character, e.g., statements of

[1] See "Synopsis of the Summa Theologiae of St. Thomas Aquinas," "Second Part of the Second Part," Theology Library, volume I, p. 276.

discipline, rules for certain states of life (penitents, virgins, widows, etc.), persuasive discourses and pastoral exhortations. The first great ecumenical councils were interested in the definitions of dogma. It is true that the mysteries of the Trinity, the Incarnation and Grace concern Christian morals in a real way; the Fathers, however, thought less, in these solemn council meetings, of the moral reverberations of the mysteries than of the scrupulous accuracy of their definition according to Christian faith.

Thus, theology's first steps moved towards dogmatic precision. And when theology acquired a scientific status, by virtue of its origins, it still retained a rather speculative character and a preference for theoretical considerations of truths of faith.

Except in quite recent times, we cannot speak of a dogmatic theology and of a moral theology. During the first centuries of the Church, theology centered on dogmatic truths. In proportion as Christian thought developed by the light of God, it utilized more and more consciously and methodically the philosophical tools inherited from antiquity, all the while perfecting them. Thus God's plan of the divine mysteries showed more clearly their ineffable source and their marvelous order.

During this time a Christian morality was born without any evident bond with this theology. It was very concerned with its own originality and responded to the exigencies of the new life opened up by Christ with its characteristic themes—unknown to the ancient sages—of universal charity, humility, penance, virginity and poverty. If, for the understanding of faith, Christian thought accepted the services of rhetoric, logic, science, philosophy, it might be said that in matters of morals neither the Academy, nor Porticus, nor Epicurus, nor even the religious gravity of a Cicero, could be of any help to a disciple of Jesus Christ. The wisdom of the pagans was deemed sheer folly at the price of evangelic simplicity, and their pretended virtues either pure pride or hypocrisy. Or else, according to a strange process, already used by Philo, man thought he could recognize in the beauties and moral truths admired in Homer, Plato, Virgil or Seneca, a few crumbs which had fallen from the table of the Lord, a few pearls hidden in the treasure of Revelation.

But this attempt itself shows sufficiently that Christian morals could not escape the effort of reflection and of scientific elaboration in Christian society. Indeed the solution of cases of conscience on the level of daily practice aroused research. At the Council of

Jerusalem, concerning the burden of Judaic observance; in the letters of St. Paul, regarding the eating of fleshmeat consecrated to idols, or behavior in regard to a public sinner; through the centuries in the presence of cases of conscience posed by fallen-away Catholics, in the administrations of the sacraments, in relations with authority as represented by the public treasury, the army, barbarian royal houses; before the problems and scandals of wealth and of misery, of games or of business, moral values needed to be analyzed and principles of Christian conduct needed to be established. Even the first sketches of theological synthesis (which we have said were concerned primarily with truths to be believed), did not reject all moral considerations, e.g., notably so in Clement of Alexandria and Origen. This movement was increased in the course of centuries with the great works of St. Ambrose, St. Augustine and St. Gregory.

However, the setting forth of a moral Christian doctrine is one thing, and a *Secunda Pars* introducing moral considerations in their necessary and organic place in a scientific theology without a break in method or ambiguity of object is quite another. In order to appreciate the exact range of this remark, it would be necessary to measure the road traveled by theology from its origins up to St. Thomas Aquinas. This progress had nothing of the inevitable in it. If it was inevitable that a Christian society should work out a more and more premeditated and methodical moral doctrine on the different levels of ecclesiastical teaching, an exceptional concurrence of circumstances was needed for this moral doctrine to fit into a theological synthesis; also there was no guarantee that the result achieved would be permanent. We even dare to suggest that the insertion of moral considerations into the unity of theology supposes so just and so lofty a conception of this science, so fine a balance in the order of these parts, that, in all probability, the teaching methods current in the schools would be unable to remain at this level. Not only does the *Summa Theologiae* of St. Thomas constitute a complete success on this point, but we must recognize that many minds have been able to read and comment on this work without suspecting the originality of it and without measuring its range!

By its practical character, Christian morality appeals to all intellects and offers a subject matter abundant enough and complex enough to justify a special study, in which we will try to organize (in view of the ends proper to the moralist) a practical science of Christian morals. Requirements or routines of university teaching, modern bent for specialization, professional distortion, all push in the same direction, and that is why, under the name of moral theology, we have seen a distinct discipline come into being and flourish.

We do not propose to write an introduction to this moral theology, but rather to point out, in line with the thought of St. Thomas, the place of moral considerations in theology. Not that we want to condemn present day methods in the name of a strict and archaic Thomism or to underestimate in the least the admirable works and the undeniable progress effected more recently. Given the fact that from the Introduction to Volume I, the *Theology Library* has deliberately placed itself in the school of St. Thomas, there is no question of an optional classification, more or less elegant or convenient. This choice is also dictated by a sound conception of theology, a science formally one and indivisible in its object and its method. In addition, quite far from harming the strict quiddity of moral studies, this choice adds a dimension of theological wisdom which controls them and affirms their certitude.

I. Place of Moral Considerations in Theology

It may seem excessive to speak of an indivisible unity with respect to a Summa which the author composed in three parts. Among these, there need be a criterion of judgment, a distinction, which implies at least a relative multiplicity and opposition. That there is a characteristic feature in the *Secunda Pars* which is lacking in the *Prima* and in the *Tertia Pars* we shall not deny. But, since this objection did not escape St. Thomas, let us examine the answer he gave to it. He recognized that the arguments relative to the existence of God, Providence and divine Government are legitimately studied in a special science called theodicy; that the nature of happiness, the order of virtues, the legal system belong to the practical science called moral philosophy. It does not follow that theology must be a collection of treatises composed of various disciplines. Strictly speaking, human beatitude as seen by the moralist is not the same object as human beatitude seen by the theologian. Any object (*ob-jicio*) is something to be had, to be known, to be loved, etc. For theology, as for the sciences or for faith, objects are conceived as objects to be known; they are thus formally distinguished as such, i.e., according to that which they appear to be to the intellect. Thus, objectivity is a formal thing; it is a relative and characteristic property of realities and phenomena in so far as they make themselves known and in the light in which they are known.

1. In the light in which they are known: this phrase describes the light under which objects are made intelligible. In theology, it is a question of the supernatural light of faith which brings our intellects to a sharing in the supremely intelligible truth which is the Divine Essence. There is no doubt but that theological knowledge is a supernatural knowledge whose principle is faith, and, through faith, the very thought of God.

2. But we are posing a second condition: *in so far as the objects make themselves known.* This condition determines the morality and the direction taken by the objects considered under a certain light (scientific, philosophical, theological). Unless we are mistaken, the distinct way for an object to take a certain attitude and to hold itself under a specific light commonly receives less attention in moral theology. Whereas we would maintain that every consideration having some bearing on morality, once seen under the supernatural light of faith, is part of the groundwork of moral theology.

It is according to their scientific order that things come to the attention of the scholar. Likewise, in the light of faith, the most diverse realities are ordered and unified by relation to that which is the only object of divine thought, the divine Essence. In the absence of this, the object would not concern faith. We may indeed consider morality without being a theologian; then we will see it not only in another light, but otherwise disposed and ordered. Without going into theology, one can be a moralist, even a Christian moralist, concerned about supernatural realities which are vital for the morality of the Christian because revealed by faith; but if we stop there, we will not have complied with the exigencies of the theological method.

Such is the impression left by many recent attempts to organize according to a new order what we believe may be called moral theology. In reality these attempts consider and order their subject matter from a moral viewpoint; that is, they have as an express and sufficient intention to direct human action in accord with its rule, and, although they take into consideration the proper activity of the Christian, with the exigencies and supernatural resources which that requires, the plan, method and outline of these studies are not less determined and governed by a moralist purpose.

To be more explicit, there is no morality, still less a Christian morality, which does not have reference to God. Theology, like faith itself, pursues only the knowledge of God. If it were possible for man here on earth to know this divine object by a simple and perfect intuition, neither faith nor theology would be put to the necessity of being formulated and reconsidered and restated. In the treatise on God we would comprehend the Trinity, Creation, the return of creatures to God, the Incarnation, and all the sacraments and Christian mysteries. The treatise on God Himself would not lead us from the existence of God to each of His attributes; it would be concentrated in the inexhaustible affirmation: God is. We well know that, under the present conditions of our human knowledge, we accede to truth only by progressive discourse. Intuition, however perfect it may be, is immovable and fills us by itself alone; in order to enrich it, to acquire more truths, in comprehension as in extension, we must proceed by reason. Such is the necessity which explains and justifies the series of numerous tracts in the three parts of the *Summa Theologiae.*

Nevertheless, the unity of theology would be ruined if we forgot, for example, that the treatise on the Trinity concerns the same object as the treatise on God, and that it furnishes to the accurate and reasoning intellect a fresh opportunity for considering the Divine Being revealed by faith with a different start. Likewise, the study of Creation and of creatures in their diversity has a theological character because it defines in explicit formulae what God is in His external activity and for the beings who are dependent on Him.

The same thing can be observed at the beginning of the *Secunda Pars,* at the point where the break is neat, and the difference more apparent. Let us not imagine that the emanation of creatures from the divine abyss ends at the moment of their being brought into existence—as the ocean's swell stops with the last billowing wave dying away on the beach, at that precise instant of immobility before it rolls back to be lost in the boundless depths. Certainly, we will not confuse divine activity and creature movement, and in order to speak of it distinctly we shall be forced to conceive of them separately and to express them successively. But this unusual demand of our discursive reason is an attempt at purification, to purify our concept of all univocal terms between these two activities. One does not really follow the other; instead of the first having to cease so that the second may begin its course, if the first ceased the second would no longer be conceivable; and if the latter truly constitutes a reality, and an increase of being, this reality is a contribution of the first. Let us say, then, that the divine tide is not content to put the creature in a position to act, to continually re-begin its own activity; this tide carries the created being to the ultimate ends of its activity and, by the act itself, it carries, contains and measures the return of the creature.

Thus, throughout the *Secunda Pars,* the theologian does not stop considering the same object, God. More precisely, the study of the return of creatures to God only causes to develop, without interruption, what their emanation from God contained and implied.

For we will not comprehend all the conditions and variations of this creation if we consider only the dependence of beings in relation to their efficient cause; we must also see that creation, a work of God, has of necessity God for its end, since God is an intelligent Being, acting by design, in view of an end and not by the blind necessity of nature or by chance. Furthermore, God being the First Cause, His works can have no other final end but Himself. On this universal ontological level, the correspondence between efficient causality and final causality is perfect; any creature which is, in the measure of its being, proceeds from the Divine efficiency and, in the exact same measure which defines its degree of perfection, is directed to God as to its end. The scholar is thus led to represent the hierarchy of creatures according to the greater or lesser participation of being, and he cannot fail to observe that the most perfect beings, in receiving more of their Creator, have necessarily more of a beginning and inclination toward the God who is their end. God as an end attracts them in the same proportion and, as it were, by the very creative act which makes them proceed from Himself. Basically, when we see things reach out to God as to their end, we foresee that in that very fact they continue and complete their emanation from Him.

We would yield to the mirage of pantheism if, neglecting the causal efficacy of the creature act, we saw in created things only apparent and fleeting modalities of the Divine Being; this is always the formidable stumbling block in the idea of participation, susceptible to a platonistic interpretation which thinks to save the transcendence of the Infinite which has been participated in, while volitilizing the reality of the participating beings.

But the idea of creation allows us to see being, the intelligibility of being, the efficacy and value of being in the created things themselves and not outside of themselves, without prejudice to the Divine transcendence. On the contrary, while recognizing in the latter enough actual efficacy to bring about something more than appearances, it makes creatures exist in their being, in their natures and their properties.

The pantheist is not interested in natures, in secondary causes, since for him they have in themselves no distinct reality, but form a sort of screen in which the fleeting shadow of a Divine reflection stands out. He cannot seriously conceive the return to God of beings who have never been able to distinguish themselves from the great All nor to escape from the abyss. But for us, created man is effectively placed in his being and in his nature by the action of the First Cause. The result is that we are invited to take into consideration created natures, to set forth their specific differences. This study is not futile, even for the theologian, who discovers in the diversity of created things both *distinct signs* permitting him to know better the ways which follow the action of the Creator, and *corresponding inclinations,* according to which Divine Goodness orients things, each one in its fashion and according to its rank, so that they may be finally attracted to Himself.

So it is that the theologian is led to consider especially certain created natures, i.e., spiritual beings, for the remarkable way in which they proceed from God and, consequently, return to Him. In the common and unavoidable necessity which wills that every creature emanating from God has God for an end, spiritual beings represent only a particular example, but a privileged one. The others come from the First Cause according to the determination of their specific nature, through the play of secondary causes which sufficiently explain their origin, even though the efficacy of secondary causes can be conceived only through Divine power. Consequently, the return of these natures toward God, Who is their end, is also reduced to an intermediary perfection. Animals and plants, in short, do indeed sing the glory of God, but it is in perpetuating their species and in fulfilling a definite function in the universe; their perfection has no value by itself; it is only one tint in a vast painting, only one note, or perhaps one pause in a symphony.

Spiritual creatures, on the contrary, are each individual by the proper and immediate effects of the Divine Causality. The spirit cannot be engendered by created causes, but it is born immediately of the Father of Light. It follows that the destiny of spiritual creatures does not turn toward God by the intermediary of more perfect

creatures, as the Neo-Platonists and Gnostics, for whom each spiritual level finds its last end and its perfection in the next higher level,
have imagined. Placed in their spiritual nature by a direct intervention from God, spiritual creatures likewise are directly ordered to
God, without any intermediary. One can, then, in regard to them,
speak with all propriety of expression of a return to God because,
at the heart of the great flux of being proceeding from God, not
only are they animated by a natural movement which belongs to
them and has God for an end, but because, more precisely, this
activity which is proper to them insofar as they are spiritual, is
dependent on no other outside cause. It is explained solely by the
resources of their spiritual nature, an immanent and direct effect
of Divine causality which places them and carries them in their being, because the bent of their nature, their progress, the achievement
of their destiny is at their disposal, and, as it were, in their hands;
because, lastly, this destiny has God Himself as an immediate end.
There is indeed a return to God, since these natures, coming from
God, go and are directed, not unknown to themselves nor by an outside force, but of their own volition, toward an end which is not
some other great divine effect, but which is directly God Himself
and God recognized as God.

One does not deny, certainly, that the ordered and complex movements of the material being present a beautiful sight, worthy of consideration and study. But they are determined and as if arranged in
advance, according to the nature of each being and the concurrence
of the influence which it undergoes from without. To express it in
a different way, the die is cast on what concerns the destiny of
each one; there is room for the unforeseen and for accidentals within
the immediate range, but, on the whole, taking into account all the
influences and given circumstances, the future of each one is limited
and there is no room for an autonomous behavior. Neither animal
nor plant are responsible for what they are; they depend upon
specific generating forces and the network of ambient causes. What
they will do follows necessarily. In regard to them the rule of correspondence between efficient causality and final causality is verified without any complication; not being masters of what is done to
them, they are not either masters of what they do and of what is
ordained by what they are. Entirely passive in their origin, they are
not directed, but are passively led. Incapable of being self-possessed,
of controlling themselves, they do not hold the reins of their con-

duct. Likewise, the theologian, from his point of view, knows enough about them when he has seen how and why they proceed from God; all the rest of their history could not bring about any surprises nor pose any theological problems.

Indeed spiritual beings subscribe no less than others to the rule of correspondence between efficient and final causalities. In a profound sense, they, too, received everything; their actions, their progressive development, their final destiny are measured in the degree of being with which they are endowed and, thus, in their way of proceeding from God. But precisely this unavoidable radical passivity, when it is a question of spiritual natures, gives them being according to their proper nature and not in just any way whatsoever. This gift of being (which, by the way, is really not a gift, since each gift presupposes an already existing recipient, whereas this gift presupposes nothing but is identified with the spiritual being considered in its bond of ontological dependency with regard to God), in short, what we call the gift, or the radical receptivity by virtue of which spiritual natures are able to do what they are, would be useless and ridiculous if the natures in question did not really possess the characteristic attributes of spiritual natures. For the spirit is free. Its immateriality opens for it the kingdom of knowledge; it understands itself intelligibly; it assumes the mastery of self according to the initial datum of its spiritual nature. Without detriment to its radical passivity, but rather in order to prove the ontological content, it is put in possession of itself, it possesses itself and it conducts itself, it is lord of itself and of its works. In this way we eliminate from the first the famous problem of conflict or of concord between the action of God and our freedom; there is no reason to take away from one what is given to another. Just as we would ruin freedom if we cut off its root, the nature which has been received and the movements and circumstances which define its position, so on the other hand, we would misunderstand this received nature and all these facts, and we would be laboring under a delusion if we denied to these spiritual beings, without subterfuge or evasion, the mastery of themselves and of their acts.

Such are the thoughts that St. Thomas condenses into an expression borrowed from Holy Scripture and already exploited in this sense by St. John Damascene, i.e., *man is made in the image and likeness of God*. To comprehend the difference which separates the image from the simple trace of God, is both to note the original and characteristic fashion by which man proceeds from God and, very profoundly, to observe the point of insertion of moral considerations into the theological synthesis. It is to be noted that the notion of an image permits the *Secunda Pars* to be tightly welded to the preceding treatise which touches on the procession of creatures. Beings are diverse according as they proceed differently from their Author; for man proceeds from God like an image. To show all that this singular manner of proceeding from God contains and announces is to complete the preceding treatise, and also to perfect our knowledge of the Divine Being. For this we cannot dispense with the consideration of the image of God. Let us understand that for the theologian to be a man, that is to say, intelligent, endowed with free will, master of himself and of his works, is to be the image of God. To work like a man, to act like a man, or, if one prefers, to return to God in a human way and according to the characteristic resources bestowed upon man by the creative flux, is literally to follow in the image of God. At the same time, to the astonishment of the simple moralist, one treats God not as a lawmaker or re-munerator, assistant, or whatever, but as an exemplar.

That this means of introducing moral considerations into theology may not be without consequence for the content and order of the treatises, we have already surmised and shall see better shortly. But at least let us hold that the inspiring idea of the *Secunda Pars,* the one which determines the entire method of the tracts, is not a moralistic proposal. The theologian touches on morality, as on the rest, without departing from his viewpoint, for he sees everything in the light of God and everything in its place, in its order, in God. Certainly he may be a moralist, even a Christian moralist, but then his viewpoint changes; for example, man, the Christian, is taken at the precise moment when the creative flux deposits him on the shores of natural and supernatural being, including the habitual qualitative resources and the movements which define his possibilities of action. Thus supplied, in possession of these gifts of nature and of grace, man faces his destiny, is invited to return to God, i.e., to resolve precisely for himself the moral problem, while directing himself by suitable means toward his true end. That man proceeds from God, that from God he has all his being, substance and accident, even to the most fleeting impressions and movements, and to the most tenuous exterior circumstances which define and color the situation; that man has no other end, no beatitude but God; that to

go to God by properly governed acts is the true perfection of man—
the moralist would indeed be left destitute if either he ignored this
or challenged it. But for him those are the preliminary facts of this
problem; what concerns him is what follows: how is this creature,
so constituted, armed, disposed, enlightened, dependent on what he
is and on all that he possesses, going to adjust his progress in order
to attain his goal? By what habitual inclinations, under what attractions, by what routes, through what obstacles, can he do so?

We will agree that this concern of the moralist is not to be
despised. Let us confess that among human affairs there is nothing
more important than the art or science of living well, of proceeding
by good acts toward a blessed destiny. But over and above the most
important human affairs, there is the knowledge of God. Now
theology, following in the wake and in the light of faith, cannot do
otherwise than to concern itself first with God, and, in one sense,
to concern itself only with God, since God Himself could do nothing
else. If moral considerations, that is, human ones, often fall under
the scrutiny of the theologian, it is necessary that, at the same time,
he have God in view.

The wonder of it is that in this way the theologian understands
man better and directs him better than if he were limited by the
sole perspective and preoccupations of the moralist; but this wonder,
which makes the believer rejoice, does not disconcert him at all, he
finds it simply normal. Things being more true in Divine thought
than seen directly by themselves, the theologian is wise in considering human morals as they are seen by God and in accord with the
Divine Being, instead of seeing them exclusively in themselves and
in their human reasons.

The moment has then come to note how morality extricates itself
from this experience; we shall note how moral considerations benefit in depth, in clarity, in soundness when St. Thomas brings them
into his theological system.

II. Originality in Thomistic Morality

Too often questions are asked of St. Thomas on such particular
problems as the extent of the right of property, the limits of com-
mercial profits, payment on a loan, whereas the fundamental problems in which the Angelic Doctor puts the very concept of morality
in a true perspective are passed over without being given attention.

Moreover, would not the most faithful Thomist be excused from taking a position contrary to that of the *Summa* on points which have radically changed over seven centuries in order to come up with solutions? On the contrary, one clings to contingent conclusions while failing to recognize positions and definitions of principle which form the foundations of doctrine. Thus one deviates from St. Thomas without suspecting it and without chance of return.

It is these initial positions of Thomistic morality which we wish to define.

1. THE ASTONISHMENT OF THE MORALIST IN THE SCHOOL OF ST. THOMAS

Surprise requires a certain vision. He who is content to gather from the *Secunda Pars* a few quotations destined to adorn his own works and to back his ideas with authority renounces all surprise. He reads in good faith what he was expecting to read, what he had in mind. A reading thus anticipated filters and rejects automatically what does not fit on first try into the preconceived system; one sees nothing, there is no surprise. The most important formulae of St. Thomas are diverted from their clear meaning or lightly treated as phrases and artifices of style. One is so sure of what one thinks he knows that there is no leeway for questioning or possibly beginning at a different starting point.

One would also avoid a pitfall if, when setting out to read St. Thomas, he could make a clean sweep of all preconceived ideas and false notions which education has instilled in him. Then he would nourish himself without harm on the teachings of the Master.

But, indeed, we do not broach the subject of moral theology with the candor of an innocent child. Since we already have certain preliminary notions about morality, clash is inevitable. Whoever begins in earnest in the school of St. Thomas and insists on the great lines of his own thought must collide with a fundamental misunderstanding; very simply, in the *Secunda Pars,* there is a concept of morality which had never been put forward.

A. The student is surprised first of all to see what a minor place is assigned to free-will in the treatise of the *Summa*. The vocabulary bears witness to it; for example, a human act, good or bad, is defined by St. Thomas as voluntary, emanating, in recognition of a cause, from the interior principle which is the will. Among voluntary acts there are some which assume the air of contingency, in the presence of which the agent enjoys a sort of indifference which he subdues in an autonomous way by his free will. These are the acts which we rightly elect or choose to do. St. Thomas, in the words of the question relative to the act of choosing, devotes only one article to the necessity or to the freedom of choice, a single article out of 94 articles which comprise the treatise on human acts.

Today, even as a Thomist, one speaks of a free act more readily than of a voluntary act. It matters little to us that the acts which the moralist is concerned with are altogether voluntary acts, and particularly free acts. What matters for our purpose is that in the mind of St. Thomas the voluntary act has all that is necessary to be moral, whereas we ordinarily speak of a free act as being a moral act. Thomistic manuals show a slight embarrassment on this point. Commenting faithfully on the *Summa,* they report carefully the definition of the will, with its conditions and its vices or impediments; but then, when they come to the morality of the human act, they recognize only the free act; freedom would be a condition *sine qua non* of morality. Outside of freedom, for them, there is physical or natural good or evil, but not moral good or evil.

B. The student of St. Thomas is surprised, secondly, to read in the *Summa* a treatise on morality in which the idea of obligation plays no role at all. Now, are we not accustomed to seeing in morality the place *par excellence* of obligation? It is true that moralists do not very readily point to this lack. Without intending to do so, they substitute the grace of blindness to which we referred earlier, while forcing on the text (with the best faith in the world), meanings and interpretations which seem to them inevitable. Be that as it may, it remains that St. Thomas did *not* include it, where he treats *ex professo* the moral law in human acts. It is of no avail to look for statements gathered here and there in the Thomist work to bring together goodness and moral malice with duty or obligation. The author does not refuse to use the same language like every one else by saying that in order to be an honest man one must do good as one should and avoid evil. This is a further reason for attaching special importance to the fact that he avoids these very simple formulae when he studies scientifically the nature and law of morality. The scientist may say in ordinary conversation that the sun rises, that it ascends and descends on the horizon and that it sets: one would be very ungracious to reproach him for the conventional formulae which do not stop him from saying in his explicit teaching that the earth revolves around the sun. We will not stop, therefore, at the *obiter dicta,* but shall take the thought of St. Thomas in the treatise which he dedicates expressly to the question of morality.

C. While reflecting on these two surprising omissions, we must concede that they exist. Modern moralists situate morality in a free acceptance of an obligation. This position seems to them not only more worthy and more recommendable, but simply obvious. One can imagine a freedom which is unrestrained and is expanding, which vaunts itself and bears fruit; in the absence of an obligation, this kind of display will have no moral character; it is a force of nature that asserts itself, scampers along and follows its inclination toward the good for which it is made and to which it aspires. Such a movement remains natural, morally indifferent. On the other hand, let us imagine a subject grappling with a knot of obligations and yielding to their pressure. If he does not assume them inwardly by a free commitment, this man would seem irresponsible, he would suffer from inner tensions; the acts to which he yields are not, so to speak, his, but those of an exterior principle. Endowed perhaps in themselves with an objective goodness, either physical or social, these good acts seem stripped of moral goodness.

Now, the Thomistic moral theologian does not dream of giving such a decisive role to freedom and obligation. Such novelty can only disconcert our minds. We ask ourselves if St. Thomas did not ignore the first principle, the fundamental problem of morality, which consists precisely in "founding" morality. Indeed, it does not stand to reason that a roving liberty which encounters the commanding obligation necessarily welcomes and accepts it. It seems to us, ordinarily, that morality is all in this viewpoint; it is an undisputed viewpoint, given empirically *sui generis* in a sort of moral sense which is not meant to be verified. Authors everywhere seek a thousand different solutions to this problem; some lean more to the obligatory command, others put more reliance in freedom; but all consider this problem as the starting point of all research on morality. That St. Thomas should build a morality without alluding to it, is what surprises.

2. ORIGIN AND CRITIQUE OF OUR FALSE EVIDENCES

If morality rules human conduct, it is clear that it is linked, in the thought of St. Thomas as in ours, to an anthropology. But our conception of man no longer coincides exactly with that which St.

Thomas had of men. Let us not go so far as to maintain that there are two different definitions. Only, the *rational animal* figures in the Thomistic work as a perfect being whose well known properties furnish for moral research a definite and certain starting point. St. Thomas does not ignore the fact that man as he actually exists is an animal who is born, who grows, whose specific development risks falling short or of becoming viciously twisted; he acknowledges that most men, if we take a census, remain, so to speak, short of their definition, rise up rarely, if ever, and then only by lightning flashes above their animality; but he does not believe for all that, that he ought to renounce the definition of man as a rational animal.

Thus we, more sensitive to immediate brute experience than to definitions laboriously extracted from experiences which have been analyzed and ground up by philosophic reflection, consider man as he leaps into our range of vision, so to speak, like an animal, later, like a child in the pursuit of his rational stature. The adult himself appears to us in an unending becoming, molded by the yearnings, impulses and pressures of his subconscious at the same time as by social pressures and legends.

Thus modern minds find it difficult to be given a fixed definition of man, that malleable being who is subject to all kind of unforeseen changes and quasi absolute new beginnings. In that case, it is true, morality is lost in the shoreless flux of perpetually changing appearance, for if we know nothing for certain about man, what can we say about human morals? We must be silent and think no more about this subject.

We can, however, correct the impression of static rigidity left by the traditional definition of man, remembering that this rational animality is not given fully developed and all at once. It is a conquest; the germs of it are carefully sown in the cradle, and even sooner, in the origin of the human being. But these promises can be fully entertained only by considering the element of time and the meeting of all kinds of eventualities—physical, psychological, sociological—which are not at all inevitable. If all men deserve this name from the fact that they belong to the species, it remains that all do not realize specific perfection effectively and to the same degree, and do not attain the full development of ontological stature which evokes the idea of a rational animal.

It is for man thus defined that St. Thomas conceives his morality. But whatever we may have said about him, he does not forget either the child, or the primitive man; he does not destroy the bridge between the rational animal and other animals, in whom he detects an imperfect kind of will and, by analogy, certain quasi virtuous or evil habits, such as an air of prudence, an air of generosity, of strength, or of pride, unchastity, etc. We know that he admits in men, on the one hand, the chief of *bona vel mala dispositio naturae,* that is, certain psychic predispositions, rooted in an organic substructure, which already condition and guide the play of the human will; on the other hand, under the heading of *consuetudo,* the effect in each one of his education, of example, of ideas received, of customs, of pressures wrought by the social milieu, not only on the child, but on the adult. He even says that in most cases voluntary resolutions are predictable, men being content most often to follow their natural inclinations and to correspond to the urgings of their environment.

Such remarks make us think that if there exists a morality made to order for the rational animal, a morality which is properly human, there can exist in it rough outlines, made for the animal, or the child, or the imperfect adult. These moralities are false, certainly, if we wish to make them the total rule of human morals; they are already rules of behavior, but still crude and infantile; they correspond to certain elementary realities in man, but not to the essential reality which defines mankind.

We must not, then, be astonished if morality begins obscurely, in the order of genesis, by actual or instinctive conformity, in which the animal kingdom offers numerous examples. It is perfected in man by a legal conformity, characterized by the idea of obligation and adjusting itself perfectly to social intercourse. On this level a behavior is good, well-regulated, if it is inserted where it should be and as it should be.

From this point of view, the goodness of acts is a matter for agreement and for justice in the broad sense; to do good is to comply with the lawful demands of another. There is a coincidence between good and duty, between evil and the refusal to do what one should. A characteristic sign of this morality is that there is a "marginal." Beyond the socially governed domain, there exists the portion of private life, of personal intimacy, which does not count socially (because it escapes control, or because, wisely, others refuse to acknowledge it) and where each one gives free reign to his tastes, to his whims, to his imaginations.

From the first outline of this rudimentary morality, we feel ourselves to be in familiar territory. The existence of the "marginal"
poses the moral problem in the eternal terms of casuistry—those of
boundary, of limit, between obligation and freedom. We will be
more or less liberal or strict, we will be able to advance or move
back the limit, no matter. The question in which everything is resolved lies in knowing how far freedom can go, and where obligation
begins.

It is indeed in this way that we as children reached the moral
life. We learned to distinguish that which seems to us good from that
which is morally good. To that which we love and hate, to that
which we do or do not do, we opposed that which we ought to
love or hate, do nor not do. This opposition is one of the first con-
quests of moral life. If we wish to do good, we exert ourselves to
pattern what we are, what we think, what we desire and do, according to the rule of what we ought to be, think, desire and do.

But this rule did not seem to us at first as the most profound wish
of our nature; it always demanded, against the indolence or the
whim of our childish spontaneity, what others were rightfully expecting of us. Good and evil rise up before us as duty and counter-
mand, and we are accustomed to this identification. Indoctrinated
from infancy and molded by society (which is the place of our relationship with others), we live marked by this lesson as by an evident
fact, that moral good is that which *must* seem good to us rather
than what seems good, and that moral evil is that which *must* seem
bad rather than what seems bad.

We have come to such a pass that the natural inclination toward
what seems to us good, the natural repulsion with respect to what
seems to us evil, would seem to us almost questionable; they must
at least await the sanction of a moral judgment before being accepted. Thus, there is introduced in man a duality of judgment and,
in the background, a twofold functioning of reason; i.e., a practical
judgment, stating purely and simply what seems good or bad, a
moral judgment, or judgment of conscience, which over and against
what I like says what I ought to like or should have liked. In order
to have a moral value, the good which I like must, on the other
hand, be that which I should like, and there is the reason moralists
need a distinct judgment of conscience to morally control and sanction the practical judgment.

Thus, we realize in the heart of man a social hierarchy in miniature, since this concept of morality requires a sovereign who rules and obliges, and a subject who is ruled and obligated. Reared as we are in a network of social relationships, it seems obvious to us that a rule of conduct has no meaning if it is not obligatory, because social rules, from the fact that they order our relationship with others, all offer this obligatory character to a greater or lesser degree. When sociology discovers in society the origins of morality, it is content to consider the latter as a collection of obligatory rules of conduct; the moralist will protest, but instead of seeking a principle of moral obligation above or outside of society, he should first ask himself if it is perfectly correct to define morality by obligations.

3. THOMISTIC MORALITY AND THE RULE OF GOOD CONDUCT

We shall never understand St. Thomas' position if we do not reach the point of throwing out the presumption that morality is essentially a matter of moral obligation, that every rule of human behavior, in order to be efficacious and definitive, must be definitely obligatory.

Obligation has its place, which is great, in morality: whenever there is a question of a legitimate bond established between a master and subject, a creditor and a debtor. Thus, to do good consists in doing what one should do. But one rightly only owes to another person, and to speak of obligation there must be two. All matters of justice, of course, bring into question obligation. But it is the same in every situation which is defined socially. As soon as we adopt a state in life, or practice a profession, a ministry, or a temporal or spiritual office, we put ourselves into perfectly defined relations; moral perfection in this respect consists in an adjustment—in fulfilling the obligations of our state of life. It is sufficient to enter, by birth or otherwise, into any society, to have a job, a role, in order to be bound and held in a network which is more or less closed and more or less defined by obligations. Hence there are rules of conduct, properly obligatory this time, because they measure our activity with regard to others according to a positive and objective determination which does not depend on us but on others. This is a matter of justice, of law, of public order, an affair of state; the others could be a family, town, society, any hierarchical organization, any order outside of us, to which we find ourselves committed.

The mistake would be to take the idea of obligation out of the

context of the restricted societies which hold us in their grips here
on earth and impose duties on us, and to apply it to the universal
society whose head is God, and to believe that we have thus resolved
the problem of a moral foundation. In reality we have founded only
a morality cut from the pattern of sociological rules of behavior
toward others. We call on the Supreme Being, Whose infallibility
and universality are beyond compare, to play the same role of other
fellowmen who hold a claim on us; we look upon God as someone
holding us in the bonds of obligation, to Whom we must answer
and give an account, Who will also apply the effects of our submission and/or our infractions by way of rewards and punishments.

Now it matters little, in brief, that this other who is legitimately
qualified to impose on us obligatory rules of conduct may be some
prince or temporal leader, public opinion, or God; we remain
always in the rudimentary scheme of a morality conceived in terms
of obligation, that is, on the level of sociological relations.

Certainly God is admirably qualified to be our Master and our
Creditor, and to obligate us. That is not the question. If we enter
into a relationship with God, no one doubts that the moral good
consists in acquitting ourselves of what we owe to Him; a special
virtue, religion, makes us capable of that. But we did not say everything about man nor about God when we spoke of dependence, of
master and servant, of king and subject, of chief and subordinate, of
judge and the one under jurisdiction, of creditor and debtor, of
sovereign landlord and the steward who is called to give an account
of his stewardship. The religious mind does not weary attributing to
God the most elaborate titles and degrees used by men, all the forms
of lordship and domination. He is not mistaken, but none of these
titles is sufficient; all are deceiving and would be blasphemous if we
understood them strictly and literally. For the morality which is
called theological, it suffices that God is the lawful Chief and Sovereign; soon we see ourselves under obligation and morality is
founded. St. Thomas is not deluded by such infantile fancies.

A theologian brought up on the Gospels sees in God our Father.
Without accenting the dependence, this consideration sets off the
vital communication, the friendly commerce which follows, an enormous and primitive fact which governs our behavior prior to any
idea of obligation. But this theologian has also freed moral philosophy from the sociological matrix in which it is buried by crude
approximations: King, Master, God is certainly all that but in the

manner of a Creator God—that is, that He is all other things and infinitely more. God can without doubt and better than anyone show Himself to us as a master and hold us under obligation; that supposes that we exist, that we have entered into a relationship with Him, that we form in some way a society with Him; this is possible, and the fact is proved by divine interventions in the history of mankind. Meanwhile, morality already has been founded.

For Adam to have received, upon awakening, certain precepts from God, it is necessary to say that morality is anterior to these precepts. Let us go back to the source. If we wish for a creature to have received orders from the Creator, let us understand Him as He is, without coarsely disfiguring the primordial event. Order is not given after the event to a creature already formed; the creating Word establishes order while placing the created being in its natural setting; it is not for nothing that *Genesis* speaks of animals and plants, each one according to its species. For nature itself is an order, precisely the principle defined and specifically differentiated according to which ways are opened to the actual movements and to the development of the created being. We well know that God did not create a heavy body in order to determine for it the law of gravity; nor a vegetable or animal, that he might order it to grow and reproduce according to its species, nor a man in order to command him to behave as a man. Only the sociological illusion makes us imagine the origin of morality as a solemn meeting between a lord and a vassal, as if it were necessary to set up first a man and then an authority charged with governing and ordering the movements of this man.

All social authorities we are familiar with give, in effect, rational orders to rational beings. They presuppose in their obligatory injunctions a human order among their subjects, that is to say, a radical order of reason which is presupposed. Now on this fundamental level of rational nature, where it is absurd to speak of obligation since we have not entered into relationship with anyone and since we have not yet encountered any agreement, not even with God, reason is already the specific principle of government in man, and of direction for human behavior; St. Thomas makes no distinction between this law and the law of morality.

For the modern mind it is not enough to be a man and to behave like one. It finds it necessary to bend human behavior to a moral law whose principle must be sought elsewhere—in God, in society, in a more or less objective ideal—whereas for St. Thomas, the law of human behavior is to be a true human behavior, it is to conduct oneself as a man, just as it is fitting that the seed of a species germinate according to that species, or for fire to burn and light to illumine.

But why give the term 'morality' to this norm which is merely human? Do we not sense the paradox: What is easier for man than to act humanly and what else can he do? It is because the epithet *morality* underlines that which is distinctive in human behavior. Man conducts himself, while non-rational natures are *conducted,* or led. Only here on earth is he capable of conceiving the idea of a rule of conduct, of reading in the order of his rational nature the regulating principle or the law of his actions. His nature is not for him a blind principle of movements determined by his species; it is his rule, he conceives it as such and he knows how to apply it as one applies a rule to direct his action. He is even capable up to a certain point, on the fringe of activities subject to his free will, of voluntarily mis-understanding and of transgressing the rule.

To speak of the moral law, of goodness or moral evil, is to point out and accentuate that which is suitable to man's distinctive and specific form, which is reason. There are in man principles and rules of different classes or levels, things which, in certain respects, seem to him (and really are) good; like all that satisfies the needs and appetites of the animal, these rules and these valuations are not false, but they do not decide, as a last resort, what is suitable to man. They still do not decide the moral viewpoint, which is rightly and specifically that of the rational animal who is man. On the contrary, if it is man such as he is who speaks and who judges, we must say that his own discretion—what pleases him, what is suitable to his taste as a rational being, what is consistent with the judgment of his right reason that is, of his reason loyal and coherent with itself and with its natural principles—is not capricious or foolish but a law of morality and that this good is specifically enough human to be morally qualified as such.

We see that St. Thomas holds neither tightly nor loosely the theory known by the name of theological morality, which makes an appeal to the authority of divine imperative in order to ensnare man in the bounds of moral obligation. For him, God is necessary to the estab-lishment of morality only because without God there would be no human nature, no rational animal, no image and likeness of God;

indeed, there would be nothing. But St. Thomas has seen perfectly that if man, having entered historically (by the ancient Law and the new Law) into relations with God, finds on his way precepts and counsels which help him to guide himself, it suffices, furthermore, that man exists, with his rational nature, so that a manner of being and of acting suits him naturally. From this moment we discern the good and the bad in this properly human viewpoint, which is the moral viewpoint, with as much determination and severity as we distinguish between a man and a monster, between a living person and a corpse.

J. Tonneau, O.P.

BIBLIOGRAPHIE [1]

Th. Deman, O.P., *Aux origines de la théologie morale,* Montréal-Paris, J. Vrin, 1951.
E. Gilson, *Saint Thomas d'Aquin* (*Les moralistes chrétiens*). Textes et commentaires, Paris, J. Gabalda, 6ᵉ édition, 1941.
E. Gilson, *Le Thomisme* (*Études de philosophie médiévale*), Paris, J. Vrin, 5ᵉ édition, 1944.
A.-D. Sertillanges, O.P., *La philosophie morale de saint Thomas d'Aquin,* nouvelle édition, Paris, Aubier, 1942.
A.-D. Sertillanges, O.P., *Le Christianisme et les philosophies,* t. I, (pp. 345 ss. *La synthèse thomiste* : *l'action humaine ou la voie du retour*), Paris, Aubier (1939).

BIBLIOGRAPHY [2]

Gilson, Etienne, *Moral Values and the Moral Life, the System of St. Thomas* (Tr. Leo R. Ward, C.S.C.). St. Louis: B. Herder Book Co., 1931.
———, *The Philosophy of St. Thomas Aquinas* (Tr. Edward Bullough). St. Louis: Herder, 1924.
———, *The Spirit of Medieval Philosophy.* New York: Scribners, 1936.
Sertillanges, Antonin D., *Foundations of Thomistic Philosophy* (Tr. Godfrey Anstruther). Springfield, Ill.: Templegate, 1956.

[1] Publisher's note. As a general policy throughout this volume, the bibliography of the French edition, when there is one, is printed first, followed by a supplementary one in English supplied by the translators.
[2] A brief general bibliography for moral theology is supplied at the end of Volume IV.

Introductory Chapter

NEW TESTAMENT MORALITY

by C. Spicq, O.P.

Introductory Chapter

NEW TESTAMENT MORALITY

When our Lord Jesus Christ taught the morality proper to the Kingdom of God which He established on earth, He defined it by references to the revealed morality of Israel, whose conceptual categories and terminology were essentially juridical. For it the will of God which must be observed is expressed in one law; virtues are practiced in obedience to certain precepts; the faithful and the saints are the just; God is a sovereign Judge; rewards and punishments are distributed in the course of a Judgment without appeal.

But within these ancient formulae, Jesus imposed on His disciples a morality absolutely unknown in all the history of religions; its establishment, unity and spirit consist of love: "Thou shalt love the Lord thy God with thy whole heart, and with thy whole Soul, and with thy whole mind. This is the greatest and the first commandment. The second is like it. Thou shalt love thy neighbor as thyself. On these two commandments depend the whole Law and the Prophets." [1] It is plain that all the other moral regulations as well as the most spiritual efforts will have the meaning or value of virtue only in terms of love; they are suspended from it as fruits are attached to the tree whose sap nourishes them. Love of God and of one's neighbor is the principle whence emanate all actions of real life, which are its flowering and fulfillment. Therein lie the originality and the fundamental unity of the morality of the New Testament, the "justice" or perfection of the Kingdom which surpasses that of the Old Testament (Mt. 5:20; 6:33) and which all the Apostles preached to converts of the early Church.

1. RELIGIOUS LOVE OF GRATITUDE

It is a matter of loving God, clearly and voluntarily. Why and how? From the creation of the world, God has shown Himself as being Goodness itself, desiring the happiness of His creatures. In the course of history, He reveals His predilection for the people whom He has chosen. He heaps on Israel His gifts and surrounds her with

[1] Mt. 22:37-40; cf. Mk. 12:28-34; Lk. 10:25-28.

a special Providence. In turn, He is presented as a wine-grower who lavishes all his care on his vineyard, a doctor who heals injuries, a shepherd who carries the lambs on his shoulder and gently leads the sheep who are suckling their young, a husband tenderly and faithfully attached to his wife, a father who educates his child, a mother who caresses the little one at her knee. All these metaphors, expressing the delicacy, the fervor and the selfless devotion of love, were chosen by the prophets to suggest the infinity of Divine charity and to prepare men for the understanding of the mystery. But the only Son of God—the true and faithful Witness—Who exists in the bosom of the Father (Jn. 1:28), was better qualified than anyone to reveal God and the secrets of His heart. Now He confirms the teaching of the prophets and He asks His disciples to consider themselves with God in the relationship of children to their Father: "You have only one Father, who is in Heaven" [2]; "When you pray, say: Father" (Lk. 11:2).

But if God reveals His charity and shows Himself as a loving Father, it is because He wishes to obtain in return the love of men. If He takes all the initiative in gifts (Rom. 11:35; Eph. 2:4) and in faithful love (II Thess. 2:16; I Jn. 4:10) it is because He counts on provoking in these whom He loves the gift of their hearts. By telling and proving His charity, He arouses their gratitude. His love is so explicit and so manifest the better to receive from His creatures the homage of their reciprocal affection, with a view to their returning love for love. Thus, charity towards God, the basis of all revealed morality, will be essentially a love of gratitude, and even a definition of the Christian: "If anyone does not love the Lord, let him be anathema." [3]

In the Old Testament, Yahweh multiplied His declarations and confirmed them by His generosity towards His people, notably His pardons. But in the New Testament He gives Himself and sacrifices His beloved Son in order to assure the happiness of all men: "God has so loved the world that He has given His only Son, so that whosoever believes in Him may not perish, but may have life everlasting" (Jn. 3:16). Not only is the theme of the Incarnation stated here, but the meaning of the Lord's Passion is revealed: "Greater

---

[2] Mt. 23:9; cf. 5:16, 45, 48; 6:1-32; 7:11, etc.
[3] I Cor. 16:22; cf. Mt. 24:12. This criterion would be that of love of neighbor in Lk. 11:42.

love than this no one has, that one lay down his life for his friends." [4]
That is what faith sees in the *fact* of Christ and of His crucifixion.
It knows, like the contemporaries of Jesus, the circumstances of His
birth, of His public life and His death, but it believes, in addition,
that Jesus is the only-begotten Son, that He came to earth and that
He sacrificed Himself in order to bear and take away the sins of
the world (Jn. 1:29), and especially that this sacrifice was inspired
and willed by Divine love (Apoc. 1:5).

From that time on, the believer—like a very innocent child who
does not question the demonstrations of affection which he receives [5]
—gives his total allegiance to the person of Jesus Christ, to His
revelation and to His work. He pledges his whole life on this conviction that God is Love—since proof has been furnished for him and
sealed in blood—, and he responds to this first love and shows it by
a love which is unceasing, that is, the gift to God of his mind, of his
heart, of his strength and energy. This is "the first love" of the
Apocalypse (Apoc. 2:4), in the sense of affection and friendship.
To the gift of God in Christ, the Christian responds with the ir-
revocable consecration of a grateful love.[6] "In this has the love of
God been shown in our case, that God has sent his only-begotten
Son into the world that we may live through him. In this is the
love, not that we have loved God, but that he has first loved us,
and sent his Son as a propitiation for our sins. . . . And we have come
to know, and have believed, the love that God has in our behalf.
God is love. . . . Let us therefore love, because God first loved
us" (I Jn. 4:9-19). Faith and Christian charity are acquiescence to
the absolutely free initiative of the love of God in Christ: "I live in
the faith to the Son of God who has loved me and given Himself
up for me" (Gal. 2:30).

2. DIVINE LOVE

When the disciple of Jesus Christ addresses himself to God as
to his Father (Lk. 11:2, 13), he does not hold onto the metaphor
of a kind and benevolent love of the Creator of heaven and earth

[4] Jn. 15:13; cf. Rom. 5:7-8. "For scarcely in behalf of a just man does
one die; yet perhaps one might bring himself to die for a good man. But
God commands His charity towards us, because when as yet we were sinners,
Christ died for us."

[5] Mt. 18:3; Mk. 10:15; Lk. 10:21-22; I Pet. 2:2.

[6] In other words, men are always in debt to God; Mt. 6:12; 18:23 ff.;
23:16, 18; Lk. 7:41; 17:10.

(Mt. 11:25; Mk. 13:19), for he recognizes only that God has truly adopted him as His child (Gal. 4:5-7). From now on, indeed, he is the son of God,[7] having been begotten—literally—by grace and baptism to divine life: "Behold what manner of love the Father has bestowed upon us, that we should be called children of God; and such we are" (I Jn. 3:1). God has communicated His nature and His life, as every father communicates his nature and his life to the one whom he begets.

In order to make this mystery understood and to emphasize its realism, St. John compares this generation to that of the children of men: "We are born of God and the seed of His nature dwells in us" (I Jn. 3:9). At the beginning of the new life, and at first from the new quality of being, there is a seed transmitted by the father, *semen Dei in vobis,* which theologians will call *grace,* just as St. Peter calls it *consortes divinae naturae* (II Pet. 1:4). As the tiny infant posses- ses at birth the human nature transmitted by his parents and makes his entrance into the world, so the baptized person, receiving grace, makes his entrance into heaven (Phil. 3:20) and possesses the nature of God: "Amen, amen, unless a man be born again, he can- not see the Kingdom of God. . . . That which is born of the flesh is flesh, and that which is born of the spirit is spirit. Do not wonder that I said to thee: You must be born again" (Jn. 3:3-7). The amazement of Nicodemus is that of all reasonable souls who are reluctant to recognize the invisible—which faith clings to (Heb. 11:1)—as the reality par excellence. But, nevertheless, these state- ments of the Lord and of His disciples are to be taken in the strict sense: "Beloved, henceforth we are children of God; and it has not yet appeared what we shall be. We know that, when he appears, we shall be like him, for we shall see him just as he is" (I Jn. 3:2). The Christian is divinized and the Holy Spirit gives him the inner conviction that he is really the child of God (Rom. 8:16).

Thanks to Christ (Jn. 1:12), the believer is a "new creature" (II Cor. 5:17; Gal. 6:15). Possessing divine life or eternal life for his own, he is "justified" [8] and admitted to society and intimacy with the Father, the Son and the Holy Spirit. He can perform acts which are reserved for God alone. He will know Him as God knows Him- self. He will love Him with the same love with which God loves Himself. It is not with his own heart that the believer can obtain

[7] I Jn. 3:2; cf. *ex. Deo nati sunt,* Jn. 1:13.
[8] Rom. 3:28; 5:8-11; 10:14; Gal. 3:11, 24; Phil. 3:9.

the object of his love, but rather, in this heart, the Holy Spirit has infused divine charity: "The Charity of God is poured forth in our hearts by the Holy Spirit who has been given to us" (Rom. 5:5). Here is a definition of a Christian: Begotten by God who is love, he possesses the nature of God, and, consequently, he also defines himself by love. We may dare to say that he is of the same race as his Father, if not of the same blood; he possesses the same characteristics of Him and must have the same activities. The morality of the New Testament rests on this rebirth: *operatio sequitur esse,* that is, as man is, so does he act. Jesus can also command weak mortals: "You therefore are to be perfect, even as your heavenly Father is perfect" (Mt. 5:48; cf. Lk. 1:17). St. Luke well understood the nature of this perfection since he translated that ideal into these words: "Be merciful, therefore, even as your Father is merciful." [9]

3. IMITATION OF GOD AND OF CHRIST

If it is true that grace is in us as second nature, it contains in itself its law of life. Noblesse oblige! Children should resemble their Father: "Be you, therefore, imitators of God, as very children—" (Eph. 5:1), "But as the One who called you is holy, be you also holy in all your behavior, for it is written: You shall be holy, because I am holy, I, Yahweh, your God" (I Pet. 1:15). But in order to imitate God, one must know Him. Now "No one has ever seen God—who dwells in light inaccessible—" (I Jn. 4:12; I Tim. 6:16). How then shall we imitate and reproduce a model which we have never seen? Actually, God has appeared on earth and has made Himself known in the person of His Son: "He has revealed Himself to us through His Son, Jesus Christ, who is the splendor of the glory of the Father, image of the Invisible God" (Col. 1:14). Christ is not only a redeemer who, in expiating sins, merits grace and introduces the elect into heaven, but He is the Holy of God, visible, tangible and imitable, the ideal of all perfection offered to the love of believers so that they may reproduce in themselves His own features and be likened to Him.

This is to say, on the one hand, that the moral life of the New

---

[9] Lk. 6:36. Perfection is an ideal toward which we lean, a state of spiritual maturity with regard to the beginning of the Christian life, which is the age of infancy; cf. Cor. 2:6; II Cor. 13:11; Phil. 3:12, 15; Col. 1:28; 4:12; II Tim. 3:17; Heb. 5:14; I Jn. 4:18 etc.

Testament is concretely defined as an *imitation of Christ,* a "mimicry" [10] as exact and complete as possible of the person and life of our Lord, since whoever sees Him, sees the Father (Jn. 14:9); on the other hand, the first activity of this divine life in us is *contemplative* (Lk. 10:38-42). It is a life of love, in effect; now, the spontaneous inclination of whoever loves is to gaze with admiration upon the object loved. Privileged in respect to Moses, who saw in some way an impersonal, invisible Being (Heb. 11:21), the faithful of the New Testament are invited to contemplate the life of the Word made flesh, just as it is described to them in the very midst of His abasements and torments (Heb. 12:2); it sees everywhere, in His slightest gestures as well as in the whole of His stay on earth, the manifestation of infinite love: "The goodness and kindness of God our Savior appeared." [11] It is in this light that the Incarnation appears in the vision of faith.

Henceforth, the moral life shall consist less in complying with the divine will expressed in a code of laws, than in imitating the thoughts, desires, actions of Christ. He Himself has determined the rules of conduct: "For I have given you an example, that as I have done to you so you also should do" (Jn. 13:15). The Apostles will have no other worry; constantly urged on, as though impelled by the love of Christ which is in their hearts, each one asks of the faithful: "Therefore, I beg you, be imitators of me, as I am of Christ" (I Cor. 4:16; cf. 11:1; I Thess. 1:6); "He who says that he abides in him, ought himself also to walk just as he walked" (I Jn. 2:6; cf. 2:29; 3:3, 5). It is a question here of exhorting the Corinthians to help the poor of Jerusalem, and as St. Paul justifies his demand by an appeal to the model which is Christ: "For you know the graciousness of Our Lord Jesus Christ . . . how, being rich, he became poor for your sakes, that by his poverty you might become rich" (II Cor. 8:9), so should you do to each other. Is it necessary to instill humility in the Philippians? "Have this mind in you which was also in Christ Jesus, who though he was by nature God, did not consider being equal to God a thing to be clung to . . . he humbled himself, becoming obedient to death, even to death on a cross" (Phil. 2:6-8). Should the Ephesians be more conscientious about

[10] The Greek work is *mimesis,* "resemblance," such as of a portrait or of a reproduction of the original.
[11] Tit. 3:4. Cf. Jn. 14:9: "Because I love the Father, I act in accordance with the command which He has given me."

the demands of brotherly love? "Let all bitterness, and wrath, and indignation, and clamor, and reviling, be removed from you, along with all malice. On the contrary, be kind to one another, and merciful, generously forgiving one another, as also God in Christ has generously forgiven you . . . and walk in love, as Christ also loved us and delivered himself up for us." [12] Even in marriage, husbands shall resemble Jesus Christ, in loving their wives with the fidelity and the devotion which our Lord showed for His Church (Eph. 5:25), and it is precisely thanks to this imitation of love that the marital union is a Sacrament, the symbol of Our Lord's union with sanctified mankind. St. Peter, exhorting the Christian slaves to be patient under the maltreatment to which they were subjected, himself appeals to the example of the Master: "Christ also has suffered for you, leaving you an example that you may follow in his steps: who did no sin, neither was deceit found in his mouth. Who, when he was reviled, did not revile, when he suffered, did not threaten, but yielded himself to him who judged him unjustly; who himself bore our sins in his body upon the tree, that we, having died to sin, might live in justice . . ." (I Pet. 2:21-24; cf. I Jn. 3:5).

This sentence of St. Peter sums up all Christian life conceived as a correlation to Christ. Our Lord died and rose again, and the Christian, in a mystical way, must die to sin and rise again "to live in justice." He lives in God with Christ (Col. 3:3). Whoever does not imitate Jesus Christ in the mystery of His death and resurrection, that is, in that which is most characteristic of the mystery of salvation, cannot be called a Christian; we cannot recognize in him the traits of the divine Model, nor, as a result, the image of the Heavenly Father, nor, finally, the character of his filial relationship. He is not, as his name indicates, another Christ.

On the contrary, whoever has understood how much he is vitally linked to Christ—"It is now no longer that I live, but Christ lives in me" (Gal. 2:20)—applies himself (in the sense of an assimilation as complete as possible) to the mystery of love and sanctity which is the life of Christ. As St. Paul expressed it, he lives "with Christ," "in Christ," expecting to be with Him in heaven and to "reign with Christ." It is a symbiosis.

Such is the real vocation of the "partakers of Christ" (Heb. 3:14). In the divine plan, it is not men, even though redeemed, who

[12] Eph. 5:2. The Apostle echoes the precept of the Master: "This is my commandment, that you love one another as I have loved you" (Jn. 5:12).

are the supreme *end* of the universe and its creation, or the ultimate purpose of Providence, but the exaltation of Christ, who is the manifestation and glorification of God's love: "Now we know that for those who love God all things work together for good, for those who, according to his purpose, are saints through his call. For those whom he has foreknown *he has also predestined to become conformed to the image of his Son,* that he should be the firstborn among many brethren" (Rom. 8:28-29). As the Son is the authentic image of God, Christians are called to resemble the Son. The faithful and persevering moral life has for its end the attainment of this resemblance begun by initial grace. Perfection, then, will be nothing else but a filial and fraternal resemblance. In other words, the goal of Christians is not so much to be proper and virtuous in the various spheres of practical action, as to acquire one by one the characteristics of their new family; they are ushered into the dwelling place of the Trinity, they who, before baptism, were *hospites et advenae* (Eph. 2:19), strangers and foreigners. There are no virtues except those which Jesus practiced and which we acquire in subjection to Him and in order to be like Him.

4. PREDILECTION AND RENUNCIATION

If the Christian vocation is the imitation of Jesus Christ, it is necessary to understand this likeness in terms of the glorious and blessed Christ—for the Christians who are called to dwell in heaven —but before that, in terms of the humiliated and suffering Christ (Rom. 6:5), since the Son of God Himself achieved glory only through suffering (Lk. 24:26). Henceforth, the children of God who are predestined to partake of the beatitude of their elder Brother (Jn. 17:24) are similarly obliged to carry their cross and to be, in their own way, crucified: "always bearing about in our body the dying of Jesus, so that the life also of Jesus may be made manifest in our bodily frame" (II. Cor. 4:10).

Suffering is an integral element of Christian morality, in the same way as love, which is indissolubly linked to it. The two poles of Christian religion are love of God and the cross of Jesus. Moreover, the very nature of the love of charity implies sacrifice. Charity, in fact, in contrast to simple friendship or ordinary affections, implies essentially a choice and love of predilection. It is not a question of instinct, nor of spontaneity, nor of sentimentality, but of a determination of the will enlightened by the mind; knowing himself beloved by his God, the Christian wishes to love Him in return, that is, to be bound to Him faithfully and exclusively, and to belong only to Him. Love allows no division. To love God implies of necessity that we hate everything else,[13] that we sacrifice whatever is opposed to the interests of Divine choice.

That is why, from the Gospels to the last writings of the Apostles, from the moment that it is a question of defining the practical moral attitude of the disciple of Jesus Christ, each author specifies the choice of his love and insists on the renunciations which it implies; e.g. when one comes into possession of a treasure hidden in a field, or of fine pearls, he sells all that he has in order to buy them (Mt. 13:44-46). "For where thy treasure is, there also will thy heart be."[14]

From his first appeal to the knowledge of the truth,[15] and to the heavenly life, man *is converted* or *does penance,*[16] that is, he turns away from idols, from error and from sin in order to turn towards God. He denies the past, sacrifices what he has adored and followed, and does not wish for more than what God wishes. The predilection of his love having been reversed, a radical change of master and allegiance is effected. Shielded from all other servitude, the Christian is answerable only to Christ, as a wife belongs only to her husband (II Cor. 11:2), as a slave to the one who bought and paid for him (I Cor. 7:22). The first Christian experience is that of a *liberation* [17] and of a transfer of ownership: "You no longer belong to yourself" (I Cor. 6:19). "For none of us lives to himself, and none dies to himself; for if we live, we live to the Lord, or if we die,

[13] In Biblical language, hate opposed to love of charity does not mean at all an abhorrence properly so-called; it is mentioned only to emphasize the preference included in charity; for the Hebrew, having no word to express preference, what is non-preferred is said to be hated. He is loved—just as Esau in connection with Jacob—but he is not the privileged man, the object of the free and singular favor reserved for the one who loves charity. All the while loving his relatives, he will hate them if the affection which he has for them is contrary to the fulfillment of the will of God. They are hated in the measure in which they are not preferred.

[14] Mt. 6:21. Cf. the "simple" heart, that is, complete in its choices and its own gift. Mt. 6:22-23; Act. 2:46; II Cor. 11:3.

[15] I Tim. 2:4; Tit. 1:2; II Tim. 2:25; Heb. 10:26.

[16] Mt. 3:1-2; 4:17; Mk. 1:4, 15; Act. 3:19 ff.

[17] Mt. 6:13; Lk. 1:74. Freedom is the privilege of the children of God, acquired from the moment of birth, Mt. 17:25; Jn. 8:31-36; Rom. 6:18-22; 8:2; Gal. 4:21-31; 5:13; II Cor. 3:17; II Tim. 1:9; Heb. 2:15; Jas. 1:25; 2:12; I Pet. 1:18.

we die to the Lord. Therefore, whether we live or die, we are the Lord's" (Rom. 14:7-8; cf. II Cor. 5:15; 8:5).

Consequently, moral life is conceived as a *service,* and Christians are servants or slaves of Jesus Christ.[18] "No one can serve two masters; either he will hate the one and love the other, or else he will stand by the one and despise the other. You cannot serve God and mammon" (Mt. 6:24; cf. Lk. 16:13). No compromise is possible; the morality of the New Testament has a horror of half-measures. This means not so much being preserved from all impurity and avoiding sin, as being loyally faithful in the dedication of one's life to Christ, sealed by love: "Do not think that I have come to send peace upon earth; I have come to bring a sword, not peace. For I have come to set a man at variance with his father, and a daughter with her mother, and a daughter-in-law with her mother-in-law; and a man's enemies will be those of his own household. He who loves father or mother more than me is not worthy of me; and he who loves son or daughter more than me is not worthy of me. He who finds his life will lose it, and he who loses his life for my sake, will find it" (Mt. 10:34-39). Charity imposes separations and detachments.

Likewise, absolute chastity will always remain the ideal of the child of God, not that sensual realities are bad or impure—since all that God created is good and since all is pure for the pure (Tit. 1:15; cf. Heb. 13:4; I Pet. 3:7),—but for the sake of perfect charity and a more exact imitation of Jesus Christ. In marriage, as a matter of fact, husband and wife are "torn" (Apoc. 14:4) between the exclusive preference which they have given to God and the legitimate affection which they keep for their mate, "and behold them distracted" (II Cor. 7:32-35). In the measure in which riches hinder the freedom to love God above all else and rivet the heart to earth, it will be necessary to renounce them: "If thou wilt be perfect, go, sell what thou hast and give to the poor, and thou shalt have treasure in heaven" (Mt. 19:21; Lk. 18:22-30).

Since love is the gift of self, charity, which orders the Christian's entire moral life, requires above all that he renounce himself; this is what is implied by poverty of spirit, the object of the first beatitude and, so to speak, the only one. The poor man, in fact, according to the Bible, is the pauper, and consequently, one who is

[18] Mt. 10:24; 24:25; Jn. 13:16; Rom. 14:18; Gal. 1:10; Eph. 6:6; Col. 3:24; 4:12; II Tim. 1:3.

hungry and aspires to be satisfied; he is afflicted in every way and
he weeps, he is lonely and helpless, or exploited and oppressed by
a hostile world, so he dreams of justice. He has only his patience to
oppose violence; unhappy on earth, he expects happiness only from
God. All his trials, far from causing him to rebel, have made him
humble and retiring; he is first of all modest; kind and affable with
men, he has a deeply religious mind, abandoning himself to Providence. Such a man is the born tenant of the Kingdom of Heaven
(I Cor. 1:26-31). Stripped of everything, his heart and soul are
completely available for love. He has already acquired his likeness
to the poor, suffering, scorned and persecuted Christ.

But whether social conditions impose or facilitate this poverty,
whether one voluntarily adopts the spirit of poverty or spontaneously
gives up earthly goods, detachment is required of every disciple of
Jesus Christ, even to the point of renouncing happiness in this world.
This is what the Gospels call "denying oneself," and one does not
understand affection for the Lord without the unquestioning acceptance of this condition: "And he said to all, 'If anyone wishes
to come after me, let him deny himself, and take up his cross daily,
and follow me. For he who would save his life will lose it; but he
who loses his life for my sake will save it. For what does it profit
a man if he gain the whole world, but ruin or lose himself?' " [19]

The seriousness of this "mortification" is such that St. Paul, who
did not want to "glory save in the cross of our Lord Jesus Christ,
through whom the world is crucified to me, and I to the world"
(Gal. 6:14; cf. I Cor. 4:2), decided: ". . . our old self has been
crucified with Him" (Rom. 6:6), and determined this absolute
law: "And they who belong to Christ have crucified their flesh with
its passions and desires" (Gal. 5:24). To his way of thinking, it
was a question, above all, of participation in the death of Christ as
realized in baptism, by which the Christian is dead to sin.

But the moral life is only the working out of this baptismal grace.
Grafted onto Christ, the believer is like a vine-shoot which can bear
fruit only if it stays on the vine. Now the heavenly Father, like a
vine-dresser who owns the plant, prunes the branches, cuts off the
suckers, and multiplies the cuttings and shavings "so that the good
branch may bear more fruit" (Jn. 15:2). It is impossible to live the
very life of Christ without being pruned, unless it be to the detriment of oneself. That is why the paternal Providence of God

[19] Lk. 9:23-25; cf. 14:27; Mt. 10:38; 16:24; Mk. 8:34.

causes so many trials destined to test the virtue of Christians and to mold them to their Savior. Does not every father train his child when he corrects him? If God treats us as sons, He will lavish us with various corrections: "Those whom I love I rebuke and chastise" (Apoc. 3:19). Certainly, these trials are not sources of joy, but they procure the fruits of justice, and this fruitfulness is a reason for courage to bear them, just as much as the certainty that they are imposed by the love of God: "But if you are without discipline, in which all have had a share, then you are illegitimate children and not sons" (Heb. 12:8). Suffering, in the New Testament, is a grace (Phil. 1:29; Jas. 5:11), an honor (I Pet. 1:7; 4:16) and a joy (I Pet. 3:14; 4:13).

5. BROTHERLY LOVE

Since God reveals Himself as the Father of all men, the latter find themselves linked by the bonds of a real brotherhood, and must love one another. Love of neighbor is one of the most distinctive features of a child of God, Who is Love. Since divine charity is thus universal, active and generous, pardons sinners and does good to those who fail to recognize it, man will need to extend his love even to his enemies, his neighbor being henceforth his brother in mankind: [20] "Love your enemies, do good to those who persecute and calumniate you, so that you may be children of your Father in heaven . . ." (Mt. 5:44 ff; Lk. 6:35). Indeed, divine love became incarnate in Jesus Christ, Who underwent death and passion in order to save His brothers. Ever since then, the consequence forces itself upon those who are already redeemed by His blood, i.e. to devote themselves to the service of their neighbor: "In this we have come to know His love, that he laid down his life for us; and we likewise ought to lay down our life for the brethren" (I Jn. 3:16). It would be contradictory to pretend to love God, whom we have never seen, and to hate, that is to say, not to love someone close at hand who can easily be the object of our attentions and services. The two rules of love of God and neighbor are so linked together that the authenticity of love towards God in the heart of a faithful man is judged by the reality of his brotherly love, certainly not by intention or by word, but in its indisputable manifestations: "My dear children, let us not love in word, neither with the tongue, but in deed

[20] Lk. 10:25-37. The parable of the good Samaritan answers the question: "Who is my neighbor?"

and in truth. In this we know that we are of the truth, and in his sight we set our hearts at rest" (I Jn. 3:18-19).

It is not surprising that Christ Jesus, who is Himself revealer, gift and living proof of divine love, has made of brotherly love at one and the same time the object of His testament and the decisive criterion for His disciples: "A new commandment I give you, that you love one another; that as I love you, you also love one another. By this will all men know that you are my disciples, if you have love for one another" (Jn. 13:34-35). Already in Leviticus 18:18, God had commanded His people to love each other as brothers. If, nevertheless, Jesus issues this commandment anew, it is that henceforth believers shall love each other *as* He Himself has loved men, therefore, after His example and still more deeply as *Christians,* in the strong sense of the word; that is, they shall live the same life as Christ, prompted by the same love. As the Father loves the Son (Jn. 13:1; 15:9; 17:24-26) and as the Son showed this love to the world (Jn. 13:1; 15:9), the faithful of the New Testament, who possess the same life and the same love, must continue this revelation. It provokes many acts of thanksgiving towards God and glorifies Him (II Cor. 9:13-15).

There, surely, is the essential part and the novelty of the morality of the Gospels, especially with respect to the morality of Israel. And so we may not hestitate to define it above all by the love of neighbor: "For the whole Law is fulfilled in one word: Thou salt love thy neighbor as thyself." [21] The proof of it is that brotherly love is the only way of salvation and of eternal life (I Cor. 12:31; 13:3; Eph. 5:2), and that duties toward God, even worship itself, are subordinate to the fidelity of its accomplishment: "Therefore, if thou art offering thy gift at the altar, and there rememberest that thy brother has anything against thee, leave thy gift before the altar and go first to be reconciled to thy brother, and then come and offer thy gift" (Mt. 5:23-24). God will always refuse to pardon the sinner who has not cancelled his debts to his neighbor.[22] Once again, in the final judgment, the separation of the good and the bad will be brought about as the workings of merciful and efficient charity, for all that we do to the least of His brethren, we do or refuse to Christ Himself (Mt. 25:31-46).

[21] Gal. 5:14; cf. I Thess. 4:9; Rom. 13:8, 10; Jas. 2:8.
[22] Mt. 6:14-15; 18:23-25; Lk. 11:4; Jas. 2:13.

6. VIRTUES

Love of charity is itself a true love; it cannot remain in the heart, but tends to act, to dedicate itself and to prove its sincerity; and its fundamental mark is to be "without pretense" (Rom. 12:9; II Cor. 6:6; cf. Mt. 23:3-32). Since Christian morality is entirely ordered by the love of God and of neighbor, all activity inspired by this love will be virtuous,[23] so the greatest sacrifices made without charity, that is, to give all one's goods, to throw oneself bodily into the flames, are of no value (I Cor. 13:1-3). To sum it up, the Christian life consists, on the one hand, in a spirit, an intention that is the reason for its acts which give the latter their moral value; and, on the other hand, it is eager for realization: "Not everyone who says to me, 'Lord, Lord', shall enter the kingdom of heaven; but he who does the will of my Father in heaven shall enter the kingdom of heaven" (Mt. 7:21-23).

The *prudence* of the disciple of Christ lies in listening to the words of the Master and in putting them into practice (Mt. 7:24; cf. Lk. 8:5-15): "For whoever does the will of God, he is my brother and sister and mother" (Mk. 3:35; cf. Jn. 13:17). A good tree cannot bear bad fruit, and it is by its fruits that we learn its quality.[24] Seeing that the Christian's whole life is infused in him by God, it must obey a law of growth and of productivity, blossom into good works [25] and bear fruit: "In this is my Father glorified, that you may bear very much fruit, and become my disciples," [26] for it is the sign of a true love: "If you keep my commandments, you will abide in my love" (Jn. 15:10; cf. 14).

The Christian is obliged to carry out all the duties imposed by natural law (Mt. 19:16-19), from honor due to parents (Eph. 6:1-2; Col. 3:20), conjugal fidelity [27] and work,[28] to respect for the established order (I Cor. 7:17-24) and obligations of justice (I Cor. 6:8-9; Eph. 5:9; Phil. 4:8), obedience to duly-constituted authorities [29] and that which is called in our day the duties of state of life

[23] Phil. 1:9. The word "virtue" is only found in Phil. 4:8; I Pet. 2:9; II Pet. 1:3, 5.
[24] Mt. 7:16-20; Lk. 6:43-44; 13:6-9; Heb. 6:7-8.
[25] Rom. 7:4; II Cor. 6:1; Eph. 5:9; Col. 1:10; Tit. 3:4; cf. the parables of the talents and the gold pieces, Mt. 25:14-30; Lk. 19:11-27.
[26] Jn. 15:7; cf. 16; Phil. 1:11-22; Jas. 3:17-18.
[27] Mt. 5:32; 19:9; Rom. 13:9; Tit. 2:4; Heb. 13:4; Jas. 4:4.
[28] I Thess. 4:11; II Thess. 3:11-12; Eph. 4:28.
[29] Mt. 22:16-21; Rom. 13:1-7; Tit. 3:1; I Pet. 2:13.

(Eph. 5:21; 6:9; Col. 3:18; 4:1). But he is especially careful to satisfy the immediate demands of charity towards his neighbor; he will be recognized by his affability, his meekness, his cordiality, his obligingness, his respect,[30] his joy,[31] the peace which emanates from him,[32] his generosity in hospitality (Rom. 12:13; Heb. 13:1; I Pet. 4:9) and alms-giving (Rom. 12:20; I Cor. 16:13; II Cor. chaps. 8-9), his reserve, his modesty and his humility.[33] He edifies his brothers,[34] corrects them in brotherly fashion in a spirit of meekness,[35] bears with them patiently (I Cor. 13:7; Eph. 4:2) and does them all kinds of good turns (I Pet. 4:10). His bearing is stamped with religious gravity (I Tim. 2:2; 3:4; Tit. 2:7); he is devout [36] and proud of his faith (Heb: 3:10; 4:16; 10:19, 35).

All that he does, he does for the glory of God,[37] that is to say "in charity" (I Cor. 16:14), which is the "bond of perfection" (Col. 3:14) in the sense that it is the way of perfection (Eph. 2:19) and leads to it, gathering and uniting all the virtues into a firmly tied bundle. It is precisely this harmonious coordination which gives each one his character of consummate perfection. Since it is, above all, a question of a morality of brotherly love, Christian morality is a *morality of the Church,* the latter being the dwelling-place of God's family (Eph. 2:19), where we live a "fellowship in the spirit" (Phil. 2:1), closely bound together (Act. 2:44-46; 4:32; II Pet. 1:7), in spite of the extreme diversity of functions (jobs, professions, tasks) (I Cor. 12:4-26; Eph. 2:18). However that may be in regard to the variety of these roles and of the numerous activities which they command, Christians walk in "the way of justice" (II Pet. 2:21), devote themselves to charity (I Pet. 2:14-15; 4:19; 3 Jn. 11) and good works (Heb. 10:24; Tit. 3:8, 14), and to behaving in a manner worthy of the Gospels (Phil. 1:27) or of the Lord (Col. 1:10) and pleasing to Him (I Thess. 4:1).

In order to behave in a manner pleasing to God "like wise men" (Eph. 5:15-17) it is essential to know His will. In the beginning of Christian life, a primary knowledge of God allows the neophyte to

[30] Rom. 12:10; I Cor. 13:4; Gal. 5:22-23; Col. 3:12-13.
[31] I Thess. 5:16; II Cor. 13:11; Phil. 3:1, 4:4.
[32] Mt. 5:9; Rom. 12:18; 14:19; Heb. 12:14; Jas. 3:18.
[33] Rom. 12:16; Phil. 2:3; I Pet. 3:8; Jas. 4:6, 10.
[34] I Thess. 5:11; Rom. 14:19; 15:2; I Cor. 8:1; Eph. 4:29.
[35] II Thess. 3:15; Gal. 6:1; II Tim. 2:25; Jas. 5:19-20.
[36] Tim. 4:7; 6:11; Tit. 2:12; II Tim. 3:12; II Pet. 1:6.
[37] I Cor. 10:31; cf. Eph. 1:12; Apoc. 16:9; 19:7.

set out on the way of salvation (Gal. 4:8-9), but he must strive diligently to develop that practical knowledge which will permit him to distinguish good from evil.[38] This will not be so much the fruit of personal considerations, nor even of investigations about the regulations of the Divine Law, but the spontaneous instinct for good which the acquisition of virtues gives (Col. 3:9-10; Phil. 3:10); notably, of the charity which "abounds in knowledge and all discernment, so that you may approve the better things" (Phil. 1:9; of Col. 2:2-3). We come thus to comprehend all the dimensions of Christ's love and its demands (Eph. 3:16-19).

To have this full knowledge of charity is to be perfect, since that is to possess God and Christ in oneself and to live in communion with them (Jn. 17:3). More directly, the Christian possesses an inner light—that is, *conscience*—which permits him to direct his moral life [39] with security. Purified by Christ,[40] enlightened by the Holy Spirit (Rom 9:14; 2:15), conscience is entitled to judge the rectitude of intentions as well as the faultless propriety of conduct (II Cor. 1:12; 4:2; 5:11; Act. 24:16). A source of convictions, morality, in drawing its inspiration from the will of God and from the precepts of His law, directs life in full knowledge of cause; [41] it is necessarily linked to charity (I Tim. 1:15).

7. THE MOVEMENT OF THE HOLY SPIRIT

What characterizes the faithful of the New Testament, in contrast to the Israelites, is that they are instructed in the will of God, not by a code of laws proposed from without, but from within, by the Holy Spirit working in their hearts.[42] The Holy Spirit, in fact, has been the agent of the regeneration of the faithful, causing them to be born into a new life (Tit. 3:5). Ever since then He dwells in them [43] and His role is to give them new life (Jn. 6:63; Rom. 8:10-11), that is, to infuse and develop the life of God in them. Having been born of the Spirit, Christians walk, i.e., behave, ac-

[38] II Pet. 1:5-8; 3:18; cf. Eph. 1:17; Col. 1:9; Heb. 5:14.
[39] Mt. 6:23; cf. the heart, giving the instinct of good, Mt. 15:10-20; Mk. 3:5; 6:52; 8:17; I Jn. 2:20-21.
[40] Heb. 9:14; 10:22; I Pet. 3:21; cf. I Cor. 8:7.
[41] Act. 23:1; Rom. 13:5; I Cor. 10:25, 27; II Cor. 1:11-12; Tit. 1:15; Heb. 13:8; I Pet. 2:19; 3:16.
[42] Heb. 8:10-11; cf. Act. 2:17; Jn. 7:39; Eph. 1:18-19; II Cor. 4:6; Gal. 5:18; "But if you are led by the Spirit, you are not under the Law."
[43] Rom. 8:9; I Cor. 6:19; Eph. 2:22; II Tim. 1:14.

cording to the Spirit, live under His direction and His control,[44] so
that "whoever are led by the Spirit of God, they are the sons of
God" (Rom. 8:14).

The Lord had prophesied that the consolation of the Spirit of
truth would teach His disciples,[45] and that His first duty will thus
be one of enlightened teaching, of instructing believers about the
will of God and of Christ, whose *alter ego* He is; for He is the
revealer and the qualified interpreter.[46] He suggests what should
be said and comprehended,[47] "Be renewed in the spirit of your
mind" (Eph. 4:23). But the Holy Spirit is quite as much a power
and a force (Act. 1:12). A principle, He is the direct agent of
divine energies infused into the Christian and, consequently, into
his spiritual processes. By virtue of this He moves, sustains and
stimulates as He comforts and consoles (Jn. 14:16; Act. 9:31).
Almost all virtues are attributed to or associated with Him: faith
(Act. 6:5; 7:55; 11:24; I Cor. 12:13), hope (Rom. 15:19),
charity (Rom. 5:5; 15:30), joy (Lk. 10:21; Act. 13:52), wisdom
(Act. 6:3), meekness (I Cor. 4:21), strength (Eph. 3:16; II Tim.
1:7), and especially, prayer, for we do not know by ourselves how
to address ourselves to God (Rom 8:26-27; I Cor. 14:15; Eph.
6:18). "But the fruit of the Spirit is: charity, joy, peace, patience,
kindness, goodness, faith, modesty, continency" (Gal. 5:22-23).

Where we see "sanctifying grace," the New Testament mentions
the third person of the Holy Trinity or one of His gifts, pointing out
that the Holy Spirit is in communication with man in a lasting and
orderly way, so that we can define life in Christ as submissive to the
Law of the Spirit (Rom. 8:2), its essential attributes being acquired
by the reception of a "spirit of filiation" (Rom. 8:5) and of freedom
(II Cor. 3:17). Nothing would be as serious as resisting the en-
treaties of the Holy Spirit, and lying to Him (Act. 5:3), grieving
Him (Eph. 4:30) or extinguishing that burning flame (I Thess.
5:19). The ideal, on the contrary, is to be filled, and as though
intoxicated, with the Holy Spirit (Eph. 5:18; cf. Act. 2:13-17).
Under His permanent motion, every Christian worthy of the name,
progressing from the state of infancy toward perfection, is literally
a spiritualist (I Cor. 2:15; 3:1; 14:37; Gal. 6:1).

[44] Gal. 5:16, 25; I Cor. 6:11, 17; 12:13; II Cor. 13:10; Act. 2:38.
[45] Jn. 14:17, 26; 15:26; 16:13; cf. I Jn. 2:20, 27.
[46] "The Spirit of Jesus" does not permit Paul to evangelize Bithynia, Act.
16:17; cf. 20:22.
[47] Mk. 13:11; Mt. 10:19-20; I Cor. 2:10-16; 7:40; 12:3.

8. PATIENT HOPE AND ITS REWARD

To be docile to the Holy Spirit, to be renewed unceasingly, to make the love of God and neighbor prevail unfailingly or without weariness in the slightest details of life, requires an uncommon strength of soul. Indeed, it is not a question merely of refusing evil desires and triumphing over sin (Rom. 3:9, 23; 6:12; 7:25), but of resisting the devil,[48] of living in a hostile and corrupting world and of being exposed like lambs in the midst of wolves (Lk. 10:3; cf. Mt. 10:22; 24:9; Jn. 17:14), of being a prey to all kinds of tribulations (Jn. 16:1-2; 33, and the entire Apocalyspe), to the point of martyrdom (Heb. 12:4). The Christian is warned of these hardships and he undertakes to face them (Lk. 14:28-33) knowingly. He is armed like a soldier ready for combat;[49] he trains like an athlete or a wrestler (I Cor. 9:24-27; I Tim. 4:8). Briefly, he develops his energies, and he is constantly urged to behave as a man (I Cor. 16:13) and to stand firm.[50]

Yet the forces of evil are so powerful that no man would be able to conquer them without the help of God and of Christ (Jn. 15:5): "Who then can be saved?" He said to them, "Things that are impossible with men are possible with God" (Lk. 18:27). It is God Himself who works in us the will and the performance (Phil. 2:13), who directs our hearts, strengthens them and guards them (II Thess. 3:3-5); He makes every good work capable of being fulfilled in accordance with His will (Heb. 13:20-21). Since every good and perfect gift comes from the Father of Lights (Jas. 1:17; cf. Rom. 8:32; I Cor. 10:13), the first means of living righteously is to implore divine assistance. On this account, prayer is the fundamental duty of the moral life, and with good reason did our Lord and His Apostles insist on it so emphatically.[51] The Christian is a man who prays, and implores God to the extent in which he has decided to do good.

God's support and protection are all the more indispensable as, over and above present difficulties, the Christian must win the en-

[48] 2 Cor. 4:4; Eph. 2:2; 4:27; 5:16; 6:12; I Pet. 5:8.
[49] I Thess. 5:8; Eph. 6:11-17; Col. 2:18; 2 Tim. 2:4.
[50] I Thess. 3:8-13; I Cor. 15:58; Eph. 6:14; Phil. 1:27; 2 Pet. 3:17; Apoc. 2:25.
[51] Mt. 6:5-15; 7:7-11; 17-20; 21-22; Mk. 11:24; Jn. 14:13-14; 15:7, 16; 16:23-26; Rom. 12:13; Eph. 5:19-20; 6:18; Phil. 4:6; Col. 3:16; 4:2; I Tim. 2:1-9; I Pet. 4:7; Jas. 5:13-18; Jude, 20; I Jn. 3:22; 5-14-16.

durance test. His battle is not that of one day, but of a whole life. How can he guarantee each succeeding day and live "upright and without offence unto the day of Christ"? [52] God alone can bring to perfection the work begun on the day of the call to faith (Phil. 1:6; cf. I Cor. 1:9). He requires His own to be vigilant,[53] after the fashion of wise virgins all ready to meet their bridegroom (Mt. 25:1-13), or of servants who await their master's return (Lk. 12:35-48; 13:23-30). It is necessary, above all, to be faithful, that is, true and conscientious, day after day, in the fulfillment of the Divine wish,[54] giving an account, like the good steward who knows he is responsible for the goods received from his master (I Cor. 4:2): "He who is just lives by faith" (Rom. 1:17; Gal. 3:11; Heb. 10:38). In other words, one must be resolved to continue his effort until death: "He who has persevered to the end shall be saved" (I Cor. 13:12).

Endurance and constancy are sustained by the hope of obtaining the good things promised by the Lord,[55] the inheritance which He is saving for His elect,[56] "for all of us must be made manifest before the tribunal of Christ, so that each one may receive what he has won through the body, according to his works, whether good or evil." [57] This patience, which does not weary of delays, made up of strength and hope (I Thess. 1:3; Rom. 5:3-5; 8:25), is one of the most beautiful fruits of the charity which trusts in its Lord and fights in His behalf (I Cor. 13:7; Cf. Tit. 2:2). The Christian life is a "running with patience" (Heb. 12:1; cf. II Cor. 1:6-7).

As he sees that the coming of the Lord is at hand, the believer must continue his race more ardently (Rom. 13:11-12; cf. I Cor. 7:25-31; I Pet. 4:7). If he works—while there is still time—with the psychology of the farmer who waits and prepares for the harvest (Gal. 6:8-10; Jas. 5:7-8), he does not stop hoping to leave this body in order to dwell near the Lord (II Cor. 5:8) and to see Him (I Cor. 13:12). This is particularly the psychology of the soldier who is fighting for victory (II Tim. 4:7; Apoc. 2:10; 3:21) with

---

[52] I Thess. 5:23; Phil. 1:10; Col. 1:23; Heb. 10:23; II Pet. 3:14; Jude, 24.
[53] Mt. 24:42-43; Mk. 13:33-37; Lk. 21:36; I Thess. 5:6; I Cor. 16:13; Eph. 6:18; Col. 4:2; I Pet. 4:7; 5:8; Apoc. 3:2-3; 16:15.
[54] Mt. 25:21, 23; Lk. 16:10; 2 Thess. 1:4; Apoc. 2:10.
[55] Mt. 5:12; 6:1-6; 6:19-21; 10:41-42; 2 Jn. 8; Apoc. 22:12.
[56] Phil. 3:14; Heb. 10:36; I Pet. 1:4; Apoc. 2:10; 3:21.
[57] II Cor. 5:10; On the salary or the reward of the good laborer, cf. Mt. 20:1-15; Jn. 4:35-36.

absolute confidence in the final triumph (Rom. 5:5; 8:35-39; I Cor. 1:7; I Jn. 2:18). Ambitious to achieve glory [58] and already absorbed in the joy of hope (Mt. 5:12; Lk. 6:23; I Pet. 1:6), the Christian knows himself to be victorious and crowned as a king (I Pet. 2:9; Apoc. 1:6; 5:10). Actually, God will put on him the crown of life (II Tim. 4:8; I Pet. 5:4; Apoc. 22:5).

The reward of true, courageous and persevering charity exceeds all description: "Eye has not seen nor ear heard, nor has it entered into the heart of man, what things God has prepared for those who love Him" (I Cor. 2:9; cf. Jas. 1:12).

9. BIBLICAL THEOLOGY AND SPECULATIVE THEOLOGY

Known facts relative to the moral life are not only scattered throughout the different writings of the New Testament, but are of dissimilar character. Our Lord and His Apostles laid down rules of conduct as they were needed in the controversy or happenings of each day, without any prepared plan. The interpreter of Holy Scripture strives to determine the shades of meaning of the original language, their use in their immediate context, the exact meaning of these principles, maxims, figures of speech, exhortations, or occasional laws. The role of Biblical theology is to take inventory of these facts, then to harmonize them and classify them while noting their respective relationships. The task is by no means easy, for, on the one hand, besides commonsense axioms, there are many paradoxical statements, peculiar to the Semitic genius; on the other hand, the literary, oratorical or hortative genre in which these precepts are laid down gives each one often an absolute, sometimes superlative value, which does not allow us to see at once its agreement with other precepts not less categorical yet of lesser importance. However, staying close to the text, the exegete cannot supplement their omission, nor state precisely what was expressed in a popular tongue, directed to readers or listeners lacking in culture. This over-all view of great themes, still expressed in their original language, constitutes the moral theology of the New Testament.

From this first elaboration, speculative theology will set up a morality, strictly speaking, by scientific construction. Reflecting on the revealed texts, it constructs a coherent, organic system, presented in didactic form. All its effort will rest on the analysis and accuracy of ideas, and it will not hesitate to use an adequate vocabu-

[58] I Thess. 2:12; Rom. 2:6-7; II Cor. 4:17; Col. 1:27; 3:4.

lary, completely foreign to that of Biblical writers. Each virtue will be presented in its proper structure, and no longer in its concrete applications nor its religious motives. From now on we see the difference in climate of the two theologies. What characterizes the morality of the New Testament is its intrinsic and constant link with faith and its object. Never is a virtue prescribed for itself, but always in view of the imitation of Jesus Christ, as an expression of charity or in view of eternal salvation.

In speculative theology, these great well-springs of inspiration— so invigorating to the heart—are not dried up, but merely rerouted in other "chapters," those on Christ or on the Holy Spirit, for example, so that it seems to the uninitiated reader that the morality of the New Testament has been secularized. Nothing of the sort! Order and clarity have simply been introduced. Where before there were only moral principles, a moral doctrine has been established. The gain is tremendous, however little the intellectual exigence may be. If, in the New Testament, for example, faith almost always implies hope and charity, without saying exactly in what these three virtues consist, their objects or their very acts are defined with exactitude by theology.

It is because theologians have classified patience with the virtue of fortitude and have stated in detail its role in the moral life, that the uses of patience (so varied and so important) in the New Testament can be correctly understood. Moreover, fundamentally it is always the desire for perfect happiness that governs all of human life, the sin which leads away from it, the grace which leads to it, the virtues which merit it and direct it. The language is different, the realities are the same; but the tiny mustard-seed has become a great tree.

BIBLIOGRAPHIE

J. Bovon, *Théologie du Nouveau Testament,* I, II, Lausanne, 1902, 1905.
A. Schlatter, *Die Theologie des Neuen Testaments,* I, II, Stuttgart, 1909, 1910.
M. Goguel, *Quelques remarques sur la Morale de Jésus,* dans *Revue Philosophique,* 1923, pp. 271-284.
F. Prat, *La Théologie de saint Paul,* Paris, 1923.
A. Lemonnyer, *Théologie du Nouveau Testament,* Paris, 1928.
M.-J. Lagrange, *La Morale de l'Évangile,* Paris, 1931.

H. Preisker, *Geist und Leben. Das Telos-Ethos des Urchristentums,* Gütersloh, 1933.
F. Amiot, *L'Enseignement de saint Paul,* I, II, Paris, 1938.
G. Thils, *L'Enseignement de saint Pierre,* Paris, 1943.
Fr. J. Leenhardt, *Morale naturelle et Morale chrétienne,* Genève, 1946.
J. Dupont, *Gnosis. La connaissance religieuse dans les Épîtres de saint Paul,* Paris, 1949.
C. Spicq, *Spiritualité sacerdotale d'après saint Paul,* Paris, 1949.
M. Meinertz, *Theologie des Neuen Testaments,* I, II, Bonn, 1950.
J. Bonsirven, *Théologie du Nouveau Testament,* Paris, 1951.

BIBLIOGRAPHY

Prat, Ferdinand, *Theology of St. Paul.* 2 vols. New York: Benziger, 1947.
Spicq, Ceslaus, O.P., *The Mystery of Godliness* (Translated by Jex Martin from *Spiritualité sacerdotale d'après saint Paul*). Chicago: Fides, 1954.
Adeney, W. F., *The Theology of the New Testament.* London: 1907.
Dewar, L., *An Outline of New Testament Ethics.* London: 1949.
Dodd, C. H., *Gospel and Law. The Relation of Faith and Ethics in Early Christianity.* New York. 1951.

The end which is last in execution is first in intention. Having to study the conduct of man with regard to his end, we must now consider, before all else, the end. It is the foundation, the keystone, the principle of all our moral theology.

What is called the end of man is that to which he is destined by his nature, that which he cannot help wanting nor seeking. It is his good, his perfection, his happiness. He can no more want not to be a man than not want to be happy.

But where is this happiness found? Some look for it in riches, some in pleasure, others in power or in knowledge . . . as believers, we know that it is in God.

In theology therefore it is our task to offer the process of reasoning to this end by placing ourselves in the faith on the level of understanding where God, who has made man to his own image and likeness, sees the things which He creates.

In this way we shall be brought to consider God and divine happiness (cf. Vol. II, ch. 2), no longer however as the exemplary type, but in the image of God according to which, being spirits, we have been made.

Chapter I

HAPPINESS

Introduction

O God, since thou dost display thy power mainly by showing pardon and pity, multiply thy mercy upon us, so that, hastening on to thy promises, we may gain a share in thy heavenly treasures. (Prayer for the 10th Sunday after Pentecost).

O God, who dost make thy faithful to be of one mind and will, grant that we, thy people, may love what thou dost command and desire what thou dost promise; so that amid the changing things of this world, our hearts may be fixed where true joys are to be found. (Prayer for the 4th Sunday after Easter).

The treatise on happiness occupies a central place in theology. It throws light on the whole doctrine of the relations between God and man. A rapid reading of the Bible, even a simple reading of the New Testament, enables one easily to justify this importance. All of the apostles, especially Peter, Paul and John, and the entire early Church, by a common movement yearn for complete happiness; they make us realize vividly that the Christian life is defined by its end, by its total attainment which is the vision of God face to face. Just as no movement is understood apart from its end, so the Christian life does not reveal its true dimensions to the mind if we overlook the fact that it gives to this life its full flowering, i.e. happiness.

In fact, happiness is nothing else than the fullness of the Christian life. Accordingly, the treatise on happiness will necessarily underlie the treatises which have to do with the Christian life. To study faith, hope, and charity, the contemplative life, any Christian virtue, to study even the work of Christ—the Eucharist, all of the Sacraments —without having happiness in view, would be to misunderstand completely these realities.

The Christian here below is defined as a man seeking happiness. Better yet, in the measure in which he is fully himself, in the measure in which he is an adult in the Paulinian sense, that is, perfect, the Christian already is in possession in the depth of his heart of a foretaste of happiness.

I. The Word of God: Our Call to Happiness

Blessed be the God and Father of Our Lord Jesus Christ, who according to his great mercy has begotten us again through the resurrection of Jesus Christ from the dead unto a living hope, unto an incorruptible inheritance— undefiled and unfading, reserved for you in heaven. By the power of God you are guarded through faith for salvation, which is ready to be revealed in the last time.

Therefore, having girded up the loins of your understanding, be sober and set your hope completely upon that grace which is brought to you in the revelation of Jesus Christ. (I Pet. 1:3-5, 13-14).

Bossuet begins his *Méditations sur l'Évangile* with these simple but splendid words:

The whole purpose of man is to be happy. Jesus Christ came only in order to provide the means for it. To place one's happiness in what one should is the source of all good; and the source of all evil is to seek it where one should not. Let us say, then: I want to be happy. Let us see how: let us find the end in which happiness consists, let us discover the means of attaining it.

The end is contained in the eight beatitudes, for in each eternal felicity is presented under a different name. In the first beatitude, it is a kingdom. In the second, a promised land. In the third, a genuine and perfect consolation. In the fourth, the satisfaction of all our desires. In the fifth, the final mercy which will take away all evils and provide every good. In the sixth, under its own name, it is the wisdom of God. In the seventh, the perfection of our adoption. In the eighth, again the Kingdom of Heaven. Behold the end everywhere, but as there are many means, each beatitude proposes one of them, and all taken together render man happy. . . . The entire doctrine on morals seeks exclusively to make us happy. The heavenly teacher begins with that. Let us then learn from him the way of true and eternal happiness. (Pp. 3 and 18).

Bossuet speaks truly; Christ placed his whole teaching under the banner of the beatitudes which, through a multiplicity of magnificent images, have in view Him who is our unique and indispensable beatitude, God Himself. It is with full knowledge of the cause that the Lord acts thus. He knows our nature, and He knows well that, created by Him in the image of God, made for Him alone, we can never be satisfied except in the possession of Him. Was not the Word of God made flesh, according to the beautiful expression of the Fathers, in order that we might become gods, by sharing in His own life? Was it not His mission to call us, in the absolute gratuity of His love, to happiness?

In the thought of God, happiness is in fact the definitive vocation of all humanity, it is the terminus of its entire destiny. To speak of happiness is really to involve the whole divine plan of salvation and to understand it in relation to the end which orders and clarifies it.

God who is communion, unity of one and the same life lived by several persons, God who is Father, Son and Spirit, wishes to extend His society so as to include us in it. He wishes to unite humanity in the communion of His life. To make use of the boldest of biblical metaphors, God wishes to be the spouse of humanity. In order to invite humanity to this total love, He has used the most astonishing words: "And the bridegroom shall rejoice over the bride, and thy God shall rejoice over thee" (Is. 62:5). "Since thou becamest honorable in my eyes, thou art glorious; I have loved thee" (Is. 43:4). In all truth, God calls us to nuptials with Himself.[1] Is there a more expressive image to convey the total sharing of life than this intimate union which engages everything in man even to the mystery of his flesh: the design of God is astonishingly simple and grandiose. It conducts us to the *beatitude of love*. But to make us perceive the prodigious richness of this divine beatitude—a sharing in His life, in His own happiness—He employs all the figures, from that of the nuptials, no doubt the most daring and the most beautiful, to those of inheritance, of kingdom, of life, of peace, etc.

1. REVELATION OF HAPPINESS IN THE OLD TESTAMENT

The Old Testament is a marvelous pedagogy. In order to lead Israel to comprehend humbly and gently, but profoundly and really, what true happiness is, it reveals its full meaning only in the light of love, in the light of the nuptials. God could not reveal the full force of His love all at once. It was necessary for Him, as a loving Father, to unveil His plan progressively, in keeping with what humanity was capable of bearing; He had to filter the light of His revelation before manifesting it in Christ. But it is clear that above everything, as Scripture tells us, God thinks of the "nuptials of the Lamb" (Apoc. 21:2-10). When God creates the world, when He creates man in His own image and likeness (Gen. 1:26-27)—and so capable of sharing in His life—it is the nuptials which he prepares!

(a) *Happiness of the Just Man*

The plan of God begins to show itself quite explicitly in the promises made to Abraham. In the transcendence of His sanctity,

---

[1] It would be necessary to cite the whole Bible. We refer to Mt. 22:1-14, and more especially to Apoc. 21:2, 9-10.

of His absolute justice, God demands of Abraham, then of Israel, a confidence, a giving up of self so total—one is reminded of the sacrifice of Isaac—that they surpass the particular occasions which draw forth acts of faith, and bring together everything that man can more or less dimly perceive of his complete destiny. It matters little that at this moment of its history Israel has a less clear view of the future life than the ancient Egyptians. In its abandonment to God, it adheres implicitly to the richness of the definitive revelation. God appears as the salvation of His people because He assures them of victory and preserves them from want, especially because He is the God of Israel, He who gives confidence and happiness because He is God: "I will take you to myself for my people, I will be your God" (Ex. 6:7). In the midst of these divine promises which involve the whole mystery of the relations between man and God, man little by little becomes aware, under divine inspiration and in a constant conflict between sin and grace, that his happiness resides in obedience to God, in alliance with Him. It is in being "just" that one is showered with divine benedictions. "The fear of God is the beginning of wisdom" (Ecclus. 1:16); happy the man who puts his hope in the Lord! Riches (Prov. 10:15; 14:20 ff.), glory (Prov. 11:16), a good and long life (Prov. 20:24; 13-14) are the signs of a life in harmony with the wishes of God. This human happiness, which certainly has a supernatural foundation, but which nevertheless *in essentials* remains earthly, came to be shattered by facts; the just did not always obtain the divine blessings which they believed they had a right to expect . . . Job proclaimed loudly his sufferings, he asserted in the face of the world that the happiness of man does not depend on man alone, but on a struggle between God and Satan. The author of Ecclesiastes himself ends up by definitively giving up in his heart all earthly happiness; he knows from experience that earthly goods, even the best of earthly goods, cannot satisfy the heart of man.

(b) *Happiness: Union With God*

Henceforth, only one way remains open, that of the prophets who more and more clearly and with more and more awareness discover for themselves and for Israel that happiness consists in the communion of man with God despite all obstacles and sufferings. In the communion of life between two spouses—God and humanity—there is realized a mutual exchange and an alliance in which the husband shows his mercy, his strength, his protection and the wife makes the gift of her fidelity. Osee, Jeremias—types of the persecuted poor—and later Ezechiel discover in the life with God and in His love the source of all happiness. "I said to God: my happiness is the Lord" (cf. Ps. 88:2; 58:4). The author of the *Canticle of Canticles* sings with splendor of the symbols of love. Thenceforth— the people of God became acutely aware—it is clear that the happiness of man is found in his response to the love of God. With what warmth *Ecclesiasticus* speaks of this love: "Wisdom inspireth life into her children, and protecteth them that seek after her . . . And he that loveth her loveth life: And they that watch for her shall embrace her sweetness" (Ecclus. 4:12-13). In the perspective of this love, stronger than death and capable of triumphing over everything, Israel finally, in the course of the Machabean crisis, becomes aware that God will raise up those who are oppressed. What matters the success of the impious, happiness comes from God alone: "Those who are faithful to the Lord shall dwell with him in love" (Wis. 3:9). The death of the persecuted just man is no longer considered as a punishment, but as a repose. To sum up in a few lines the teaching of the Old Testament on happiness, it would perhaps be best to cite the expression of Moses demanding of God to show him His Glory, that is to say, to show him by a sensible presence His divinity in the radiance of His power and His grandeur. "If therefore I have found favor in thy sight, show me thy face, that I may know thee, and may find grace before thy eyes: look upon thy people this nation . . . And he said: show me thy glory." God answered: "I will show thee all good, and I will proclaim in the name of the Lord before thee: and I will have mercy on whom I will, and I will be merciful to whom it shall please me" (Ex. 33:13-14; 18-19). Is there not here the strongest presentiment that happiness is the vision of God, that it is God known by an intimate knowledge of love, in His Goodness?

2. THE GOSPEL REVELATION OF HAPPINESS

Israel prepares and announces the Messianic work of the Gospel. When Christ appears, He makes Himself known as the One who comes to fulfill the promises, but by going infinitely beyond them. Only the manifestation of the love of God [2] can reveal to us the

---

[2] The expression is from St. Paul. Here are certain texts: II Thess. 2:8; I Tim. 6:14; II Tim. 1:10; 4:1-8; Tit. 2:13.

fullness of our happiness. With Him, the source of happiness is there, in the midst of the world, in the heart of humanity, within the reach of all. To possess it in itself, it suffices to believe in Him, to give oneself to Him. Presence of the Kingdom of God among us, Christ is the heir who comes to share with us the gifts of God.[3] He is the spouse who comes to share with us the life of God. As Bossuet so well divined, Christ is our happiness, at once consolation, satiety, mercy, knowledge of God, divine filiation. Christ is always preoccupied with recalling to His apostles that, more than the gifts of healing, and the power over devils which he granted to them, the source of their joy should be the kingdom of God itself: "You do not rejoice in this, that the spirits are subject to you; but rejoice in this, that your names are written in heaven" (Lk. 10:20). During His life He has no other concern than to call men to partake of divine beatitude, and all through His preaching, it will always be the entrance into the kingdom—therefore into beatitude—which will constantly be given as a motive for acting, as the supreme motive which alone justifies disdain for all the rest. This entrance into the kingdom can require the most exacting sacrifices because God Himself is at stake, the unique goal of our life. Let us recall the parable of the treasure or that of the pearl (Mt. 13:44-45): everything must be sacrificed—riches, kinsmen, integrity of body, life itself. Happiness is then the supreme good. It is a participation in the very goodness of God in an intimate society with Him, the entrance into His joy. All men are called to know this happiness, all men can enter into the kingdom through faith in Christ; even here on earth they know the beatitudes, the happiness of a nuptial feast, of a eucharistic banquet. They will however come to know perfect happiness, absolute happiness, only in the feast in heaven, the feast of the nuptials with Christ, in the eschatological banquet in which all together the children of the heavenly Father will taste God. (Lk. 22:17-18; Mk. 14:25; Mt. 26:29).

(a) *According to St. Paul*

It is of this definitive happiness, in the fullness of Redemption manifested in the risen bodies, that St. Paul thinks. When Christ will have restored everything into the hands of His Father, "God," he said, "will be all in all" (I Cor. 15:28). Happiness for him is

[3] Christ is the heir; cf. especially St. Paul. Christ is the spouse: cf. especially St. Matthew, 22:1-14; 25:1-13.

to be with the Lord: "And so we shall ever be with the Lord" (I Thess. 4:17). It is, even at this point, the great reality in his life that he yearns to die in order to be with Christ. Paul often thinks of this incredible, unique and unheard of intimacy which he will have with his God, fullness of a personal knowledge in the supreme embrace of divine love: "We see now through a mirror in an obscure manner, but then face to face. Now I know in part, but then I shall know even as I have been known" (I Cor. 13:12). This happiness is really the object of Paulinian teaching. Is it not for it that he left everything: "I count everything loss because of the excelling knowledge of Jesus Christ, my Lord. For his sake I have suffered the loss of all things, and I count them as dung that I may gain Christ and be found in Him . . ." (Phil. 3:8)? Again it is the same reality which permits him to proclaim to the world, through all his tribulations and all his sufferings:

> Who shall separate us from the love of Christ? Shall tribulation, or distress, or persecution, or hunger, or nakedness, or danger, or the sword? Even as it is written, 'For thy sake we are put to death all the day long. We are regarded as sheep for the slaughter.' But in all these things we overcome because of him who has loved us. For I am sure that neither death, nor life, nor angels, nor principalities, nor things present, nor things to come, nor powers, nor height, nor depth, nor any other creature will be able to separate us from the love of God, which is in Christ Jesus our Lord. (Rom. 8:35-39).

Without the perspective of this beatitude St. Paul would acknowledge that "We are of all men the most to be pitied" (I Cor. 15:19). Caught up by the vision of Christ, the hope of glory for all Christians, Paul yearns for the moment in which the Church will have attained her full stature in the light of face to face, in charity (Eph. 4:13), and in which the entire creation will tremble with joy at participating in the full redemption of the children of God (Rom. 8:19-22).

(b) *According to St. John*

St. Paul is fully sustained by the most extraordinary hope, that of the final beatitude in which all men, united in Christ, will see God face to face; St. John himself manifests this same aspiration in a more tranquil manner. He too is impatient to see the full realization of the divine plan, but he is acutely aware that happiness is already here; eternal life, which will be consummated in heaven, is already begun on earth. "Now this is everlasting life, that they may know thee, the only true God, and him whom thou has sent, Jesus Christ" (Jn. 17:3). It is the common life with the three divine Persons; it is the entrance into the trinitarian society. "Our fellowship may be with the Father, and with his Son Jesus Christ" (I Jn. 1:3). It is, we must have the courage to say, a veritable possession of the divine Persons, whom we can enjoy as we will. "He who abides in the doctrine, he has both the Father and the Son" (II Jn. 10). "He who keeps his commandments abides in God and God in him" (I Jn. 3:24). "He who has the Son has life" (I Jn. 5:12). "I will give you another Advocate to dwell with you forever" (Jn. 14:16). "God is charity" (I Jn. 4:9), St. John tells us, and He communicates Himself to men in order to make them share in the happiness of God. Christ prayed for just that:

> Yet not for these only do I pray, but for those also who through their word are to believe in me, that all may be one as thou, Father, in me and I in thee; . . . and that the world may know that thou hast sent me, and that thou hast loved them even as thou hast loved me.
> Father, I will that where I am, they also whom thou hast given me may be with me, in order that they may behold my glory, which thou hast given me because thou hast loved me before the creation of the world. Just Father, the world hast not known thee, but I have known thee, and these have known that thou hast sent me. And I have made known to them thy name, and will make it known, in order that the love with which thou hast loved me may be in them, and I in them. (Jn. 17:20-21; 23-26).

Eternal life in its perfection is the vision of God. "Beloved, now we are the children of God, and it has not yet appeared what we shall be. We know that when he appears, we shall be like him, for we shall see him just as he is" (I Jn. 3:2). This is why the whole Church yearns for the nuptials of the Lamb: "The Spirit and the bride say, 'Come!' And let him who hears, say, 'Come!' " (Apoc. 22:17).

The Word of God, manifested in Christ, present in the Church, reveals to us the incomprehensible splendor of the divine plan for the world: we are beloved of God to the point that He desires to make us enter into His mystery, into His repose, that He desires to make us partake of His life, His happiness. Our happiness is indeed the mystery of the nuptials of Jesus, it is the mystery of the kingdom of God, it is the possession of the divine Persons in joy and peace, it is the triumph of divine charity.

> In an absolute communion with Christ there will be realized perfect unity in perfect distinction, a single image in a profusion of images, and in each

of the images, each of the members, each of the sons, perfected in their being by their full relation to the Father and the Spirit, in the Son, like the Son, and Himself eternally perfected in His absolute relation with the Father and the Spirit. Because they will be in Christ, Christ in them, the Father and the Spirit in Christ, men will be one in the Three, and not in any sense absorbed, but consummated in the very act which unites them and forms them into one body: *"Consummati in unum"* (Jn. 17:21-23).[4]

All assembled together in a single love, sons of the same Father, modeled after Christ, our first-born brother, the perfect image of the infinite love, we shall give glory to God by sharing in the happiness of the love with which He has loved us from eternity.

Such is the objective to which God leads us. It is His desire to unite us to Himself in the most complete union, in perfect light and in perfect love; He desires that this union flow over into our bodies and glorify them; that it unite us to one another, and that, assembled as one—in the image of the divine Persons—we may form with Christ our head the perfect body of the Lord. Then will finally appear perfect happiness: "God himself will be with them as their God. And God will wipe away every tear from their eyes. And death shall be no more; neither shall there be mourning nor crying, nor pain any more . . ." (Apoc. 21:4). In our Christian hearts sing the most extraordinary hopes—"Father, thy kingdom come, thy will be done" (Mt. 6:10; Lk. 11:2-3)—and also the most extraordinary gratitude, for nothing, unless it be the gratuitous love of Him who has first loved us, could make us worthy of our extraordinary vocation:

Blessed be the God and Father of our Lord Jesus Christ, who has blessed us with every spiritual blessing on high in Christ. Even as he chose us in him before the foundation of the world, that we should be holy and without blemish in his sight in love. He predestined us to be adopted through Jesus Christ as his sons, according to the purpose of his will, unto the praise of the glory of his grace, with which he has favored us in his beloved Son. In him we have redemption through his blood, the remission of sins, according to the riches of his grace. This grace has abounded beyond measure in us in all wisdom and prudence, so that he may make known to us the mystery of his will according to his good pleasure. And this his good pleasure he purposed in him to be dispensed in the fullness of the times: to re-establish all things in Christ, both those in the heavens and those on the earth. In him, I say, in whom we also have been called by a special choice, having been predestined in the purpose of him who works all things according to the counsel of his will, to contribute to the praise of his glory—we who before hoped in Christ. And in him you too, when you had heard the work

---

[4] J. Mouroux, Sens chrétien de l'homme, p. 130.

of truth, the good news of your salvation, and believed in it, were sealed
with the Holy Spirit of the promise, who is the pledge of our inheritance,
for a redemption of possession, for the praise of his glory. (Eph. 1:3-14).

II. Human Experience of the Call to Happiness

"Thou hast made us for thyself, and our heart is restless until it
rests in Thee!" (St. Aug., *Conf.,* I, 1).

1. THE CALL TO HAPPINESS

The little bird leaves its nest, takes to flight, it flies a little on the level
of the street, soon from leaf to leaf, then higher, and finally you see him
balance himself on the summit; you no longer see him, but a crystal clear
song seems to fall from the sky; he sings, he sings, he will sing until his
death, every morning; the little bird does not know sweet joy, the friendship
of other animals, peaceful contemplation. The child also takes to flight; with
his limpid eyes, he walks, he sings, he mounts upward, and then one day he
is stopped, he sings no more.[5]

Tragic human experience! Man is made for happiness, but man
is unhappy. How hard it is to join these two assertions! Still truth
obliges us to do so. Who in fact knows whether it is better to hear
the prodigious appeal of happiness which excites humanity time after
time, or the unforgettable complaint, so sad and so weary, which
makes itself heard by this same humanity, falling back upon itself?
"Sleep my baby, and let the sea sleep, and let our immense misfortune sleep. . . ." [6]
Man is made for happiness, and man is unhappy; would he only
be unhappy because he yearns for happiness?
After having heard the divine message of hope, let us now hear
the human experience of the call to happiness. Nothing is so moving
as this quest for happiness, tirelessly taken up by all humanity.
Nothing, it seems, can turn it aside from this quest, as if beyond
all defeats and misfortunes, it had at the depths of itself an unfailing
instinct, an absolute certainty of being promised the fullness of
happiness, namely beatitude. We all know it from experience, sometimes from a painful experience. It is from the depths of our heart
that the secret promise of happiness springs. Pascal was right: "All
men seek to be happy, even he who is going to be hanged." A paradox perhaps, but full of enlightenment. Even till death, happiness is

[5] Festugière, *Socrate,* Flammarion, Paris, p. 166-167.
[6] Simonide Fr. 27 Eden, cité par le P. Festugière dans *l'Idéal religieux des
Grecs et l'Évangile,* Coll. *Études Bibliques,* Gabalda, Paris, 1932, p. 168.

what attracts man. The animal itself which does not think of happiness, does not think of death. Man alone finds that he has need to realize a life which for him has completeness of value and meaning, a life which for him consists of joy, achievement and perfection. Astounding dignity of man, the source of all his misfortunes! Man needs to realize his vocation as man. There is in him an exigence and a duty upon which his happiness depends. This is why the terrible and lamentable despair which leads to suicide testifies more than anything else to the irrepressible demand of the appeal of happiness, for, the suicide believes it impossible to attain happiness in this life.

2. THE VOCATION OF MAN

Made to attain happiness, man finds himself called to become greater, to fulfill himself through being more and more receptive to the jubilant exuberance of being, and to *realize* himself in *communion with the all*. Attracted by the total and radiant presence of the mystery of being, he feels himself called to open to it with all of the powers of welcome which are in him. What appeals resound in his heart! The difficulty for him no doubt is to understand at what level is found the appeal which will polarize all other appeals and, without mutilating them, will be capable of integrating them by unifying his whole life! Should he say: "My happiness is God," or "My happiness is enjoyment!" This is a question of paramount importance because life is at stake. The desire for fulfillment is in him so profound that unless it is realized in a chosen line, life becomes a veritable scandal.

A presence entirely directed toward the world and toward others, in a perspective opening on the absolute and the universality of being, little by little man becomes conscious that he will be able to realize himself fully only in two apparently contradictory movements, though in reality they are complementary: that of renouncing himself and of possessing himself.

To remain faithful to this desire of total fullness in the gift and the mystery of himself, without diminishing it or denying it, constitutes for man the whole problem of happiness.

3. THE FLESH, SOURCE OF HAPPINESS

Total fullness, certainly! But it is only slowly that man forms a definite view of what this means. This is the reason why his most spontaneous ideal is an ideal still undifferentiated from total actualization, an ideal filled with activity, with intervals of rest, an ideal of joy flowing from this intensified activity, a vague ideal of communion with others.

This ideal cannot remain undifferentiated, and this is why almost immediately it most frequently inclines him toward an ideal of riches, of health, of serenity, of enjoyment, of happiness, of a happiness which might be defined as a constant and indefinitely renewed state of pleasure.

First of all, man thinks that he cannot be happy without a certain carnal fulfillment; and there is here a part of the truth which Christianity, affirming the resurrection of the body, does not deny. Man yearns to be perfect even in his body. He feels himself in need of robustness, of health, of possession of the physical world, of well-being, of which riches themselves are only the prolongation. He runs the risk certainly—an easy temptation—of yielding to this appeal in a quite superficial search: happiness is the satisfaction of sensual cravings, happiness is the money which permits this satisfaction. Pitifully poor as it may be when left in its rough structure, this satisfaction can be maintained only by the heroic work of the imagination. Art also can play a great role:

> We are moving toward nothingness, precisely because we are moving toward everything, and everything is attained at the moment in which all our senses are ready to set out. Days are fruits, and our role is to eat them and to taste them, moderately or voraciously according to our own nature, to profit by all that they contain, to make of them our spiritual flesh and our soul, to live; to live is nothing else but that! [7]

And the exclamation of Montherlant is well known: "Let the senses live! They alone do not deceive!" [8]

Would not the flesh then be the fountain of happiness in its immediacy and its proximate ideals? Not at all, for it leads to defeat; suffering is there and especially death is there; and man desires in vain a kind of fairyland of a sensible world in which everything would correspond to his desires, man dreams in vain of an ideal corporal transcendence which would allow him to escape from all servitude, from every limitation of his carnal condition. It is not the flesh which can realize this kind of liberating escape from self. On the bodily level happiness is never anything more than pleasure,

[7] J. Giono, *Rondeur des Jours,* "Art et Médecine," February 1935.
[8] Montherlant, *Aux fontaines du désir,* Presses de la Cité, Paris, 1946, p. 12.

that is, the satisfaction of a need or a tendency, and so something partial which passes over in us whole areas—and the most vital— in a state of dissatisfaction. How often the incessant searching for pleasure reveals a profound despair which is ignored! Pleasure, and at a much greater depth, sensual pleasure, seems to promise infinite prospects! How many men believe that sensation is the way of access to the absolute of being in its concrete fullness! Rimbaud has sung of it in the famous text of the *Lettre du voyant:*

> The poet is made by seeing through a long, immense and reasoned disorder of the senses all the forms of love, of suffering, of folly. He seeks in himself, he uses up in himself all the poisons in order to retain only their quintessence. Ineffable torture in which he has need of all faith, of all super-human force, in which he becomes the greatest sick man, the greatest criminal of all—and the supreme savant—for he has arrived at the unknown, since he has cultivated his own soul which is richer than any other.[9]

It is impossible to maintain this intensity without descending into folly. Most frequently, however, a middle position is adopted in which the concern becomes that of finding the means for preserving sensual pleasure and prolonging it indefinitely. Numerous texts of Gide or of Montherlant would easily enable us to accept this point of view. Whatever may be the voluptuous attitude, extreme or medium, there is always the problem, as Mr. Guitton so well saw, of annulling the present moment, of enjoying oneself, for all sense enjoyment tends to be turned into enjoyment of the essence of self, of which the senses are merely a symbol. 'Enjoyment of self' is a perfect expression for concentration upon oneself! We dare say that sensual pleasure is in the last analysis self-contradictory. One of the masters of contemporary eroticism has admitted it: "Sensual pleasure," he says, "is the greyhound course of desire, on which the pursuer always falls before the end, before having attained his prey." [10] And he adds observations like these: "If the concept of time were totally abolished from sensual pleasure, man would die. Complete sensual pleasure would make us eat in the palace of another; how far we are from this ideal and from this sublime end!"

Thus caught up by an ideal of happiness which fills all his being, man does not perceive that his quest for bodily and sensual pleasure

---

[9] Rimbaud, *La lettre du voyant.*

[10] Malcom de Chazal. Text cited by Bataille: *Le bonheur, l'érotisme et la littérature,* in *Critique,* April 25, 1949, p. 302 and 303.

falls short of his total bodily welfare, and, turned toward exteriority, leaves a certain lack of fulfillment. He does not even perceive that he drives away the very happiness to which he aspires. If in fact it is true that the role of pleasure is simply that of perfecting the tendency which has attained its object, of being a surplus which is added like the bloom of youth, it is clear that it cannot be the end, since the man who pursues it becomes engaged in a vicious circle, an absurd effort to attain an objectless satisfaction. Whoever is willing to reflect and to judge in the light reaches the certitude that the most profound denial of the ideal of fullness, inherent in the heart of every man, is to believe in the flesh as the sole source of happiness; and yet whoever loves the truth, to the point of knowing how to find it even where men pervert it, must admit that in this quest of sensuality and of pleasure there is something like an effort to live sensibly in the dimension properly called spiritual. This quest yields evidence of the aspiration of the flesh to bear in itself the very seal of the spirit and of the infinite.

4. POWER, SOURCE OF HAPPINESS

Would not power lead us closer to the end? Would it have happiness for a fruit? To be able to do what one wishes, at the moment one wishes, as one wishes, in complete freedom, is not this the summit of human fullness? Does it not seem that the life of man at this point is ruled by the will for power, that man renounces pleasure voluntarily in order to exercise power? Riches, honors, glory, ability, all the sources of power are but so many strong attractions for man. Who would dare deny the dignity of man seeking the exaltation of himself in power, in the transformation of nature, in the employment of all his faculties? And yet who would dare deny that merely the development of our powers of conquest, sacrificing essential parts of ourselves, draws us to the surface of ourselves and renders us strangers to ourselves by sowing in us a monotonous boredom? Who does not discover the astonishing limits of the desire for power? The best of ourselves and the best of others escapes the clutch of its grasp; spiritual beings do not reveal themselves to us except inasmuch as they wish to do so. Force can do nothing against spirits, it breaks against their freedom. The rejection of pressure is still the only means of penetrating into their intimacy. It is easy to stimulate freely the sensual pleasures which one desires, thanks to the necessary excitants, but it is impossible to stimulate this total joy, this profound joy for which man longs, and which would coincide with his very being. Absolute power—deploying in its service the most extraordinary of modern techniques—allows us better than ever to realize that the most profound and the most exquisite sentiments transcend every technique and demand an attitude of welcome which is really the inverse of the instinct of domination. There is perhaps nothing which expresses so cruelly the failure of the will to power as the Apologue of Tolstoy: "The ground a man needs":

> A man was promised as much land as he could circumscribe before sundown; he makes haste, he runs; the sun begins to go down, he runs faster. Finally he arrives at the end of the great circle at the moment in which the sun falls below the horizon. Exhausted, he too falls: he dies. He will be allowed the few feet of earth which he needs for a grave! [11]

5. CAN MAN BE THE HAPPINESS OF MAN?

If pleasure or power fails to procure happiness, perhaps at least man should be able to find his supreme fulfillment in the gift of himself to humanity which would permit him to transcend his own destiny in the collective destiny of all humanity. Would not the way of happiness be discovered in the remark of Marx: "The supreme being of man, is Man"? Let us try to measure the full import of this statement.

To understand the statement of Marx in the sense of a closed humanism which wants to make of man the measure of all things recalls that man, open to the mystery of being, cannot find his end in himself, even though it were in his own virtue. To see there the profession of faith of a philanthropist leaves him the burden to explain why the gift of himself to others is justified. This justification in fact is due either to nothing else than goodheartedness or to some ulterior motive. Willy-nilly, he must go beyond private interest to find a reason for the meaning of the existence of each individual! When, however, there will no longer be anything to do for others, what will he live for?

Just as idealism escaped the impasse by hypostatizing man (who becomes creative intelligence, reason), by erecting an idol which parodies the true God, so Marxism gets around it by affirming that its mystique of human liberation is not addressed to such or such

---

[11] Charles Baudouin, *Où la virtu d'humilité reprend ses droits,* in *Ma Joie terrestre, Où donc es-tu?* in *Études carmélitaines,* Desclée de Brouwer, Paris, 1947, p. 175.

an individual, but to humanity as a whole. Individual men have no more right than I to my devotion and to my immolation. From man to man, from one group of men to another group, there is no essential difference. At the level of individuals there is no absolute base for the founding of human life.

Moreover, for the Marxists to speak of man, is to speak of a personified humanity which already exists in the gradual progress of the present revolution and which some day perhaps will subsist in a kind of eternity. It is to this present and perhaps future humanity which they immolate themselves—to which they immolate others— as to an absolute before which a human life has only to yield and submit itself.

Let us frankly admit what there may be in this commitment which, from the point of view of the subject, is similar to commitment with God: in humanity the Marxists find the fulfillment of great human values, and God is the judge of the secret of the consciences of those who keep faith with humanity. It is however clear that in this gift to deified humanity, man does not comprehend the deepest and most authentic of human values, those of the world of personal relations with God and through God with other men. In short, man sacrifices to the task for which he needs be immolated; man remains in his isolation, without interior and personal contact with other men; he is in contact with comrades, he is not in communion with friends. The effort for liberation and so for development fails because it does not reach the heart of human reality.

6. KNOWLEDGE, SOURCE OF HAPPINESS

Neither the flesh, nor riches, nor glory, nor power, nor even dedication of oneself to humanity opens one up to the world and to others and makes one self-possessed in freedom. Would not the mind—through knowledge and love—be the only thing capable of bringing happiness?

It is an undeniable fact: man desires to know. In addition to pleasure and to sensuality, he seeks a liberating knowledge; in addition to power, an appeal for the sovereign liberty of the mind comes to light! The ideal of a synthesis of all his experiences in a single act: what fascination for man!

But how great the distance from the desire of knowledge to its realization! What leisure is necessary in order to think! What self-denials, what fatigues must be incurred in order to conquer truth humbly, bit by bit! Certainly, this knowledge is in us the cause of a real happiness, but how imperfect. How far we are from the total plenitude which would fill our hearts.

Is there not moreover reason for distinguishing in the mind a practical aspect and a contemplative aspect? The practical aspect of the mind understands only by organizing a logical process, by setting up a mode of acting, by creating a product which can manifest its intent through signs. The contemplative aspect of an intelligence is not master of itself and depends upon that deep interior which remains transcendent and which it tries to contemplate through certain signs in which it discovers only an uncertain and always changing mirage.[12]

It is through the practical aspect that we subject to ourselves everything created, and there is in it certainly a victory for the mind, a source of joy which, however, cannot lead to complete joy. It resembles too closely power which, as we have seen, does not reach to the depths of being.

It is through the contemplative aspect, on the contrary, that our knowledge gains entry to mystery. In an attitude of welcome and of assent, there is a possibility of being open to the richness of being. But in that, we discover the weakness of our insight. We are open to the mystery of God, but in some negative sort of way; God does not reveal His face to us. But we can already note that perfect happiness can come only from this receptive attitude of the mind. Let us reflect upon this for a moment. In order to recognize the beings that have for us the value of an end, a purely intellectual receptivity is not enough; the whole being must be available or receptive with an attitude of welcome and fidelity. Things exist for us only to the degree in which we open our minds to them, to the degree in which we already love them. There is an affinity which precedes acceptance and knowledge; and it is here that we perceive the bond that links intelligence and will.

For our total and absolute happiness a total knowledge, exhausting the mystery of reality and the mystery of its origin, is necessary. It would be necessary to know God and to know him not from without, as the creator of things, but from within through personal communion with His own mystery, in light and in love. If absolute hap-

[12] G. Madinier, *Intelligence et mystère*, XXVI es Journées universitaires. Supplément aux *Cahiers Universitaires catholiques*, p. 77.

piness is somehow possible, it can only come from a luminous encounter with God. Is this not the ideal which Plato perceived?

What would not the destiny of a mortal be to whom it would be granted to contemplate absolute beauty, not clothed with flesh and with colors destined to perish, but in its purity and its simplicity, to whom it would be allowed to see beauty face to face, in its unique form—divine beauty.[13]

In the intelligible world the Idea of the Good is perceived as something far-fetched and with difficulty, but it cannot be perceived without concluding that it is the *cause* of everything, of everything that is upright and beautiful; that it has, in the visible world, engendered light and the sovereign of light; that in the intelligible world it is it which is sovereign and dispenses truth and understanding; and that it is necessary to see it in order to conduct ourselves with prudence in public and private life.[14]

7. LOVE, SOURCE OF HAPPINESS

If it is true that knowledge enables us to perceive something of happiness, if it is true that there is no personal knowledge except in love, it is evident that love is a source of happiness.

Not certainly the egotistic love of the senses, of brute possession, but a love entirely spiritual, depending on a spiritual knowledge which bears upon the mystery of the other. Is it not here exclusively that one possesses himself in denying himself? It is true, the human heart aspires to a total possession, to an ecstasy in the other, but men learn by experience that a love which is only human leads sooner or later to deception. If there can be for another the revelation of an absolute, a human being cannot be for him the absolute source of happiness. We demand more of human love than we have a right to expect of it.

As the mind in fact yearns for a knowledge which is completed in God, so it yearns for a love whose source is in God.

8. GOD, THE HAPPINESS OF MAN

We have need of a total union—through knowledge and love—with God, and in God with our fellow men. If beatitude is possible it can be only in a union with God and with all our fellow men, in the fulfillment of a call which comes from the depth of the mind and the heart.

The conclusion forces itself upon us: the human person who by his mind transcends every determination, every conditioning, dis-

[13] Plato, *The Banquet,* 211 c and 212.
[14] Plato, *The Republic,* b. 7, 5-17-a d.

covers in and through his action on the world, in and through his relations with others, that no created good can totally satisfy him. If one day he should see this aspiration for happiness, in its plenitude and perfection, fulfilled, it is clear that this will be possible only in God. Certainly, humanly speaking, we cannot be assured that this absolute of happiness will be given us. It depends, as is evident, on the divine goodness. We cannot penetrate into the intimacy of others without being invited to do so, neither can we have access to the divine intimacy without being introduced into it by God Himself. Revelation alone tells us that this happiness is possible. It confirms this immense human aspiration—always unsatisfied— and surpasses it in its total vastness. As Christians, we can then say that man is made for happiness, for the fullness of joy. But let no one deceive himself. Happiness for us is the total perfection of man in an encounter with God. Let us not speak of happiness in the case of the comfortable state of a self-centered individual, let us withhold the name "happiness" from the state of self-satisfaction which hides the most frightful defects, from the state in which too great human assurance and equilibrium isolate authentic values. We know well that the expression "happiness" can be "the habitual expression of egotists, sensualists, profiteers, exploiters, thieves, traitors, cowards, misers; of places, of honor, of glory, of those who, ready for apostasy, today deny the soul, womanhood, fatherland or the God of yesterday, in order to offer incense to a new idol destined tomorrow for the same abandonment." [15] But we also know that it should signify this spiritual plenitude, fully expanded in God and in others, this denial of self in the perfect possession of self which always implies here below a constant progress, but which should attain the absolute of perfection in the next life. Let us then restore to the word happiness its true meaning. We are made for happiness and for joy, for absolute happiness and joy.

Is this absolute possible? An absolute happiness without constant betterment would seem to be contradictory. A whole segment of modern thought seems unwilling to grant this absolute happiness. Whether it be Mr. Le Senne:

There is no final state. We must then set aside the teachings which treat of time as though it were a passage through which the mind would be introduced into a state in which it would be filled and from which it could never defect.

[15] Van der Meersch, *La petite Sainte Thérèse,* Albin Michel, Paris, 1947, p. 258.

No idea has perhaps had a greater attraction for man than that of a paradise, of a kingdom of ends; where there would be nothing to do but to enjoy, for he would then be dispensed from willing. Sometimes also, one imagines that consciousness is like a short history between a state of obscurity which is not yet it and a state of possession in which it would no longer be, a less than consciousness, a more than consciousness; but when we try to conceive precisely either the one or the other, we can no longer find anything but death, for let one try to furnish an Eldorado with the contradiction of the essential play of enjoyment, and he forgets that it gets its whole value from the struggle of which it is the victory. (*Le Devoir,* p. 287).

Or whether it be Gide:

O Lord, protect me from a happiness which I could attain too quickly! Teach me to defer, to withdraw my happiness even unto Thee.

However blessed it may be, I cannot wish for a state in which there is no progress. I picture to myself celestial joy, not as a confusion in God, but as an indefinite and continued approach to him. If I did not fear a play on words, I would say that I despise a joy which would not be progressive. (*La porte étroite*).

Or whether it be Simone de Beauvoir:

Paradise is rest. It is transcendence annihilated; a state of things which is given and which is never to be surpassed. But in this case, what shall we do there? It would be necessary in order that the air be respirable there, that there might be occasion for actions, for desires, that we would have to surpass it in its turn: that it might be no paradise at all. The beauty of the earth gives promise, it is because it promises some new things. An unchanging paradise promises us only an eternal boredom.

Literature has often described the deception of the man who has just attained the end so ardently desired. And then? One does not fill a man; he is not a vessel which meekly allows itself to be filled; his condition is to surpass everything given. As soon as it is attained, his fullness shades off into the past, leaving vacancy, that always future hollow of which Valéry speaks. (*Pyrrhus et Cinéas,* p. 87).

Or whether it be Montherlant:

"Happiness is the desire, the progression, the expectation, the first contact: let no one go further" (*Aux fontaines du désir,* p. 230).

All of these men concur in essentially the same objection—paradise is impossible, happiness is unthinkable, for man is a being on the march who cannot stop marching without annihilating himself. The Christian can understand the partial truth in the objection. More than anyone else, in fact, the Christian knows that there can be no question here below of absolute happiness; more than anyone else, he knows that this earthly life requires constant progress, and more than any other also, he knows that this constant progress is the sign of his lack of happiness; furthermore, he aspires to perfect happiness and he thinks that to deny the absolute overflowing end is to render unintelligible the very movement of progress whether we wish it or not. To relegate human effort for the infinite without granting man the possibility of attaining the absolute he aims at, is to set up the absurd in the heart of man. A march has no meaning except from the end of the movement! To speak of a stage in it, while forgetting the point of arrival, seems to destroy the very idea of stage, which only makes sense if there is already found in it, through hope, a foretaste of the end.

In truth, the whole force of the objection comes from a lack of meaning as to what God is. He is made over into a sort of object—similar to other objects—which comes to hamper the indefinite movement of the mind. He is imagined to be a reality which is placed on the same level as other realities. It is not understood that God is not a good, a good alongside of other goods, but *the Good* which fills the mind completely, precisely by satisfying the aspiration for surpassing every limit.

Perhaps to comprehend how God, and God alone, can perfectly satisfy the desire of man, it will be well to listen to Augustine:

I have wandered around like a lost sheep, seeking thee without, but thou art within. I have gone to great pains to find thee outside of me, but in vain. Thou art within me, if I have at least desired thee. I have tramped through the streets and the open places and the cities of the world seeking thee and I have not found thee. I sought thee badly without, since thou art within me. I sent messengers, that is, my external senses, in search of thee. I did not find thee! I searched badly, I see well now, O my Light, O God, who has illumined me, for I sought thee badly by the senses, since thou art within me. Moreover, they have never heard me say where thou hast entered into me. My eyes say: "If he is not colored, it is not through us he has come." The ears say: "If he makes no noise, he does not pass through us." Smell says: "If he has no perfume, he does not enter through our canal." Taste says: "If he has no savor he does not enter through me." Touch says: "Since he is not a body, don't ask me anything about him." These things are not in thee, O God, neither physical beauty, nor passing brilliance, nor radiant light, nor color, nor agreeable sound of any sort, nor the perfume of flowers or of unguent or aromatic, nor honey, nor delightful manna, nor anything pleasing to the touch or embrace, nor anything subject to any sense whatever. No. I seek nothing of that kind when I love my God. Far from me the folly of taking as my God these things that my senses, which I share with the animals, seize upon. And yet, when I look for my God, I look for a light superior to every light and one which the eye does not see; a voice superior to every voice, but one which the ear does not hear; a perfume transcending every perfume, but yet not perceived by the smell; a sweetness which knows no taste; an embrace above every other embrace, but one foreign to the touch. (*Confessions* I. X. c. 6.).

Fullness of Christian life, if man must pass by everything and therefore die to everything in order to attain God, is but to rediscover everything in God, completely illumined by the light of love. What choice of images could better reveal the personal experience of Augustine?

What do I love in loving thee? It is not the beauty of bodies, nor their perishable grace, nor the brilliance of the light so pleasing to my eyes, nor the sweet melodies of worldly songs in their various keys, nor the suave odor of flowers, their perfumes, and aromas, nor manna, nor honey, nor bodily members made for the embraces of the flesh. No, it is not all of that which I love, when I love my God. And yet, it is Light, a Voice, a Perfume, an Embrace that I love, when I love my God. It is the light, the voice, the perfume, the embrace of the interior man which is in me, there where shines for my soul a light that is limited by no extension, where issue melodies that are not carried away by time, where perfumes are exhaled and not dissipated by a breath of wind, where one may taste a food that no voracity can cause to disappear, and embraces that no satiety ever deserts.[16]

Who, better than Augustine, knew the tragedy of human experience in its appeal to happiness? Who knew better how to discover that happiness is God Himself?

In this misery without respite, in which spirits fallen straight downward show by their nudity the division of the darkness that is never clothed with thy light, thou showest clearly how great thou hast made thy spiritual creature, him who is in eternal rest, for whom nothing that is inferior to thee suffices, nothing, I say, not even himself. Yes, it is thou, our God, who shalt illumine our darkness. From thee emanates the light which clothes us, and our darkness will then be as the sun at noonday.[17]

Throughout human experience, we thus find the same drama of the Bible, that of the personal relations of man with God, the great drama of grace and of sin. To discover the true God, the living God, man must destroy all his idols which risk hiding from him the ineffable mystery.

It is time to take theological note of this appeal to happiness.

[16] St. Augustine, *Soliloquies,* xxxi, n. 1,2,3. We cite these two texts, according to an article of P. Lavaud, *Béatitude et Vision de Dieu* in *La Vie spirituelle,* Suppl. of July 1, 1931, pp. 5 and 6.
[17] St. Augustine, *Confessions* I, XIII, c. 8-9 to 25.

III. The Theology of Happiness

The glory of God is the life of man,
The life of man is the vision of God.
S. Irenaeus

Our whole analysis of human experience bears witness that there is in man an absolute exigence for progress which demands of him, since it is not possible for him to perfect himself by his own powers, that he open his mind to the mystery of this transcendence on which he and the world depend. There is in man the aspiration to be like God, and this aspiration is what Christian metaphysics and theology have keenly analyzed for a long time.

1. ASPIRATION TO HAPPINESS

All creation is lifted up by an immense urge which, from its very depths, impels it toward God. It is shot through and through by a dynamism of structure, by a love of nature which relates it to its source. Created by God, dependent on Him for its whole being, every creature, by the very fact that it is, finds itself directed toward God who is the principle and the end of its being.

Man does not escape this vast aspiration which elevates creation toward God. He discovers in his deepest consciousness his existential relation to Him who has given him being, and who from the interior recalls to him this upsurge of nature so utterly irrepressible, of which he is not the master, and which is at the very source of his being and, by that very fact, of his mind.

It is his duty, in creation, to take note of this call of God, which is essential to his very nature. It is thus that he perfects this creation.

We have already analyzed this human experience, and we have seen that man could find out through constantly renewed deceptions that, in his desire to perfect himself, it is radically impossible for him to fix any limits to his willing without, by that fact alone, going beyond them.

2. THE NATURAL DESIRE TO SEE GOD

But he may also become aware of it by an analysis properly metaphysical. Intelligence is open to all being, it has an unlimited capacity, and God alone can fill this desire of all being. The will, that is, the dynamism of an intelligent being, is also open to the unlimited horizon of the good. Made for universal good, nothing consequently can wholly satisfy it but God, the universal Good.

From the fact of this opening to the mystery of all being, there is in the heart of man an aspiration for a perfection of self which is of the spiritual order, of a dimension in some sort angelic, even divine. There is in him a higher dimension which some minds, such as Plato or Augustine, have analyzed, and which certain modern thinkers, even those the most lacking in faith, Nietzsche, for example, or Dostoievsky, and certain existentialists have rediscovered. It is clear that one has not said everything of the human being when, with Aristotle, he has defined him as a rational animal. His specific dimension thus set forth does not exhaust his grandeur.

This astonishing dimension of man, where it is fully explained, is what St. Thomas calls the natural desire of seeing God. It is in it, we dare say, that the great mystery of man consists, a mystery which we have never fully explained, before which we can assert a priori that all our efforts will fail, for it is the mystery of man as spirit, of his soul considered not so much as form of the body, but as spirit.

May we try to explain somewhat what this natural desire of seeing God is?

It is a desire of the will to seek the good proper to the intellect. To possess God by intelligence is for man the object of love, and since the object of this love is not present in this life, love tends toward it and desires it. It is a natural desire because it flows from the intellectual nature as such, commanded by a natural knowledge.

Knowing God by reason, we aspire to know Him in His essence, in Himself.

St. Thomas has often set forth this argument from natural desire. Let us summarize its elements. Setting out from created things, we can affirm the existence of God, but we cannot know *what* He is. We affirm the existence of God as cause of the world, as it were in darkness, without perceiving Him as He is in Himself. Unsatisfied, the created mind aspires to a knowledge of the divine essence in itself, by a desire which is at the same time a thirst for beatitude. We might say that the natural desire as such merely reveals the nature of the mind itself. Is not the strength of the proof from natural desire actually the desire to know essences and causes, and is not this latter but the simple manifestation of the opening of the mind to all being? We might say again that this natural desire is a desire which, in accord with the structure of the created mind, manifests itself in the consciousness of disproportion between the intellectual nature in its essence and the partial determination which actuates it. We insist on the fact that the desire of knowing God in His mystery is always present with reference to our knowledge of beings. We certainly cannot therefore conclude to the beatific vision which the theologian holds exclusively by faith. We reach a simple philosophical conclusion which cannot prejudice in any manner the essential supernaturality of the beatific vision. But for us this philosophic conclusion has its importance, for philosophy appears here as going to meet the theologian, who accepts its teaching because it agrees with Revelation.

We do not say, as some do, that the spirit should be defined, as the desire of God, but simply that, being spirit, the human being is directed by its nature to searching for its spiritual identity beyond its own limits.

What we discover is that God causes in the created spirit the desire for being united with Him and for participating in His mystery.

St. Thomas assures us that no natural desire can be useless. Does that mean that this desire must without fail find its realization? Certainly not, but it does mean that this desire cannot be disordered, that the existence of such a desire points to the affirmation that it can be satisfied. To say that the desire of seeing God cannot be vain is to say that it is possible for a man to see his desire realized if its object is presented as the end product of a superior gift. It is to affirm that there is in the created mind an intrinsic possibility of the realization of the vision of the divine essence. The soul is by nature capable of knowing God, *"capax gratiae, capax Dei."* In other words, the nature of the created spirit testifies to the desired receptiveness, in line with its proper perfection, of that supernatural elevation which would be the vision of the divine essence, whose realization depends on the divine good pleasure. To speak of natural desire is then to affirm rigorously the ontological orientation of the human mind toward God. Since God has brought certain minds into being He has oriented them to return to Himself.

The desire of seeing God is a desire which moves when aroused because it depends on the transcendent cause, namely God. Not having in itself the necessary resources to realize this desire, the mind which as such faces the transcendence of God and so His gratuity,

must abandon itself to the sovereignly free design of God. If God
gives Himself, it will be as an additional gift, inaccessible of itself
and beyond desert. There is no necessity that God should satisfy
this demand.

To sum up, man is constantly attracted by a beyond. He yearns
to see himself perfected by the gift of infinity. Outside of faith, however, we could not affirm that this lack of fulfillment is "remediable."

3. HAPPINESS, THE LOVING VISION OF GOD

God freely corresponds to the attraction which He has placed in
human nature. He comes—it is, as we have seen, His whole plan
for the world—to communicate to us His beatitude. God loves us,
He speaks to us, He enters into personal communion with us, He
desires to lead us to that fullness of communion which the symbol
of nuptials suggests.

Can we go beyond the image and explain what our happiness will
be? Certain texts of Scripture invite us to do so: "We see now
through a mirror in an obscure manner, but then face to face. Now
I know in part, but then I shall know even as I have been known"
(I Cor. 13:12). And: "Beloved, now we are the children of God,
and it has not yet appeared what we shall be. We know that, when
he appears, we shall be like to him, for we shall see him just as he
is" (I Jn. 3:2).

According to these texts, then, our happiness will be a personal
meeting with God, in the fullness of light and of love. Beatitude
will be the act by which we will take possession of God in the face
to face vision. It is clear that this taking possession of God can
take place only in knowledge and love! We must, as we have already seen, transcend all our partial acts in order to live by the
spirit. Beatitude will be the act in which God, entirely penetrated
by our mind and raised up by the light of glory, will offer Himself
to us. *Beatitude is the vision of God* in the fullness of charity.

In the vision, act of intelligence and act of will are wholly simul-
taneous. In the actuation of man by God, there is an indivisible participation of the intellect and the will in the divine act—if it is true
that man in the simplicity of his unity is act in terms of his capacities.
No doubt, in this simultaneity of act there is a priority of *order* of
intelligence over will in the ontological order; just as in the trinitarian life, there is a relation of origin of the spirit to the word, so
in beatitude there is a relation of origin of the act of the will to the

Our beatitude is not the paradise which Mohammed announces in the Koran:

"For those who believe in Allah there will be in the kingdom of their Lord gardens beneath which streams run. . . . There will be for them pure women and the favors of Allah.

"Perfect women with large black eyes, similar to pearls, will be the reward of their faith." (Sourates 3 and 56).

But what awaits us does not arise from a platonic ideal of separated souls in which happiness seems to be bound up with the loss of our condition as man. To what purpose then should Christ have risen? And yet: "if Christ be not risen, our faith is vain" (I Cor. 15:14).

As the symbol of paradise on the opposite page expresses it—in the wholly human, joyous and sensible terms of the Christians of the 11th century who painted it—our beatitude is at the same time heavenly and earthly. It is "a new heaven and a new earth" (Apoc. 1:1).

Again, as this fresco shows, our happiness is where Christ is: the risen Christ sitting at the right hand of the Father, amidst the angels and celestial principalities. It is here that He has prepared a place for us (Jn. 14:3). It is here that the best of us reside, since He has given us the baptism of the Spirit, the Spirit of the risen Christ, the guarantee of our future glory (Eph. 1:13-14), who lives in us, and whose final action will be to restore life to our bodies (Rom. 8:11). It is here where is found the veritable altar on which, living by His Spirit, we shall meet the Father and where on our earthly pilgrimage, we will nourish ourselves with His body under the sacramental sign of the Eucharist.

This happiness with Christ, in the same Spirit, with the Father, commands the whole movement of the present life. It is our end. On it is founded and is built our whole moral theology. (Fresco of the vault of the Saint-Chef, Isere, France. End of the 11th century.)

act of intelligence. In simpler terms, let us say that man, whole and entire, shares in the simplicity of his being in the life of the intelligence and love of God.

We shall know from the inside the mystery of trinitarian life. In the immediate knowledge that we will have of God, each person will be revealed to us in the relations which he maintains with other persons. It will be the heart of God which will be found adapted to our own.

Let us not imagine that the presence of God in us is according to the manner of intelligible objects which afford us a conceptual grasp. It is the spiritual essence of our being which, objectively, will be found conformed to the divine object. Changed in God, we shall possess God Himself in full light, in an absolute interiority. Humanity will be the married woman of the Apocalypse, and she will be able to say to God in very truth: "Whatever is thine is mine," for she will make but one with God, pierced through by the very life of God, even while remaining in the bosom of this immanence mysteriously distant from God, the distance which there is between the Creator and the creature. Thus she will live in society with God in a mystery at once of union and unity. The happiness which can be realized after death is then essentially the vision of God in love.

Only the vision of God satisfies the deepest and most persistent aspirations of our spiritual faculties. It guarantees the fullness of our filial life through the full enjoyment of its paternal inheritance. This glory which personalizes us fully by making us happy is in fact a participation in the eternal glory of the Son of God. It is He who, receiving from His Father the divine nature, communicates to us through His sacred humanity a share in His own nature, makes us like Him of whom He is the resplendent image, and makes us return lovingly to the Father in the Spirit. As Bossuet said: "One day we shall be like him by the effusion of his glory, and loving in him only the happiness of resembling him, we shall be inebriated with his love. This will be the last and perfect consummation of the work for which Jesus Christ came" (Meditations on the Gospel, Part 2, 72nd day). And he adds: "Thus the Father sees in them only Jesus Christ and this is why he loves them with the same effused and universal love which he has for his Son" (Ibid. 75th day). It is from this communion in the life of God at the summit of our spirit that all the other gifts which will render man totally happy, flow.

4. HAPPINESS AND THE RESURRECTION OF BODIES

If we say that the essence of happiness is this union with God, it is not for the sake of denying the happiness that the resurrection of bodies bring, the sharing of life with our fellow men in Christ, but it is simply to reveal the ultimate basis for all of these superabundant beatitudes. Illumined at its highest point by the beatifying presence of God, our whole being will be in the light. The divine vision is at the root of our corporal glorification. The body of man, we have seen, yearns for spiritualization and would like to be fully transparent to the light of the mind, interior to the soul and enveloped by it. The vision of God through love has rendered possible the resurrection of bodies which finally attain their full stature. The spirit causes the body to participate in its own spiritual conditions; it clothes it with light according to the degree of its luminosity; it conditions it to the point that its sensibility no longer vibrates except to the appeals of the spirit:

"The body is spiritual, that is, incorruptible like the spirit which makes it live, glorious like the spirit entirely swept up into the divine light, powerful as the spirit sharing in its triumphal creative liberty." [18]

5. HAPPINESS AND COMMUNION OF LIFE WITH OUR FELLOW MEN

Happiness through the presence in them of the divine Persons whom they enjoy, beatified in their bodies which are become perfect instruments of expression and of action, glorified in their bodies in the image of the First-born, sons of the same Father, all men will participate in the knowledge and the love by which they are loved by God. Knowing God as He is known, loving Him as He is loved, they will know each other, they will love each other in an incredible intimacy, in absolute transparence. They will know and love one another from within. They will be interior to one another in the light of love and their lives will take on the breadth of all their fellow men. In fact, in the heart of each man will beat the heart of God and of all his companions. Moreover, happiness will be the beatitude of a fraternal society in which, related to God, men will

[18] Mouroux, *The Meaning of Man,* Sheed and Ward.

be united among themselves by the same life of the Trinity. Did not St. Thomas, in his commentary on Chapter 17 of St. John, write that "the end of all the gifts of God is that we may be united among ourselves with a unity similar to the unity which obtains between the Father and the Son"? (Com. on St. Jn., Ch. 17).

Is this not what Scripture suggests in describing happiness as a feast in which everyone shares in the joy of all, not only within himself, but also in the sight of all?

6. HAPPINESS AND CREATION

Being one with God and their fellow men, men will once more be in accord with all of nature which, transfigured, will tremble from the joy in their hearts. In the hymn of thanksgiving of humanity beatified, it is creation which will give glory to God. Everything in its place will contribute to the universal harmony. In beatitude, it is the jubilation of a single happiness, of the whole heavenly Jerusalem. All things are taken up into the unity of light and love; everything is interiorized in God, wisdom, light, love, rest for all humanity. Man and the whole of creation have definitively entered into the joy of God, become forever all in all.

IV. The Realization of Happiness

"God has made temporal things in order that man maturing in them, might yield his fruit of immortality" (St. Irenaeus).

Humanity is therefore called to happiness, to that fullness of communion with the three divine Persons in the transparence of a perfect knowledge and love, which will have repercussions even on their bodies. To be created in the image of God is for mankind the root of that calling which must reveal all its richness in the celestial light of the kingdom. Then, having attained its perfect expression, this image which was given to it in order to be developed by its freedom, will become resplendent in the beatifying encounter of the face to face meeting with God.

From this vocation to beatitude, which is really the most profound truth about man, naturally flows the deepest spiritual attitudes, those which govern the whole development of our lives even to its final perfection.

1. HAPPINESS IS A GRATUITOUS GIFT OF GOD

In beatitude God gives Himself as a person in love. Recall the figure of the nuptials. Happiness is then the finest gift of God, the most absolute, incomprehensible and gratuitous that there is. Only the free love of God was capable of filling the infinite distance between creature and creator. As we have seen, nothing in the creature, even the spiritual, necessarily calls for this gift from on high. Happiness is connatural to God alone. He possesses it by nature, by right of birth, if one may use the expression, and no creature—angel or man —can possess it except as a gift from God, an absolutely free and gratuitous gift which we cannot know except by the revelation of the divine good pleasure. We say then that happiness is a *supernatural gift,* that is, a gift which can come only from on high, meaning by that that our vocation to happiness, that is, a sharing in the divine life, is not a necessity of nature, but a purely gratuitous call of God. Thus it is a wholly vain effort to try to obtain it by our own powers, for we are radically incapable. Our natural resources are of no assistance in regard to supernatural happiness. How often have Christ and the Apostles insisted on this fact that every grace comes from on high, from the Father of lights! This is why the only possible attitude with regard to this gift of God, when it is revealed to us, is to open ourselves to it, in a disposal of our whole being, in an attitude of welcome which permits divine revelation to enter into us. This implies necessarily an attitude of humility, of poverty, of self-denial which is really the constant message of the gospel.

God alone can make us a gift of Himself. No intermediary, except perhaps as an instrumental cause, can be of the slightest aid to us. Nothing conveys to us more forcibly the most radical purity of hope. Only God is its possible foundation. What great dignity is man's who, awaiting the happiness of God alone, has even the angels for his servants!

2. WE MERIT HAPPINESS

Beatitude is a gift of God, but a gift which does not make our efforts useless in acquiring it. God who created us free, wishes that His gift become ours. He wills that beatitude come entirely from Him, yet also that we collaborate under His influence in His realization in us. As the Fathers constantly say: God who has created us without our help will not save us without it! After having been introduced by the action of divine grace to the life of the three Persons, we will, under this same influence, cooperate by our free action in the development of the germ of happiness deposited in us. We will merit happiness. Each of our acts must have happiness for its goal. This implies an attitude of vigilance, of patience, of activity, for man goes to God only by a long human detour, a long pilgrimage. It is by each of his acts, deepening in him the image of God, that he tends toward happiness.

The whole meaning of human morality is to generate in time this active consent to beatitude, this acceptance, this vital and free disposition to understand it more profoundly from day to day.

The whole Christian life tends toward happiness, toward the last days, in a constant upward striving. It consists in receiving God inwardly in a movement which must be intensified day after day, and which gives to time its genuine dimension; it consists in an infinite yearning which has God for its object, and which none of our actions will ever be able to fulfill. More than anyone else, the Christian discovers the truth of the expression of Nietzsche: "Man is made to be surpassed," and he well knows that the way which leads to happiness is a way which demands his whole attention, a way in which to do his own will he must do God's will and that of his neighbor and the world, without hoping to attain God in plenitude before the last days, a way which will throw him tirelessly from one impulse to another, from one gift to another, from one sacrifice to another. It is the hard way of humility and of sacrifice, of renunciation and of poverty, but also the joyful way of perfection, of happiness, of peace, of spiritual freedom. It must be said without reserve: the law of all genuine spiritual life is to prefer to everything else this active consent to God, to subordinate to Him our whole life, in the interests of a progress which is constantly renewed. In a sense, everything is already won when, beyond all transient concerns, we have awakened in ourselves the desire for paradise, when we have said "yes" to the invitation to eternal goods, for this earnest "yes" releases a latent spiritual energy capable of drying up in us all the sources of egoism. In the life of children of God, of sons of light, of heirs of Christ, happiness appears to be the very keystone of the arch.

3. HAPPINESS BEGUN: THE BEATITUDES

A true consciousness of this constant attraction for happiness—law of incessant growth which constitutes the basis of the Christian life—leads to the understanding that Christian beatitude is not purely teleological. It is not a goal in which we would in no way participate. It is already given us in germ in faith and charity. Happiness or to speak like St. John, eternal life has already begun in this life. Certainly it is still hidden and the life of which we are the bearers is not yet manifest, but it is already possessed. It comes from God, it finds its nourishment and its principle of development in God, it tends towards its full unfolding in the celestial life. Certainly in this life our knowledge, our faith, are not on the level of our love and our charity. There is here a principle of imbalance which will only disappear in that simultaneity of the act of knowledge and of love established on the same plane (of which we spoke in the theology of beatitude) but which, henceforth, makes us aspire to know as we are known, that is, to know in vision. In the precise measure of our charity we will aspire to the face to face vision, but also, in the exact measure of our charity, we shall discover at the heart of our life a foretaste of beatitude, and this foretaste consists in the beatitudes. The true Christian, here below, as Holy Scripture leaves no doubt, is he who lives the beatitudes, who lives by God and by all things in God, who already tastes the glorious goal of hope. The constant tension toward final things and the beatitudes are two complementary aspects of the Christian life:

And seeing the crowds, he went up the mountain. And when he was seated, his disciples came to him. And opening his mouth he taught them saying, blessed are the poor in spirit, for theirs is the kingdom of heaven. Blessed are the meek, for they shall possess the earth. Blessed are they who mourn, for they shall be comforted. Blessed are they who hunger and thirst for justice, for they shall be satisfied. Blessed are the merciful, for they shall obtain mercy. Blessed are the pure of heart, for they shall see God. Blessed are the peacemakers, for they shall be called children of God. Blessed are they who suffer persecution for justice' sake, for theirs is the kingdom of heaven. Blessed are you when men reproach you, and persecute you, and speaking falsely, say all manner of evil against you, for my sake. Rejoice and exult because your reward is great in heaven; for so did they persecute the prophets who were before you.

You are the salt of the earth; but if the salt loses its strength, what shall it be salted with? It is no longer of any use but to be thrown out and trodden underfoot by men.

You are the light of the world. A city set on a mountain cannot be hidden. Neither do men light a lamp and put it under the measure, but upon the lampstand, so as to give light to all in the house. Even so let your light shine before men, in order that they may see your good works and give glory to your Father in heaven. (Mt. 5:1-16).

O the happiness of the perfect Christian upon whom falls the blessings of the Lord! In accord with God, a vibrant love in his heart, in accord with himself and with his fellow men, in accord with all creation, the genuine Christian lives in the very joy of God. He permits the Lord, more present to him than he is to himself, to deliver him from evil and to reconcile him to all things. Gladdened by the divine presence which makes him adopt God's view of the world; gladdened in the peace and hymn of thanksgiving which corresponds to the word of God in his life, the Christian destroys in himself this tendency which he has to see evil everywhere, to blame things, events, his neighbor and even himself. He whom the spirit has instructed to see in all things the hand of the heavenly Father who loves him is happy. He can say with St. Paul that Christ has enlightened his life. He knows that through his actual humiliation, through all sufferings and miseries, divine glory is at work to lead him on to final happiness. He knows that, in hope, he is the heir of eternal life (Tit. 3:7). He has a foreknowledge of the final triumph of love at the end of time; already he tastes the joy of this final triumph; already he tastes the joy of God.

Let us be frank about it, the Christian life begins with the most extraordinary prospects of happiness which it has ever been given to man to conceive. Henceforth, it is a life of happiness. "Happiness would be a word inconsistent with our exile, if loving the infinitely perfect and happy Being, we should not be happy in his happiness," [19] as Charles de Foucauld tells us, his face transfused with joy. Julian Green was right when he wrote:

I felt that happiness was near, humble as a beggar and magnificent as a king, it is always there (but we know nothing about it) knocking at the door that we might open and that it might enter and sup with us.[20]

"Our citizenship is from heaven" (Phil. 3:20). In this life we are but pilgrims and sojourners, on the march toward our fatherland, and we yearn for happiness with all the power of our love.

[19] Charles de Foucauld, *Lettres à Henri de Castries,* Grasset, 15th edition, Paris, 1938, p. 185.
[20] Julian Green, *Journal,* Vol. 3 (July 29, 1940).

"Thy kingdom come, thy will be done, on earth as it is in heaven" (Mt. 6:10; Lk. 11:2-3). With the whole Church we are going to the Nuptials of the Lamb, and in our hearts sing the words of the Apocalypse: "Come, Lord Jesus, Come!" (Apoc. 22:20).

REFLECTIONS AND PERSPECTIVES

The Morality of the Good

To put the treatise on happiness at the head of the whole of moral theology indicates a decisive choice. We have preferred a morality of the good (happiness being the total good, the conscious end of the rational creature) to a morality of duty, of social obligation or precept, or a morality of pleasure, of sentiment, etc.

Why this choice? Because theology is a science (wisdom even) whose end is to seek, in the faith, a final understanding of things. Now the activity of man has no meaning nor any "reason" apart from the notion of good. The good is what all beings desire and cannot help but desire. It is their "poids de nature." Whatever man does, whether alone or living in society with his fellows, he seeks his good. The first inquiry of the moralist then arises immediately: what is the total supreme good, i.e. the final end of man? The good which is the happiness of man being discovered, all moral activity is found determined by it.

But will this inquiry into happiness laicize theology? Would it not be simpler to begin with the commandments of God which are a *datum,* inscribed in the law of Moses? We answer that a morality of commandments *explains nothing.* It can well have an explicit opinion of the *datum,* but it will still have to look for *reasons* to support it. A morality which ceases to look for reasons, properly speaking, no longer deserves to be included in a theology. The concept of precept or of obligation is after all a sociological notion and man is not merely a social animal; a morality of commandment or of law or any sociological morality (of the type of Durkheim) touches man only under one of his aspects.

On the other hand, a morality of the good, while satisfying the intelligence, itself gives a reason for the *datum.* We have spoken of the "inquiry." It is only a manner of speaking; for the believer does not need to search for his final end, i.e. his happiness. He knows where it is: "We know that we will be like him, because we will see him as he is." "This is eternal life to know Thee and him whom thou hast sent, Jesus Christ. . . ." Now man knows numerous desires and these apparently are presented as something absolute—pleasure, thirst for power, knowledge, love. . . . How can we instil order among these desires or these appetites? How can a single desire underlie all of these disparate desires? Such are the questions to which the "inquiry" should bring an answer. It establishes order among all the desires of men.

Moreover, absolute happiness which is presented as the total good of man is for the theologian something quite different from the happiness which the philosopher might discover at the end of an apparently similar inquiry. We know that the happiness of which we speak is not an abstract end, it is the Kingdom of God which the gospel promises us, the communion of the saints and eternal life with Christ in the Holy Spirit in the presence of the Father. In a word, beatitude is the evangelical Kingdom of God with all its divine, spiritual, yes even social, corporal, earthly and cosmic dimensions. And if the necessity of analysis compels us to consider for a moment this end in itself, apart from every consideration of means or of ways, this does not mean that we might attain it without Christ. (Cf. Vol. 5).

The Antinomies of Morality

The morality of the good resolves the following antinomies: interested and disinterested morality (beatitude promised is my happiness, but at the same time it is only by losing myself that I find it); gratuitous gift and merit (beatitude is a gift of God and at the same time an object of merit); person and society (a morality of precept can be liberating for society and constraining for the individual; a morality of pleasure can be liberating for the individual, constraining for society; a morality of the good is necessarily liberating both for the person and for society.)

A morality of law or of precept is always somewhat abstract and is inevitably tempted to become casuistic. In fact, the law is concerned only with what is general; and it may be that one act, even commanded, may become bad as a consequence of the circumstances in which it is posited. Again the moralist is left to envisage the largest number of cases possible. But it is impossible that he should envisage all of them. A morality of the good on the contrary is never abstract. The good refers not only to the essence of the act, abstractly considered, but to the act such as it is, with all its circumstances. *Bonum ex integra causa, malum ex quocumque defectu:* an act is good if it is entirely good, bad, at least relatively, if it has the slightest defect.

The Good and Duty

If duty is defined as an exterior law which is burdensome to me and which I do not like, it is itself disagreeable and burdensome to me, and it does me no good (it is not a good for me) so long as my heart remains a stranger to it. If duty is defined by what is good, there is no longer an antinomy between duty and good. Duty is to do what is good, and the more I desire, the more I love what is good, the more I shall discover the good in it. It is better to do what is good by loving it than to do it without love. Likewise if we define the object of the will as duty (in the first sense), the will is a slave and does not find its own good, it cannot expand. On the contrary, if we define the object of the will as the good, purely and simply, there is no longer any antinomy between duty and good (not even any difference) between to will and to love. We might study in the perspective of these antinomies the perfecting of the old and the new law.

Dogma and Moral

A morality of the good, as we have learned, cannot be defined as "the sum total of the commandments to be observed." The good is not only what is commanded; and what is accomplished by obedience to human law, can, in a given circumstance, not be good. Obedience is not the only moral virtue.

The morality of the good is inserted quite naturally into that part of theology which is called dogmatic, and superficially if this distinction seems to oppose it to the theology called moral. In particular it is inserted into the theology of divine government with which we terminated our second volume. God, principle and end of all beings, conducts each creature according to the end which he has assigned to it and the nature which he has given it. God moves the animal to act instinctively and man to act freely. Man, whom God has made conscious and master of his acts, will be able to discover the end which was given him and to determine the means which will enable him to reach it. God attracts him since He is his end and his happiness, and leads him since He is the principle of action. A morality of the good is a morality of nature which is developed and unfolded according to its own internal law, such as God has made and willed it. Moreover there is no dichotomy between dogma and moral theology. Nothing of what dogma presents is indifferent to morality. The great "dogmatic" treatises, because they furnish morality with its principles and its foundation, are also most necessary to the moral theologian; first, the treatise on God, since the whole of morality is commanded by the intuitive vision of God and eternal life with Him: thus, the theology of St. Thomas, who, in presenting to us the divine processions of knowledge and of love, shows us that God does not create us nor lead us through any necessity, but in His wisdom and His love, and that, having created us to His own image, we must resemble Him. Finally, the study of original justice shows us the state in which God created us and to which He wishes us to return, more marvelously still, through Christ. In a general way, the study of man, of his nature, of divine government, presents us with the same principles and end of our moral action.

Inversely, morality considered as a study of the acts of a nature, implies nothing which can distinguish it in itself from the theology called dogmatic.

Natural and Supernatural Morality

The morality which we present is not "natural" even though it begins by a study of the "natures" which are principles of our action, or is presented as a morality of development, of the unfolding of natures. The place which we give to natures has the advantage simply of calling attention to the fact that the nature of man is not destroyed or changed by grace and the latter remains a "help" given to the former.

The hub of all the relations between nature and grace in morality is to be found in the famous case of "the natural desire to see God." Is there in our nature a desire to see God face to face? In other words, is there a natural desire for the supernatural? Certain theologians wishing to safeguard the transcendence of the supernatural deny that there is a natural desire to see God. Others, on the contrary, wishing to safeguard the providential ordination of the mind toward the supernatural, while maintaining the gratuitousness and the transcendence of the supernatural, are opposed to every formula which would seem to indicate a complete heterogeneity of the mind and of its supernatural end.

Outlines of Additional Study

Beatitude and beatitudes. Show the bond between the evangelical beatitudes and the Beatitude which is eternal life. Show the role of relative beatitudes (glory of the body, society of friends, etc.) in the fulfillment of happiness. Note this remark of St. Thomas: "The created being added to the uncreated good does not make a greater good; neither does created happiness added to uncreated happiness make a greater happiness . . . just as two heats added one to the other cannot make a greater heat; but if there exists anything which is "heat by essence" realized in the concrete, it could not be affected by the addition of a hot element. And since God is the very essence of the good . . ." (*De Malo,* Q. 5, a. 2, ad. 4 m.). Beatitude does not exclude other beatitudes, it provides a basis for them.

Compare in the New Testament the elements of Beatitude. Compare the future paradise of Christians: 1) with paradise before the Fall (is there not already in the intention of the author an intention of an eschatological description?); 2) with paradise in the Koran; 3) with the wholly human and natural happiness as Aristotle conceived it in his Ethics and his Politics.

Formal and objective beatitude. We call objective beatitude (finis cujus) that which is the object itself of the beatitude of man, i.e. essentially God as known and loved. We call formal beatitude (finis quo) the act by which man is made happy. Compare the elements in each of these and make a synthesis of them. Note well that beatitude is an act, an operation, the type and exemplar of all human acts. Show the respective roles of intelligence and of will in happiness (beatitude formally is intellectual vision, the joy which results from the will's being entirely dependent on the impregnation of intelligence by God).

Happiness and Joy

Is not joy an accident of a good act? a quality inherent in a good act, something which necessarily accompanies it? Can joy then be sought for in itself outside the act which is its basis? Can there be a good act without joy? What is to be thought of a pure morality of joy and happiness? What is required that it be true and Christian? Does it not frequently happen that the deepest joys are not those that are sought for? Is there not in that a kind of law of joy (in the measure in which joy is not sought for its own sake, but accompanies the good act which has been willed, and so gets all its strength)? Are these considerations valid for beatitude? What should we then seek before all else? Would there be any evil in seeking personal happiness, everything else being excluded? Might one however desire his end by excluding from his desire every accompaniment of happiness? Likewise, can we desire a good act while systematically excluding every accompaniment of joy or even of pleasure? If this question appears to be impossible and contrary to the nature of a good act, show the place and the part of renunciation, mortification, sacrifice, and the cross in Christian morality. If mortification—or the cross—is a "good act" does it still necessarily imply some part of joy? Show the possible psychological deformations of this doctrine: (no longer joy, but masochistic pleasure).

Beatitude and Eschatology

Is all our beatitude a future enjoyment? Did we not receive the guarantees and the first-fruits of it at Baptism? What are they?

Beatitude and Capital Sins

Capital sins are those to which other sins are more or less closely attached. Does not the domination of a capital sin and its seduction come from the fact that sinners are attracted in these seven sins by their aspects of beatitude? Answer yes or no, and justify your position. If there is occasion for it, indicate what would be the aspect which would correspond to each capital sin and make of it a "capital" sin, source of sin.

Certain Universal Principles of Morality (Where the Latin endows these adages with precision and an untranslatable conciseness, we have first stated them in that language.)

Omnia agentia necesse est agere propter finem: Whenever any being acts it acts for an end.

Unumquodque appetit suam perfectionem: Every being seeks its own perfection.

Natura non tendit nisi ad unum: Nature tends toward only one end.

Unumquodque in tantum perfectum est, in quantum est actu: In everything, the measure of being, or the measure of actuation is likewise the measure of perfection.

Objectum voluntatis est finis et bonum: The object of the will is the end and good.

Contemplatio maxime quaeritur propter seipsam: actus intellectus practici non quaeritur propter seipsum, sed propter actionem: Contemplation is desired for its own sake; the act of the practical intellect is not desired for its own sake, but for action.

Actions properly called human are those of which man is the master, or those which proceed from a deliberate will.

Quanto operatio potest esse magis continua et una, tanto plus habet rationam beatitudinis: The more continuous and unified the operation can be, the more it approaches the perfect operation of beatitude.

Beatitudo est perfectio humani boni: Beatitude is the perfection of the human good.

De ratione beatitudinis est quod est per se sufficiens: It is characteristic of beatitude to be self-sufficient.

Omnis delectatio est quoddam proprium accidens quod consequitur beatitudines: Delight, or joy, is a proper accident which accompanies beatitude.

Delectatio consistit in quadam quietatione voluntatis: Delight consists in a certain repose of the will which has attained its object.

BIBLIOGRAPHIE

Le traité de la béatitude, en tête de la morale, peut être considéré de deux manières. D'une part, en effet, il donne les principes de toute la théologie morale et est un traité de la fin de la vie humaine (ou de la fin de la morale); d'autre part, il est un traité de la béatitude considérée on elle-même.

Sur la fin de la vie humaine, et la finalité en morale, on consultera d'abord les ouvrages de synthèse:

M.-S. Gillet, *La morale et les morales,* Paris, 1925.

Ét. Gilson, *Saint Thomas d'Aquin,* dans la coll. *Les moralistes chrétiens,* Paris, 1925.

A.-D. Sertillanges, *La philosophie morale de saint Thomas d'Aquin,* Paris, Alcan, 1922; *L'esprit de la philosophie médiévale,* Paris, Vrin, 1932.

A. de la Barre, *La morale d'après saint Thomas d'Aquin et les théologiens scolastiques,* Paris, Beauchesne, 1911.

Puis monographies claires et simples, comme:

Th. Deman, *Aux origines de la théologie morale,* Montréal, Inst. d'ét. médiévales, 1951.

A.-D. Sertillanges, *Vrai caractère de la loi morale chez saint Thomas d'Aquin,* in *Rev. des sc. phil. et théol.,* 31 (1947).

M.-S. Gillet, *Le fondement intellectuel de la morale d'après Aristote,* Paris, 1905.

J.-B. Dumas, *Theologiae moralis thomistica,* Paris, Lethielleux, 1930.

B.-H. Merkelbach, *Summa theologiae moralis,* Paris, Desclée De Br., 1931.

D.-M. Prümmer, *Manuale theologiae moralis,* Fribourg, Herder, 1915.

L.-J. Fanfani, *Manuale theorico-practicum theologiae moralis ad mentem S. Thomae,* Rome, Lib. Ferrari, 1951.

et enfin le livre récent de J. Maritain. *Neuf leçons sur les notions premières de philosophie morale,* Paris, Téqui, 1951, sans oublier l'ouvrage de caractère historique de:
J. Rohmer, *La finalité chez les théologiens, de saint Augustin à Duns Scot,* Éd. de philos. médiév. XXVII, Paris, Vrin, 1939.
Sur de béatitude en particulier, on lira d'abord l'article de A. Gardeil, dans le *Dict. de théol. cath.* (Art. *Béatitude*) Paris, 1905, et les nombreux "sermons" parmi lesquels la série des "Conférences de Notre-Dame du P. A.-M. Janvier en 1903 (Conférences sur *La béatitude*).
On lira aussi l'article du P. M.-D. Roland Gosselin, *Béatitude et désir naturel d'après saint Thomas d'Aquin,* dans *Rev. des sc. phil. et théol.*-XIII, 1929, pp. 193-222. Et l'on consultera la très intéressante controverse sur le désir naturel dont la bibliographie critique a été établie par le P. A. Motte dans le *Bull. thomiste,* IX (1932), pp. 651-675. Voir enfin M.-J. Le Guillou, *Surnaturel,* in *Revue des sc. phil. et théol.,* XXXIV, 1950, pp. 225-243.

Enfin, sur la synthèse des deux points de vue (fin de la morale et béatitude proprement dite), on lira avec fruit les œuvres et les Commentaires de saint Thomas d'Aquin. Parmi ces derniers, citons:
A.-D. Sertillanges, *La béatitude,* Coll. *Somme théologique,* aux Éd. de la Revue des J., Paris, 1936.
Le bon ouvrage de J.-M. Ramirez, *De hominis beatitudine, tractatus theologicus* 3 tomes publiés à Madrid entre 1942 et 1947 au "Consejo superior de investigaciones científicas."
Enfin, R. Garrigou-Lagrange, *De beatitudine, de actibus humanis et habitibus.* Commentarius in Summam theologicam S. Thomae, I a II æ qq. 1-54, Turin, R. Berutti, 1951; et *L'éternelle vie et la profondeur de l'âme,* Paris, Desclée De Br., 1950.

BIBLIOGRAPHY
Books
Buckley, Joseph, *Man's Last End,* St. Louis: B. Herder Book Co., 1949.
Connell, Francis J., C.SS.R., *Outlines of Moral Theology,* pp. 7-12, Milwaukee: The Bruce Publishing Company, 1953.
Farrell, Walter, O.P., *A Companion to the Summa,* Volume I, New York: Sheed and Ward, 1940.
Garrigou-Lagrange, Reginald, O.P., *Life Everlasting,* St. Louis: B. Herder Book Co., 1952.
Gilson, Etienne, *Moral Values and the Moral Life, the System of St. Thomas Aquinas* (Trans. Leo R. Ward, C.S.C.), St. Louis: B. Herder Book Co., 1931.
MacGillivray, G. J., *Moral Principles and Practice,* pp. 1-25, New York: Sheed and Ward, 1938.
McHugh, John A., O.P., and Callan, Charles J., O.P., *Moral Theology, A Complete Course,* Vol. I, pp. 9-10, New York: Joseph Wagner, Inc., 1929.

Articles
Donnelly, P., "Gratuity of the Beatific Vision and the Possibility of a Natural Destiny," *Theological Studies,* 11:374-404 (Sept., 1950).
O'Connor, W. R., "Natural Beatitude and the Future Life," *Theological Studies,* 11:221-239 (June, 1950).

The necessity of analysis leads us to introduce all sorts of definitions in theology. After the study of God, of His creation, and of His divine government, we pass to another treatise which we have entitled moral theology. In all this there is however no break in continuity. There is always question of God, of the acts of God, of His providence, and of His government, and everything continues to be seen in the light of God who gives us faith, i.e. in the manner in which God sees all things.

God governs everything according to its nature, i.e. according to what He made in creating it. God leads animals toward their end by the instinct which He has given them and which is in them. God conducts man toward his end by the reason which he has given him and which permits man to guide himself while being led by God. For man is capable of knowing the end for which God made him and of seeking it by himself. Man is moved, even while being himself and for himself his own principle of movement. This is true on the level of nature, but equally so on the level of grace, for if man does not find in himself, at least in his nature, the special aids which God grants him in order to obtain the happiness of a child of God, at least he can appropriate these aids, and thanks to them, act and merit by himself. In short, man gains his end, the universal good for which God made him, in being governed by God by the same title as other beings; but since the government of God leads him through giving to him the power of guiding himself, man gains his end by certain acts which are proper to himself and for which he is personally responsible.

At grips with these elements of his destiny, man cannot resist being plunged into a deep inquiry. Since he is capable of knowing his end, what is this end? What is his true good, his universal good, that good for which he is made and which we call "happiness" as it is the good of an intelligent and free creature? (vol. II, bk. 1). Then having recognized that God is this end, the theologian considers the different characteristics and exigencies of this happiness which is his (id.). Nothing else remains for him now than to study the acts by which with the aid of God he attains his final happiness (vol. II, bk. 2).

We must recognize the "theological" character of this development. The moral theology which we seek to organize is not founded on the principle of external obligation and of law. Had we organized it in this way, we would still have to understand these laws and accommodate them to ourselves. The theologian is a believer who has difficulty understanding and yet a law must be understood like everything else. Moreover who will blame him since St. Paul tells us that we are no longer under the law but under grace, that we are children of freedom? Our moral theology is then based on the principle of the good which the ancients defined as what all creatures desire. Where does our natural desire lead us, the most basic desire which God has placed in us? This is the question and no one can excuse himself for dodging it. It entails in its response the whole foundation of our morality.

We return to our thesis. We have now to study the acts by which we attain to divine happiness. Following the English arrangement of moral theology in two volumes, we shall develop in this volume the study of the general principles of human acts and in the companion volume IV, the study of particular human acts, i.e. the virtues.

The universal consideration of acts in this volume is divided as follows: 1. human acts in themselves (chapters 2 and 3); 2. the internal principles of these acts: virtues and vices (chapters 4 and 5); and 3. the external principles of these acts: law and grace (chapters 6 and 7).

Chapter II

HUMAN ACTS

by J. Dubois, O.P.

I. INTRODUCTION: Sources and Position of a Theology of Acts
    1. Moral philosophy or theology?
    2. Sources of a theology of human acts
    3. Current value of a theology of human acts
    4. Place of the treatise on acts in theology
    5. Plan of the study

II. THE WILL
    1. Will and appetite
    2. Spiritual affectivity and the desire of the good
        Its object
        Interiority
        Breadth
        Spontaneity
    3. Principle of love and principle of energy

III. VOLUNTARINESS
    1. Voluntariness and omission
    2. Voluntariness and involuntariness; the conditions of voluntariness:
        Violence
        Fear
        Concupiscence
        Ignorance
    3. Contemporary aspects of the problem of involuntariness

IV. THE CAUSES OF VOLUNTARINESS
    1. Whence comes the impulse of the will?
        Intelligence
        The sensible appetite
        The will
        God

2. The modes of voluntariness
    What we cannot help but will
    The good and goods
    The indetermination of the will

V. FREE WILL AND LIBERTY

1. Freedom of choice and indetermination
2. Freedom of choice and psychological determinism
3. Reason and will in the free act
4. The free act, act of the person
5. Free will and liberty

VI. PSYCHOLOGICAL STRUCTURE OF THE HUMAN ACT

1. Origin
2. Phases of the human act
    Phase of intention
    Phase of choice
    Phase of execution
3. Remarks on the voluntary act
    Strong moments and weak moments in the voluntary impulse
    Elicited and commanded acts
    Order of intention and order of execution
    Interior acts and exterior acts

VII. MORALITY OF THE HUMAN ACT

1. The rule of good and evil
2. Conformity to reason
    The ontological and the moral order
    Synderesis and right reason
    Reason and divine order
3. How can a free act be bad?
    Status of the problem
    Reference to a moral rule

VIII. THE NORM OF MORALITY

1. The sources of good and evil
    The object
    The circumstances
    The end

Chapter II.

HUMAN ACTS

For a man not to act is not to be. Lord, Thou hast promised us joy, and joy is something else for us than to be idle and to sleep. It would not be to represent Thee, Thou who art pure Act, if there remained in us, as too often happens here below, so many principles of movement not employed, if, finally, what is an obscure beginning did not issue forth and if we should not exist, for there is no other happiness for man than to give his all. (Claudel, *Feuilles de Saints,* p. 56).

I. Introduction:

Sources and Position of a Theology of Human Acts

Though happiness is written in the depths of human desire, it cannot be possessed in this life. It is impossible for a being subject to the limits of time and of bodily condition to embrace God by a changeless and beatifying act. God alone, pure Act, is seized and loved by a unique and eternal gaze.

And yet man is moving toward beatitude. As Aristotle had already noted, it is in the multiplicity of his acts that he tends toward the possession of the good. Man performs in time the acts inspired by the urging of his desires.

This is an inferior condition, certainly, subjected to the limitation of multiplicity, but a condition which reflects a real dignity because it is already pregnant with a desired good. Man is in fact engaged in each one of his actions, attaining by his action a certain absolute: he acts well or ill; on the other hand, the merit attached to this undertaking roots it in its perfection, furnishing him a guarantee of his final development.

The treatise on human actions fits in, then, immediately with the one on happiness; man tends toward his end by his actions. Their good or bad quality is already a foretaste of his final destiny, and beatitude itself will be the richest and the most perfect of human acts.

1. MORAL PHILOSOPHY OR THEOLOGY?

To tend toward beatitude, to receive in the very goodness of acts accomplished a guarantee of the happiness sought: the Christian

74

approves these formulas, but rightly judges them insufficient, abstract, even equivocal. If faith confirms their certitude, it infinitely changes the meaning of it by giving to their words a complete content. Further back we associated beatitude with the kingdom of God; the Christian knows the object of his hope, he knows that God is his end. More yet, he knows that this end is already in his possession: "The kingdom of God is within you." Paradox of divine life in us! Pilgrim of the Kingdom, man is on the way, each of his acts is a step in his journey toward God, who already dwells in him by faith and love. Charity is the mysterious bond of grace and glory. The Kingdom of God is given like a talent which must be evaluated. The acts of the faithful servant fructify in the riches of eternal life, they are already riches of eternal life. Through charity, the life of the Christian is then supernatural in its unfolding as well as in its terminus. In charity, beatitude, final end, merit, take on a divine significance. Our end is the possession of God in the beatifying vision before being the unfolding of our personality as man; merit is no longer merely a guarantee of virtuous fulfillment of this personality, it is the edification of our being in glory.

This initial awareness is very important. Philosophical reflection must remain open as far as the concrete mode of its realization—the divine mode of supernatural economy—is concerned.

In the abstract analysis of the development of the morality of a human act, the Christian will be obliged to restore to words their true meaning. The treatise on human acts is not properly a subject of theology. Every man should reflect on his commitment to the good. Before knowing the word of God and despite their groping in the discovery of the true good, philosophers have studied the moral activity of man.

The treatise on human acts arises from natural ethics. It is one of the places in which the theologian takes his stand on philosophy. Certainly, man restored by grace knows another law than the principle of pure reason, the economy of the Christian life knows some more efficacious powers than strict natural morality, but grace, virtues, gifts, do not overthrow the natural structure of the human act. Under the special influence of God, the act of man is a free and deliberate undertaking. The light of choice is more intense, the vigor of decision is greater, but even though inspired from on high, the choice does not remain less a human action. Theology presupposes moral philosophy precisely as grace presupposes nature.

2. SOURCES OF A THEOLOGY OF HUMAN ACTS

There is, then, no reason to be astonished if the "sources" of the treatise on human acts, such as Christian reflection has organized it, are found in the philosophers.

Certainly, Holy Scripture shows that man is, by his acts, the master of his destiny. It sanctions good acts and bad acts. From Genesis onward man is presented as conscious and free when confronted with divine precepts.[1] The sapiential books contain very profound reflections on the destiny of man and his liberty.[2] To those who consent to follow Him Christ demands precise acts by which He will judge their fervor and good faith, acts which procure happiness.[3] He distinguishes simple inclinations from efficacious intentions.[4] He weighs the gravity of the secret desires to which man has given his consent.[5] St. Paul has described in the following terms the struggle between

[1] "Yahweh says to Cain: Why art thou angry? and why is thy countenance fallen? if thou do well shalt thou not receive? but if ill, shalt not sin forthwith be present at the door? but the lust thereof shall be under thee, and thou shalt have dominion over it" (Gen. 4:6-7).

[2] "God made man from the beginning and left him in the hand of his own counsel. He added his own commandments and precepts. If thou wilt keep the commandments and perform acceptable fidelity, forever, they shall preserve thee. He hath set water and fire before thee; stretch forth thy hand to which thou wilt" (Ecclus. 15:14-17).

"God created man of the earth, and made him after his own image. . . . He put the fear of him upon all flesh, and he had dominion over beast and fowls. He created of him a helpmate like to himself: he gave them counsel and a tongue, and eyes and ears, and a heart to devise: and he filled them with the knowledge of understanding. He created in them the science of the spirit, he filled their hearts with wisdom and showed them both good and evil. He set his eye upon their works to show the greatness of his works . . ." (Ecclus. 17:1, 4-7).

[3] The whole of Chapter 5 of St. Matthew will suffice to show this. And throughout His preaching the Lord demands of those who hear Him to prove by their conduct their adherence to God. In Mt. 7:21, we read: "Not everyone who says to me, 'Lord, Lord' shall enter the kingdom of heaven, but he who does the will of my Father in heaven shall enter the kingdom of heaven." The parable of the talents (Lk. 9:11; Mt. 25:14) and that of the faithful servant (Lk. 12:35-47) repeat the same demand. The Lord insists on it in His last discourse (Jn. 14:15): "If you love me, keep my commandments." St. John seems to have been so struck with this appeal that he made of it the theme of his epistles. The love of God must be manifested in concrete and daily undertakings, in particular in the love of our neighbor.

[4] Cf. the parable of the two sons (Mt. 21:28-31).

[5] Mt. 5:28. "But I say to you that anyone who even looks with lust at a woman has already committed adultery with her in his heart."

the flesh and the spirit, the drama of human action under the law: "It is not what I wish that I do, but what I hate, that I do" (Rom. 7:15).

In truth, as soon as man considers his destiny in the world he begins to reflect upon his own nature, to analyze the end and structure of his acts. The consciousness of freedom is given in the very experience of acting, it is within the reach of every man. From Confucius to Pythagoras and Socrates the great spiritual men of all times have experienced this effort of introspection and of psychology. Here as in the whole of morality Christian thought is indebted to Greek thought, and in particular to Aristotle, scientific culmination of Socratic fervor.

The treatise on human acts, in its rigor and precision, was constituted rather recently. We see it maturing in the immense movement of theology in the 12th and 13th centuries. The great stages of its evolution are marked off by the work of St. Augustine and by the entrance into the West of the translations of Aristotle and then of St. John Damascene. The former had been struck by the mystery of human endeavor under the influence of the divine call and by the desire for happiness. He also examined lengthily the psychology of love, of consent and of enjoyment. Christian morality survived for a long time on the riches of the Augustinian treasury. The great master of the medieval schools, Peter Lombard, fixed the tradition of it. But little by little Aristotle was introduced into Christianity, and theologians found in the *Nichomachean Ethics* an organized morality, Book III of which furnished a splendid analysis of the human act. The play of intelligence and of the will at the point of the act of choice, such as Aristotle presented it, nourished speculation on free will.

It is the appearance in the West of the translations of St. John Damascene which made possible the union of the two currents. The *De Fide Orthodoxa* had the advantage of offering an analysis of the human act sufficiently refined to show agreement of the thoughts of Augustine with those of Aristotle. This synthesis was the work of St. Thomas Aquinas. The treatise on human acts of the *Summa Theologiae* is a reduction to perfect order of the conceptions which underlay a very profound view of the voluntary act. Despite its analytic and abstract aspect, the exposition of St. Thomas is certainly, in the whole history of philosophy, one of the most vigorous and penetrating. We shall follow his example by inaugurating this moral part of the theological synthesis by a philosophical analysis. Some may be repelled by his relative abstractness. It will be evident here with a particular clarity that a rigorous philosophy is indispensable to the theologian whose steps and ultimate definitions it serves to clarify.

3. CURRENT VALUE OF A THEOLOGY OF HUMAN ACTS

St. Thomas was the first to develop a scientific treatise on human acts. The categories which he introduced were a lasting acquisition for theology. It would still live by them if, under the influence of a moral theology called "practical," the treatise on human acts had not been displaced, deformed and abridged. Since the 16th century the demand for a psychological and moral analysis at the level of the very principles of morality has been lost, and writers have fallen into the morass of casuistry, that niggardly economy of moral conduct which Pascal so cruelly ridiculed. In this perspective, or rather lack of perspective, the treatise on human acts no longer appears as necessarily bound up with that of happiness. It loses henceforth its fundamental role. It also loses the axis of its intelligibility. The essential concepts are devaluated and suffer damaging confusion: those, for example, of conscience, of voluntariness and of free will.

It is important to restore to this treatise its rights: For that the method of philosophy will suffice. We shall try to work on this plane and to reflect on the human act in the light of a conception of the nature of man.

At any rate, it is on this plane only that the treatise will remain living and susceptible of rejuvenation. Everything that modern psychology discovers—biological conditioning, patterns of behavior, exploration of the unconscious, characterology—helps to nourish and to illustrate a view of man profound enough to judge and to assimilate the new results. The moralist can sharpen his insight even while remaining in the light of the same principles.

4. PLACE OF THE TREATISE ON ACTS IN THEOLOGY

Once the necessity of the ultimate end has been accepted, the study of human acts becomes fundamental. It is precisely the object of morality to consider how the acts of man are ordained to the end which he intends. All later reflections on the conditions of morality presuppose this preparatory study. We will even say that their various streams converge to throw light on all of the aspects of this central reality, the action of man on the march toward his happiness. We shall consider the *passions* because human action emanates from a complex being depending partly on the reactions of a sensible body. Moreover, by his own action, man conditions his future; his acts leave behind them, in the soul as well as in the body, certain traces of the present action, viz. *habitus;* thus dispositions acquired for good and for evil are the *virtues* and *vices* which have a moral value with regard to the acts which they facilitate. Finally *law* is nothing else than the regulation of human action, especially in the relations of the latter with the common good. When *grace* comes to animate it with a new life, this whole moral organism subsists; the acts of man supernaturalized preserve the same psychological structure. The study of psychology, and the morality of the human act considered as it were in the pure state, must be retained in the study of morality as a whole.

5. PLAN OF THE STUDY

For the philosopher and the theologian, human action asks two kinds of questions. Some concern its development and psychological structure, others its moral value. This explains the division of our study in this chapter (parts II to VI; parts VII to IX).

The psychological part will help us to perceive in good order: 1) the power from which principally the human act emanates, *the will;* 2) what characterizes *the voluntary;* 3) its *modes;* 4) the voluntariness of the human action being a free voluntariness, the application of the results of the preceding analyses to a study of the *free act* and of the *free will;* and 5) a brief glance at the *psychological unfolding* of the human act. These elements will be sufficient to enable us to approach the morality of the voluntary undertaking.

As to its moral value we shall inquire into 1) the *moral rule;* 2) the application of it to the measure of the *goodness* or the *malice* of acts; and 3) the particular case of the determination of merit. These elements will permit us certain reflections on the state of happiness in our action, thus leading us back to the point from which we started.

II. The Will

The lucid and loyal analysis of the least of my acts enables me to discover the will's true dimension. My capacity to love is infinitely greater than the content of the realities which I grasp. Among various possible uses of my time, I have today the choice of reading, of, perhaps, reading a work of theology. My choice involves a more or less profound desire, one that is more or less explicit, but it is definitely this desire which animates interiorly my action and determines my attitudes. I choose on the basis of what appears to me to be my good: my relaxation, my duty, my culture, my spiritual advancement.

The power of the soul which confronts the good and brings to bear upon it all its force is the will. The intellect is defined as the faculty of being and of the true; the will in a parallel way is defined as the very *desire* of the *good*. It is a conscious and rational desire. The will is a *spiritual affectivity*.

Only those acts are characteristic of man that are effected by the dynamism of the will. We distinguish *human acts,* voluntary and conscious, from the *acts of man,* i.e. mechanical or spontaneous acts which man performs without either thinking of them or exercising his profound affectivity.

1. WILL AND APPETITE

The will has been defined as a "desire of the good." Being pure tendency toward the good, the will is an appetite. The appetite is really an internal principle which inclines a being toward its end. The desire of man has this characteristic of tending toward the good consciously grasped as such. This is why we immediately added: conscious, rational desire. In saying that the will is an appetite, we place ourselves among those beings which tend toward an end, and in specifying that it is a *rational appetite,* we indicate its place in the hierarchy.

The concept of appetite introduces an overall view of the world. It suffices to examine nature to see that everything around us is tendency. Every being is animated by a natural dynamism which makes it incline toward its own perfection: germination, growth, flowers, fruits, desire, love; this inclination appears with evidence in living things. The ancients found this impulse in the beings which we set down as inert. Rocks, heavy bodies tend downward, light gases tend to rise, because, they said, they seek to find a place which is suitable to their nature as heavy or light. Appetite is then the internal need of a being to discover its place, its fulfillment, its plenitude.

Though it is common to all beings, this natural dynamism is realized in unequal modes: from the mineral to the living, from the living to the being endowed with knowledge and to man, the hierarchy of appetites is superimposed on that of natures. *Interiority, breadth, spontaneity* of appetite increases with the degree to which we rise in the scale of beings. Interiority tends toward immanence, breadth toward universality, spontaneity toward initiative and independence. True enough, since we ourselves approach God who loves Himself in a perfect immanence, with a love which embraces all being, and which, far from being determined, is inexhaustible outpouring and infinite liberty.

We do not speak any more of the *natural appetite* of inanimate beings: that a stone follows gravity, that grain tends to mount upward in a stalk, the bud to open up. We qualify this surge of nature rather freely by the term tendency or dynamism, because, no doubt, these beings do not know the terminus of their tendency. The tendency is imprinted on their natures, but like their natures, it is strictly determined and imposed from the outside by the will of the Creator. The term appetite is more commonly reserved for tendencies consequent upon knowledge: the sensible appetites of animals, the rational appetite of man, the will.

Cognitive beings in some sense look out upon the universe. By its eyes, ears, smell, its whole sensible organization which is often so delicate, the animal is open to external realities. They, in some way, come to dwell in it. It knows them. Thus the pleasurable object no longer stimulates desire by an external attraction; known by the senses, it becomes an internal principle of inclination. The cat leaps upon the mouse. It pursues it. The mouse is the term of its desire, but it is the image of the mouse known, and desired because known, which activates interiorly its hunt. There is a progress in the interiority of the appetite, yet the animal is not master of its inclination. As with beings deprived of senses, the inclination is imposed from without. The affectivity of the animal presents an automatism, greater perhaps, but still similar to that of nonliving things: automatism of instinct, determinism of the useful and the harmful. The cat cannot not *desire* to crush the mouse which suddenly appears in its range of vision. John Damascene rightly said: "non agunt, sed magis aguntur," they are acted upon more than they themselves act. Judgment of what is to be done is not within their power. Nature has judged for them; they but obey the will of their Creator. Sensible affectivity is then the movement released by sensible knowledge, an impulse toward the useful, flight from what is harmful. Bound to the sensible, animal appetite shares in its relative interiority, that, namely, of representations. It is subject to their limits, for its scope does not exceed that of bodily organs, and its spontaneity is only a response to exterior solicitations.

Through the whole corporal part of his being man shares in the sensible nature, he is subject to its affective movements, the passions. But he escapes from their limits because of a superior power. Man is spirit. What the appetite of the animal is to sensible knowledge, that the will is to intellectual knowledge. The degree of knowledge indicates the dignity of the corresponding appetite. The will is the power of desire of a conscious and reasonable being. It is a rational appetite, a spiritual affectivity.

2. SPIRITUAL AFFECTIVITY AND THE DESIRE OF THE GOOD

On the level of the spiritual being, interiority, breadth and spontaneity—criteria of which we have already observed the increasing excellence as we pass upward on the scale of being—are presented in a much more perfect mode. Their similarity to the divine model becomes clearer as we approach Him. Man is the image of God.

Its Object

But this image is incarnate. Through my body I am in contact with things, and it is apparently toward them that my will is borne. Do I not find here the object of my affectivity? No. In reality, I ask far more of things than they can give me. The spirit within me accomplishes an over-extension in order to discover through and beyond itself its proper object: the good. Sensible affectivity confronts corporal realities apprehended by the senses. Spiritual affectivity confronts the very essence of the good; it is defined as the desire of the good.

Should I say that my desire has for its object a universal value? Yes, but in the sense in which intelligence has for its object the *being* of things that *are*. In the will as in the intellect there is the fundamental complexity inherent in the condition of man. My mind discovers the object in the light of being; I desire everything under the aspect of good, according as each participates in the sovereign good.

Interiority

It is the intellect which effects this fundamental penetration. It apprehends the measure of the good of beings which are proposed to my desire. The animal is moved infallibly, he is acted upon, without consciousness. Being man, I know what is useful for me, I know what is good for me, I judge, I am aware. This intimate bond between intellect and will, to which we shall have to return, merely causes to be expressed on the plane of spiritual affectivity what we have seen in sensible affectivity. The surge of desire follows upon knowledge. It is the condition of interiority. The intellect discerns and detaches the good from things which I encounter, it presents it to the will which is moved. Love is born, springing up from the depths of my person, because another has entered into me.

Breadth

Bound up with intellectual knowledge, the will like the intellect has a universal range. While sensible desire is limited to particular things, the desire of man tends toward the good, i.e. being as desirable. This basic indetermination, due to the particular and limited character of the things which surround us, constitutes the foundation of our free will.

Spontaneity

Indetermination in the presence of *goods* does not exclude necessity with regard to *the* good. Confronted with this transcendental object, the will behaves like a nature. The desire of the good is as necessary in man as is falling for a heavy body. It is a natural and spontaneous movement. It is not within man's power not to desire the good, and if he seemingly desires something evil it is still because he finds in it his happiness.

3. PRINCIPLE OF LOVE AND PRINCIPLE OF ENERGY

The tendency toward perfection inherent in every being takes on in man a spiritual mode. In him the will is the profound desire for happiness. This is why it is called spiritual affectivity. More precisely, if we allow for the fact that the spirit in man is reason, we may call it a rational appetite. One definition sums up all the others: The will is the love of the good.

Now it appears that modern thought has lost the deep optimism of this view. Since Kant especially, the will is referred to as an energy which faces up to duty. Through the "education of the will" moralists understand by the formation of "character," strength, manliness, courage, generosity.

If we go to the bottom of things, the will-love does not exclude but rather surpasses the contemporary conception of the will. The latter has retained only one aspect, the energetic and almost violent aspect. To call for *volunteers* for some dangerous mission is, according to common understanding, to solicit the services of those in whom moral energy will triumph over interior reluctances. Now, what is this energy if not a surplus of generosity, if not a force which forestalls spiritual dislocation? Such a force draws its dynamism from the very dynamism of love. The willing of a good must set itself in opposition to the obstacles that may arise. In the upsurge of love, a power must maintain the unity of affective life. It is this intimate energy which the current conception of the will retains. Moreover, it is easy, through the middle term of generosity, to grasp the displacement effected from love to "sense of duty." Generosity is the expansive virtue of a healthy love. Moral energy is a force which issues from generosity.

For the life of man, a morality of duty is rich in fidelity and nobility. But it runs the risk of not satisfying it, it does not seek deeply enough for the source of human action. Man is not moved first by an imperative, but by a desire. Not "the good must be done," but "I want the good." In speaking thus we do not reduce morality to an easy hedonism. To will the good is to be faithful to reason, a fidelity which has its demands. Love has its obligations and its struggles, and the ideal of man is to integrate duty into the stream of his personal choices. "The sign of a free man is to be able to make joy coincide with his most habitual actions, the sign of a slave is to separate them." [6] Similarly one might say: the sign of a free man is to be able to make love coincide with duty.

The voluntary act is one which is animated by love.

III. Voluntariness

The will is an affectivity conscious of its end. What proceeds from it will be defined by the same characteristics of interiority and of knowledge. The voluntary is one that has its origin in an inner principle, the end being known.

[6] L. Lavelle, *La conscience de soi,* Paris, Grasset, 1933, p. 113.

1. VOLUNTARINESS AND OMISSION

It will be noted that we say the voluntary is *that which is,* not *is an act which.* This detail has its importance. The voluntary does not necessarily presuppose an act. The non-willing also enters into the category of the voluntary. There is a *direct* and an *indirect* voluntary, or if you prefer, a positive and a negative. We impute to men the effects of their omissions. The pilot responsible for a ship is the cause of the shipwreck if he is not at the controls. But, someone will say, his abstention is voluntary because he has *willed not to act.* Beneath the external omission there is a positive interior act. The pilot has willed to omit, that is why his omission is voluntary.

Certainly to will *not to act* is voluntary. But aside from this *direct* voluntary, there is an *indirect* voluntary. What appears is the omission, and it may be that it was voluntary, but we go beyond the exterior act. It may be that the pilot *did not wish* to intervene, quite simply because at the moment he willed something else. *Not to will* therefore what one should is indirectly attached to the will. Not to act then and not to will are voluntary.

Now each time that I wish something, I omit to wish all other things. These possible acts are infinite in number. Are these omissions voluntary? No. For in reality there is no infinity of choice. We have only to consider the acts possible *for me.* This evaluation will vary with circumstances and duties. The conflict of the voluntary and of the juridical order is then rich in questions of casuistry.

2. VOLUNTARINESS AND INVOLUNTARINESS: THE CONDITIONS OF VOLUNTARINESS

Such is the domain of the voluntary. It is important to fix its limits. The reward for this effort will be to furnish us with elementary conceptions indispensable for explaining the imputability of acts and the responsibility which they involve whether from the moral point of view or even from the juridical point of view.[7] First we shall compare the voluntary with the willed (volitum), a conception closely resembling *velleity.* The *non-voluntary* is that which, not proceeding

---

[7] The jurist takes equal account of fear and of error and he works out a definition of them for his own use (cf. can. 103-104). It will be noted that in the case of marriage, for example, the considerations of the jurist and the moralist do not concur. Grave fear does not annul the morally voluntary but it can create a juridical impediment (can. 1087).

from the will, is a stranger to the voluntary. One should carefully distinguish also the non-voluntary from the *involuntary*. Here there is question of what is no longer foreign to but *contrary* to the will, what it wishes to prevent. It is important to determine the part of the voluntary and of the involuntary in the human act. For this the elements of the definition given above may be consulted: interiority, knowledge of the end.

Violence

Violence is a force or a constraint applied from without. By throwing a stone into the air I impose on it a movement contrary to nature. The violent is opposed to voluntary movement just as to natural movement. It would be contradictory that an act interior by its very nature should be totally conditioned by something exterior. Violence can have no effect on the act itself of willing (the elicited act).

But the will commands the faculties in the exercise of their acts (commanded acts). These can be constrained, without the will, from the exterior, e.g. the *forced* deeds of the martyrs who did not wish to adore the emperor. Beneath the involuntary external deed, the only possible way of applying violence, consent remains unaffected. Between violence and voluntary there is open contradiction.

Fear

Our times are acquainted with violence in its most subtle forms. But let us not on that account hasten to the conclusion of involuntariness in situations of weakness. True violence is rare, and it is often confused with fear.

The latter is a trepidation of mind in the presence of some imminent and dangerous evil. The act to which it gives rise is complex. It is that of the captain who in order to save his ship throws the cargo overboard. Ideally, on leaving port, he certainly did not wish to do this. In face of the tempest, however, he does will it. Thus the decision made in the face of danger is repugnant to my prior wishes. Fear has made me will in a particular case what, theoretically, I did not will at all. I do wish it nevertheless. Here is a mixture of the involuntary and the voluntary in which the latter predominates, since it bursts forth in an act welling up from the interior in perfect consciousness.

Concupiscence

Contrary to common opinion, passion is not violence. Lust, desire proceeding from our sensible nature, increases voluntariness. Concupiscence is in fact an attraction which strengthens the voluntary movement, warping it toward the appetite of the delectable good. In other words, the will fulfills with greater alacrity and ardor what it does under the stimulus of a vehement desire. One should note, however, that we speak here of voluntariness and not of liberty. It will be seen that with regard to the sin of passion, the intensity of the passionate movement even while reinforcing the voluntary, obscures the light of judgment. Passion prior to deliberation diminishes the freedom of the will and consequently the sin. We conclude then with this paradox: by reason of concupiscence, there is less of liberty and yet more of voluntariness.

Ignorance

In the three preceding cases voluntariness was estimated in terms of function of the interiority of the principle. In the case of ignorance the yardstick will be taken from knowledge.

Ignorance is not *error,* false judgment, nor *forgetfulness,* knowledge once possessed but actually lost. It is the absence of knowledge which normally would be required. Moralists have distinguished degrees in their qualifications of ignorance: from *invincible* ignorance due to the incapacity for learning, to *crass* ignorance, resulting from laziness, and to *affected* ignorance, the fruit of mental fuzziness and contempt. There is one distinction which interests us here more particularly, for it shows ignorance in direct union with voluntariness. With regard to the act of the will, it may be antecedent, concomitant or consequent.

An act which results from antecedent ignorance is involuntary. I buy a stolen object. Not knowing its origin, I cannot will it as a stolen good.

Concomitant ignorance accompanies the act without being its cause and without being itself voluntary. Thus the accomplished act is neither voluntary nor involuntary, but non-voluntary. I wish to kill my enemy. Believing that I see some game, I kill him. I would have done the same thing if I had known what I was shooting at. I was ignorant of this. Did I will to kill him? No. I did not kill through ignorance but in ignorance. My intention is blameworthy but my act escapes the category of voluntariness as it does of involuntariness. This ignorance neither excuses nor accuses me.

As for consequent ignorance, since it is voluntary, it renders voluntary the acts of which it is the cause. There will be shades of difference according as it was directly or indirectly willed: from the impassioned which "does not wish to know," to the negligent which did not believe it a duty to know, the degree of voluntariness is more or less high; this is true for the measure of voluntariness for the act which results from igorance. Very often, had one known, he would not have acted. Consequent ignorance is then the cause of voluntariness, but some admixture of involuntariness remains possible.

3. CONTEMPORARY ASPECTS OF THE PROBLEM OF INVOLUNTARINESS

As we have just defined them, the voluntary and the values which limit it are considered in their abstract state, in their relation to the very nature of willing. Such a reference guarantees the permanence of these conceptions.

Still, modern moralists approach human activity through the measure of its concrete realizations. Moved by juridical or casuistical preoccupations, they formulate the problems of voluntariness more readily in terms of imputability and responsibility.

For about a century, psychology has moved in this direction. The problems raised by criminology, moral rehabilitation, education, have sparked the researches of the psychiatrist and the psychologist. They asked themselves what could be the limits and the conditions of responsibility. But approaching the human reality exclusively in an experimental fashion, these theorists have gone so far as practically to dissolve morality into pathology. They get rid of responsibility by substituting a given form of determinism. The determinism of constraint and of social pressure for the sociological school, the psychological determinism of heredity for Lombroso and the partisans of "moral insanity," the psychic determinism of the subconscious for Freud and the psychoanalysts.

Whatever may be said of the philosophies of man too hastily removed from experience, it cannot be denied that psychological exploration by pathology and the divers methods of observation have restored the position of the problem of the voluntary act. The results of these works help to make us aware of the limitations which determinism imposes on the voluntary and through it on liberty. Man is conditioned and sometimes imprisoned in a network of social complexities—economic, physiological, psychic—which it is the duty of the moralist to take into account.

But the human soul is an incarnate spirit, and the final secret of the spirit escapes all measurement. Some have found this spiritual dimension embarrassing because it flows over into their experience and into their scientific framework. But if determinist theories eliminate the voluntary as something too elusive for the mind to grasp, the spiritualist conception of the voluntary is not unaware of determinism.

For him who has perceived the spiritual nature of his activity, lucidity of consciousness and mastery of will, there can be no question of suppressing liberty. The real problem is to discern as well as possible the fringe at which determinism will allow it to have play. This is why the moralist will have recourse to the experimentalists.

IV. The Causes of Voluntariness

I have decided to read. A few moments ago I was not reading. I then began to will. What force moved me to do so? This question raises the problem of my liberty. Before approaching it, a preliminary answer is possible on the grounds of psychological analysis. Let us try to discern more accurately the components of the voluntary act. Assigning the will its place in the order of beings, we have defined it as a rational appetite. This placement allows us to explain both what the causes of the voluntary are and what are its modes.

1. WHENCE COMES THE IMPULSE OF THE WILL?

Psychological analysis distinguishes two aspects in the voluntary movement: first, I act or I do not act; secondly, If I act, I do this or that. The first aspect, the pure fact of acting, concerns me as a subject. We shall call it the *exercise*. The second involves an element of *determination* which comes from the *object* willed. This distinction between exercise and determination permits us to discern what comes from the intellect and what from the will in voluntary activity.

Intelligence

A pure efficiency without determination is inconceivable. At any rate, it is not reasonable. Movement has to have a terminus, and there is none for willing except the good. It is knowledge which makes the good present to the will. It is the intellect which presents to the will its object. I want this or that because I have appreciated its goodness.

To estimate the value of a good is nothing else than to seize a certain relation, for the good includes a relation, namely, being inasmuch as it is desirable. Whether the object immediately is indisputably good, or whether it be necessary to establish this goodness by reasoning, or whether one would have to recall some teaching received or fall back on some traditional evaluation, reason measures the goodness of things and proposes them to desire. We may say then that intellect moves the will after the manner of a final cause.

The Sensible Appetite

But we shall see that this judgment of measurement is subject to warping. The passions sometimes upset us to the point of disturbing the serenity of our judgments. Under the lash of a violent love, of anger, of hunger, a man judges differently about the suitability of an object. It is through this bias and so on indirect grounds that the sensible appetite can be included among the movers of the voluntary act.

We must recall here that the voluntary is, through the sensible appetite, more or less under the immediate influence of everything that conditions the physical being of man. Health, heredity, climate, customs, conditions of life, influencing the passions, increase or diminish the lucidity of judgment.

The Will

Objective motion has the characteristics of a final cause and has priority over it. The will cannot put itself in act if no good is presented to it. Exercise presupposes a previous determination.

Nevertheless, once tending toward the good proposed, the will activates by its prompting all the acts necessary to acquire it. In the order of exercise the motion comes from the will. The case is the same with it as with a king who recognizes only the total good of his kingdom and who by his commands moves the ministers of each department. In the realizing movement of human activity the will moves the other powers, and it is in this dynamism that it itself is moved.

The willing of a good implies in fact the willing of everything that is related to it. Because I willed to read, I willed everything that could bring about this end. I changed my work, I took up a book, I isolated myself, I willed each of these acts. I was moved in each one of these particular volitions by my desire to read. By the fact that the will tends toward an end, it is the motive power of the volitions which concern the means. We may conclude then that the will is itself moved in the order of exercises in the manner of an efficient cause.

God

But is this the final explanation of voluntary dynamism? I am not perpetually in a state of willing! My successive acts of will have beginnings. Whence comes the energy that enables me to actually will? Only a metaphysical consideration can answer this question. Shall we attempt, on a purely psychological plane, to attach each act of will to the movement of a preceding act? In that case, we would be threatened with the necessity of an indefinite regress without ever finding the origin of the efficiency sought.

The will is power of desire, and it requires an actual reality to cause it to pass from potential to actual willing. When I desire something that is presented to me, my voluntary impulse has its origin in a motion which surpasses me. Who is the author of this impulse if not the very cause of the will: God at once the transcendent and immanent mover.

God is Himself present to the work and in the work of each being and He is also the final mover of my acts. The least of my acts of will draws its vigor from the divine motion. Creator of the universe, God alone can move beings from their interior, showing respect for their natures. He moves his creatures intimately and without violence, or at least He makes them move themselves, according to their natural endowment. Heavy bodies tend downward, the rose blossoms, man desires, chooses, enjoys. God is present at each of these acts. Creator of the human soul, cause of the will, God is the final mover of the voluntary act.

In the voluntary act there are three types of motion: one objective, through the act of reason, the other subjective, the very energy of the will, the third transcendent while remaining also profoundly intimate, the divine motion. It is easily seen that this last motion includes in an eminent way the objective order and the order of exercise. In its energy as well as in its end, all voluntary activity is under the influence of a divine dynamism. "In him we live and move and are" (Acts. 17:28).

2. THE MODES OF VOLUNTARINESS

Does not this influence destroy the autonomy of the voluntary act? No, for God respects its modes. The voluntary act can really be either necessary or free.

What We Cannot Help but Will

Let us consider the will in the very urge of its being. Being essentially appetite for the good, it is moved necessarily by the good. This necessity is that of every natural inclination. Just as infallibly as the rock is moved by its weight and the animal by its instinct for the useful, the will tends toward happiness. Once the spiritual appetite is exercised, it is unable not to will the good. To will happiness is a necessary act of will.

How far does this necessity extend? The will necessarily wills whatever maintains with happiness a necessary relation. There are goods which, without being themselves our final end, are attached to it by a necessary bond. It is by one and the same love that a music enthusiast cherishes what is related to his art and the means for practising it. He loves the great musicians, he seeks out everything which can serve the call which is in him. Thus everything that immediately throws light on the ultimate end, all the necessary means or privileges, share in its irresistible attraction.

The will then enters into the play of a determinism, let us call it a necessary spontaneity; it necessarily desires the sovereign good.

The Good and Goods

But what is the sovereign good? For the creature there is here introduced a radical indetermination. In God who knows perfectly His own goodness, which is absolute and infinite, Love wells up in a necessary act of will, infinitely satisfied. The condition of the Blessed shares in this fullness. Seeing God face to face, the elect adhere to Him infallibly. Their will is fixed in a necessary choice, plenitude and fulfillment of the voluntary.

In its earthly condition, human nature escapes from this superior determinism, which is also fulfillment of liberty. Only an infinite and perfect good can appear to me to be suitable from every point of view and fill the infinite capacity of my will as a man. As a Christian, I know who is my good! But reason alone does not immediately and with certainty reveal that this good is in God. I am determined to seek the sovereign good without knowing with evidence this absolute capable of necessitating my choice. I aspire toward it, but I do not encounter among creatures any but particular, partial, and mixed goods. *Some goods* or good things, and not *the Good*. Determined to desire the latter, I am indetermined with regard to the former. My native impetuosity makes me desire happiness and to seek the absolute through things. Before knowing God, man locates where he can his sovereign good, he chooses his ultimate end, and is frequently duped by a happiness whose misery he does not even suspect. Happy the man who discovers the vital insufficiency of what he grasps and sets out to discover the absolute which it suggests. "All our yearning is but a question" (Rimbaud, in a poem, *Les soeurs de charité*). Happy the man who discovers in the perfection of God the satisfaction of his desire. "Irrequietum est cor nostrum, Domine, donec requiescat in te." [8]

The Indetermination of the Will

Except for the good known with certainty, our will is never necessitated to choose what it wishes. This is the consequence of the irreducible gap which separates for us the *Good* from goods. We constantly experience this indetermination, experience of choice, of indecision, the bitter experience of sin; and how often it happens that we choose what is evil! We can account for this indetermination in the three orders of motion distinguished earlier in this chapter.

First, in the objective order: we have already commented on the ignorance in which we naturally were of our final end. Because of this radical indetermination of the creature we have to choose the concrete object of our desire, and what diversity do we find among the choices of men before they are captivated by God!

We have seen moreover that in man spiritual affectivity was subject to the limitations of matter. The breadth of the spirit must accommodate itself to a body limited by narrow perceptions, subject to the illusion of the sensible, subjected to the passions, tempted by inferior pleasures. This carnal condition costs man many errors. By it, he is even more indetermined in his search for the good.

Even if we succeeded in stabilizing our will in its desire for an end,

[8] St. Augustine, *Confessions,* bk. 1, chap. 1. "Thou hast created us for thyself, O Lord, and our hearts are restless until they find rest in thee."

indetermination remains with regard to the means. Not all of them are necessarily connected with the end. We must choose among the possible ones. In this we differ from material beings which a natural automatism has determined to unique reactions or at least more circumscribed ones; we escape from the lower determinism of physical law or instinct.

In the order of exercise, the will likewise escapes from necessity. It can will or not will. Certainly, when I think of beatitude, my will cannot not will to desire to possess it. But it is possible for me to omit thinking about the sovereign good. The will is not determined to will to think of the good, it being the function of the latter to stimulate it to action.

Finally, God respects this indetermination, this earthly condition of our voluntary nature. He moves each agent in conformity with its condition: from necessary causes there must come necessary effects, from contingent causes, contingent effects. He therefore gives to the will a movement naturally indetermined. To object that this indetermination of the will suffers defeat by the necessity of the divine motion is to suppose the will capable of choosing something else than that to which God moves it. It is to overlook the metaphysical nature of divine causality: God is immanent in each of our acts. Divine movement is infallible, but it is applied to the action of a free nature. Far from destroying liberty, the divine movement is its best guarantee. God creates us free, and He looks upon us as free. We freely will what God wishes that we should will. Divine necessity, liberty of human choice—"we must hold to both ends of the chain." The divine impulse maintains us in our radical indetermination.

The voluntariness of our deliberations and of our choices is a free voluntariness.

V. Free Will and Liberty

1. FREEDOM OF CHOICE AND INDETERMINATION

In the indetermination of the will, man becomes aware of his liberty. Before I opened this book the use of my time was indetermined. I might, indifferently, have gone to a movie, listened to the radio, gone to a church service, but I *freely* continue my reading because it is always possible for me to change my occupation. In that, I am aware of being free. Not being under the necessity of willing this rather than that is for most men the meaning of liberty.

In truth, however, this is no more than a first approach, superficial and provisional, to the mystery of liberty. Liberty cannot be defined in terms of indetermination alone. That would be to identify it with pure contingence. To be free on Sunday is not to be indifferent to all possible forms of leisure. The liberty which would find me as indetermined in the evening as in the morning would be quite ridiculous. Indetermination is no more than the field for the exercise of liberty, the occasion of its manifestation. My liberty does not consist in a radical indifference in the presence of all the things which surround me. If that were true, I should be a victim of chance, more miserable than the beings deprived of knowledge. Liberty of choice is a positive reality, closely allied with a spiritual condition. Among material beings, nature has somehow fixed by a pre-established judgment the terminus of movement. As a man, I myself judge the terminus of my desire, I weigh and measure the goodness of things. Free will is precisely the power to compare a given good with the absolute good, even though only a partial good is chosen. To be free then is *to be able* to judge of the good actually and immediately desirable. Through free will, I escape from indifference: many things were offered a moment ago to my choice. I chose that of reading. I determined myself.

To say that the will is not necessitated to follow the good thus proposed to it would again equate liberty with indifference. It would claim that the appetite does not desire the good judged to be so, and therefore to contradict the very conception of appetite. I cannot will the contrary of what I have finally judged to be preferable. This would be nonsense; appetite follows judgment.

2. FREEDOM OF CHOICE AND PSYCHOLOGICAL DETERMINISM

The real problem is then to ask ourselves what force activates free judgment in order that it may exercise on the will a determining influence. The illusion of indifference rests then on an experience, alas a current one, which seems to deny this thought: "I do not do the good that I wish and I do the evil that I do not wish." How often it happens that I choose a part while *knowing* that the good lies elsewhere! The doctor forbids me to smoke. I know that smoking is harmful to me. I am perfectly aware of it at the moment when a friend offers me his cigarette case. Nevertheless, I accept one. It is the same in all of the cases in which, *knowing* what the law is or what would be the good, I rob myself. Popular language expresses this very human duplicity thus: "He has acted contrary to his conscience."

To act contrary to conscience is to go against a calm and deliberate judgment, one which I form quietly, as a moralist. Still, even when I act contrary to my conscience, I follow a judgment. Every choice implies a deliberation and a judgment that are more or less perceptible. Human action can be analysed in the form of a practical syllogism whose general structure would be like this: the good is to be chosen; but this act is good; therefore this act is to be chosen. The major is necessary. It expresses the very nature of the will defined as the desire of the good. The conclusion is the final decision which immediately ordains my act. The free choice then resides in the minor; it is made real in the judgment in which I affirm; this is my good.

I always choose then what seems to me to be the better thing, what seems to me to be good. But is this not to admit, as opposed to a liberty of indifference, a determinism of the better? This was the position of Leibnitz. For him, freedom was only a psychological determinism. Would not man be merely a spiritual automaton under the lash of a moral necessity?

This illusion arises from the fact that one juxtaposes, as though distinct persons, an abstract intelligence and a will acting in a void. I do act according to a judgment, to be sure, but it is not the result of a group of ideal reasons. To affirm: this is my good, is to attribute to a limited being the determining value of the good in itself. Now, as we have seen, God alone exhausts the fullness of good. There is between *the* Good and goods an irreducible margin in which the play of reason is indetermined. My judgment of a good does not depend solely upon the resources of pure reason. I choose the better, but the better that is chosen is not necessarily the better according to reason. My choice cannot be placed in rigorous equation; something of the non-rational enters in. This non-rational is no other than the very impetus of affectivity. The final practical judgment is already saturated with will.

3. REASON AND WILL IN THE FREE ACT

It is not enough then to say that the will acts conformably to the judgment which proposes the good to it. It concurs of itself with the efficacy of this judgment. The free will is the mistress of the choice in the judgment which determines it.

The intellect is determined with respect to particular goods. The surge of affectivity comes to fill the gap between the abstract and the concrete, between the universal conclusion of morality or of conscience, and the reality of the present in which I live. The will gives to judgment its value of existential efficacy. Among all the goods which were proposed to my free choice a moment ago, I was able to examine which of them was preferable. I judged that the reading of an austere treatise on theology was the most suitable means for attaining the higher end which I pursued. But this conclusion, quite ideal and reasonable, did not in itself have any grip on my action. It was merely a matter of being reasonable, it alone did not have the power to make me act. My will had to intervene.

The judgment which makes me act is no longer a simple speculative conclusion: this is to be done, it is preferable to read; it is an order: do this, you must get to work. The affective movement which carries me toward action gives to my reason a hold on the concrete reality of action. The moral proposition is no longer universal and abstract, it determines me efficaciously now. The judgment which has determined me is that which *I have experienced* in opening my book and in beginning to read.

Thus the judgment does not become final except in virtue of the will itself. The presence of this affective dynamism appears clearly in all the cases in which it warps the reasonable decision. Reason tells me clearly that I should not smoke, but in the circumstances in which I find myself the temptation is so strong, it seems so desirable to me. Smoking harms me, I know, but in the present case I consider this pleasure as a good. It injures my health, disturbs my habits, even overturns my moral principles. The final practical judgment nevertheless determines me in this direction.

The better thing chosen concretely is no longer necessarily the better thing in itself. I am inclined to perceive in these particular goods only the aspect that pleases me, refusing to consider any other aspect. The false good can then have the nature of a good. All the disorder which the inferior affectivity can bring into the moral judgment is here seen. The vilest kind of pleasurable object can take on the appearance of the desirable. The concupiscence which increases the voluntary likewise dulls its impetus.

It is true then to say that the strongest motive prevails, but it is not the strongest from the point of view of pure reason, abstractly. It is the one which my affective dynamism has allowed to be the strongest.

4. THE FREE ACT, ACT OF THE PERSON

The causality of the abstract motive is then only relative. In order to pass from the rational conclusion to the absolute of the act the will itself has to be called upon. The judgment determines the will, the will conditions the judgment. To all appearances we have gone full circle!

No, for the mystery of free will lies precisely in the intimate relationship of intellect and will. Earlier, we pointed out the respective role of the two powers in voluntary activity. The intellect moves the will by presenting to it its object. The will, possessing the initiative of its exercise, moves the intellect and pushes it to its final conclusion. Objective motion, motion of exercise—we must make this analysis carefully; let us see what it may imply.

Evidently there is no question of separating the two powers of the soul as two antagonistic individuals, though the human mind tends to such severities. Intellect and will are powers of the same soul and they are mutually enveloped in this essential unit. The soul acts *through* them. As in the mysterious interaction of soul and body, so there is between intellect and will a living reciprocity, a vital but not a vicious circle. The analysis of their respective roles permits us to distinguish the components of a unique act, the act of the person who is the *whole* that acts. It is by virtue of this analysis that the free act has been situated with regard to the two extremes. It is neither the radical indifference of a blind will nor the determinism of a rigorous judgment.

The mystery lies between the two extremes. One can no more give an explanation of the secret of the free act than of knowledge or of love. The purpose of an analysis is not to remove the mystery, but to see into it as far as might be possible. As the result of the reciprocal action of two spiritual powers of man, the free act is a willed judgment or judged will.

Of the two, Aristotle preferred the second. Of the two components of the voluntary act—the light of reason, the dynamism of the will— the latter seems to play the major role. The free will is an enlightened dynamism. This is why it has been defined as the mastery of the will over the judgment which determines it.

I choose according to what I am. There is in the depths of my person a secret complicity with certain goods with which I am identified. This tendency defines me, it reveals my intimate character, it creates in me an affinity which conditions my judgment. The secret of the free act is that of the person desiring and willing. Freedom reveals and measures my person.

5. FREE WILL AND LIBERTY

Free choice reveals the person, but if my free act betrays what I am, it is also my free act which constitutes me. The experience of this fact is one of the initial perceptions of existentialist thought. It is what J. P. Sartre means by saying that man is liberty. But his system requires him to interpret the free act as an unforeseeable choice which defines him who posits it, giving meaning to the present situation, and a new meaning to the past, setting up his being and creating his moral rule and his entire universe. Thus man is "nothing but his project." [9] He identifies himself with the choice presently experienced. This is to discover under a more subtle form the freedom of indifference carried to the most radical of contingencies, that of the absurd.

In addition to a scorn for transcendental values, there is in such a philosophy a misunderstanding of the durable character of our acts. These leave in us their traces, they mold us. Our personality is built up in becoming. It is by acts of free will that we fashion it.

By their intensity or their repetition free acts create in us new aptitudes for action. They leave in our souls inclinations to desire the end freely chosen. There is no question of the automatism of bodily habits but of an eagerness of the soul which becomes more and more lively. By the sole power of our free will we can establish in ourselves a state of liberty. This liberty desired and constructed can constantly be refused or destroyed, but my liberty of yesterday influences my liberty of today. It remains true that I act according to what I am, but I also become in acting.

The virtuous man who has ardently chosen the good and who perseveres in his choice gains by an increasing facility, he moves toward the perfect liberty of him who, freed from the slavery of his passions, tends without obstacle and without resistance toward the

[9] J. P. Sartre, *L'existentialisme est-il un humanisme?* Nagel, Paris, 1946, pp. 22-23.

reasonable good. Free will is the instrument of this liberation, it is at the service of spiritual freedom.

This last assertion requires an explanation in which moreover we shall sum up our theory of the voluntary act. Free will can be called freedom of choice, but this freedom of choice does not exhaust the whole richness of liberty. We can push our reflection further and do justice to the philosophies which closely bind liberty to the person.

Beyond the freedom of choice, at the very source, there is a metaphysical liberty which we readily call freedom of spontaneity.[10] Freedom of choice is the absence of necessity; freedom of spontaneity is the absence of constraint. It is the freedom of a being which follows without violence its natural movement. The stone falls freely, the bird freely builds its nest, so long as nothing intervenes to oppose the spontaneous and necessary movement of their natures. The freedom of spontaneity is nothing more than the possibility of of a being to tend freely toward its end. It is identical with the necessity which comes from within.

Freedom is a necessity! What a paradox! Our proposition will be understood by reference to the outline sketched in part II of this chapter. By remounting the degrees of being we observed a growing and parallel unfolding of interiority and of spontaneity. On the level of conscious beings, interiority becomes immanence, spontaneity becomes initiative, independence, mastery of oneself. Freedom of spontaneity in spiritual natures is the necessary and natural welling up of will. In God it attains its sovereign perfection. The necessary love which He has for Himself is an urge toward perfect liberty. In man, freedom of spontaneity is the necessary desire of the good.

Unfortunately, we too often dissolve our freedom of spontaneity into our freedom of choice. We wrongly believe that man can choose his essential end as he chooses his avocation, his distractions, his loves, his means of action. There is in fact in the heart of man an undeniable desire to imitate the divine model, to attain the perfect independence of divine liberty. Man is made for a liberty of spontaneity.

What will this spontaneity be if not the very desire of God, for there is only one final end, the object not of our choice but of our

[10] The expression is from Jacques Maritain, in his article on *L'idée thomiste de la liberté,* published in the *Revue Thomiste,* July-September, 1939 and since then in the volume of essays *De Bergson à saint Thomas d'Aquin,* Paris, Hartmann, 1947.

natural and necessary impetus. The perfectly free man is he who has discovered what the sovereign good is, he whose will merges with the very will of God. Perfect liberty is then a perfect compliance with the Creator, a handing over of oneself to God.

For us this liberty is the terminus of a progressive liberation. We must disengage ourselves freely from the slavery of sin and of the flesh. Each one of our choices involves a consent and a detachment. Free will, liberty of choice, is the instrument of this liberation. When choice is absorbed by spontaneity, then genuine liberty, the determinism of the final end, will reign.

Left to our own powers as men, we would have the tragic certainty of tending toward an impossible fulfillment, a liberation never attained. The Christian knows that this liberation is acquired and that he does not attain it solely by himself. He possesses in grace the germ of a sublime liberty, the liberty of the children of God, and he goes forward towards its accomplishment. The Holy Spirit is in him—light and power, lucidity and intelligence, mastery of will, the divine spontaneity of Love which cries out to the Father. The celestial Jerusalem gives birth to free sons of genuine liberty: "Where the Spirit of God is, there is liberty."

VI. Psychological Structure of the Human Act

We have seen that the human act is the fruit of an interior life. Theologians very early began to trace out its maturation, for this psychological analysis is at the service of a more exact and refined moral appreciation. Certain stages were distinguished in the unfolding of the human act.

1. ORIGIN

In the Middle Ages the Augustinian distinction of the *uti* and the *frui,* and the still confused analysis of the *consensus,* of the *intentio* and of the *voluntas* [11] had facilitated the reflection of the theologians. Little by little, however, Aristotle was introduced into

[11] It is difficult to find for these Latin expressions, entered as such into the technical language, rigorous English equivalents. One might suggest for the *uti:* usage, the fact of using; *frui,* enjoyment, the fact of enjoying a good. St. Augustine opposes one to the other by showing that sin consists in the enjoyment of what one should not use, or in the use of what should be a pure object of beatitude. *Consensus, intentio* and *voluntas* are defined later on, cf. par. 2.

Christianity. There was found, particularly in the third book of the *Nicomachean Ethics,* a description of the human act in which choice (*electio*) and deliberation (*consilium*) were analyzed with care. The harmonious fusion of the two currents was accomplished by St. Thomas Aquinas. The system of the Angelic Doctor was moreover favored by the arrival in the west of the texts of the *De Fide Orthodoxa* of St. John Damascene. The latter had drawn up a refined plan of the steps of the will moving towards its end. The contribution of the oriental doctor enabled St. Thomas to complete and to expand Aristotle.

The plan proposed by St. Thomas was imposed on Moral Theology by his penetration and skill. It is important to understand its design, for it will be presupposed in further developments, particularly in the whole of the psychology of the virtues. Moreover, it will be seen that this analysis employs and presents with precision what has been said of the free act.

2. PHASES OF THE HUMAN ACT

We distinguish *certain acts* in the human act. Not that one should imagine a discontinuous development, nor that we wish to introduce arbitrary gaps in the genesis of the voluntary. We wish simply to express in exact terms the interaction of the intellect and the will and to indicate the *time* of their mutual fertilization. From desire to pleasure, from intention to decision, the movement is one. But if there is a movement, there is progress, progress whose phases are moreover perceptible when the act undertaken falls short: there are some desires without sequel and some intentions not efficacious.

Phase of Intention

In each of my deliberate acts I can discern what is the *end* and what are only the means. I read these lines *in order to* realise a plan which transcends my precise act. I wish to know doctrine. This plan can itself be ordained to a higher one: I wish to deepen my knowledge of Christianity. In every way, I act by virtue of a reason which motivates me; I have an end, a purpose.

What has made me active is an initial act of awareness, the fruit of a seeking or of an illumination. I have discovered this good which is a deeper spiritual insight. This good has aroused my desire. I have loved it. A certain moral sense, something which in me is most upright, has suggested to me that this good was suitable to me, and the intimate affirmation of this suitability produced the intention in me. Henceforth there is in me a willingness for the end perceived and desired.

Such is the order of *intention*. It confronts the end which motivates my action. We have studied the natural and spontaneous reaction of the intellect and the will in the presence of the good. The four acts which have been distinguished in the birth of the intention express its development. The voluntary movement begins with *cognition* (a): I discover the goodness of a thing. The will is spontaneously moved toward it and this act is so natural to it that there is given to it, by autonomasis, the very name of the power from which it emanates: it is the *simple will* (b). In its impetus this willing is, as it were, controlled by a *judgment* (c). There is no question of a choice but of a reasonable appreciation—even though reason be falsified or perverted—for the end will seem to me to be suitable or not according to the equilibrium of my tendencies or my affinities. The seal of this judgment confirms my will in its first impetus. Desire becomes *intention* (d), the willing of the end already quite tensed toward accomplishment.

Phases of Choice

A popular saying claims that "hell is paved with good intentions." Such in fact is the intention. It itself does not insure realization. One must pass from the universal to the particular of the concrete action. This passage is effected by the choice of the means, a choice which is accomplished in election.

At this moment my desire for spiritual deepening is realized in the effort to assimilate dry doctrine. Before beginning I had to decide on my immediate action. Divers means were presented to me— to pray, to render some service, to arouse myself to a new effort. But theoretically they were all of equal value with regard to my intention. The problem was to choose the one that suited me best in the present case. We see here the final maturation and opening up of the free act.

In the second phase we distinguish four acts in which intellect and will alternately share the initiative.

First it was necessary for me to become aware of the means, to deliberate, to hold *counsel*, to speak with myself. This is a work of knowledge (a).

But the voluntary dynamism which urges me to action cannot remain at the theoretical and abstract stage of this deliberation. From the fact of their connection with the end, all of these possible acts take on a certain attractiveness. That is so true that the reading did not immediately attract my adherence, I was undecided among the various possible objects to which I myself had attached this attraction. I had *consented*. This *consent* is a voluntary movement that draws its vigor from the intention which animates me and which I apply to the means of realization (b).

It is from this state of maturation that the decided *judgment,* or the judged *will* of which we spoke earlier, can develop. Among all the means available I *choose,* a complex act of which judgment is one aspect (c), and the voluntary undertaking the other (d). In this *election,* I have decided with finality that I am going to read.

Considered comprehensively, the phase of election is extremely complex. In it is realized the passage from the absolute of the end to the relative of the means. The analysis of St. Thomas, who harmonizes the analyses of Aristotle and St. John Damascene by going beyond them, is here extremely precise. Deliberation or counsel (a), consent (b), practical judgment (c), election (d) make evident the successive attitudes of intellect and will—though they may not always be chronologically discernible.[12] It is in the following manner that we plot with greater precision the moments of a reciprocal action. Consent furnishes the collected means in the deliberation with a value which renders them desirable and introduces the practical judgment. The elective judgment, enlivened by consent, prepares the choice. Thus one sees how, animated by the force of an intention, an abstract deliberation culminates in a concrete and true to life choice.

Phase of Execution

The choice has determined me with regard to the means. There was a question then of passing over to the actual. Having decided to read, I withdrew to a quiet place, I took up the volume which suited my purpose, I completed a series of precise bodily move-

---

[12] There are cases in which the *means* for realizing the end are *unique.* Consent is not a substitute for election. The final adherence to the means adjudged the best is here adherence to a unique means. That is what would take place if I had no other means of fulfilling my intention than to work at theology. In such cases the phase of election loses its aspect of discernment of the means, but it retains its essential value, the adjustment of the intentional dynamism to the realization of a concrete action.

ments. All of these were commanded in virtue of my final choice.

Contrary to what one might believe, this *command* is the work of intellect (a) which immediately ordains and commands my action. Some have seen in this an act of the will, and we must admit that the distinction is a delicate one. In truth, the *imperium* is only an intimation to the powers of the decision toward which the choice is being borne, it is an order: a work of reason.

On the other hand, it is the will which applies this order to the powers (b). This is why each of my acts was the bearer of a voluntary dynamism issued from the intention and channeled by choice. If presently I read, it is in virtue of this same impetus.

The phase of execution then presents four characteristic acts: intelligence *commands* (a), the will is stirred to movement (b) and, under the influence of this movement, the intellectual and sensible powers, the bodily members, act (c). An act of will lies at the end of this whole procession: fruition (d) or enjoyment—that is, repose in the possession of the end.

To the degree in which I am aware of approaching this term of my initial desire, of being on the road to a richer spiritual life, my present study bears with it something of this joyous certitude. The final end of man being the possession of God, he will not attain perfect *fruition* before that blessed fulfillment. The realization of his desires is only an image, sometimes clear, sometimes obscure, of this supreme possession.

We receive the guarantees of this sovereign good in the very acts which guide us toward it.

3. REMARKS ON THE VOLUNTARY ACTION

An analysis of the movements of intellect and of will which culminate in the perfect human act has permitted us to single out twelve moments. Still we should be careful not to give to each of these stages the same value, nor to enumerate them in a rectilinear fashion. The human act is presented rather as a curve where both strong and weak moments may be indicated.

Strong Moments and Weak Moments in the Voluntary Impulse

The unfolding of the human act is enlivened by an initial will of the good, but this dynamism does not show at every stage with the same clarity.

We regroup first the three acts which immediately confront the end: simple will, intention, fruition. We have seen that from the first to the second there was progress in efficacy: canalization of voluntary energy in the desire through acquiescence in the end known. Between the second and the third there is all the difference between the power and the act, all the distance from desire to possession, from hope to joy. In this separation the free activity of man comes to be inserted.

The three other acts of the will: consent, choice, the command of other powers, confront the means. It is easily seen that psychological intensity attains its maximum in the election which regulates the intensity and directs the current of voluntariness which issues from the intention. In the complex of practical judgment and of choice, where free will is exercised, the will appears under its most typically human form—freedom of choice.

Elicited and Commanded Acts

It will be easy now to distinguish the elicited and the commanded acts. The first are those which emanate directly from a power, in the present case from the will. They are therefore spontaneous movements of spiritual affectivity in the presence of the good of the end or of the means. We have just seen their particular forms: desire, intention, enjoyment, consent, choice, the initiating of activity.

The *commanded* acts are voluntary, but only in the sense that they are the point of application of the will. They are acts of the powers: intellect, sensible powers, bodily members (the will itself when its acts are decided and commanded) which voluntary efficacy sets in motion by pushing them to action. We were able to see that the application of the voluntary influence on the powers was effected after the stage of the imperium.

Order of Intention and Order of Execution

A beautiful life is a dream of youth realized at a mature age. A perfect human action is one in which the initial desire is satisfied in beatifying fruition, that is, one in which the execution realises and fulfills the intention. We will say then that the end is first in the order of intention and that it is last in the order of execution. There is in every human act a passage from the ideal to the real which is effected in the unity of the end pursued. It is at once the germ and the fruit, it initiates the action and it is also its terminus.

Henceforth, we emphasize the importance which the end will take as a criterion of moral judgment.

Interior and Exterior Acts

We will express the passage from the *ideal* to the *real* by distinguishing in the total human act the *interior* and the *exterior* act. Interiority and exteriority are here taken in their relation to will, and thus we desire to contrast the immanent act of intention with the commanded acts of the will.

The interior act is really the act which regards the end. It is the intention which animates the decision and the realization, that in whose name and in view of which I choose and act.

The exterior act is one which, proceeding from this interior inspiration of the will, fulfills its design and employs the means. We may remark that every commanded act is exterior to the will: a voluntary thought, an inner satisfaction, an imagination consented to are on this ground *exterior* acts.

It is clear that this distinction is inspired by two preceding distinctions, and sums up the fruit of the psychological analysis to the benefit of a more refined judgment of the human act. It enables us to account for the spread, inevitable and sometimes crushing, between the means employed and the ideal that animated the action— between what *I do* and what I wish to do. Genuine justice is that which can judge man from within, measuring the intention before the realization. We shall grasp the importance of this discernment when the question of judging the morality of the human act comes up.

VII. Morality of the Human Act

The justice of the world, public opinion, the memory of the centuries blame or praise human actions according as they judge them to be good or bad, and each of us examining his conduct interiorly sees in them good and evil. Still one really wills only the good, as we have tirelessly repeated in the course of these chapters. How can this division be justified? The contradiction is only apparent, it is in fact a sign of progress. With the terms good and bad we enter the domain of moral judgment. We, however, still account for this progress. This will be the task of the last part of this chapter.

1. THE RULE OF GOOD AND EVIL

Why is my action good or bad? If I refer to the manner in which the world dispenses justice or even to the manner in which I closely examine my own conduct, I will be tempted to reply: from its conformity with law. That is good which is in agreement with the moral law.

Now, to make conformity to the rule the norm of good or bad is already to take up a position on morality. It is really to admit that the goodness of a human act is not to be found in its pure spontaneity. Nietzsche placed the morality of superman "beyond good and bad." In doing this, however, he abandoned morality and pretended to become God. Closer to us, Gide sees in the sincerity of successive desires the criterion of the goodness of the acts which they solicit. Does he escape from all morality? No, for it would be easy to show that fidelity to sincerities, even though successive or contradictory, arises from an antecedent principle—the very absolute of sincerity. Every metaphysics, as well as every mysticism, entertains a conception of man and of life. So it is in vain that the amoralist tries to escape from good and evil.

That is good which conforms to a moral rule. This is certainly true, and the expression, "to act according to one's conscience," formulates this familiar datum of experience. Conscience is the interior voice which dictates the rule to be followed.[13] Is it always sufficient? This affirmation leaves many questions open. What is the origin of this rule? its foundation? It is known that systematic philosophies have given the most diverse answers to these questions. All pay their respects to the expression "moral conscience," but to say that the rule of morality is dictated by conscience merely pushes the question back. Beneath the unity of the expression there is hidden a deep divergence of conception.

[13] In the vocabulary of modern philosophy, the term conscience has a very broad meaning, all the way from psychological conscience to moral conscience. The latter has itself a confused content and in general implies a sense of obligation, of duty, or, or good and bad (cf. the view expressed by Le Senne in his *Traité de Moral générale,* Presses Universitaires de France, Paris, 1946). For St. Thomas and the Scholastics, conscience is never confused either with synderesis or with right reason, it is only the *application* of the first principles of morality to particular cases of action. This act of the *practical judgment* is fallible and it has in view a singular instance, while the rule of morality is an objective, speculative, universal and infallible principle. It is not the technical meaning which we employ here.

Deeply impressed by the reality of duty, Kant made of the moral law a categorical imperative imposing itself on the conscience from without. To posit the moral rule as an absolute transcending and dominating man, is not lacking in nobility. The austere and worthy respectability of this morality has made a strong impression, and the more so because it comes close to a certain conception of Christian morality. It also satisfies a certain sense of order and of greatness. It strongly influenced the morality of the last century. More or less consciously, the different forms of rationalist thought have felt its impact. In order to admit the Kantian morality or rationalist ethics, however, one would have to believe in the absoluteness of the mind. A certain scientific spirit has lost this faith. Positivism in all of its forms has called in doubt the transcendence of the moral ideal. The effort has been made to explain the genesis of conscience; for some the moral law was the prolongation of biological forces, for others the product of social pressure. The success of the sociological morality of Durkheim was well known, and is still current. Moral conscience would merely be the expression in each individual of the collective conscience, and the meaning of good and bad would simply coincide with social necessity.

The step from positivism of the sociological kind to materialism was quickly made. The morality of the totalitarian states or of historical materialism is simply a transition to unlimited social determinism. The rule of good and bad there becomes the will of the people or of the leader who represents them. Moreover, the historic dynamism which presides over the evolution of society constantly changes the meaning of the moral rule. Man is henceforth crushed by the collectivity, he is dominated by history. The ego is no longer anything more than a "grammatical fiction." [14] The only rule of conscience as well as the only freedom is to permit oneself to drift in the determinism of the event.

Such moralities develop logically the principles which are born of the misunderstanding of the spiritual or of the negation of God. They can however only deceive those who have perceived the absolute of the mind and the autonomy of the self. The wholly material pressure of the collectivity leaves man crushed under a fatalism which is imposed upon him from without. Even though he was op-

[14] This is the expression by which in *Le zéro et l'infini*, the prisoner Roubachof designates the spiritual dimension denied man by historic materialism. The final pages of the novel by A. Koestler are very suggestive in this respect.

posed to materialism, Kant really deserves the same reproach, for the impersonal transcendence of the categorical imperative likewise makes of the moral law a precept exterior to man.

It was the peculiar merit of Bergson to restore the spiritual dimension of man by affirming the spontaneity of the person and the interiority of conscience. Without in any way misunderstanding the reality of social *pressure,* he saw in *aspiration* the superior and truly human source of morality. This spiritualism provides an escape as well from Kantian obligation as from sociological determinism. Was it satisfactory as a basis for the moral rule? No. For Bergson does not account for the spontaneous surge of the spirit. If it is true that morality is essentially biological, it cannot be defined in terms of this trait. Moral regulation should be based upon nature, but on this point Bergson's effort leaves us unsatisfied.

As for existentialist thought, if it has perceived the absolute of the ego, it still seems to be searching for the moral law. Can a thought which arrests a man "in the world" or defines him as a pure choice culminate in a universal morality? One has a right to ask such a question.

None of these moralities appears to be satisfactory because they all miss something belonging to the human reality. This lack varies somewhat, but to consider the moral rule as an exterior dictate laid upon man from without, or inversely, to exalt the anarchical impulse of an ego delivered over to his own choice, is likewise to misunderstand the profound nature of man.

These uneasy and drawn out efforts contrast strangely with the serenity of a Socrates who saw in the nature of man himself the criterion of just and unjust. True morality is in fact the one which delivers up man to himself and makes him seek the rule for his conduct at the very source of his own dignity. Now every excellence of man is in his reason which shows him his end and manner of living. The good of man is then the fulfillment of his spiritual nature, and the rule of morality is nothing else than conformity to reason. In such a conception, the "voice of conscience" is not the repetition of precepts imposed or acquired, it springs up from the depths of nature whose law it translates. Christian morality is inscribed in the great Socratic tradition which it enlivens with new breath by introducing the idea of God into it.

Reason is a gift of God and the reflection in man of the Creator. The final basis of human morality is conformity to the divine order.

2. CONFORMITY TO REASON

The Ontological and the Moral Order

The moral distinction of good and bad is based on the very nature of man and his spiritual affectivity. As rational appetite and conscious desire of the good, the will tends necessarily toward the good which reason presents to it. Ontologically, whatever *is* is *good,* for being and the good are convertible. On this level the good and the end are identified. To desire evil is unthinkable. I desire whatever seems to me to be good.

In passing from the ontological to the moral order, the good and the end—one might say desirable realities—take on a new relation which introduces a fundamental difference—that which separates the *moral* good from the *moral* bad. This relation is precisely conformity to reason.

To say that it is characteristic of man to act according to the good presented by reason is to affirm that it is his nature to do what is conformable with his ultimate finality as a reasonable being. Among the lower animals the end is inscribed into their nature; evil is what is repugnant to it. The lightning that shatters the fir-tree ruins its harmonious growth and deprives it of its perfection as a full grown tree. It is the same with man. His finality is inscribed in his spiritual nature. For him evil consists in whatever is repugnant to this perfection. But if the fir-tree struck down by lightning or the insect crushed on the pavement, undergoes evil from without, man himself introduces evil into his own actions. Endowed with reason, man has the power to propose to himself his own good. This dignity involves a risk. Man can, under pretext of embracing apparent goods, direct his desire toward objects that are contrary to his final end. The winds and the currents of the open sea powerfully carry along the sailboat launched on the water. But not all are equally favorable to him who sails toward the Antilles, and some will certainly be *contrary*. It is the end of the cruise which enables one to pass judgment on it. Similarly, it is in the good contrary to the end that moral evil resides. In the order of morality evil is then pure privation, it is a false good, a positive reality not conformed to the finality of man.

The rule of my acts as man is then inscribed in the heart of my reasonable nature.

Synderesis and Right Reason

It is easily seen that there is no question of a series of innate principles. The moral rule is not a code, even a very general one, whose first articles man carries about with him.

The law of morality is inscribed in man as the law of a living organism is inscribed in its very functioning. The biologist evolves the theory of it, but the organism lives it without formulating it. Likewise, as soon as he acts, man evolves the law of his spiritual nature. In the speculative intellectual order, for example, the act of knowing is for me the occasion of becoming aware of the great laws of intellectuality: the first principles. I put them to use in my contacts with objects, i.e. in the knowledge of being, and through a concomitant conception, I can intuitively evolve them. Thus there becomes clear to me the first truth that "that which is cannot at the same time and under the same aspect be itself and something different." Similarly in the moral order, I come in contact with the rule of morality as soon as I realize a voluntary act. I can perceive intuitively, in the functioning of rational action, the great principles of morality. Traditional theology speaks of the *habitus* of first principles, the natural powers of intelligence which enable us to grasp them intuitively. It especially designates under the name of *synderesis* the original possession of the first principles of morality.

I carry inscribed in myself the necessity of acting in view of an end worthy of me. Synderesis is the intellectual translation of this. It is synderesis which suggests to me, in the very exercise of the will, that the action must respect the order of nature, that the good lies in fidelity to reason, that I should be prudent, just, courageous and temperate. It is as it were the inner sense of the moral rule.

Right reason is reason enlightened by synderesis and is inspired to direct itself in action by the first principles of morality (we say likewise that a just mind is one that judges in the light of the first speculative principles). Still we should be on guard not to conceive of this dependence as though it were a deduction. From the first principles nothing is deduced, they are immanent in everything that is inspired by their veracity. Reason renders them present to human activity; its work is to judge in the various domains of morality in the light of this superior clarity. It is said that the reason of a temperate man is *rectified* in the presence of goods of the sensible order, because he has an understanding of what, in this domain, is suitable to his nature as a man. In each area of morals, reason receives its rectification from some particular virtue, and at the summit of this virtuous organism reigns prudence, the virtue par excellence of right reason.

The virtuous man is then he who habitually lives in the light of synderesis. His interior lucidity comes from a fidelity to conscience. "To act according to conscience" is to follow the secret inclination of right reason. It is clear that the current notion of moral conscience designates the inner meaning of the good of human nature and its application to action. It recovers in a confused way the notions of synderesis and of right reason.

Reason and Divine Order

It is said of Christian morality that it delivers a man over to himself. The Christian meaning of creation is extended to the limit in this assertion: Christian morality delivers man over to God.

Through the categorical imperative, Kant located the moral law "between heaven and earth" without grounding it in either the one or the other. As we have set it up, the moral law is at once immanent and transcendent, entirely in man because entirely from God. It is really *in* my nature, but it was *given* me with my nature. Being like the latter the work of the Creator, it is, like it, a gift of God. If reason is a participation in the light of divine intelligence, the moral law is a participation in the knowledge of God, of God contemplating and dictating the eternal order of the universe. Inscribed in our nature, the moral law is the reflection in us of the eternal divine law. This is why the beauty of the virtuous life comes from its conformity to the divine order.

The philosopher who scrutinizes nature can foresee this divine value. He prepares the way for the Christian whose faith, under the guidance of God, can go on much further. In truth, God has deigned to give more. In order to enable us to participate more fully in His light, He has spoken. The Decalogue dictated to Moses was the first gift made to His people. This was still only a figure of what was to come. The ancient law had been fulfilled to perfection when the Word itself of God came among us. Through the mouth of His son, God gave us the law of love. Those who recognized this voice have received, along with a more precise rule of life, a more delicate feeling for the good and the bad.

For all that, nothing is disturbed in our psychology, but henceforth everything is played in a key transposed to the infinite. A new moral rule, more divine and more interior, has become ours. Right reason is enlightened by law, nature has been elevated to supernature. We know our destiny as children of God. For the Christian, the natural law and the revealed law coalesce in the unity of a single moral rule. The identity of their author is the guarantee of their continuity; the order of creation is expanded into the order of charity.

3. HOW CAN THE FREE ACT BE BAD?

We now have the necessary elements for resolving a delicate problem. Since the will infallibly desires the good and since right reason proposes to the will a good conformable to our nature, how can man will evil? In other words, how explain the defection or the first sin of the virtuous man? Such is the problem of evil in the voluntary act.

Status of the Problem

Among beings that do not possess reason it is easy to account for evil in their action. It finds its origin in the evil of the being which acts. Evil is a privation and a privation in the cause leads to a privation in the effect. If I am afflicted with laryngitis I will sing in a deplorable manner.

But the problem is more complex when there is question of the voluntary and free act. We again have recourse to a previously invoked principle: the evil of an action has its origin in the evil of the agent, but the application is more delicate.

Since the question concerns a voluntary and free act, the defect mentioned in the agent should itself also be voluntary and free. To suppose the contrary would be, by denying the freedom of the agent, to suppress liberty of choice and thus to desert the problem. We do not consider as free the acts of those whose will is defective or acts imposed by violence.

On the other hand, this voluntary and free defect which influences the will, the cause of evil, cannot be itself a moral evil. If it were, the defect of the will would already be a bad free act for which we should have to account. Thus we could retrace our steps indefinitely from bad act to bad act and nothing would be explained.

Reference to a Moral Rule

What we have said of the moral rule and of its immanence in the action provides us with a solution. The source of evil in the free act is a free deficiency prior to choice: the nonconsideration of the moral rule. St. Thomas Aquinas was the first to make this precise answer. He proposed as an illustration of the case, the example of the artisan and his rule. The carpenter makes use of a rule in order to draw lines on the wood. It happens that one day he fails to use this rule, the lines which he draws are no longer straight. This deficiency of design is explained by a previous deficiency—forgetfulness or negligence in using the rule. It is the same with human action. The regulation comes from right reason, but it errs when reference is not made to it.

Thus at the moment in which, despite the advice of the physician, despite previous resolutions, I accept the cigarette offered me, I act without considering the rule. Through a participation due to passion or through the inertia of my will, I neglect, before choosing, to make reference to reason which should measure the act. There is the defect in which evil originates. Sin is not in this nonreference, it is in the fact of acting without reference to reason. Its cause is in this preliminary deficiency.

It is in this way that we reply to the objections raised. This deficiency is free and it is not an *evil*. That it be free is due to the very nature of the will, which, as we have seen, possesses the initiative in its exercise. But this free deficiency is not an evil, for we do not demand of the will that it always consider the rule. All we ask of it is that it never act in contradiction to it.

I hold a light to guide my steps in the darkness. I am not bound to carry it constantly in my hands, but if I want to walk without taking chances and without stumbling, it is better that I should carry it. Sin is falling without having recourse to the rule.

The richness of human experience implicit in this metaphysical explanation is admirable. Many defections are explained by a lack of preliminary reflection. It is difficult for a man always to consent to exigencies required for a perfect interior lucidity. At one time haste, at another laziness makes him neglect to have recourse to the light, which is nevertheless his privilege. This resignation does not fail to disturb the movement of the will.

A profound view of the human undertaking inspires this solution.

The will has the initiative of its intentions. It is always lawful for it to escape from the precepts of the law and divine solicitations. This is not a bad will, it is an insolvency. At the root of every sin, there is a resignation of the will.

Inscribed in the heart of rational nature, the moral rule is the sign and the condition of the dignity of man.

VIII. The Norm of Morality

Having explained the nature of the moral rule, let us see how it is applied in the specification of human action.

1. THE SOURCES OF GOOD AND EVIL

Considered as the development of the potentialities of being from which it emerges, action is a concrete reality which establishes it in the world: it is a form of being. Hence it possesses the goodness inherent in being, the ontological goodness or excellence which will be proportionate to its perfection.

Now, to be perfect, every action requires a group of conditions. It is the integrity of their realization that will make one say of an apparatus that it functions well or of an organism that it reacts well. In the same sense we say of an athlete that he plays well, of a lawyer that he pleads well, if their acts present a certain required completeness. To play football presupposes a precise object, limited by the rules of the game. The activity of the player is animated by the *end:* it is in view of winning the game that he spends himself on the field. Finally, the game presupposes certain *circumstances,* accidental elements which can increase or diminish its perfection. For the football player whether or not he is properly shod, whether the field is dry or muddy, or whether the equipment is complete are not indifferent matters. The object, the circumstances and the end are components of every action. By them we can measure its perfection or its defects. Through them will enter the weaknesses which render the action deficient.

But so far the problem has been only one of ontological excellence. We have considered human action independently of its deep finality, that is, in its sole fullness of physical being. In reality the action of man enters immediately into the moral order. Compared with the immanent rule of reason, the components of human action are going to be the sources of its morality.

The Object

A movement is first qualified by its end. Now the object is the end of willing. An act is good or bad according to the conformity of the object willed with the moral rule. To will what is objectively forbidden by the rule based on reason, as lying, stealing, etc. is a bad action. A still more delicate appreciation will make me reject as evil or as less good whatever is repugnant to my profound finality or my personal vocation. At the time I am writing these lines, the reading of a novel or some easier activity would perhaps be a defect with regard to my ideal.

The Circumstances

On the other hand, every act is posited in a pattern of conditions of person, place, time and manner. These accidental relations, affecting human action from without, are its circumstances. Aristotle mentions eight of them. Here, placed in order, are the questions which identify them. First, those which affect the act itself: *Where? When?*—Circumstances of time and place. *How?*—The manner of acting. Then those which concern the effect of the action: *What is it that one does?* (quid). Finally, those which regard the causes: The principal agent, *Who?* The final cause: *In view of what?* The means employed: *By what means?* and the matter which has undergone the action: *With regard to what?* The nonconformity of circumstances to the rule of morality becomes a source of evil for the actions which they affect, for they themselves can also sustain a special relation with reason. This is evident in the cases in which a circumstance itself becomes the object of will. To work on Sunday is an act whose whole malice consists in the circumstance of time. Moreover, in every event the human act takes on a new malice from the fact of untoward circumstances. In a period of famine the black market, though always forbidden, is aggravated by the circumstance of time. The offense given a superior, in public and with outrage, is by so much the more blameworthy as the malice born of the circumstances of person, of place and of means builds up.

The End

Of all the sources of morality, the end is, as one might guess, the most important. Principle and goal of willing, the end initiates the action. It communicates to the acts which it inspires its own rectitude, or its own defects. We will say also that the end is the object of intention and of desire and we shall apply to it what has been said earlier of the object in general, that is, that its goodness or its malice conditions the goodness of the will. The end is in some way a target-object which faces up to the interior act, and which I pursue across and beyond the immediate objects. The same act of studying can take on many different values according to the end which motivates it: disinterested culture, preparation for a career, obligation of a profession, more or less legitimate ambition, sordid interest. The agreement or disagreement of these particular ends with my final end as a reasonable man and a child of God is the source par excellence of the goodness or the malice in my activity.

2. MORAL INTENTION AND MORAL EFFICACY

The intention faces the end. Can we conclude that the qualification of a human act is determined by that of the intention? The whole question is to measure the relations of the interior act to the will. This measurement is delicate; we must examine it.

Interior Act and Exterior Act

These were defined above by comparing their objects. I study my theology in order to understand better my condition as a Christian. The interior act faces the end, it is my desire to know. The exterior act is the one that I execute after the decision: I study. It faces the concrete act or the immediate end.[15]

We shall consider separately these two acts, or rather these two aspects of the human act, and we shall make use of a different criterion to weigh their moral value. The goodness or the malice of the will comes from the object. The moral qualification of the interior act comes then from its object, the end. That of the exterior act comes from the objective appreciation of the action and of its circumstances, what is properly called the object of the act. In itself, to give alms is a good act; to steal from your neighbor is a bad act. The same act can then be considered inasmuch as *willed,* i.e. inasmuch as borne on the current of an intention, and inasmuch as it is

[15] It will be noticed that in the very unfolding of the interior act there is a dichotomy between the act of intention and the act of choice. We shall not insist on it here. The reciprocal goodness and malice of these two interior acts are measured by rules similar to those which compare the interior and exterior act. With regard to intention, choice is in fact already turned toward the exterior, for it faces the means.

presented objectively. How are these two criteria of evaluation going to get along together?

Their points of contact are rich in casuistry. We shall give here only the broad principles which should guide the judgment in such matters.

In the order of action, the end is first. The exterior acts are produced in the impetus which it sets up. It is then the intention which bears in germ the goodness or the malice of the complete act. It is enough that it be antecedent. To give an alms through vainglory is an act vitiated by the intention that it elicits. To give an alms through charity is on the contrary clothed with a double excellence; the good object is placed in the service of a good end.

Thus the exterior good act becomes doubly so through the fact of the good intention; it is corrupted by a bad intention. The solution is not symmetrical insofar as the bad exterior act is concerned, for the good is more demanding than the evil. A small defect suffices to destroy its integrity. The bad intention aggravates with its malice the bad exterior act—for example, the act of stealing to procure the means of doing evil; the good intention on the contrary does not suffice to render sound a bad exterior act, bad, that is, in itself. Whatever public opinion may hold, the end does not justify the means.

Intention and Execution

Thus the goodness of the will does not repair the malice of the exterior act; at most one could say that the latter receives from it some excuse. This should suffice to justify Christian morality against the reproach sometimes made against it of being a *morality of intention.*

Still this reproach has some foundation, and the Christian cannot try to justify himself entirely. He can ask only that his thought be thoroughly considered and that the morality of intention be not reduced to a morality of mere velleity.

To accept the primacy of intention does not mean that intention alone suffices. The normal destiny of intention must be realized. In the voluntary movement the intention is a germ, it is rich in every dynamism, but its whole reality is in its fruit. The will does not find quietus except in the end. Perfect joy is that of the accomplished work.

Then there is also the social value. The will realized introduces into the world the good and evil with which intention was pregnant. In the world of material things in which man moves this aspect is important. Without modifying the proper value of the intention, the external act supplies a good or a bad surplus, that of its effects. Moreover these visible consequences, the only ones that man can evaluate with certainty, are the references on which human justice rests. The intention escapes the judge. Material life, social life, the exchanges among men are possible only on condition that their will be efficacious.

Nevertheless, it is the material conditions themselves, through the chance encounter of causes, which sometimes render sterile some intentions pregnant with efficacy. Such would be the case of one who wished to give an alms or to found a social work, but who loses his fortune. Another, he who wished to take vengeance and saw his enemy disappear before he could do so. But even if the realization fails, the moral value of the intimate will remains. It is not modified in any way by the failure or the success of the external work. "Anyone who even looks with lust at a woman has already committed adultery with her in his heart" (Mt. 5:28). The external act is only the prolongation of the interior impulse, which already possessed all of its moral quality.

More profoundly, since what one *does* is merely the expression of what one *desires,* and in the final analysis of what one *is,* the authentic measure of a man is that which touches his person. If this measure escapes the judgment of human justice, it does not escape the judgment of God. He it is who "searches the heart and proves the reins," who knows our most secret desires.

Psychological Echo of the Exterior Act

When it is said that the external act adds nothing morally to the internal act, it is abstractly assumed that the intention *remains the same.* But it is important to distinguish moral analysis from psychological analysis. Concretely, in the psychological play of the action, the will is modified by the external act. The execution re-echoes the intention. It may happen for example that several external acts are necessary in order to reach a realization; it is necessary to return to the work several times. The *number* of the acts engages the will in a new way. On the other hand, it cannot be denied that the fulfillment of the voluntary act increases the interior will in *extent.* The application of the intention to some particular choices and to efficacious undertakings confirms its initial proposal. Finally, the *intensity* itself of certain external acts is not without disturbing effect on the will, which finds more joy or fervor in acting. Thus the fire of the battle arouses the ardor of the combatants, the energy required for the employment of a decision increases the firmness of the resolution. Through the bias of their psychological re-echoing, the number, the extent, the intensity of the external acts have therefore an *indirect* influence on the morality of intention. But this remark really only underlines the *moral* priority of the interior act.

The Consequences of Our Acts

The comparison of intention with efficiency raises a final question relative to the effects of the external act. In what measure is the goodness or badness of the latter modified by its consequences?

The principles enunciated and utilized earlier make the answer easy. On the one hand the objective criterion of the moral value of the effects is their conformity to the rational order. On the other, in order that the effects have a moral value and that they may be able to qualify the external act, they must enter into the domain of the voluntary. The moral good or bad presupposes the voluntary. Thus, the goodness or the malice of the effects qualify the external act in the measure in which they have been *premeditated* and *willed* with it.

This is evident for all the cases in which the external act is posited consciously as a cause. But there are cases in which the author of the act has not reflected on possible effects. Are they morally imputable to him? Cases can be distinguished according to the more or less close connection with their cause.

When the consequences are quasi-natural or follow inevitably an act, it is clear that, explicitly willed or not, they follow from the will which has placed their cause. For example, the drunkard knows from experience the absurd acts which the state of drunkenness causes him to commit. Even though he does not explicitly wish them, he accepts in the very act of drinking to excess the criminal effects which will follow from it.

In other cases the effects are not foreseeable. If nothing is foreseen, nothing is willed. Such effects have no influence on the moral value of the external act.

This is the case of the hunter who accidentally kills a man in the forest which he thought was deserted. The unfortunate consequence of his shot cannot be imputed to him; for it was not foreseeable.

It is obvious that from the foreseeable to the unforeseeable the scale mounts to infinity. Many questions of casuistry can be argued concerning the voluntary in *cause*. The principles here recalled suggest solutions.

IX. The Merit of Human Action

We have seen that morality consists in the specification of human action. According to the harmonious or dissonant relation which the action bears to the moral rule, it can be called just or sinful, worthy of praise or of blame. We measure in this way the intrinsic value of the act considered in itself; but the whole act has a reverberation on others and, more profoundly still, it is inserted in the universal order. On this ground, it enters into relations with justice and falls under the head of retribution. The measure of *merit* is the measure of retribution.

1. MERIT AND HAPPINESS

Is not the retribution of a human action the same as beatitude itself? It has been said that for man action was the means of acquiring beatitude. It would seem then that its acquisition or loss would be the sanction of our acts according as they are good or bad.

A certain conception of happiness would lead one to think that this is so. It is observed that man by instinct turns toward his interior to find there a just sanction for his acts. There is a secret joy in acting in conformity with the rational order. Many a pagan philosopher has experienced this intuition. Nearer to us, the moral rationalists and the moralists of value still live by it. Happiness consists in the practice of virtue, the latter being conceived as a setting in order of the powers of man according to reason. For the moralists of "interiority," good action is beatifying in the measure in which it produces the perfect man, in whom it causes the order of reason to prevail. Man perfectly rectified, his powers established in reasonable equilibrium, possesses the conditions of happiness. This is what Aristotle wants to say when he affirms the identity of happiness and of virtue. According to this view, the sanction of our acts is in the very quality of the being which they build up; our acts model by their impress the effigy of our moral being, they bear in themselves their recompense or their punishment according as they are virtuous or vicious.

We must acknowledge the portion of truth which this position on morality retains. We discover in fact a profound perception. Happiness consists in conformity with reason and there is an affinity between the good act and beatitude. Far from denying this optimism, Christian thought gives it a perfect formulation and foundation. But as the pagan philosophers or the moralists without God live it, this optimism is strangely contradicted. A bond is asserted between the good act and happiness, the unfolding of the virtue of man, but one must recognize the precarious character of this beatitude: it is limited, difficult and rare.

Limited, because if there is question of the development of man, it is in the narrow range of this life. Aristotle wished the contemplation of the eternal as a superior ideal, but he admitted that the chances for it were slim.

Difficult to attain, for the road which leads to virtue is rendered painful and rough by the insufficiencies of man, his slowness, his failings, nis bodily condition. It is strewn with many obstacles placed there by the exterior world, matter, other men. Could a man be happy if he alone existed? The happiness of each one demands that all the members integrated into the total order be virtuous at the same time.

These difficulties make virtue quite rare, as also they make perfect happiness quite rare.

This happiness is then sadly precarious and the moralists of whom we speak cannot escape an admission of defeat. What becomes of retribution in this case? These philosophic moralities ignore merit. If merit had any meaning for them, it would consist in capitalizing on the good acts which make up the totality of virtue. Each act inscribed in the being which it posits has its own value and renders easier those acts which follow. But the fragile character of beatitude removes from the acts all certain value of any happiness to come. Hence it is the goodness or the malice of each undertaking which is the immediate sanction. Happiness is no longer a term toward which one tends and whose merit is the seed and promise. It is in conformity to an interior rule, to reason, to mind, to the universe. There is in this moral attitude a cold and austere grandeur, a sufficiency which tragically shuts out God. Wonderful human specimens are born of it: unselfish, stoic, even disciplined, but their sadness and resignation can scarcely be missed by anyone who is acquainted with Christian joy.

To escape these shortcomings, we must break the circle of moralities limited to man. Faith in immortality and in the existence of God, from which Christian philosophy in particular benefits, makes possible this liberation. Christian morality also affirms the beatifying value of activity in conformity with reason, but it goes beyond the human limitations of this philosophic conception: "Credo in Christum qui judicaturus est vivos et mortuos . . . Credo in vitam aeternam." Faith gives us the certitude that beatitude is possible and that there exists "Another," who transcending time is present to His creature. A new moral reality then comes to fill the gap between the act and happiness: merit. Beatitude is already present in the heart of the good act. Through merit the moral specification of our acts is a guarantee of the possession of happiness.

2. THE BASIS AND NATURE OF MERIT

Let us try to clear up the origin and the nature of this new moral value. Merit is derived from a consideration of the human act from the point of view of retribution which introduces us to the domain of the relations with others, a domain peculiar to justice.

Merit presupposes *otherness* and *integration* in an order. The acts that we posit have a repercussion in the universe, they influence other men, favor or hinder the legitimate development of their own personality. Man cannot be withdrawn from his social context. Even if he retires into solitude, he is a member of the human community, responsible to it for his acts, even if it is merely an accounting for his choice of isolation. Moreover, certain more restricted communities, with ranks more or less tightly drawn, quite often envelop a man with their codes and their obligations. A person is French, a soldier, member of a labor union, member of a club. The fact of being favorable or harmful with regard to others who surround me, makes me a creditor or a debtor in the equilibrium of the whole body. And that by a twofold title: with regard to the members whom I meet individually, and also with regard to the whole which they constitute. The fact of injuring or of benefiting a member re-echoes indirectly on the community as a whole, and conversely the good or the evil inflicted on the whole reflects back on each of its members.

Merit is precisely the sanction of the good and the bad which my acts have procured in these two forms for others. It results from the relations which bind me to each of my fellow men and to their community. A part of the whole, I am under the force of the reactions of other parts and of their group. Merit is retribution according to justice.

The preceding considerations are immediately applicable to human justice for whose sanctions they are the basis. Reward and punishment are society's way of recognizing merit and demerit. But experience teaches us the insufficiency of these social sanctions. Human justice is doubly limited. In the first place, it cannot evaluate genuine virtue. Its judgment is liable to error, for the real value of acts escapes it. It is obvious that it cannot know the intention of the agent. In the second place, it is incapable of furnishing a compensation which might suffice for the happiness of man. It is exterior to the profound result of the human action. In its worth as in its reward, social justice does not exhaust genuine justice and it leaves man unsatisfied.

3. MERIT AND THE DIVINE ORDER

An equitable determination of merit presupposes then *Another* whose judgment is not subject to error, which penetrates to the depths of the heart, which takes in with one glance the total order of the universe in which the action of man is inserted, and finally, whose retribution transcends time without being limited by the hazards of this earthly life.

To find a perfect evaluation of merit, we must have recourse to that divine *Other*.

Basis of Merit in God

We have seen that merit requires otherness and integration into an order. The foundation of divine retribution can be analyzed from this two-fold point of view: God is at the same time the other par excellence and the principle of universal order. God in His transendence is first of all the ultimate end of man, the Other to whom all our acts must be referred. He is Himself the supreme rule of the will. Moral goodness and malice mean nothing other than rectitude or deviation with respect to this divine rule. My acts are good or bad according as they are homage or denial in respect to the divine good. Who could judge better than God Himself of the honor or the offense done to Him?

On the other hand, God governs the totality of beings and especially the world of spiritual beings. Creator, He is author of the order of the universe. Providence, He presides over the common good of all. He evaluates therefore at their true measure the repercussions of our acts on the good of the whole.

Merit and the Natural Divine Order

So the ultimate foundation of merit is the judgment of God "who renders to each one according to his works." Let no one be misled here by the appearance of heterogeneity and exteriority in divine retribution. The defenders of moralities of interiority sometimes reproach believers with weakness and resignation which this recourse to the *Other* and this need of recompense represents. Their humanism finds in the fidelity to reason or to the universal order the sole sanction worthy of the demands of conscience. According to them, God is for the believer either a paymaster or a policeman, and merit is merely an extrinsic evidence of satisfaction.

Such a conception would be a great caricature of Christian morality. If in His transcendence God is the *Other* par excellence, He is also the perfect immanent present in the heart of His creature. The order of reason in which some rightly see the foundation of morality is based on God Himself. Conformity with reason is but conformity with the divine order. To realize in oneself the perfect balance of virtue, to place in hierarchical order ones desires and tendencies, to assure in oneself the reign of reason, is to introduce the kingdom of God.

For him who believes in God, beatitude is the fulfillment of the divine order, the order of which God Himself is the author. The initial assertions of the moralities of interiority remain, but they take on a new depth, they finally attain their complete truth. It becomes possible from then on to capitalize in some way their good. This totalization is always realized, even if here below it is not fulfilled in a human perfection; for all our acts remain present in the memory of God in eternity. So merit is not *first* a recompense added from without. It is not sought as such. There is an immanent retribution which consists in the value of the act itself, but it is over and above the promise of a transcendent compensation because the moral value is estimated by God. God is immanent and He transcends time. For this reason, merit is the guarantee of the realization of the order postulated by the good act.

As for being certain whether man could by his own powers alone know in its fullness the divine order to which he naturally aspires, the answer is misleading. History shows that man has but very vaguely foreseen natural beatitude, even when he had the sense of the divine. He discovered the relations of man to God, but he ignored the relations of God to man. Very few men are led to the knowledge of a personal God. Philosophers have not dared to hope for it, nor believed it possible. Israel itself was awakened only gradually to the consciousness of immortality. In such conditions, merit remains extrinsic to human action: men seek favors from the gods, they ask Yahweh for a just compensation for their misfortunes.

Supernatural Merit, Promise of Glory

It is the supernatural order which realizes perfectly the harmonious relationship between man's acts and their final end. It is in the light of this perfect realization, which infinitely surpasses human reason, that we have been able to reflect on the obscure condition of merit in natural beatitude.

Supernatural merit is a guarantee of divine life. Jesus Christ came to make known to men this sublime vocation to eternal life and to provide them with the means of attaining it. We are called to share in the happiness of God Himself, to see Him face to face, to know Him and to love Him as He knows and loves Himself. Such is the revelation of the perfect divine order.

This eternal life has already begun, for grace is in us the germ of glory. Merit takes on its true dimensions and the interiority of eternal life assures the perfect coherence which would be impossible without grace.

It always remains true that good acts find their immediate sanction in the virtuous being which fashions them, but it is the very image of God which shapes them in us. Little by little, they prepare our whole being for beatifying possession, constructing even from the present moment, our being in Glory.

In supernatural merit we possess the pledge of our beatitude.

CONCLUSIONS

"And God made man from the beginning, and left him in the hand of his own counsel" (Ecclus. 15:15).

With his condition of creature, man received from God the gift of a strange dignity at once magnificent and perilous. The return to God which the lower creatures effect in the passivity of determinism, is realized in man by conscious choice. If he is similar to the beings subject to divine movement, he must nevertheless recognize sovereign good and tend freely toward it. The destiny of man is to choose, to persist in his choice and throughout his life, in the multiplicity of his acts, to derive the greatest possible advantage from his freedom to constantly question his free choice. Freedom is the means proper to man to realize in the universe the order willed by God.

But "before man is life and death, good and evil, that which he shall choose shall be given him" (Ecclus. 15:18). Man really possesses the fearful privilege of disposing of the divine movement to the point of having the power, if he is unfaithful to it, of dissipating it in nothingness. In a world created for the good sin is nothingness —an infidelity and a failure. This infidelity to the light which God has given us is a giving up of the mastery which He has left us over our will. Sin is the fruit of a dynamism coming from God but which was dissipated in creatures instead of returning to its principle. It depends on us that God be the Alpha and the Omega of our human acts, as He is of all things.

The Christian knows that he finds in God Himself the strength and the light to make a return to Him without confusion or deviation. Christian experience lives by this certainty. Each morning at the beginning of work, the Church offers to God the works of the day, beseeching Him to be the beginning of them and the end:

Anticipate, O Lord, by thy inspiration and follow with thy assistance all our actions, in order that our every undertaking may always have its beginning in thee, and that thus begun in thee, may also end in thee. Through Christ, our Lord.[16]

REFLECTIONS AND PERSPECTIVES

Here is a short sketch of the questions which should still be treated or investigated.

Apropos of the Nature of Voluntariness

1. THE UNCONSCIOUS OF THE PSYCHOANALYSTS AND VOLUNTARINESS

If, as Freud claims, mechanical and automatic acts or defective and disturbed acts give evidence of a deeper psychism, one may wonder how much of spiritual activity the agent exerts in them.

[16] Actiones nostras quaesumus, Domine, inspirando praeveni et adjuvando prosequere, ut cuncta nostra operatio a te semper incipiat et per te coepta finiatur. Per Christum Dominum Nostrum. [Quatiarum Actio post Missam]

This point arises from a more extensive critique than the presuppositions of Freudianism. The question is in fact one of knowing what may be the relations of the spiritual soul to the lower psychic mechanism of complexes and tendencies. This is suggested by the treatise on the passions which has undoubtedly been enlarged and enriched by psychoanalysis. Cf. R. Dalbiez, *La méthode psychoanalytique et la doctrine Freudienne,* 2 vols., Paris, Desclée de Brouwer, 1936.

2. BIOLOGICAL DETERMINISM AND VOLUNTARY ACTION

We have seen that free will is the property of a person. To what degree does man escape from the determinism which the physician discovers in the rhythms and movements of the body? Certainly, in the composite which is man the primacy is held by the spirit, but it may be asked: under what conditions can the spiritual will of a man, subjected to a strong bodily determinism (hereditary, pathological, habit, etc.) emerge and dominate these lower and contrary tendencies?

Cf. Dr. René Biot, *Le corps et l'âme,* in the collection "Présences," Paris, Plon, 1938. Dr. Charles Odier, *Les deux sources, conscientes et inconscientes de la vie morale* "Être et Penser," Neufchatel, Éditions de la Baconnière. 1943. E. De Greef, *Notre Destinée, et nos instincts,* Paris, Plon, 1945. J. Boutonier, *Les défaillances de la volonté,* Paris, P.U.F., 1945; *L'angoisse,* Paris, P.U.F., 1945. Let us recall also one of the works which reminded the public of the synthetic view of man: Alexis Carrel, *Man, The Unknown,* New York, Harpers, 1935.

On character and personality, the importance of which we have already emphasized in the knowledge of the determinism which conditions the free act, the best work is that of E. Mounier, *Traité de charactère,* Paris, Édition du Seuil, 1945.

3. VOLUNTARY ACTION AND PROPAGANDA

The presentation of truth to crowds is a modern form of violence. It seems that the action of man bombarded by intensive propaganda is no longer fully voluntary. There is in fact wanting in it an objective knowledge of the end which it pursues. This raises the question of the morality of propaganda as a means of teaching the masses and of soliciting their efficacious action. Should the procedure of politicians who use the results of crowd psychology for just ends be condemned?

With Regard to Liberty

A problem constantly represented with regard to free will is that of predestination. It has occasioned great controversies in Christian thought throughout history: Augustine and the Pelagians, Luther and free will, Thomism and Molinism, Baianism and Jansenism. The solution involves both the treatise on God and the treatise on Grace, for it is especially the mystery of the divine will and salvation which has raised the question.

The solution must be based on a metaphysics of the divine will and of divine movement (cf. Part IV). There is a copious bibliography on this subject. Beyond the articles in the dictionaries, we mention only Garrigou-Lagrange, *La prédestination des saints et la grâce,* Desclée de Brouwer, Paris, 1936.

On the Moral Obligation of Conscience

We have not yet approached a problem which is of great practical importance. Is one bound to follow an erroneous conscience? The answer draws on elements supplied by the treatise on human acts.

1. Conscience is judgment relative to particular cases of action. It applies the moral law, but it is subject to error in this application.

2. An erroneous conscience must be followed. Even if conscience is deceived, it promulgates a law to me. One must follow reason even when it is in error. It is not the materiality of the fact which judges me, but the value which my will gives to it (cf. Part VIII, the morality of intention).

3. This does not imply that the will which does evil through error is always good. Everything depends on the attributes of the error— voluntary or involuntary, vincible or invincible (cf. Part III, relations of the involuntary to ignorance).

The comparison of states of consciousness, right, doubtful, certain and moral obligation, are discussed in the treatise on prudence (Question of probabilism).

On Spiritual Liberty

Finally, we may give some thought to Christian liberty. What is the meaning of Christian liberty when compared with metaphysical liberty? Christian liberty is the freedom of a liberated slavery. The Christian enjoys, in the Holy Spirit, a new dynamism: faith is the beginning of lucidity, grace the beginning of selfmastery, love the gift of self. Cf. the beautiful pages of J. Mouroux, *The Meaning of Man,* chaps. 6, 7, 8, New York, Sheed & Ward, 1948.

The most penetrating synthesis "on spiritual liberty" is no doubt the article by P. Guérard des Lauriers, published under this title in le Cahier de la Vie Spirituelle consacré au *Saint Esprit,* Paris, Édition du Cerf, 1943, pp. 130-152.

On Certain Phases of the Human Act

It might be useful here to recapitulate what we have said thus far about the different categories of acts which can be classified and enumerated in the perfect "human act."

I. Acts which are referred *to the end*

A. *Phase of Intention*

We distinguish here:

a. Act of intelligence: the general idea found in every man of a good capable of perfecting himself.

b. A love (act of the will) of complaisance for this general good.

c. An act of intelligence which is a judgment culminating in the determination of moral duty.

d. An act of the will, which is efficacious, for this good; that is the *moral intention* (this intention will make of the act a meritorious act or a sin).

II. Acts which are referred to *the means*

B. *Phase of Election*

a. Act of intelligence searching for the means for realizing the moral intention. This is inquiry or *counsel.*

b. Act of the will which approves in proportion to the means. This is *consent.*

c. An act of *practical judgment.* One judges of the most suitable means for attaining the end desired in the moral intention.

d. Act of the will which decides upon a means. This is *efficacious* choice.

C. *Phase of Execution*

a. The intellect decrees the use of this means. This is *order* or *command*.

b. The will moves the faculties suitable for its realization. This is active *use* (*usus activus*).

c. To what does the *execution* by these faculties of the commanded moral act correspond? The *commanded act* (*usus passivus*).

III. Acts with Reference to *the End*

D. *Phase of Possession*

a. Complaisance of the will, fruit of the normal fulfillment of the human act. It is *fruition* which is enjoyment or repose.

PRINCIPLES AND DEFINITIONS

We present here a group of definitions and principles from the moral theology of St. Thomas (Ia IIae).

1. Certain Great Principles of Moral Theology

Objectum voluntatis est finis et bonum (1,1,c.): The object of the will is the end and the good.

Natura dicitur quandoque principium intrinsecum in rebus mobilibus, quandoque quaelibet substantia vel quodlibet ens (10,1,c.): Sometimes *nature* is called the internal principle of realities subject to movement, sometimes a given substance or being.

Se habet finis in appetibilibus sicut se habet principium in intelligibilibus (8,2,c.): In the order of things desirable and moral, the end plays a role similar to that played by a principle in speculative things.

Finis est primum in intentione rationis, postremum in executione (18,7,ad.2): The end is first in the order of intention, last in the order of execution.

Sicut esse rei dependet ab agente et forma, sic bonitas rei dependet a fine (18,4,c.): Just as the existence of a thing depends on its efficient and formal causes, so the goodness of a thing depends upon its end.

Bonum causatur ab integra causa, malum ex singularibus defectibus (19,6,c.): What is good comes from an integrally good cause; evil appears as soon as something particular is lacking (for example, a human act is "good" when the end, the means and the circumstances are good; it is "sinful" when one of these elements is defective).

2. The Will and the Human Act

Actus humani proprie dicuntur qui sunt voluntarii, eo quod voluntas est rationalis appetitus qui est proprius hominis (Q. 6, Prol.): Properly speaking, only voluntary acts are human acts, for the will is the rational appetite which is proper to man.

Hoc importat nomen voluntarii quod motus et actus sint a propria inclinatione (6,1,c.): The word voluntary implies that the movements and the acts planned come from a personal inclination.

Actus voluntatis est inclinatio quaedam procedens ab interiori principio cognoscente (6,4,c.): The act of the will is a tendency or inclination which proceeds from an internal principle of knowledge.

Ad rationem voluntarii requiritur quod principium actus sit intra cum aliqua cognitione finis (6,2,c.): In order to be voluntary the act must come from within and from a certain knowledge of the end.

Appetitus naturalis est quaedam inclinatio ab interiori principio et sine cognitione (6,4,c.): The natural appetite is a certain tendency or inclination whose principle is interior but which does not imply knowledge of the end.

Illa vero quae ratione carent tendunt in finem propter naturalem inclinationem, quasi ab alio mota, non autem a seipsis. Proprium est naturae rationalis ut tendat in finem quasi se agens vel ducens ad finem (1,2,c.): Beings not endowed with reason tend toward their end by a natural inclination, as though moved by another, and not by their own initiative. It is proper to a rational nature to tend toward its end by directing itself toward that end.

3. The Voluntary and Its Limits

The indirect voluntary: *Voluntarium dicitur non solum quae procedit a voluntate directa, sicut ab agente, sed etiam quod est ab ea indirecte, sicut a non agente* (6,3,ad.1): We call voluntary not only that which proceeds directly from the will of the agent, but also that which results from something not directly willed.

Violentum est motio quae procedit a principio extrinseco contranitente passo (6,6,ad.1): Violence is motion which proceeds from an external principle and contrary to the will of him who suffers it.

Concupiscentia est appetitus delectabilis et est proprie loquendo in appetitu sensitivo (30,1,c.): Concupiscence is the appetite for what is delectable. It is really a part of the sensitive appetite.

Ignorantia tripliciter se habet ad actum voluntatis: concomitanter quando ignorantia est de eo quod agitur, tamen etiam si sciretur nihilominus ageretur; consequenter inquantum ipsa ignorantia est voluntaria. Uno modo quia actus voluntatis fertur in ignorantiam sicut cum aliquis ignorare vult, et haec dicitur ignorantia affectata. Alio modo dicitur ignorantia voluntaria eius quod quis potest scire et debet; antecedenter quando non est voluntaria et tamen est cause volendi quod alias non vellet (6,8,c.): Ignorance affects the act of the will in three ways: It is *concomitant* when it has to do with the object of the action in such a way that even if one knew he would nonetheless act. It is *consequent* when it is itself voluntary: whether the act of the will bear on the ignorance itself, as when one desires to be ignorant—affected ignorance, or whether the ignorance is that of someone who could and should know. It is *antecedent* when it is not voluntary, and yet is found to be the reason why one wishes what otherwise he would not wish.

4. Certain Important Pairs of Terms in Moral Theology

Elicited and commanded acts. *Duplex est actus voluntatis: unus quidem qui est eius immediate, velut ab ipsa elicitus, scilicet velle; alius qui est actus voluntatis a voluntate imperatus et mediante alia potentia exercitus* (6,4,c.): There are two kinds of acts of the will: one which proceeds from it immediately as its direct fruit (elicited act), namely, *to will;* the other is an act of the will commanded by the will and carried out by means of another power.

Interior and exterior act. *In actu voluntario invenitur duplex actus, scilicet actus interior voluntatis et actus exterior, et uterque horum actuum habet suum objectum. Finis autem proprie est objectum interioris actus voluntarii; id autem circa quod est actio exterior est objectum eius. Sicut actus exterior accipit speciem ab objecto circa quod est, ita actus interior voluntatis accipit speciem a fine sicut a proprio objecto* (18,6,c.): The voluntary act is made up of an interior and an exterior act, and each of these has its own object. The end is the object of the interior act. The immediate term of the action is the object of the exterior act. Just as the exterior act is specified by the *object* with which it is concerned, so the interior act is specified by its *end* which functions as its proper object.

Actus humani species formaliter consideratur secundum finem, materialiter autem secundum objectum exterioris actus (18,6,c.): The formal aspect of a human act is determined by its end, the material aspect is determined by the object of the exterior act.

Exercise and specification. *Dupliciter aliqua vis animae invenitur esse in potentia ad diversa: Uno modo quantum ad agere vel non agere; alio modo quantum ad agere hoc vel illud. Indiget igitur movente quantum ad duo, scilicet quantum ad exercitium vel usum actus; et quantum ad determinationem actus* (9,1,c.): There is a twofold way in which a power of the soul is capable of divers acts: 1) It can act or not act; 2) it can in acting realize this or that. In both cases it has need of being moved, both as to the *exercise* of the act and as to its *determination.*

Intelligence and will. *Voluntas movet intellectum quantum ad exercitium actus, sed quantum ad determinationem actus, quae est ex parte objecti, intellectus movet voluntatem* (9,1,ad.3). *Intellectus movet voluntatem sicut praesentens ei objectum* (9,1,c.): The will moves the intellect with regard to the exercise of the latter, but with regard to the determination of the act, which comes from the object, it is the intellect which moves the will. The intellect moves the will by presenting to it its object.

Id quod apprehenditur sub ratione boni et convenientis movet voluntatem per modum objecti (9,2,c.): What is intellectually grasped as good or suitable moves the will by an objective motion.

Necessary voluntary and free voluntary. *Quantum ad exercitium actus voluntatis a nullo objecto ex necessitate movetur; quantum ad specificationem actus, voluntas ab aliquo objecto ex necessitate movetur, ab aliquo autem non* (10,2,c.): As for the exercise or the production of its act, the will is not moved necessarily by any object. As for the specification, certain objects necessarily move the will (in exercise), others do not.

5. The Good and Evil of Human Acts

General principles: *Omnis actio inquantum habet aliquid de esse, intantum habet de bonitate* (18,1,c.): An action has as much of goodness as it has of being. The measure of the being of an action is the measure of its goodness.

Inquantum vero deficit ei aliquid de plenitudine essendi quae debetur actioni humanae, intantum deficit a bonitate et sic dicitur mala (18,1,c.): To the degree in which an action lacks fullness of being which is due to a human action it is deprived of goodness and insofar is called evil.

Dicuntur aliqui acti humani vel morales secundum quod sunt a ratione (18,5,c.): Acts are called human or moral to the degree in which they spring from reason.

Omnis actus habet speciem ab objecto, et actus humanus (moralis) habet speciem ab objecto relato ad principium actuum humanorum quod est ratio (18,8,c.): Every act is specified by its object, and the moral human act gets its specification from the object as related to the principle of human acts which is the reason.

In actibus honum et malum dicitur per comparationem ad rationem (18,5,c.): The good and evil of human acts are determined by comparison with reason.

The measure of morality. *In actione humana bonitas quadruplex considerare potest: Una quidem secundum genus, prout scilicet est actio, quia quantum habet de actione et entitate tantum habet de bonitate. Alia vero secundum speciem quae accipitur secundum objectum conveniens. Tertia secundum circumstantias, quasi secundum accidentia quaedam. Quarta autem secundum finem, quasi secundum habitudinem ad bonitatis causam* (18,4,c.): The goodness of a human action can be considered in four ways: 1) Generically, i.e. inasmuch as it is action. It has as much of goodness as it has of action and of being (this is generic goodness). 2) According to its species, which is determined according to the object which is suitable. 3) According to circumstances which are as it were "accidents" of the act. 4) According to the end, i.e. its relation to the cause of its goodness.

The object: *Ipsa proportio actionis ad effectum est ratio bonitatis ipsius* (18,3,ad.3): The proportion of an action to its effect is the reason of its goodness.

The end: *Quantum ad actum voluntatis non differt bonitas quae est objecti a bonitate quae est ex fine* (19,2,ad.1): In what concerns the act of the will, the goodness that comes from the object does not differ from that which comes from the end.

Bonitas voluntatis dependet ex intentione finis (19,7,c.): The goodness of the will depends on the intention of the end.

Unicuique rei est bonum quod convenit ei secundum suam formam, et malum quod est ei praeter ordinem suae formae. Patet ergo quod differentia boni et mali circa objectum considerata comparatur per se ad rationem; scilicet quod objectum est ei conveniens vel non-conveniens (18,5,c.): That is good for a thing which is suitable to it according to its form, evil which is outside the order implied by its form. It is clear then that the difference between good and evil in what concerns the object is essentially referred to reason. It consists in this that the object agrees or not with reason.

Bonitas dependet a ratione ex modo quo dependet ab objecto (19,3,c.): Goodness depends on reason in the same way that it depends on the object.

Rectitudo rationis consistit in conformitate ad appetitum finis debiti (19,3,ad.2): The rectitude of reason consists in its conformity to the desire for a suitable end.

Ratio est regula voluntatis humanae inquantum derivatur a lege aeterna (19,5,c.): Reason is the rule for the human will because it derives from the eternal law.

Ad hoc quod voluntas sit bona requiritur quod conformetur voluntati divinae (19,9,c.): In order that the will of man be good, it must be conformed to the divine will.

The bad act: *Dicimus malum communiter omne quod est rationi rectae repugnans* (18,9,ad.3): In general we call everything that is contrary to right reason bad.

Peccatum proprie consistit in actu qui agitur propter finem aliquem, cum non habet debitum ordinem ad finem illum (21,1,c.): Sin, properly speaking, consists in an act which, accomplished in view of a determined end, does not maintain with it the order which is due to it.

The erroneous conscience. *Conscientia est quodammodo dictamen rationis; est enim quaedam applicatio scientiae ad actum* (19,5,c.): Conscience is in a certain sense the verdict of reason; it is really a certain application of knowledge to action.

An erroneous conscience obliges: *Simpliciter omnis voluntas discordans a ratione, sive recta, sive errante, semper est mala* (19,5,c.): Strictly speaking, the will which sets aside what reason proposes, whether the latter be true or erroneous, is always bad.

An erroneous conscience does not always excuse: *Si ratio vel conscientia erret voluntario, vel directe vel propter negligentiam, quia est error circa id quod quis scire tenetur, tunc talis error rationis vel conscientiae non excusat quid voluntas concordans rationi vel conscientiae sic erranti sit mala* (19,6,c.): If reason or conscience is deceived in consequence of a wilful error, whether this be directly or through negligence, the error does not excuse, for it has to do with something that one should know. And the will which acts in conformity with this reason or this erroneous conscience, posits a bad act, without in any way being excused.

Merit and demerit: *Meritum et demeritum dicuntur in ordine ad retributionem quae fit secundum justitiam. Actus bonus vel malus habet rationem laudabilis vel culpabilis secundum quod est in potestate voluntatis; rationem vero rectitulinis et peccati, secundum ordinem ad finem; rationem vero meriti et demeriti secundum retributionem justitiae ad alterum* (21,3,c.): Merit and demerit are categories of retribution which is an act of justice. A good or bad act is qualified as worthy of praise or blame according as it is in the power of the will; upright or sinful, according to the manner in which it is ordained to the end pursued; meritorious or demeritorious, from the point of view of retribution which, in justice, is due to others.

(J.D.)

BIBLIOGRAPHIE

1. La base la plus sérieuse et la plus abordable de toute réflexion sur la conception chrétienne de l'action humaine et de la liberté reste l'exposé magistral du P. Sertillanges dans sa *Philosophie de saint Thomas,* Tome II, liv. VI. Aubier Édit. Montaigne, Paris, 1940. Le même auteur donne dans la *Philosophie morale de saint Thomas d'Aquin,* Aubier, Paris, 1942, un exposé plus détaillé et plus technique des problèmes et des notions.

2. Instruments de travail.
   - Situation historique du traité.

Le spécialiste de ces travaux est Dom Odon Lottin qui a exploré tous les auteurs médiévaux des préscolastiques à saint Thomas d'Aquin. Une bonne partie de ses articles a été rassemblée dans *Psychologie et morale aux XII*^e et *XIII*^e *siècles,* Tome I, Problèmes de psychologie, Gembloux, 1942. On lira en particulier: "La psychologie de l'acte humain chez saint Jean Damascène et les théologiens du XIIIe siècle occidental," pp. 393-424 (Revue Thomiste, 1931, pp. 631-661).
   - Ensemble du traité.

Merkelbach, O.P. *Le traité des actions humaines dans la morale thomiste.* Dans *Revue des Sciences philosophiques et théologiques,* 1926, pp. 185-206.
M.-S. Gillet, O.P. *Les actes humains,* traduction française du traité de la Somme théologique, Paris, Éd. de la Revue des jeunes, 1926.
Quelques pages denses et précises de É. Gilson dans son *Thomisme,* 4e et 5e édition, Vrin, Paris, 1942.
   - Problème du libre arbitre et de la liberté.

Outre les ouvrages du P. Sertillanges cités plus haut, on pourra se reporter à un article du même auteur dans *La Vie intellectuelle* du 25 avril 1937: *Le libre arbitre chez saint Thomas et chez Henri Bergson.*

R. Garrigou-Lagrange, O.P. *Dieu, son existence, sa nature,* Paris, Beauchesne, 1929, pp. 589-656.

J. Maritain, *L'idée thomiste de la liberté* dans *Revue Thomiste,* juillet-septembre 1939, pp. 440 seq. Article repris dans le volume: *De Bergson à saint Thomas d'Aquin,* Paris, Hartmann, 1947.

J. Mouroux, *Sens chrétien de l'homme,* coll. "Théologie" N° 6, Paris, Aubier, 1945.

Pour l'analyse psychologique de l'acte de libre-arbitre, il faut rappeler les remarques très pénétrantes de J. Laporte dans ses trois articles sur *La liberté et l'attention selon saint Thomas d'Aquin* dans la *Revue de Métaphysique et de Morale,* 38 (1931), pp. 61-73, 39 (1932), pp. 201-227, 41 (1934), pp. 25-57.

- Problème du mal moral.

Se reporter à la bibliographie proposée au terme du traité du mal, tome II, pp. 245-246.

J. Maritain, *Saint Thomas d'Aquin et le problème du mal,* dans *Vie intellectuelle,* juillet 1945, pp. 30-49. Repris dans le volume de la collection "Présences," *Le mal est parmi nous,* Paris, Plon, 1948, et dans *Raison et raisons.*

Le P. Sertillanges a été surpris par la mort alors qu'il achevait un grand ouvrage sur *le problème du mal.* Le premier volume, partie historique, était achevé. Paris, Aubier, 1949. Le tome II, *la solution,* est inachevé et ne comporte que quatre chapitres: Paris, Aubier, 1951.

- La conscience.

H.-D. Noble, *La conscience morale,* Paris, Lethielleux, 1924.

Pour une confrontation des différentes doctrines morales avec la morale chrétienne, on pourra se reporter à l'ouvrage de M. Le Senne: *Traité de morale générale,* coll. "Logos," Paris, P. U. F., 1946. Chacune des grandes positions philosophiques est présentée en quelques pages et la bibliographie est abondante. C'est d'ailleurs le seul service que puisse rendre au théologien cet ouvrage dont l'éclectisme est confus et décevant.

On trouvera un intéressant panorama des théories contemporaines dans les *Actes du IVe congrès des sociétés de philosophie de langue française,* Neufchatel, 1949, dont les rapports et communications étaient consacrés à *la liberté* (13-16 septembre 1949). Collection "Etre et Penser," Neufchatel, la Baconnière, 1949.

L'exploration psychologique de l'engagement moral est au centre des philosophies existentialistes et personnalistes. Le théologien se doit d'en connaître les essais, sinon pour en adopter les conclusions, qui restent par principe au plan phénoménologique, du moins pour prendre acte des questions posées et des analyses souvent pénétrantes.

On pourra se faire quelque idée des présupposés d'une morale existentialiste dans le petit volume de J.-P. Sartre, *L'existentialisme est-il un humanisme? (Pensées),* Paris, Nagel, 1946. Pour une étude plus approfondie:

L'être et le néant, 2ᵉ partie et 4ᵉ partie, Paris, Gallimard, 1943. Simone de Beauvoir, *Pour une morale de l'ambiguïté* (Les essais). Paris, Gallimard, 1948. Une critique a été esquissée de cet humanisme par B. Pruche, *L'homme de Sartre (structures de notre temps),* Grenoble, Arthaud, 1949. L'initiateur du personnalisme, É. Mounier, en a résumé les grandes thèses dans son volume: *Qu'est-ce que le personnalisme? (La condition humaine),* Paris, Éd. du Seuil, 1947. Dans cette ligne N. Berdiaeff a présenté une très suggestive analyse de la liberté: *De l'esclavage et de la liberté de l'homme (Philos. de l'esprit),* Paris, Aubier, 1946, tandis que G. Madinier et M. Nédoncelle réfléchissent plutôt sur la conscience comme dimension de la personne: M. Nédoncelle, *La réciprocité des consciences, essai sur la nature de la personne,* Paris, Aubier, 1942; G. Madinier, *Conscience et mouvement,* Paris, Alcan, 1938.

Quant aux conceptions grecques de la béatitude et de l'engagement humain, le maître ouvrage reste celui du P. Festugière: *L'idéal religieux des grecs et l'Évangile* ("Études bibliques"), Paris, Gabalda, 1932. Du même auteur: *La sainteté,* Paris, P. U. F., 1942.

Pour étudier l'entrée des doctrines helléniques dans l'univers moral du christianisme primitif: Dom David Amand, *Fatalisme et liberté dans l'antiquité grecque* (Recherches sur la survivance de l'argumentation morale antifataliste de Carnéade chez les philosophes grecs et les théologiens chrétiens des quatre premiers siècles), Louvain, Bibl. de l'Université, Desclée de Brouwer, 1945.

BIBLIOGRAPHY

BOOKS

Augustine, Saint, *Divine Providence and the Problem of Evil.* New York: Cosmopolitan Science and Art Service Co., Inc., 1942.

Davis, Henry, S.J., *Moral and Pastoral Theology,* Vol. I, pp. 11-113. London: Sheed and Ward, 1941.

Garrigou-Lagrange, Reginald, O.P., *God, His Existence and Nature* (trans. Dom Bede Rose), pp. 589-656. St. Louis: B. Herder Book Co., 1936.

Maritain, Jacques, *St. Thomas and the Problem of Evil.* Milwaukee: Marquette University Press, 1942.

McHugh, John A., O.P., and Callan, Charles J., O.P., *Moral Theology, A Complete Course,* Vol. I, pp. 22-62. New York: Joseph Wagner, Inc., 1929.

Mouroux, J., *The Meaning of Man.* New York: Sheed and Ward, 1948.

———, *The Christian Experience.* New York: Sheed and Ward, 1954.

Sertillanges, Antonin D., O.P., *Foundations of Thomistic Philosophy* (trans. Godfrey Anstruther). Springfield, Ill.: Templegate, 1956.

Slater, Thomas, *Manual of Moral Theology,* Vol. I, pp. 17-57. New York: Benziger Bros., 1908.

ARTICLES

McCarthy, John, "Imputability of Effects Voluntary in Cause," *Irish Ecclesiastical Record,* 64: 409-415 (Dec., 1944).

Rockey, P., "Morality of Exterior Acts," *Modern Schoolman,* 31: 213-221 (March, 1954).

Chapter III

THE PASSIONS

by A. Plé, O.P.

I. THE GIVEN DATA OF FAITH AND TRADITION

1. Holy Scripture
2. The Fathers

II. THEOLOGY

1. The animality of the passions
   - (a) The passions are movements of the sensible appetite
   - (b) The passions entail or follow certain psychological modifications
   - (c) The passions of the sensible appetite in the hierarchy of passions
2. The passions are human acts
   - (a) The sensible appetite of man should remain under the dominance of reason
   - (b) Morally, the passions are either good or bad
   - (c) How the passions are controlled
3. The eleven principal passions
   - (a) Classification of the passions
       1. The concupiscible and the irascible
       2. The stages of passionate movement
       3. The objects of the passions
       4. Internal contrariety of irascible movement
   - (b) Love, the fundamental passion

REFLECTIONS AND PERSPECTIVES

BIBLIOGRAPHY

Chapter III

THE PASSIONS

The theological study of man would be seriously incomplete if it neglected these physiological phenomena, this conscious and unconscious life without which man would not be a man, but a pure spirit.

As we saw earlier, man consists of a substantial union of body and soul. Human acts are then not only those of his reason and of his free will; they include also those of his affective powers, the whole life of the mind "in its bodily setting." The body is also human, to the degree in which it receives animation from the soul.

The passions are the most intense manifestation of this affective life. They remain until death, as inseparable from the life of reason as our body from our soul. In their physiological phenomena as in their conscious or unconscious psychism—the rage of anger, the tears of sorrow, the constriction of fear, the tension of hope, the warmth of joy—all the passions are of interest to the theologian for, neither angel nor beast, it is with all the powers of his being, body and soul, that man attains eternal happiness or that he shuts himself out from access to it.

Man does not work out his destiny solely by acts of his free will; he seeks it also by his passions, and it is most frequently there that failure surprises him, for he finds in them powerful and artful adversaries against whom he must fight fiercely and without weakening. Most men, St. Thomas states, are overcome in this fight and often without even having to put up a struggle (Ia IIae, q.81, a.2, ad.3 and IIa IIae, q.95, a.5, ad.2).

Revelation and Catholic tradition re-echo with the din of this struggle and of these failures, to the point that one might ask oneself (as some think) whether the passions are not intrinsically opposed to reason and to God and whether the solution would not be purely and simply, to eradicate them.

But is it necessary to do violence to our nature and no longer tolerate in ourselves any activities except those of the spirit? If not, then in whom and under what conditions can the passions, good or bad, lead us to God, our last end and perfect happiness?

Such are the questions which we ask ourselves in this chapter.
Before giving the answer of theology, we shall first inform our-
selves briefly on the data of our faith and of Catholic tradition.
Theology has no other tasks than to mint their riches.

I. The Given Data of Faith and Tradition

1. HOLY SCRIPTURE

God has made man "a little less than the Angels" (Ps. 8:6),
having created him in His "image and likeness" (Gen. 1:26). But
he is at the same time a being formed of clay which was then
animated by the "breath" of Yahweh (Gen. 2:7); it is from the
side of Adam that Eve is born, bone of his bones and flesh of his
flesh (Gen. 2:21). Man is a divine "breath" in a flesh, and so a
being of passions.

And the inspired text teaches us at once how the sin of Adam is
bound up with his flesh, and how much his fall affected him in it:
pains of childbirth and subjection of desire, the sweat from hard
work in a hostile world, and then death and dissolution of the body
(Gen. 3:16-19).

Thus in the first three chapters of the first book, the Bible
acquaints us with the role of the flesh and the passions in our creation and in our Fall. Throughout Revelation this teaching never
varies. On the one hand, it is our very nature to be "in the flesh,"
and on the other our flesh, since the Fall of Adam, is rebellious.

There is no need of accumulating texts of Scripture to teach us
that man is a spirit in the flesh. Experience will suffice, confirmed
as it is by the sciences of man. Language itself is a witness to it,
especially that of Revelation, which constantly associates the most
spiritual of human thoughts and affections with parts and organs
of the body, even the most carnal: the face, the members, the liver,
the entrails, the kidneys, etc.[1]

Over against this, Revelation adds to our human experience some
decisive lights by teaching us that the flesh is closely associated with

---

[1] Cf. Dhorme, *L'emploi métaphorique des noms des parties du corps en
hébreu et en accadien* (Gabalda, 1923), taken from a series of articles which
appeared in *Revue Biblique* from 1920 to 1923. Prat, *Théologie de St. Paul*
(Beauchesne, 1929), II, pp. 53-60 and 486-487; and Antoine Guillaumont,
Les sens des noms du coeur dans l'Antiquité, in *Le Coeur "Études Carmélitaines,"* 1950.

the Fall of Adam. Since then, the flesh is not only "weak" (Mt. 26:41) but corrupted and corrupting: "For out of the heart come evil thoughts, murders, adulteries, immorality, thefts, false witness, blasphemies" (Mt. 15:19). "Now the works of the flesh are manifest, which are immorality, uncleanness, licentiousness, idolatry, witchcrafts, enmities, contentions, jealousies, quarrels, factions, parties, envies, murders, drunkenness, carousings and such like" (Gal. 5:19-21). "But everyone is tempted by being drawn away and enticed by his own passion. Then when passion has conceived, it brings forth sin; but when sin has matured, it begets death" (Jas. 1:14-15). "All that is in the world is the lust of the flesh and the lust of the eyes, and the pride of life; which is not from the Father, but from the world" (I Jn. 2:16).

Must we conclude from these texts, selected from among many others,[2] that the flesh is essentially bad? Our faith answers no. For if the flesh were the irreconcilable enemy of God, how could the Son of God have been "made flesh" (Jn. 1:14) or made "in the likeness of sinful flesh" (Rom. 8:3)?

It was through the flesh that sin came; it is in the flesh—that of the Son of God—that God does justice to sin, it is in it that God was glorified on the day of Easter; it is this flesh which is given to us as a food for life (Jn. 6:53-65).

Our flesh in its turn has already received the guarantees of its resurrection. It is called to participate in the divine life, not only in the future, at the time of the resurrection, but from this present life since our baptism.

It remains true that "flesh and blood can obtain no part in the kingdom of God" (I Cor. 15:50); it is true that "I myself with my mind serve the law of God, but with my flesh the law of sin" (Rom. 7:25); "the Law, in that it was weak because of the flesh" (Rom. 8:3); "for the wisdom of the flesh is hostile to God" (Rom. 8:7); and contrary "to the desires of the Spirit" (Gal. 5:17). But this is true only of the flesh left to itself and abandoned to the "guilty passions," to this "law of sin which is in my members" (Rom. 7:23).

In revolt against the spirit, the flesh welcomes to itself the law of sin; but subjected to the spirit, it is good and holy. "As you yielded your members as slaves of uncleanness and iniquity unto

[2] E.g., Rom. 8:6-7; 13:14; Gal. 5:16; I Cor. 1:20; 2:5; 3:19; 6:13; II Cor. 1:12; Col. 2:18; Eph. 2:3, etc.

iniquity, so now yield your members as slaves of justice unto sanctification" (Rom. 6:19).

It is the pagans and sinners, says St. Paul, who are "without affection" (Rom. 1:31). On the contrary, because it is subjected to the spirit, the flesh of the Christians, even before the Resurrection, participates in salvation, but always on condition that it die to itself and be placed on the cross with Christ: "Walk in the spirit, and you will not fulfill the lusts of the flesh . . . But the fruit of the spirit is joy, charity, peace, patience, kindness, goodness, faith, modesty, continency . . . They who belong to Jesus Christ have crucified their flesh with its passions and its desires. If we live by the spirit, by the spirit let us also walk . . ." (Gal. 5:16-25).

To live by the spirit, under the guidance of the Holy Spirit, is then not to cease to be man, to cease to have flesh, a heart, to cease to know their warmth and emotions. The inspired text gives testimony that God made flesh was not "impassible." He sighed with sadness (Mk. 8:12), knew anxiety (Lk. 19:41; Jn. 11:35), the groaning of sorrow (Jn. 11:33). Though He stiffened against trial by "hardening his countenance" (Lk. 9:51), He was acquainted with trouble (Lk. 22:44); He cried out as one dying alone (Mk. 15:37). He experienced too the unleashing of anger (Mk. 3:5; Mt. 21:12-13), the emotion of pity (Mt. 7:36; Mk. 1:41; Lk. 7:13), tenderness (Mk. 10:16; Lk. 13:34), hunger (Lk. 4:2) and thirst (Jn. 19:28).

After the example of Christ, the Christian should not then plan to smother in himself all sensibility and all passion. His faith assures him that since his baptism his body is "for the Lord" (I Cor. 6:14); his body is the temple of the Holy Spirit (I Cor. 6:19) and member of Christ (I Cor. 6:15). His heart is inhabited by the Holy Spirit (Rom. 5:5; II Cor. 1:22) and by Christ (Eph. 3:17). His heart knows comforting (Col. 2:2; II Thess. 2:18), affection (II Cor. 7:3), tenderness (Rom. 12:10), the desire of seeing those whom he loves (I Thess. 2:17), joy (Lk. 24:52; Acts 5:42). The heart of the Christian likewise knows sorrow and torment (II Cor. 7:12; Rom. 9:2), affliction, anguish and tears (II Cor. 2:4), jealousy (II Cor. 11:2) and the devouring fire of apostolic zeal (II Cor. 11:29). "The work of the flesh" itself is declared good in marriage (I Cor. 7:2-5) and St. Paul goes so far as to enjoin husbands to love their wives as their own flesh, as Christ loves the Church (Eph. 5:28-29).

That is the teaching of our faith. The flesh and its passions are not radically bad, they are creatures of God; but since the Fall, sin has entered into them (and first of all into our minds); it is sin that has "corrupted the ways." [3] But in the person of Christ, the flesh of man and his passions find not only their healing and their liberation, but their exaltation and divinization. The Christian, moved by the Holy Spirit and nourished by the sacred and glorious flesh of Christ, should crucify his flesh only in order to subject it entirely to the Spirit and to enable it to bring forth works of life: "Glorify God and bear him in your body" (I Cor. 6:20).

2. THE FATHERS

The teaching of Revelation on the flesh and its passions, which we have just recalled, when proposed to Greco-Latin minds and experienced by them, is very soon found in conflict with the seductive tenets of the current "philosophy" (Col. 2:8). For this philosophy the flesh was only a weakness, failure, and illusion, a unique obstacle which separates us from the divine world; the Platonic myth of the cavern characterizes rather neatly the turn of mind which then prevailed.

The proponents of Docetism, the first heretics known to us, were slaves of this mentality; they could not admit that the Son of God, since He was God, could have taken to Himself veritable flesh. He merely clothed Himself with its appearance, they said. The Church will have to combat for centuries the excesses of such a mental attitude by condemning a whole family of heresies (encretism, gnosticism, manicheism), already anticipated by St. Paul (I Tim. 4:1-5). For these marriage is essentially bad, as is likewise the whole world of bodies, whence the prohibition under pain of sin of the use of certain foods (meats, wines, etc.) and the practice of an inhuman asceticism rigorously enforced. On the contrary, but for fundamentally the same reason, certain Gnostics will push so far the opposition between the flesh and the spirit as to advise the satiating of the passions in the thought that, thus set free, the spirit might be able to rise with ease to contemplate God.

It is remarkable to note that in the century of Descartes when again the prevalent philosophy separated contemptuously the flesh

---

[3] "It is the perverse will which stirs up passion, it is subjecting it to passion which creates habits, and it is the non-resistance to habit which creates necessity" (St. Augustine, *Confessions,* 8, 5, 10; Pl. 32, 753).

from the spirit, something of the same error appeared again in Jansenism and in Quietism.

The Catholic Church has carefully preserved herself from this whole family of errors. She thinks with St. Augustine that if we had no passions, we could not live properly (*City of God,* 14, 9).

No doubt certain of these spiritual masters, more "Greek" on this point than authentic witnesses of the faith, emphasize strongly the opposition of the flesh to the spirit. They go so far as to claim that "among the perfect," movements of the flesh are "quite dead and annihilated." [4] They speak of "killing the body" (Palladius, His-toirie lausiaque, P.G. 34, 1023 B) and wish to be freed from "this dangerous envelope" of the body.[5] Finally, they borrow from the vocabulary of the Stoics one of its most characteristic expres-sions: the "apatheia," i.e. a perfect indifference to things, total impassivity. Here is, for example, what Clement of Alexandria writes of the "gnostic," that is, according to his vocabulary, of the perfect—today we would say of the contemplative or the mystic:

Having already become established through love in the good which he will possess, having anticipated hope through the gnosis, he does not tend toward anything since he possesses everything toward which he might tend. He seems then to remain in a unique and unchangeable attitude, loving in gnostic fashion, and he does not have to desire to be rendered similar to beauty, for he already possesses beauty through love. What need has he any more of courage and of desire, this man who has conquered loving intimacy with God without passion and who has himself been inscribed among his friends through love? It is necessary for us to separate from the perfect gnostic every passion of the soul. For the gnosis effects the exercise; exercise estab-lishes a stable disposition, and the latter culminates in the suppression of the passions ("apatheia"), not in the mastery of the passions; for the complete suppression of desire produces the "apatheia." Now the gnostic will have no part either in the goods which are everywhere vaunted, in the passional goods coming from the passions, for example, the joy which follows upon pleasure, the dejection connected with chagrin, in the caution which is dominated by fear, not even in pride, for the latter accompanies anger. Some think that they are no longer evils, but already goods. But it is not possible for anyone once perfected by love and who has tasted for eternity and without satiation the endless joy of contemplation, to again find pleasure in these small and jejune goods. What possible causes still remain to pursue anew these worldly goods for any one who has seized the inaccessible light, even though it be neither in time nor space, but by this gnostic love through which there come to him also the heritage and the complete restoration, a reward of which the gnostic takes possession in advance for having chosen it and hastened

[4] Origen, *Com. in Rom.* 6, 9: P.G. 14, 1102 B.
[5] Saint Ambrose, *Des avantages de la mort,* P.L., 14, 548 A.

toward it by love? Or indeed, by moving toward the Savior through the love he has for him, even though perceiving his tabernacle on earth, does he not leave life (for he no longer has any confidence in it)? Does he not deliver his soul from passions (for they accompany life)? Does he not live by killing off desire, by no longer obeying his body? (*Stromates,* 3, 9, 73 to 75; P.G., 9, 293).

To be well interpreted, texts of this sort must be understood in the light of the teaching common to the Fathers of the Church who unanimously assert, following St. Paul, that we must not hate our own flesh.

Here are some texts, e.g. from St. Augustine who, as is known, was himself a convert from Manicheism:

The fact that the flesh lusts against the spirit, that the good does not dwell in the flesh, that the law of our members is opposed to the law of our mind, does not indicate a mixture of two natures issued from contrary principles, but the division of only one against itself in punishment of sin (*De la continence,* 8, 21).

Somewhat earlier St. Augustine had written:

The flesh has no lust unless it be by means of the soul; but it is said that the flesh lusts against the spirit when the soul through carnal lust opposes the spirit. We are both; and the flesh itself which dies when the soul leaves it, even though a very inferior part of our being, is not thrust aside as though one would flee from it, but it is laid away in order to be taken up again, and once recovered, it will never again be abandoned. 'We sow a material body; we shall arise a spiritual body.' The flesh will no longer lust against the spirit when it will be called spiritual, for, without any resistance, and even without any need of bodily food, it will be subject to the spirit in order to be eternally vivified. These two elements which are present oppose each other in us, let us pray and so act that they will come to agree with each other, for we are made of them both.

We should not think that one of them is our enemy. Our enemy is the evil which the flesh covets against the spirit. Once this evil is healed it then disappears. Both substances will be saved, and there will no longer be conflicts between them . . . (The flesh) then is not our enemy, and when we resist its vices, it is the flesh we love because we heal it. (*Ibid.* 19).

There is no question therefore of killing the body but, as St. Ambrose says, of "making use of it as a skilful artist" (*Des avantages de la mort,* P.L. 14, 609 D). The flesh, to cite St. Augustine again, is a servant and even a spouse who must be made subject:

Your flesh is your spouse, your servant. Whatever name you may give it, you must make it subject to you; and if you combat it, the combat must bear some fruit. For it is fitting that the inferior be subject to the superior in such wise that he who demands the submission from one inferior to himself be, in his turn, subject to him who is his superior. Respect the right order of things and seek for peace in it. You, subject to God; the flesh, subject to you. What is more just, more beautiful? You, subject to a greater, and the lesser subject to you. For the order that we recognize, the order that we recommend, is not: the flesh to you, and you to God, but you to God, and the flesh to you. If you scorn the first term: you to God, you will never obtain the second: the flesh to you. If you do not obey your Lord, you will be tortured by your slave. (*Ennarations sur les Psaumes,* Ps. 143; P.L. 37, 1860).

Baptism cleanses us from our sins, but the lust remains with us. We must resist it, but this offers no occasion for destroying the flesh. What should be destroyed "are the vices of the flesh, and not the flesh itself" (St. Greg. the Great, *Morales,* 20, 41, 78; P.L. 76, 185 C). If the flesh, says St. Gregory, is for us at times a "seductress for evil," it can also be "an aide to good" (*Hom. sur Ézéchiel,* 2, 7, 18; P.L. 76, 1024 D). Our body is the temple of God and each of us is the priest, says St. Isadore of Pelusus (*Lettre à Théodose,* P. G. 78, 781 D).

The Christian "apatheia" is not the death of the heart but the presence of "a heaven in the heart":

For me, apatheia is nothing else but a heaven that one has in his heart and mind, which makes him regard as playthings the snares of the devil. He then really possesses apatheia, and is recognized as possessing it, who has purified his flesh from every stain, raised his mind above creatures, subjected all of his senses to reason, placed his soul before the face of God in a constant tendency toward him who transcends all our powers. Again, some have defined apatheia as resurrection of the soul preceding that of the body; others, as a perfect knowledge of God, inferior only to that of the angels. And so, this perfection consummated, and still unfulfilled, according to some who have tasted it, so satisfies the soul and so detaches it from matter, that after having placed it in a celestial port, while still permitting it to live in the flesh, it lifts it toward a kind of rapture to heaven itself, there to contemplate God." (St. John Climacus, *L'Échelle du paradis,* 29; P.G. 88, 1147 D).

Such are the end and the means of Christian "mortification." To succeed in it, the struggle is necessarily long, demanding and difficult. Catholic tradition has constantly described all the details of its strategy; they can be found in works on asceticism.

Thus, enlightened by Holy Scripture and Patristic tradition (the liturgy has also supplied us with valuable data), at once reassured and disquieted on the role of the flesh in our salvation, the theologian asks himself for an exact account of the passions, of their moral goodness and of their control.

II. Theology

The Fathers of the Church never speak of the passions except in connection with temperance or mortification. The *Sentences* of Peter Lombard, which was the manual of theology for the Middle Ages, allude to the passions only in the treatise on the creation of man and in that of original sin.

The introduction into the West of the works of Aristotle was, on this point as on many others, a decisive event. Taking his stand on the first attempts of Albert the Great [6] to integrate Aristotle with Christian thought, St. Thomas was able to develop the first treatise on the passions and to firmly integrate it with the whole of moral theology. The place assigned to the passions in the *Summa Theologiae* (as the second part of the treatise on human acts) is of itself quite significant.

Far from rendering antiquated this Thomistic treatise on the passions, the later development of psychological science rather showed with greater clarity its exactitude. The modern theologian is invited to an effort of transplanting and of applying the positions taken by St. Thomas. This is why in the pages that follow we take our stand on St. Thomas, without thereby neglecting the works undertaken in contemporary psychology.

As we have already seen, the theologian is directly interested in human activities in the degree in which they bring us nearer to or remove us farther from happiness.

These acts can only be "human acts," i.e. such as proceed from the free will of man. As a rational animal, man does not work out his eternal destiny on the plane of reason alone, but also of "animality," to the degree always in which reason can and should be present in it. It is such acts that we must now study.

It is in the passions that the activities of the human composite are manifested in their complete intensity and complexity. Not only the psychological conscience but also the moral conscience itself is

[6] Cf. P. Michaud-Quantin, *Le traité des passions chez St. Albert le Grand,* in *Recherches de Théologie ancienne et médiévale,* v. 17, Jan.-Apr. 1950, pp. 90-120; Dom Odon Lottin, *Psychologie et morale aux XII⁰ et XIII⁰ siècles,* Éd. Duculot, 1942-1949.

involved in them, at one and the same time with the physiological movements of our body. The interest that the theologian takes in passions has its source here: all the elements, from the physiological disturbance to the intervention of our liberty, which decide the moral goodness or badness of our sensible life are deployed and bound up with them.

We divide our study into three parts:

1. The animality of the passions.
2. The passions are human acts (hence they have a moral value).
3. The eleven principal passions.

1. THE ANIMALITY OF THE PASSIONS

(a) *The Passions Are Movements of the Sensible Appetite*

In the treatise on man we saw that a sane psychology interprets the play of our passions and our activities by the conjoining of two pairs of distinctions—of knowledge and appetite, on the one hand, and of reason and sensation, on the other.

We studied in the preceding treatise the human acts which are proper to man because they are to be found on the plane of reason, and more especially on the level of rational appetite, i.e. of the will.

We place ourselves here on the plane of the human composite taking an interest in the acts of the soul inasmuch as it animates the body; in the acts, consequently, which man has in common with the animal. We study especially the sensible appetite, i.e. the appetite which tends toward objects perceived by the senses: the five external ones—sight, hearing, taste, smell and touch, and the four internal senses—common sense, which in some way integrates interiorly the partial data of the external senses, imagination, memory and instinct (the so-called *vis cogitativa,* corresponding to the *vis aestimativa* in the animal). The sensible appetite is, as it were, the power of judgment of sensibility.

The knowledge and appreciation of sensible objects releases in us movements of the sense appetite. These are the passions (love or hate, desire or aversion, joy or sadness, hope or despair, daring or fear, and anger).

Before bearing upon particular sensible objects, the sensible appetite exists in a state of tendency. Each one of our powers naturally aspires to exercise its act—our intelligence to know, our eye to see colored objects, our taste to savor food, etc. These inclinations are laws of our nature which direct our powers toward their respective ends, even before they know what they are.[7]

These inclinations which St. Thomas identifies with natural appetite (*De Ver.* 25.1) can be likened to the primitive energies which the contemporary psychologists and psychiatrists seem to call instincts (MacDougall, Guénot, etc.), compulsions (Freud), functional motivations (Charles Odier), etc. These compulsions are considered by them as "the psychic representations of an excitation whose source is in our organism." [8] They constitute as it were the unconscious subsoil of our affective tendencies which expend all their powers in the passions. (Of this unconscious subsoil we cannot become aware even by directing our whole attention toward it, unless it be indirectly through some of its effects.) This pulsational energy, which constitutes the motive power of human activity and which subtends in the unconscious our affective tendencies, normally requires, say the psychiatrists, "to be objectified." That is to say, to sublimate the primitive self-love, it needs to be given an extramental object and in that way be adapted to the real in order finally to attain to "oblativity," that is, to a gift of self.

Unfortunately we cannot elaborate upon the important contribution which contemporary psychology might make to the moral theologian in his study of the passions. The major part of a scientific development of this relation still remains to be made. We think however that we have said enough about it to impress the reader with the importance of the relation. At the same time, the student will see how easy it is for the Thomistic conception of the human composite to welcome the valuable discoveries of modern psychology.

If these compulsions can be compared with what the Thomists call the inclinations of the natural appetite, neither the one nor the other constitutes what, following St. Thomas, we here call the passions. In fact, passion is the act of the sensible appetite which, already inclined by nature toward its object, even before having come to know it, is borne toward it as soon as sensible knowledge perceives and evaluates it.

In giving its object to the appetite (whether this object be perceived by the external senses, or whether it be imagined or recalled

[7] H. D. Noble, *Les passions dans la vie morale,* v. 1, pp. 30-31.

[8] Docteur Parcheminey, *Le problème de l'ambivalence,* in *Amour et Violence,* "Études Carmélitaines," 1946, p. 26.

by memory) and in evaluating it (by the *vis cogitativa*) as good or bad for itself, sense knowledge gives to the appetite both its object and its actuation, that is to say, it releases its natural potentiality. We then have to do, and only then, with a passion.

We can even say that hereditary or acquired dispositions of temperament are, if the expression is permissable, only the materials of the passions, and not the passions properly so-called. We reserve the use of this word for *acts* of the sensible appetite and we refuse to apply it to these tendencies and to all of these potentialities. This does not mean, however, that the theologian is indifferent to the complex play of all these potentialities.[9]

(b) *The Passions Entail or Follow Certain Physiological Modifications*

Our exposition would be gravely wanting if we were content to define passion as an act of the sensible appetite confronted with its object. There would be lacking to it any mention of the physiological movement which intrinsically is a part of this act, and is found bound up with it as matter is with form or the soul with the body.

It is essential to passion, an act of the human composite, to include bodily movements: divers gesticulations, alteration in facial expression, rise or fall of the temperature, quickening or retarding of the heart beat, etc. Contemporary medicine permits us to go further in the study of these physiological phenomena of passion and to measure their exact effects on the nervous systems: endocrin, sanguinary, respiratory, muscular, etc.

To reduce passions to mere appearances is to fall into the error of Materialism. The opposite error—that of "angelical" spiritualism—is to ignore them or to regard them as an independent system more or less parallel and accidentally bound up with "emotive thoughts." Physiological and psychological phenomena are two aspects of the

[9] For modern philosophers and psychologists passion is (as one may read in the *Vocabulaire philosophique* of Leland) "a tendency of a certain duration, accompanied by affective and intellectual states, particularly of images, and strong enough to dominate the life of the mind (this power being able to manifest itself either through the intensity of its effects or by the stability and permanence of its action)." Malaquert (*Éléments du caractère,* p. 219) writes thus: "Passion is an exaggerated inclination, especially one which takes up permanent residence, opposes everything, subordinates other inclinations to itself and pulls them in its wake." In the Thomistic terms which we have adopted here, passion is not merely an "inclination which is exaggerated." It is rather, to use the expression of Théodule Ribot, an "emotion-shock."

same reality; it is characteristic of passion to unite them in a manner so profound and essential as to suppose that if one of the two should be wanting, there would be no passion, just as a body without a soul is only a corpse and as a soul without a body would not be a man.

This unity of psychology and physiology is so great that in the detailed study of the passions and the virtues which moderate them, St. Thomas does not regard it as idle to point out the useful role of gesture and of mimicry in order to arouse or to moderate passion. He does not think it unworthy of the theologian to take an interest in the bodily dispositions of persons, according to age, sex, the native disposition of organism, etc., which make some of them for example more prone than others to anger, hope or despondency, etc. St. Thomas points out similarly the importance of stimulants, like alcohol, for stirring up courage and that of some maladies which suffice of themselves to arouse certain passions, such as sadness or fear. In question 38 of the Ia IIae, devoted entirely to remedies for sadness, St. Thomas enumerates side by side the contemplation of the truth and free flowing tears, friendly conversation, sleep and bathing.

Because the demons are capable of acting on our "bodily humors," says St. Thomas again, they can arouse or excite in us passions, and so induce us to commit sin, even though, being unable to touch our liberty, they can never force us to do so (Ia IIae, q. 80). It is by reason of a similar action that St. Thomas recognized in the stars an influence over our lives, an influence which itself can be overcome, for it cannot touch our freedom. The astrologers themselves recognize with Ptolemy that "the wise man dominates the stars,"—in the measure in which he controls his passions, comments St. Thomas.

We are not astonished that the progress of science has lengthened the list of physiological causes of the passions, nor that medicine can at will, by a simple injection, excite or calm a passion, even provoke or arrest it. We see in it the happy confirmation of the essential role played by our body and by the physical world in our passionate life. We hasten at once to remark that, even though essentially bound up with physiological phenomena, the passions are nonetheless human actions. Man can and should act with them inasmuch as he is a rational and free being. The good order of reason is not contradictory to the functional disturbance of passion (Ia IIae, q. 24, a. 2, ad. 2) even if this disturbance embarrasses or prevents the exercise of it. Suspension of reason comes normally and naturally in sleep. Why should this tying off of reason be against nature in the case of anger, for instance, that passion in which the physiological disturbance is so great that it necessarily entails a certain prevention of reason? (Ia IIae, q. 48, a. 3). This inhibition of reason is not necessarily unreasonable. This is also the case in the pleasures of the conjugal act which are so strong as to bind reason, but in which St. Thomas sees neither mortal nor venial sin. He thinks, however, that this suspension of reason is a consequence of original sin. It did not exist in the state of innocence (Ia IIae, q. 34, a. 1, ad. 1).

Before studying this intervention of reason which makes of the passions human acts, we might inquire why these acts of the sensible appetite are called passions. By doing so we shall discover in them one of the essential traits of their nature.

(c) *The Passions of the Sensible Appetite in the Hierarchy of Passions*

The word passion belongs to the vocabulary of metaphysics. When one being acts on another, its activity is called action in the acting cause and passion in the recipient. Thus the one receives from another that which it did not have. It is this reception that is called a passion.

The more the acting cause is dominating, the stronger is the passion of the subject. It is already "to suffer" to receive the effect of an exterior cause. The same is true if this effect excludes whatever might be contrary to it in the patient. It is still more true if this effect is contrary and drives off the natural dispositions of the patient.

Knowledge is a passion in the measure in which to know is to receive "intentionally" the form of the object known. But the object exercises a causality more dominating when it makes itself to be loved. Known, it was present in the knower; loved, it attracts him to itself and models him after itself. There is therefore more passion in the appetite than in knowledge.

There is still more passion in the sense faculties: first of all because intellectual cognitions are added to former ones, while sensible cognitions displace one another; in addition because sense perceptions have for organs corporal elements and their physiological phenomena. Passion is still stronger in the sensible appetite, where the disturbance caused by the object loved produces necessarily a certain physiological commotion and where, moreover, each movement drives out the preceding one and can even contradict the natural tendencies of the appetite—joy, e.g. which is naturally suitable to it is suddenly displaced by sadness.

Of all the "passions" of which man is capable, those of the sensible appetite are then the strongest. It is to them that the moralist reserves especially the term passion.[10]

The passions then are movements of the sensible appetite aroused in the soul by the knowledge and appreciation of a sensible object causing in it a physiological commotion.

It is not with impunity nor without deep servitude that our spiritual soul is united substantially with our body. It knows through it the passivity of matter, aggravated still more by the effects of original sin. In such conditions, can the soul safeguard its independence and impose its rule over that part of itself in which it is by nature substantially united with a body rendered rebellious by sin?

2. THE PASSIONS ARE HUMAN ACTS

(a) *The Sensible Appetite of Man Should Remain under the Dominance of Reason*

He who refuses to distinguish in order to unite the components of the same being, can only parcel them out on one plane or confuse them on another.

Not distinguishing the rational plane from the sensible, the Stoics and Cartesians (and all who fall into an extreme dualism of body and soul) isolate and confound at one and the same time the components of the passions. On the one hand they see only thoughts, and on the other certain mechanical movements.

It is thus that in his "Discours des passions de l'amour," Pascal (if indeed he is the author, the matter is disputed) says:

The greater one's mind, the greater his passions, because the passions being only sentiments and thoughts belong exclusively to the mind, even though

[10] In addition to these "animal passions," the theologian is acquainted with "bodily passions," those which the body experiences not inasmuch as it is the instrument of the soul, but its matter. A wound, e.g. the amputation of a member, touches the soul and causes it to undergo a passion. These bodily passions do not interest the moralist except insofar as they may arouse the "animal passions."

occasioned by the body; it is clear that they are only mind itself and that thus they fulfill their whole capacity (Oeuvres, collection "La Pléiade," p. 314).

In such a conception, as soon as reason intervenes in passions, there is no longer any passion, but only a thought (though occasioned by the body). Hence there is no passion unless reason be wanting and, in this case, every passion, of whatever kind it may be, is, as Cicero said, a malady of the rational soul. Every passion is morally bad.

The Aristotelian-Thomistic conception of passion is quite different, for it distinguishes in man reason and sense, and unites them without depriving them of anything proper to their existence. The intervention of reason, far from suppressing passion, simply gives it the regulation of which it stands in need in order to become "human," without thereby ceasing to be "animal."

No doubt it can happen that the disturbance of passion may be such as to make any exercise of reason impossible. This is the case, e.g., in madness, drunkenness, "paralyzing" fear, etc. In this case, passion is an "act of man," not a "human act." Reason, ligated, does not and cannot intervene. The case is of no interest to the moralist (except insofar as reason might have been able and bound to intervene to avoid the cause of this passion).

Most often passional perturbation leaves some field of action for reason. At that point some voluntariness is introduced into passion which then becomes a human act. Man finds therein fulfilment of his destiny.

In what does this intervention consist? It is not a suppression of passion. It is a regulation, one from within, the natural fulfilment of the animation of the body by the soul, a participation of sensible life in reason. The same man thinks and feels emotion. The passions of man are not those of the animal (despite all their points of resemblance). They share, without ceasing to be themselves, in the life of reason just as the cogitative power which, because it shares in reason, is not wholly like the estimative power of the animal, though it may have the same objects, the same functions and the same fundamental processes.

In the language of the psychoanalysts—may they pardon us for this transportation—: reason, in its moderation of passion does not need to aim at the creation of a "super-ego," i.e. a regulation imposed from without—education and social pressure—unassimilated by the genuine self, the source of psychic energy; it aims rather at the prevalence of the oblativity of the self over primitive narcissism and lawless compulsions, which the extrinsic regulation of the super-ego dangerously throws back into the unconscious without succeeding in integrating them with the profound wishes of the self (Cf. III *Sent.*, 23, 1, 1. c). Thus the psychoanalysts state that among the neurotics "we find ourselves in the presence of a veritable disentanglement of compulsions (Triebentmischung). In other words, the saturation of negative valences by the positive does not take place, rather each valence appears isolated (Dr. Parcheminey, art. cit. p. 39). "When in the midst of the sphere of psycho-motive expression, a superior instance undergoes a functional weakening, the instance which is immediately inferior to it recovers its independence, and begins to function according to its own laws, its primitive rules." [11]

The theologian says nothing different, even though he transposes it to his level, when he affirms that the passions in man, in order to be fully themselves, need to participate in the superior faculty, that is, in reason. If this participation fails at the point where it is expected, passion follows its own laws, its primitive laws. Like a cancer, it is dissociated from the self at the same time that it dissociates the self; it is, at least, a nervous disorder, if not a sin.

On the contrary, if passion in man participates in reason from within, far from losing anything of its nature, it finds it in its fulness (it is a *human* passion). Becoming completely an act of the human subject who experiences it, integrating itself fully in its unity, passion really adds to the nobility of man, the rational animal. Rational he must be, not only on the plane of pure reason, but in everything that he is, including the movements of the flesh. It is thus that vassal states enrich and glorify the sovereign nation that rules over them and are benefited by it without being reduced to servitude.

St. Thomas, following St. Augustine, compares the empire of reason over passion to that of the husband over his wife (*De Ver.*, 15, 2, obj. 9). Imitating Aristotle, he likewise compares it to the rule of a prince over free men. The soul governs the members of its body as slaves who have but to obey, for they do not belong to themselves; but it must govern the passions like free men who

---

[11] *Ibid.*, p. 36. Cf. A. Plé, *Saint Thomas d'Aquin et la psychologie des profondeurs*, par. 3: *L'unité de la personne*, in *Suppl. de la Vie Spir.*, Nov. 1951, pp. 422-434.

have rights, including that of contradiction and of resistance (Ia, q. 80, a. 3, ad. 2).

It is interesting to note that this liberal government is exercised on the level of knowledge and of appetite.

On the level of knowledge. We have seen that if there is passion it is because the cogitative power has judged an object good or bad for the subject. Through the functioning of this judgment the appetite tends toward the object or away from it. The cogitative power (Ia, q. 80, a. 3) is moved and directed by reason and thus is distinguished from the instinct of the animals. It is, then, by elevating the cogitative (which St. Augustine very accurately calls the particular reason) above the laws of simple instinct—and not by suppressing it—that reason (the superior reason for St. Augustine) is called by man's nature to control his passions. Thus, it is necessary that the judgment of reason be incarnate, if one may use the expression, in the sensible judgment of the cogitative: or, if you prefer, it is necessary that the cogitative, while remaining itself, that is, while remaining on the level of the senses which is its own, judge of itself (and not against itself) in accord with reason, because it participates in it. The solution lies in an "assumption" of the instinct (which becomes in that way cogitative) and not in its annihilation, or its rejection.

On the level of appetite. In the animal, the sensible appetite is simply borne toward the object which the senses present to it and which is evaluated by instinct. In man, this appetite participates in the superior appetite, that is, the will. It is in fact a principle of universal metaphysics that, in a complex being, the inferior powers are moved only by a superior power. Naturally then in man the sensible appetite lends itself to the impulsion of the will; it has need of the will in order to be itself. We find here transposed, the law of assumption: the sensible appetite is made for participation in the rational appetite; the norm is that it desire in an affective way in conjunction with the spiritual desires of the will.

Such is the order of nature. God has not given us a sensible nature in order that we might have no other task than to kill it. Insensibility, declares St. Thomas, is a vice. It is against nature (IIa IIae, q. 92, a. 1).

But this order of nature has been disturbed by original sin and further by the effects of our personal sins. That is why our passions lend themselves so reluctantly to the participation of our superior powers. Nevertheless, in order to find the full equilibrium of their own activity as well as their harmonization with other human activities, they require this participation.

It is, then, by the participation of the passions in reason and not in their annihilation that man must find his moral success. Human passions are not intrinsically bad, they are natural, and therefore good. They normally seek a regulation of reason, a fact which causes them to enter the moral sphere. When this regulation is absent, or when it is perverse, passion is immoral; when on the contrary it is exercised and is sound, passion is moral. This is what we must now examine.

(b) *Morally the Passions Are Either Good or Bad*

For details on this question we refer the reader to the treatises on sin, grace and each of the theological and moral virtues, especially the virtues of fortitude and temperance whose object is precisely to regulate the passions which are most difficult to control.

We shall limit ourselves here to general principles which permit us to judge of the moral goodness or malice of the passions.

First, let us recall that a passion does not deserve the qualification moral except insofar as it is a human act, that is, an act in which there is found something of the rational and the voluntary.

There are cases, as we have already pointed out, in which the disturbance of passion is so great that the rational and the voluntary can no longer find any place. Consequently no morality is found in them unless the will is able and bound to act upon the causes which arouse this very violent passion.

We note that, by themselves, the passions can have their objective goodness or badness, e.g. when their object agrees or is at variance with reason. This is the case, for instance, with modesty, which is not a virtue but a virtuous passion, or with fear (reasonable) of impurity (IIa IIae, q. 144, a. 1). It is the case also with jealousy, which is sadness (unreasonable and so, vicious) due to the happiness of others, or with a righteous anger in which personal vindictiveness would be found fully justified (IIa IIae, q. 158, a. 1).

In all of these cases in which the regulation of reason can be exercised and is not there is moral disorder. If this negligence is wilful, the fault is essentially commensurate with the malice of the will; if it is not wilful there is fault also, though less grave, e.g. the sin of sensuality which, of itself, is only venial.

In the most frequent cases, passion is doubled by a movement proper to the will. The two appetites, the sensible and the rational, bear upon the same object. If it is the rational appetite which starts the movement, the passion is called consequent; otherwise, it is called antecedent.

The morality of consequent passion is that of the will: either passion makes manifest the intensity of a will strong enough to draw the sensible appetite after it, or, if this enticement is willed, passion merely increases or diminishes the goodness or badness of the will to which it permits a more prompt or a more vigorous execution. It is, e.g. more virtuous for a man to love his neighbor not only with all theological charity, but also from a full charitable heart (cf. *De Ver.,* q. 27, a. 6), with mercy.[12] Inversely, a passionate fury voluntarily stirred up by a hateful will aggravates the perversity of it. Moreover, the absence of anger can bear witness to the weakness of a love of justice (IIa IIae, q. 158, a. 8).

Antecedent passion tends to disturb the rational judgment which follows it and to entail a decision which will not have for its sole motive a serene and objective decision of reason.[13] In this case the goodness or the malice of the will in the matter are found somewhat diminished. It is, for example, more virtuous to decide on an act of charity through the very movement of this virtue than through the sole urge of the passion of mercy. Conversely, it is less perverse to allow oneself to be enticed by passion into an act of impurity than to decide to do it coldly and deliberately.

Thus it is seen how passion, to the degree in which it is and must be human, enters into the field of morality, whether it possesses by itself its own malice, or whether it augments or diminishes the goodness or the malice of the will which is borne toward the same object.

[12] For St. Thomas, mercy is a passion. Cf. IIa IIae, q. 30, a. 3.

[13] There is a case, that namely in which antecedent passion is already by itself morally good (e.g. modesty), in which the judgment of reason is not vitiated by passion, but rather happily prepared. It is "anticipated" but not falsified. It can even be rendered less perspicacious, as happens in "knowledge through connaturality" which enables the chaste person to judge spontaneously and exactly of things pertaining to chastity, even though he may not be able to give the reasons for his instinctive judgment. Such knowledge requires (if not to be rectified) to be confirmed and clarified by science.

(c) *How the Passions Are Controlled*

The passions by their very nature must be controlled by reason, not indeed as slaves by their master, but as free men by their chief —a delicate task which sin has come to make quasi-impossible. The help of God's Grace in this matter is particularly indispensable.

In the light of what we now know of human passions, it is possible for us to trace out the great principles by which they are to be governed.

Never forgetting that one does not dispose of his passions as he would of the mobility of his feet or hands, but that it is proper to respect their own consistence, our reason and will united can act:

1. On the bodily factors of the passions. We have seen their importance. Good physical and mental health and, if need be, an adapted therapeutic, an intelligent mortification can, within certain limits, correct an hereditary or acquired temperament, moderate or excite a passion. To be pointed out also are the role of gesticulation and of expressive mimicry. The Church, in her liturgy, has not forgotten it.

2. On external and internal sensations. We can forbid ourselves to see, hear, feel, taste or touch a desirable object, we can refuse to imagine it or to call it to mind. The view or the recall of the object is, as we have seen, one of the causes of the passions.

3. On the evaluation furnished by the *vis cogitativa*. It is the judgment of value which definitively decides the direction of the passion. Since original sin the judgment of the cogitative power has but too great a tendency to impose itself on that of reason instead of orientating itself in its direction. The very effort of the control of passions is here not only one of safeguarding the full independence of the judgment of reason, but also of making it descend, as it were, to the level of the sensible judgment of the cogitative power. Everything will be resolved if the cogitative power shares sufficiently in the power of reason to appreciate, as it does, sensible objects.

4. On the sensible appetite itself which, since original sin, lends itself with difficulty to the motion (psychologists would say the prevalence) of the will and tends not only towards independence but also to subject the will to its caprices. The will, like reason, confronted with the cogitative power, is obliged to safeguard its independence of the sensible appetite, and must seek to "assume" it, without ever claiming to suppress it. In the last analysis, the

moralization of our passions does not consist in choking them under the pressure of the interdicts of a "super-ego" or a moral legalist, but rather is effected by the force of our spiritual love and the power of contagion of our lower loves; that is, by loving strongly, and with all our powers of loving, from the noblest to the most "animal," in harmonious unity and in the hierarchical order of their dynamism.[14] This is the proper effect of our virtues and especially of the virtues of temperance and of fortitude. St. Thomas calls attention to the unfortunate effects of a tyrannical regulation of reason: it becomes a source of difficulty and of distress. On the contrary, a regulation of reason rightly virtuous becomes inherent in passion; it becomes a quality of passion. We would even say that reason animates from within the dynamism proper to passion. The latter is then permanent and is exercised with ease and with joy; it is virtuous (III *Sent.* 23, 1, 1).

3. THE ELEVEN PRINCIPAL PASSIONS

A treatise on the passions would be incomplete if it did not try to introduce some order into the category of human passions. Based on the nature of things, a judicious classification will complete our knowledge of the passions and facilitate our control over them.

St. Thomas' classification terminated in the recognition of eleven passions, or rather of eleven passional families, specifically distinct from one another, whose nature, causes, effects, remedies and morality he analyzes with great psychological finesse (Ia IIae, q. 26, a. 48).

These analyses cannot be summarized. They must be read in the text. We shall limit ourselves here to establishing the Thomist classification of the passions, and will conclude with some reflections on the passion which may be called the mother of them all— love.

(a) *Classification of the Passions*

To classify the passions, St. Thomas appeals to a series of principles drawn from the nature of the appetite and of the objects, a fact which lends great interest to his classification. Here, step by step, is how he proceeds:

[14] Cf. *Loi et amour, Suppl. de la Vie Spir.,* No. 17, May, 1951.

1. The Concupiscible and the Irascible

Recall the distinction made by St. Thomas between the natural appetite and the sensible appetite. The first is an unconscious inclination, preliminary to all knowledge, which moves each being toward the good proper to its nature. The second is the inclination to different goods known and evaluated by sense knowledge.

The natural appetite is capable of two movements: one by which it preserves itself in existence, the other by which it triumphs over what is opposed to it. On the one hand, it profits by what is suitable to it, and on the other, when the possession of this good meets with some obstacle, it reacts, it overcomes and it sets itself against it.

This distinction of natural appetite is necessarily found in the sensible appetite, which is not simply borne toward the object which the imagination and the cogitative power present to it as good—or, in the contrary circumstance, turns away from it—but if there is any difficulty, it reacts against it. According as the passions belong to one or the other of these two movements, they belong to the concupiscible or the irascible category.

In the case of the concupiscible passions, the sensible appetite merely lends itself to the passion which its object exercises over it. It loves it or it hates it, desires it or flees from it, finds joy in it or sadness according as the object of the appetite is good or bad.

In the family of the irascible passions, the object of the appetite is good and bad at once. It is good, but something offers an obstacle to it and it takes on the aspect of evil, or it is bad, but something of good can be found. I hope or I despair of a difficult object, I dare attack the difficulty, or I fear to do so, I take vengeance on some obstacle which gets in my way by becoming angry.[15]

[15] This distinction of the concupiscible and irascible appetite cannot be rightly compared with the distinction made by Freud at the end of his life between the two instincts to which according to him all compulsions can be reduced. The libido (by which must be understood all the compulsions of tendency or constructive compulsions) and aggressiveness, or instinct of death which groups together all our compulsions of destruction (sadism, masochism).

The Thomistic and Freudian distinctions cannot be confused, for several reasons: not only, as we have said, because the compulsions of Freud are not the passions of St. Thomas, but also because the aggressiveness of psychoanalysis is in no way comparable with the irascible of St. Thomas. The latter is specified by the contrariety of its object, good and bad together, and that which results from the movements of the appetite. The "hardiness" of the irascible is not the destructiveness of aggressiveness.

2. The Stages of Passionate Movement

The passions are movements of the sensible appetite. In every movement we can distinguish the principle of the movement, the direction of its progress toward its good, and finally rest at the point of arrival.

In passional movement, the *principle* is love, that is, the suitableness to itself which the object awakens in the sensible appetite, the *progress* is the movement of desire, the *rest,* at the point of arrival, is pleasure.

3. The Objects of the Passions

A third principle of classification of the passions is borrowed from their objects. This is a classic method employed by St. Thomas for whom the powers and the acts are specified by their objects, i.e. by things in their relation to the subject who knows them.

Whether the object of the sensible appetite be judged good or bad is what establishes a specific difference of the object and so of the passion.

We come now to distinguish in the concupiscible three specifically distinct passions, two at each stage according as the object of each is good or bad:

Object good		*Object bad*	
It is suitable to me:	love	It is not suitable to me:	hate
It attracts me	: desire	It repels me	: aversion
I find rest in it	: pleasure	I suffer it	: sadness

4. Internal Contrariety of the Irascible Movement

We have said that objects of the concupiscible are good or bad, while the objects of the irascible are both good and bad at once. Hence the passions of the irascible will not be distinguished solely by the goodness or the badness of their object but also according to the prevalence of one of two contrary movements that an object, in which there is a mixture of good or bad, provokes in the appetite. A good attracts me, but a difficulty repels me. If this difficulty does not exceed my powers, I hope; in the contrary case, I despair.

Some evil menaces me. If the threat does not seem to me to be too great, I dare; in the contrary case, I fear. We point out in this respect that it reverts to the cogitative power to determine whether the difficulty to be overcome exceeds my powers or not. The cogitative then has a role of the first importance to play in the passions of the irascible, even more important than in those of the concupiscible.

Finally, if instead of being future and menacing, the evil is present and sustained, it is no longer a time to fear or to flee. A (relative) good remains possible, that of protesting and of seeking vengeance. To oppose and to sustain oneself at the same time really defines what is called anger, in which the contrariety of movements, which characterizes the irascible, is pushed to its maximum. Neither of the two predominates. Since anger brings together with violence the two opposite movements which up until then moved separately and divides the mutually opposed passions of the irascible, anger has no double, it is alone in its species.

It is thus that St. Thomas counts five passions specifically distinct in the irascible appetite. Two—hope and despair—face a good but difficult object; two others—daring and fear—have for object an evil that threatens. Anger, the last, is opposed to an evil being suffered.

In adding these five passions to the six that we have distinguished in the concupiscible, we have a total of eleven specifically distinct passions. Neither more, nor less. Still it would be more exact to speak of eleven different families of passions, each of which is able to bear upon particular objects. Thus, the passion of mercy is a species of sadness, that of others considered as our own; envy is another species of sadness, modesty a species of fear, etc. It will be noted that this distinction of eleven specific passions is not at any point based on either their physiological phenomena or on their quality of imitation. Contemporary works undertaken in this field never succeed in clear cut specifications. These phenomena often appear similar for very different passions. The system of classification of St. Thomas, with its philosophical basis, appears to be more precise and more easily applied in moral theology. Still it does not forbid anyone to look for a physiological system of classification, although such a system is yet to be discovered.

(b) *Love, the Fundamental Passion*

Not forgetting that St. Thomas never distinguishes except in order to unite, we will not consider these eleven passions as separate and independent entities.

Their reciprocal relations are profound and multiple. The irascible passions are ordained to those of the concupiscible and presup pose them. Their relation consists in removing the obstacle which arrests the movements of the concupiscible, already enticed by love or hate, and permitting them to rest in pleasure or sadness.

Moreover those concupiscible passions which have evil for their object can be no more than secondary with regard to those which tend toward the good. If I hate, it is because I love.

Finally, of these last, love is the principal one. If I desire or take delight, it is because I love.

Thus love is at the beginning of every passional movement. It serves as the mover or the principle. Love is the first "passion" which directs an object to the sensible appetite. It arouses in it (and by so doing it merely defines the tendencies of the natural appetite) what St. Thomas calls by turns a likeness of itself, an aptitude, a complaisance, a connaturality—in short, not yet the attraction of desire, but its mover.

If I love a given object, it is because it meets in me, it awakens in me and fashions in me an image of itself, an expectation, a likeness—whether it bring me what I confusedly expected or whether I find in it what I already possessed. In the first case it enriches me, and I desire to incorporate it in my being, for it actualizes one of my potentialities, it satisfies the initial tendency of my natural appetite and, more profoundly, the universal law of all being, which is confounded with my being, for which to exist is a good.

In the other case, I love this object as another self. It is a good for me that also exists for itself.

These two loves cannot be separated. We must even say that all love is both, for the object of all love is twofold. To love, says Aristotle, is to wish well to someone. In all love there is therefore the good which I want and that for whom I want it (myself or another). The good that I want is not loved for itself but for him whom I love; it is loved for its own sake. I love him out of friendship, while the good that I want for him, I love out of concupiscence.

We will close this all too short analysis of love by calling attention to its "unitive" power.

The union of the lover and the beloved is at once the cause of love; love itself is its effect. The substantial union of the subject with itself or its union of likeness with another thing than itself, is the cause of love. The affective union which actualizes in the appetite the object loved is what defines love. Finally, the real, effective union which the lover seeks with the object loved in order to be made one with it is the object of love.

In conclusion, the reader will need little reflection to grasp the importance of the passions in human life.

These human acts, in which are united in man what he has of his own with what he has in common with the animals, epitomize in him his beauty and his misery, his mystery and his drama, his eternal destiny.

The theologian is interested in the passions not only for the sake of the morality which is inseparable from them, not only because love, queen and mother of the passions, is the psychological factor of unity and union, but also because the theological virtues are rooted in them and must enliven them.

In what way do the human passions play a role in our life of union with God? However spiritual the union may be, it appeals also to our passions.

REFLECTIONS AND PERSPECTIVES

The Passions in Theology

The treatise on the passions is entirely characteristic of theology. Many theologians, however, by-pass this treatise; others treat the passions quite simply as an evil, a disorder and a sin. The effort of a sane theology is to discern their role and to determine with accuracy their morality (good or bad, as in every human act). And first of all, not to forget their existence.

In fact, the passions have an enormous importance in every human life. Man is neither a pure spirit nor flesh without a soul, but an incarnate spirit. Passion, which is not purely voluntary (or of pure virtue), but the voluntary incarnate, or more exactly, an act of the sensible appetite of man comprising a psychological reaction is, by that title, entirely characteristic of "human affections." Besides, every spiritual growth is accompanied by a mastery of greater and greater strength of the spirit over the flesh and every degradation of the sinner, of a servitude more and more narrow of the spirit to the flesh. At the extreme limit, the blessed at the resurrection will be spirit even in their flesh, while sinners will be flesh even in their spirit.

This mastery, however, should not be understood as a tyrannical regency, in the stoic manner. Passion, or at least the movement of the sensible appetite, comprises for the will a *datum* of which the latter must take account. The ancients loved to compare spirit and passion to two principles, masculine and feminine, in order to show that if there should be between the two an order of precedence and of government, there should not be servility, to show the ascendancy (and the limits) of liberty over the passions.

The passions have received in Christianity new titles of nobility from the fact that they can be assumed into theological life itself. The words of faith, hope, and love are words which signify passions before they signify theological virtues. And if these latter virtues transpose in the spirit the movement of these passions, it is not denied—it is even normal, without its ever being necessary—that they should have an authentic passional reverberation in all being. At the end of our earthly theological life, beatitude will assume in our resuscitated bodies and in our glorious sensibilities, all the elements of the passion of joy.

It would be interesting to show in the Gospel, in the sacraments and the liturgy, the role of the passions in the conduct of human life. Let us set up certain landmarks:

In the Gospel, point out all the "passions" of Christ: for example, the joys of friendship, sorrow at the death of Lazarus (sorrow accompanied by tears); fear in the Garden of Olives, anger when he drove the money changers out of the temple, joyous emotion in the presence of children, in the presence of the rich young man, etc.

Among the sacraments, analyze the genuine character of passion in marriage. Show that "conjugal faith" which is a passion must be assumed by the theological charity of each spouse for the other. God shows that there is not in it the sublimation or the refusal of passion, but on the contrary, integration and spiritualization. (Let us note that spiritualization does not mean the elimination of what is carnal, but signifies that the carnal act is also wholly penetrated by spirit.)

In the sacramental rites or the sacramentals, note the place assigned to the passions of man, particularly in Baptism, at the birth of the new man; notice all the rites which confer on the senses an equally spiritual role: "I bless thine eyes with the sign of the cross that thou mayest see the splendor of God; I bless thine ears with the sign of the cross that thou mayest hear the word of God; I bless thy nostrils, etc." Observe the parallel rite of analogous anointing in Extreme Unction: the anointing of the eyes to erase all the sins of sight; the anointing of the lips to erase all the sins of the mouth; etc.

Finally, show the role of the liturgy (where gesture, speech, music, song, the agreeable odor of incense, colors, etc., concur in one and the same prayer) in educating the passions of men—in earlier times and today.

Love. What is love? The psychology, physiology and the theology of love. The place and function of love in animal life, in human life (birth, growth, maturity, education), in the life of God.

Finally, granted the importance—which it is not possible to exaggerate—of the joy toward which the Christian moves, show the role and the place of joy in Christian life. What is to be thought of the saying: "We are worth what our joys are worth"? Explain and comment on it. Joy and mortification. Joy and the cross in the life of the Christian. Joy and the resurrection.

The Passions and Psychoanalysis

Psychoanalysis in its first positions has been doomed to most unhappy situations. It has become the scandal of the honest man, the mud hole of pornographic literature, the cast off of the materialist doctor and the spiritualist philosopher. It has been characterized by betrayals in popularization, absurdity of fashion, exaggerated therapeutic claims, incompetent excursions of psychoanalysts into the domain of philosophy and ethics, fratricidal struggles of the pupils of Freud, etc.

Can the non-professional man be his own guide in the midst of such a confusion?

He should know that for several years, in France and abroad, the concern for serene objectivity, which does honor to and gives fruitfulness to science as to theology, is inclining—or constraining—numerous investigators to grant to Freud the very prominent place which he deserves. He really discovered a new continent, but it was seen at the same time that he prospected only a small part of it and that the caravel which carried him there is now sunk. Or, to speak without metaphor, it is more and more recognized that fidelity to the scientific spirit of Freud (he gave a magnificent example of it, correcting, resuming, abandoning from work to work his hypotheses of research) invites one to "surpass" him: separating Freudian psychology and therapeutics from the materialistic and atheistic philosophy of Freud, continuing the observations and scientific researches which are capable of improving the therapeutics and the psychology.

Among Catholics, honor goes to M. R. Dalbiez for first having made the effort (*La méthode psychoanalytique et la doctrine freudienne,* Desclée de Brouwer, 2nd Ed., 1949). Recently, the validity of the distinction between doctrine and method made by Dalbiez has been hotly contested (cf. P. Gemelli, in the Italian review "Vita e Pensiero," May, 1950); Louis Jugnet, *Un psychiâtre philosophe: Rudolph Allers, ou l'anti-Freud,* Éd. du Cèdre, 1950). A recent article of Dr. Lagache, "Définition et aspects de la psychoanalyse," (*Revue française de psychoanalyse,* July-Sept. 1950), showed that a distinction can be made between Freudian therapeutics and psychology. But does this permit us, as M. Dalbiez proposed, to distinguish the wheat from the chaff in the works of Freud? It may be doubted.

Moreover, for several years now different lines of research have been variously directed. In loyalty to the scientific spirit of Freud himself, effort has been made to purify his observations, to multiply and to develop them, to improve his method, to limit his psychology to a phenomenology, in short, to emphasize the scientific rigor of psychoanalysis, thanks to which a sane spiritual conception of man can easily accept and respect him.

It is notably in this direction that the following works proceed: Dr. Odier (Protestant), *Les deux sources consciente et inconsciente de la vie morale,* Éd. de la Baconnière, 1943; Prof. De Greef, *Notre destinée et nos instincts,* Plon, 1945; of Prof. Charles Baudouin (especially *De l'instinct à l'esprit,* Desclée de Brouwer, 1950); Canon Nuttin (Louvain), *Psychoanalyse et la conception spiritualiste de l'homme;* Dr. Gregory Zilboorg, *Sigmund Freud, His Exploration of the Mind of Man,* Charles Scribner's Sons, N. Y., 1951; and the efforts made by the "Études carmélitaines" (R. P. Bruno de Jésus-Marie, O.C.D.), les Cahiers Laënnec (R. P. Larère, S.J.), the Études (R. P. Beirnaert, S.J.) and the *Supplément de la Vie Spirituelle* (especially, no. 19 of Nov. 1951). We mention also the "Association Catholique pour l'étude des problèmes de thérapeutique, psychiâtrique et psychologique," which groups Catholic theologians and psychiatrists (neurologists, psychiatrists and psychoanalysts), and also the "Congrés Catholique internationaux de psychologie clinique et de psychothérapie." Similar researches are being carried out abroad, notably by the Institute of Psychology of Montreal (R. P. Mailloux, O.P.).

One result of these works is that the more psychoanalysis is purified from all alliance with philosophy, and the less there is asked of it that a science of observation and a therapeutic method cannot give, the more it can on the one hand have useful relations with organized medicine, and on the other be integrated with a conception and a treatment of man as a whole, body and soul. Scientifically studied, psychoanalysis is far from undermining the morality and the freedom of man. On the contrary, it permits us to remove the false appearances of virtue and of liberty, and in that way to enlighten our moral effort—cf. N. Mailloux, *Déterminisme psychique, liberté, développment de la personalité* (*Supple. de la Vie Spir.,* Sept. 1952). We may hope that psychoanalysis will soon be able to improve our science of the control of passions, our Christian and Pastoral pedagogy.

But we may well moderate this optimistic perspective. While waiting for psychoanalysis to attain the development that we wish for it, its practice remains dangerous, especially if one possesses only a superficial and bookish knowledge of it. Like every science, in order that it may be exercised properly, many years of theoretical and practical work must precede. Those who cannot give these had better practice prudence and modesty.

Psychologists and moralists are at work. We might wish that they were more numerous, better qualified scientifically and better equipped, and that their efforts would not be compromised by amateurs and by journalists.

Powers of the Soul

Perhaps it would be useful to sum up here the different "powers" and "faculties" of the soul that we have been led to consider:

I. Powers of knowledge:
  1. Sensible
      a. external senses $\begin{cases} \text{common sense} \\ \text{imagination} \end{cases}$
      b. internal senses $\begin{cases} \text{cogitative or "particular reason"} \\ \text{memory} \end{cases}$
  2. Intellectual

II. Powers of appetite:
1. Sensible

a. concupiscible
{
love
desire
joy or delectation
hatred
flight
sadness
}

b. irascible
{
hope
despair
} Before a *difficult* good

daring
fear
} Before an evil *difficult* to overcome

anger { Before an evil considered as insurmountable and demanding vengeance.
}

2. Intellectual: the will.

It will be noted that the irascible is referred to its object (which is presented to it by the cogitative) not absolutely, but insofar as it is *judged difficult* to attain or repel. Then too, the good and the bad, objects of the irascible, are not good and bad simply perceived, but *estimated* to be good and bad relative tᴗ the resources of the subject. The irascible is then already mingled with the rational and in this respect its passions are nobler than those of the concupiscible. But the latter are more fundamental and richer. The irascible is founded on the concupiscible and is at its service.

BIBLIOGRAPHIE

Les pages qui précèdent auraient atteint leur but si elles avaient incité le lecteur, et l'avaient préparé, à lire lui-même le texte de saint Thomas (*Somme théologique*, Ia IIae, questions 23 à 40). Rien ne vaut en effet le contact direct avec ce maître psychologue. On pourra s'y aider par la lecture du chapitre quatrième du *Saint Thomas d'Aquin* de M. Étienne Gilson (Collection *Les moralistes chrétiens,* Lecoffre-Gabalda, 1925).

Le lecteur moderne ne peut manquer de se trouver dérouté par cette division des passions établie d'après leurs objets ainsi que par l'ensemble de cette psychologie plus philosophique qu'expérimentale. Et en effet les sciences physiologiques et psychologiques ont fait depuis le moyen-âge des progrès importants dont le moraliste est invité à bénéficier.

Une première synthèse a été tentée, au sujet des passions, dans l'ouvrage du Père Noble (*Les passions dans la vie morale,* Lethielleux, 1931), qui vaut encore d'être lu, quoique depuis ce temps la science ait fait de nouveaux progrès. Toute documentation sur ce point risque d'être très rapidement dépassée. Grandes en effet sont les perspectives d'avenir que pourront apporter à l'étude des passions les découvertes que l'on sent proches et qui nous donneront meilleure connaissance des phénomènes nerveux, sanguins et endocriniens. On peut signaler notamment les travaux, à peine ébauchés, de la médecine "psycho-somatique." A titre d'illustration, l'ouvrage du Dr Robert Wallis, *Passions et maladies* (N.R.F., 1950) peut être utile, malgré ses conclusions confuses. On voit sans peine tout ce qu'apporterait à l'étude théologique des passions la parfaite connaissance de leur genèse et de leur croissance, l'unité encore si mystérieuse de leurs éléments physiologiques et psychiques, tant au plan conscient qu'inconscient; une étude systématique de la mimique et du comportement du passionné, enfin le rôle si important de la vie sociale dans l'éveil, la maturation et l'expression des passions humaines.

Pour l'instant toutes ces recherches, à peine commencées pour la plupart, souvent viciées par un préjugé matérialiste, n'offrent au moraliste que des matériaux très fragmentaires, incertains ou précaires. On en trouvera un bon ensemble dans le dernier ouvrage de Georges Dumas, *La vie affective, physiologie, psychologie, socialisation* (P. U. F., 1948).

Certains livres de la collection "Que sais-je?" pourront être utiles comme première et généralement solide mise au courant des questions (cf. notamment les numéros suivants: 8. *Le système nerveux;* 24. *Les rêves;* 39. *Les Hormones;* 50. *La sexualité;* 52. *La folie;* 188. *La psycho-physiologie humaine;* 252. *La douleur;* 277. *Physionomie et caractère;* 285. *L'inconscient;* 322. *Les sentiments;* 333. *Physiologie de la conscience;* 350. *La mémoire;* etc.) Il y a, enfin, beaucoup de choses à prendre dans les traités modernes "du caractère"; signalons:

Le Senne, *Traité de caractériologie,* Coll. *Logos,* Paris, Pr. univ. de France.

E. Mounier, *Traite du caractère,* Paris, Éd. du Seuil.

E. Peillaube, *Caractère et personnalité,* Paris, Téqui, 1935.

BIBLIOGRAPHY

BOOKS

Aquinas, St. Thomas, *Summa Theologiae,* Ia IIae, Questions 23 to 40.

Connell, Francis J., C.SS.R., *Outlines of Moral Theology,* pp. 16-17. Milwaukee: The Bruce Publishing Company, 1953.

Farrell, Walter, O.P., *A Companion to the Summa,* Vol. II, pp. 232-237. New York: Sheed and Ward, 1940.

Gillet, M. S., *Education of Character* (trans. B. Green). New York: Kenedy & Sons, 1941.

Gilson, Etienne, *Moral Values and the Moral Life, the System of St. Thomas Aquinas* (trans. Leo R. Ward, C.S.C.). St. Louis: B. Herder Book Co., 1931.

McHugh, John A., O.P., and Callan, Charles J., O.P., *Moral Theology, A Complete Course,* Vol. I, pp. 39-45. New York: Joseph Wagner, Inc., 1929.

O'Brien, Patrick V., *Emotions and Morals.* New York: Grune and Stratton, 1950.

ARTICLES

Farrell, Walter, O.P., "Man's Emotional Life," *Cross and Crown,* 6: 178-198 (June, 1954).
Ginunez, V., "Training the Emotions," *Catholic Mind,* 43: 612-617 (Oct., 1945).
Keenan, A., "Emotions in the Whole Man," *Integrity,* 7: 25-30 (Oct., 1952).
Miller, L. G., "How to Control Your Passions," *Liguorian,* 41: 227-233 (April, 1953) and 293-298 (May, 1953).

Having studied human acts, it remains for us to consider the principles of those acts.

First, interior principles. These are the habits (habitus) which in us are species of powers, of capacities for spontaneously doing well (virtues) or ill (vices). These considerations on the habits (habitus), their role, their origin and development are as valid for virtues as they are for vices. Still our study would not be complete if we did not come to a particular analysis of the virtues on the one hand, and of vices on the other, or more especially of "vicious acts," which are worse than the vices themselves, and for that reason must be considered separately (Sin, Chap. V).

Secondly, external principles. These can be distinguished according as they incline us to good or evil.

He that inclines one to evil is the Tempter, the devil, of whom we have already spoken in the second volume of *Theology Library*.

He who aids us in doing good is God. First of all, God instructs us by His laws (Chap. VI), and we understand well that in this "instruction" are brought together in summary form all formation, all education, familial, social and religious, and all "direction." But God is not content with merely instructing us; since the end which He proposes for us transcends our natural powers, He furnishes us with a more efficacious aid to attain it. He intervenes in our heart and aids it from the interior by setting up in it a second and more perfect principle of action, grace (Chap. VII).

One further remark: most of the "manuals," and even the catechisms, divide theological material into Dogma, which they define as "a body of truths to be believed," and Moral, which according to them, is "a body of commandments to be observed." It is clear that in such an arrangement the "treatise on grace" would be inserted into the dogmatic part, the part which as such is opposed to Moral. But we do not conceive of Moral in this way, just as furthermore we do not divide our Theology into Dogma and Moral. We grant, if you wish, that grace is a subject for dogmatic treatment, but this is no reason why it should not also be an element of moral theology. For us, the latter is in fact the science which studies the end of human life, the acts which lead to it and the principles which govern our activity in view of that end. And it is for this reason that we study grace in "Moral."

Chapter IV

HABITS AND VIRTUES

by A. L. Mennessier, O.P.

INTRODUCTION

I. HABITS

1. Discernment of habitus
2. What a habitus is in its subject
3. The role of habitus
4. Where habitus are located
5. Acquired and infused habitus
6. Development of habitus
7. Morality of habitus: vices and virtues

II. THE MORAL VIRTUES

1. Role of the moral virtues: their necessity
2. Distinction of virtues
3. Aspects of the distinction of virtues:
    (a) the "medium rei"
    (b) the "medium rationis"
4. Courageous virtues and temperate virtues
    (a) temperate virtues
    (b) courageous virtues
5. The cardinal virtues

III. THE SUPERNATURAL ORGANISM OF VIRTUES AND OF GIFTS

1. Infused virtues
2. Theological virtues
3. God, the object of theological virtues
4. The infused moral virtues
5. What sort of capacity for action do the infused virtues bring us?

Chapter IV

HABITS AND VIRTUES

Introduction

The moral reality par excellence is virtue. In the over-all plan of his general Moral Theology, St. Thomas calls it an interior principle of good action. We shall see how, in the conduct of moral life, it is needed for the assured discernment of the good as well as for its prompt and firm accomplishment. Especially in studying virtue we discover not indeed an abstraction, but the virtuous man himself, organizing, developing his life in constant progress. Virtue is a living reality; it is man in the course of constructing himself morally, it is a moral ideal incarnated in the living forces of action. Such is the meaning of the classical definition which makes of virtue a "habit (habitus) of good." Moreover, the general study of the virtues, if it is carried out in theological completeness with a consideration of the infused virtues and of supernatural grace, begins necessarily with a preface of wholly philosophical allure—the tract on *habitus*.

This philosophical approach should not disconcert the reader who is solicitous about Christian sources. If he looks for the Gospel or St. Paul, and is given Aristotle, it is because in the effort to construct a theological synthesis, in this case our own, we take doctrine at the point of systematization where all its branches converge. Virtue is a human reality, even though it is also, in the domain of grace, a gift of God. When there is question of defining its psychological sources, or even its ontological reality, philosophy has a contribution to make.

The call to the Kingdom which the Gospel proclaims, presupposes a conversion of the heart, as well as the magnanimous response through daily humble fidelity. The ideal of the new man that St. Paul traces, and which faith, hope and charity animate, "these three" . . . (I Cor. 13:13) is accompanied by a whole moral behavior in which the principal Christian virtues enter into the picture.[1] But what reality in us corresponds to this life according to

[1] See Lemonnyer, *Théologie du nouveau Testament*, Bloud et Gay, 1928, Ch. 3.

179

the Spirit? That is the theological problem. Lactantius defined the Christian concept of virtue in function of philosophical notions. Virtue is not simply knowledge, but an interior principle and will of the good. The Book of Wisdom mentions the four virtues of the Greek philosophers: "Her labors have great virtues. For she teacheth temperance, and prudence, and justice, and fortitude, which are such things as men can have nothing more profitable in life" (Wis. 8:7). St. Ambrose, taking up this enumeration of the Greek philosophers, gave to these four virtues the name of cardinal, retaining however the idea of the connection of the virtues. St. Augustine adopted the definition of Cicero: "Virtue is an habitual disposition of the soul (*habitus*) which puts it as though naturally, in accord, with reason." But such a disposition is not, according to him, a virtue except it proceed from the faith and be ordained to God. Peter Lombard, gathering together the texts of Augustine, furnished the classic definition of the Middle Ages: "Virtue is a good quality of mind (*bona qualitas mentis*) which insures rectitude of life, which no one can use badly, and which God alone works in man." St. Thomas accepted this definition, though he reserved the last part of it for the infused virtue. He achieves an integration in the moral synthesis of the Aristotelian doctrine on habitus. It is at this point that the doctrine on virtue takes on its full dimensions—hence the many references to St. Thomas in the course of this treatise. In this matter, St. Thomas is the most authentic theological source. Since his comprehensive work only commentaries have been added.

I. Habits

1. DISCERNMENT OF HABITUS

By using the word *habitus,* in preference to that of habit (*habitude* in French), we intend not only to guard against a certain technical character in this term, so important in philosophy, but to indicate immediately everything that distinguishes the spiritual reality from the current idea which makes of habit a simple mechanical groove. In fact, even the most apparently mechanical habit implies, as J. Chevalier so well showed in his book on habit, something quite different from the automatism of a groove. In concrete life, habit itself always has all the complexity and all the mystery of life.

"Theories of habit," writes Dwelshauvers, "have been falsified for fifteen years by a careless remark of Leon Dumont, taken up and propagated by William James: habit is of a physical nature, or, if you wish, mechanical. In other words, a habit that we form might be compared to a crease that we make in a piece of paper and which remains even after we try to smoothe the paper out again, or again to a shape which a garment takes on in adapting itself to the form and the movement of the body." [2] Habit is a phenomenon of life which attains its full complexity in the living person.

Also, in order to discern its nature, we must first sketch the external traits in which the presence of habitus is recognized.

A first distinction, which Aristotle had suggested, is that between custom and habit itself: συνήθεια and ἕξις. It is possible for one to do something habitually without for that matter being as yet properly speaking habituated. "In this case," writes J. Chevalier, "it would be better to say of a man who generally rises early without being habituated to it that he has a custom, or better still, that 'he is accustomed' to rise early, and that by reason of a medical command, a rule of life, lack of sleep, in short, for any reason you wish but habit. On the contrary, habit is a permanent, internal disposition of the subject himself, which, born of custom, becomes in its turn the cause and the principle of the accustomed activity. It is a principle of spontaneous action which reveals itself in a diminution of effort."

This internal source, habit, we are invited by St. Thomas to recognize by the following traits which henceforth clothe the action which proceeds from it: *firmiter, expedite, delectabiliter operari.*[3]

Firmiter. Habit stabilizes us. But we do not take it to be a simple repetition. If there is any fixation, it is not in the sense of any stereotyped hardening of action, of any ossification which would impoverish it and reduce it to a mere routine. In reality the problem is one of orientation given to our activities, of a slope where the whole psychological richness will go on being damned up, but without therefore losing its complexity. "Habit is not the light tendency of a heart which hardly oscillates to the right, which the least attraction causes to oscillate to the left, it is a clear-cut and well

---

[2] Georges Dwelshauvers, *L'exercice de la volonté,* Payot, 1935.
[3] Cf. R. Bernard, *La Vertu,* vol. 1, Ed. of the Rev. des J., pp. 282 ff., a good commentary on this triple aspect of the re-echoing of habit in action.

drawn slope on which our ideas and affections flow." [4] We add that in the Thomistic conception of habitus, this stability distinguishes it from what would still be a simple "disposition," insufficiently established to be called a habit.

Expedite. We are dealing here with a spontaneity of action, similar in many ways to that of instinct, of a facility of action which allows us to go straight to the end without either hesitation or delay. It is a correctness of adaptation, whose importance we see in the case of moral virtue, which calls into play, unlike pure instinct, our most ·profound spiritual resources. This "neatness" of action (R. Bernard, *op. cit.,* p. 383) denotes not only a spontaneity but also a mastery. Thus the very idea of *habitus* implies possession: One has things at one's finger-tips.

Delectability. "The third trait," writes R. Bernard, "is the pleasure which one finds in action. This is a sign that there is in us as a second nature, that which enables us to accomplish with liking and approbation, as though it were an activity natural to us, things which are normally above our native powers or against our innate or acquired tendencies."

Connaturality, which again stamps the living character of habitus.

These characteristics of stability, of ease and of pleasure in acting, of joy, reveal in habitus something quite different from the routine automatism from which we should carefully distinguish it.

To cite Dwelshauvers once more: "It has not always been noticed with sufficient precision that it is necessary to distinguish in human conduct a class of habits which tend to become automatic, to make us do things mechanically, and another class of habits, quite different from the first, which are distinguished by a more intellectual character, a greater richness and a more intimate collaboration with what is superior in our mind. To designate this second class of facts, we borrow a term from Aristotelian-Thomistic tradition and speak of *habitus.*"

Over against the habits which tend to become routine, the *habitus* appears to us as implying a growing mastery of our action and an increasing suppleness of adaptation. While mechanical habits are often only a particular impulse which tends to isolate such or such an individual trait, the *habitus* seems to us to be an integration of our activities in a synthesis of the whole, elements in the construction of a personality.

[4] Janvier, cited by Dwelshauvers, *op. cit.,* p. 56.

2. WHAT A HABITUS IS IN ITS SUBJECT

For Aristotelian-Thomistic philosophy, what precedes is still only a rather exterior view of the reality of habitus. A more philosophic reflection will force us to think in terms of *being,* the nature of the enrichment which it brings to our actions; and at the same time a deeper analysis will discern in it an essential manifestation of our spiritual life.

Habitus, it is true, influences directly our activity, giving to it a delightful perfection of firmness and pleasure; it is more true that essentially habitus remains in the subject which acts and procures in him a perfection of *being,* a richer being, and thus a richer activity.

Habitus is defined then as a certain state of the being which acts, rather than as a certain capacity for action. To acquire habitus is to perfect oneself, and it is important to note that, in Thomistic perspectives which we here make our own, habitus is something quite different from certain superadded powers of action. Aristotle classified habitus in the predicate of *quality,* and the definition held by St. Thomas is: *Dispositio qua bene vel male disponitur dispositum secundum se vel ad alterum,* or more simply, *dispositio secundum naturam.* Hence it is not directly the order toward activity which defines habitus, but the disposition affecting a subject in a stable way, and determining him in regard to his nature.

To understand this, we might recall that according to this philosophy a being is first constituted in its substance as a definite being having a given nature. It is through activities in conformity with its nature that it develops itself and acquires its final perfection. All the activities of any being whatsoever are for it as so many means by which it actualizes itself and reaches its full flowering. These activities themselves do not proceed directly from the substance, but from the powers of action. This simply means that the activities being differentiated, we recognize in their principle certain faculties themselves differentiated, and so distinct from the simple substance. All that we wish to say is that our habitus are not new powers added to our powers of action, but a perfecting of the being which acts. This perfecting affects it principally in its powers, but also, in certain cases, in its essential make-up.

Hence the distinction between *entitative* and *operative* habitus, according as the "subject" which the habitus perfects is directly the power of action or radically the substantial being.

Operative habitus, having for their subject a power, produce an immediate echo in the quality of the activity which proceeds from it, since the whole reason for the power is the operation.

As for entitative habitus, if these modify the being in its substantial behavior, they produce no less of echo in the activities which proceed radically from its nature. St. Thomas gives health as an example of an entitative habitus, which seems to him to be the result of a good balance of material elements. But our theology retains throughout this notion of entitative habitus in order to define original justice and the state of grace. Original justice is then conceived as a harmonious equilibrium of all the powers, relative to the ideal of human nature, even while presupposing a supernatural principle of this harmony. Grace is conceived as a kind of super-elevation of nature itself. Now this reference to nature—*dispositio subjecti secundam naturam*—makes of the entitative habitus a reality of the dynamic order. To the radical super-elevation of nature by sanctifying grace corresponds, in the powers, the supernatural operative habits: infused virtues—which qualify them as activities proper to the participated divine nature.

It follows that to define habitus, even in its relation to the more perfect action which it makes possible, as a quality perfecting the subject, is not without consequences. We will understand it better when we see in what this perfection which brings habitus to our powers of action consists.

3. THE ROLE OF HABITUS

There is no need of habitus when we speak of a power naturally determined to its act. Such are the natural activities which proceed from instinct. The latter needs neither to be perfected nor trained. The bee constructs its hive perfectly. The need of habitus does not make itself felt except where there is complexity and indetermination of power. The role of habitus is to reduce this indetermination and to introduce order into the complexity.

Habitus appears first of all as a manifestation of spiritual life and of voluntary activity. Not only because it is in this domain that we meet with natural indetermination, but also and especially because to *move itself* is the character proper to the human act. We are masters of our powers of action. The will moves itself and moves the powers subject to it. Now the fruit of this actuation of powers is not only the act, but also a disposition in the power itself to act in the same way and to lend itself anew more easily to the commands of "practical reason," whose analysis of the human act should have brought into relief the role of mover. The doctrine of habitus appears here as a corollary of the structure of the human act such as Thomist philosophy describes it. Habitus then is nothing else but this disposition of our powers of action to lend themselves more readily to acts to which a superior power moves them. It is in this submission to the moving power that habitus continues to develop. Thus it appears not only as a determination of the confused potentiality of the passive power, but also as a phenomenon of synthesis: a coordination of our powers. Far from being a routine impoverishment in the manner of a purely mechanical habit, a habitus is a phenomenon of adaptation, in which spirituality plays the lead and constructs our spiritual life. This aspect of synthesis comes to light in the habitus called intellectual—science, wisdom— in which under the active light of the active intellect, and in function of first principles, the whole order of our thoughts is organized. On the moral plane, we see good habits, which are virtues, being developed in a way which makes for a true spiritual organism of our moral virtues.

This setting in relief of the rational and voluntary activity in the hierarchy of powers which provide occasion for the formation of our habitus, permits us more than ever to distinguish them from routine automatisms. Far from being a diminution of voluntary life, habitus is an integration of the whole psychological richness with voluntary life. We gain increasing mastery of this richness by damming it up.

Thus are joined together the two classic definitions of habitus: *dispositio subiecti secundum naturam:* disposition of the subject according to his own nature—and *quo quis utitur cum voluerit:* something which is used at will, a mastery over self.

4. WHERE HABITUS ARE LOCATED

Some new definitions are furnished by the special study of the various "subjects" of habitus.

We note first that *entitative habitus* are located in the substance itself. This may appear rather contradictory, for substance, by itself, has no need of habitus, all development being here of the accidental order. We may grant then that habitus in this case is met with only on the level of the material conditioning of our existence: health. There could be no entitative habitus affecting the very substance of the soul unless there were question of rendering it radically capable of activities corresponding to a superior nature: sanctifying grace.

As for *operative habitus,* we have said that they were an actuation of what remains naturally undecided in our powers of action— a determination which Scholastic philosophy calls "first act" in relation to the second act which is the operation itself. We reached the conclusion on this question that it is especially relative to voluntary activity that habitus are established. To discern what in us is capable of becoming "habituated" is therefore primarily to recall how far the domain of the voluntary extends and how far the different aspects of the government of ourselves are involved.

When the problem is one of the activities of the bodily order tied in with the organism itself, we could speak more freely, it seems, of *habits* than of *habitus* properly so-called. According to St. Thomas, there are no habitus which, properly speaking, have their locus in the body.

But there are in the bodily organism certain inclinations which our habitus more or less serve and which are there integrated so far as to make them, in a secondary way, a part of it. Thus, for example, to the virtue of temperance is joined the physiological habit of fasting.

To discern the motor habits capable of being integrated thus with habitus properly so-called, we shall, with Dwelshauvers, here distinguish three kinds of habits: the motor automatisms for good deeds, the injurious automatisms, and the habits called passive.

It is important to exercise the first; it is necessary that certain of our acts not require a new effort each time that they are renewed. And it is to be noted that these automatisms themselves are not a pure mechanical repetition, but a supple adaptation. It is this which distinguishes them from the injurious automatisms which are merely routine, or from the purely "passive" habits which, having been unconsciously formed in us, take up their abode under the form of manias or tics.

Sensible affectivity—the *appetitus sensitivus* of the Scholastics— is the seat par excellence of habitus. These emotive activities which Thomistic philosophy classifies within the list of the eleven passions are integrated in a human psychology, in which they must be subjected to the spiritual and be placed at the service of our rational ideal. Our sensible affectivity thus becomes the seat of habitus in the measure in which there is question of its being raised above pure instinct, of becoming spiritualized. These habitus are nothing else than the growing submission of the "sensitive appetite" to the commands of reason and of will. It is a veritable spiritualization which makes of this docility of the sensibility not simply a passive submission to an external restraint or a harsh command, but a suppleness and a spontaneous orientation in the direction of rational objects. Every ideal of moral virtue is there, as we shall presently see.

In the will itself, the necessity of habitus makes itself felt to a lesser degree than in the other powers. Without a doubt habitus are related principally to voluntary activity, but this does not mean that it is the will itself which is the principal seat of habitus, but rather that the powers which are not *naturally* voluntary need to be adapted to its rule. There is in the will a natural inclination to rational good. The difficulty is not so much in willing the good as in discerning what is really reasonable and in lending all the sensible powers to its fulfillment. This is why the moral virtues have their seat in the practical intellect and in the sensible affectivity rather than in the will itself. There is no necessity of virtue in the will except where it has to choose things which are no longer in the direction of its quite natural movement (to will in a disinterested way the good of others is not spontaneous for our fallen nature, always in tow of our private good, whence the need of an habituation to justice), or when one has to deal with a good which is superior to nature (the charity which loves God supernaturally).[5]

The education of the will consists then principally, according to this point of view, in the education of the practical intelligence (prudence) and of sensible affectivity (moral virtues).

On the question of habitus properly intellectual, about which we must here likewise say a word, their necessity depends on the essentially potential character of human intelligence. Thomistic philosophy then shows us the *intellectus possibile* determined, under the active light of the active intellect, by the *species* which, to the precise degree of this active power of the intellect, are organized into habitus. Habitus of the first principles, first of all, and secondly habitus of science and of wisdom which are something more than a growing capacity of intellectual synthesis.

[5] R. Bernard, *op. cit.,* p. 355.

5. ACQUIRED AND INFUSED HABITUS

Habitus are a living reality. We have already noted: they are acquired, developed, and can be ruined or lost.

On the origin of habitus we ask what part nature plays, what part our personal acquisitions play. Scholastic philosophy notes on this subject that if it is true that no habitus is properly innate, some among them are nevertheless realized, such as the habitus of first principles of knowledge, as soon as the activity of the mind is awakened. Just as in the moral order the first principles of practical reason are established in the status of habitus (synderesis) as soon as conscience is exercised.

These are not, properly speaking, innate, in the sense that the operation is prior to their establishment in the power. But they are natural in the sense that they are realized by the very fact of the spontaneous play of our intellectual nature and of these first evidences which, once perceived, are installed in us, so to speak, as the principle of all further "habitual" developments.

Our other habitus will be developed less spontaneously, by a voluntary exercise more or less laborious.

We may ask, however, if here again nature does not furnish certain dispositions more or less variable according to the individual for the acquisition of habitus. No doubt these individual conditions exist, but we must be careful not to understand *habitus,* such as we have defined it, as synonymous with the passive habits which appear in us, almost without us, and which can take their point of departure from this or that natural inclination or temperament. True habitus presuppose the integration of these natural inclinations in the equilibrium of the whole of our rational and voluntary life. This is why we shall soon say that habitus cannot escape the moral qualification of good or bad. If virtue, which is a good habitus, is facilitated at one point by a natural propulsion, it will generally have to be exercised with much greater care in another complementary domain. In any case, habitus is an aspect of self-mastery.

The part played by personal acquisition is then preponderant. Because we are not only masters of our activities, but also of the powers from which they proceed, the latter are modified by the very use we make of them. We see then that to establish a habitus, a whole series of acts is normally required, more precisely, acts so intense that the orientation given them may have the stability which, in Aristotelian terminology, distinguishes it from the simple "disposition." It is certainly more a question of intensity than of repetition. The important thing, in order that a habitus be acquired, is to see accurately and clearly and to will strongly. A single vigorous act, a deep psychological reaction, though generally not sufficient to establish a habitus in a permanent way, can at least efficaciously inaugurate its development.

Our theology, having determined the part of nature and of our personal acquisitions, points out also the part of God, by indicating the existence of infused habitus which we discover in speaking of the virtues. Let us say here, in a few words, that the latter habituate us to acts which surpass the normal capacity of nature. We note especially, according to the definition given previously of habitus, that they are not the addition of new powers to our natural powers, but an orientation of the latter toward superior activities. This is to say that our capacities for supernatural action are not something which would come simply to be super-added to our human psychology. If habitus is a determination of the power itself, supernatural habitus do not escape this law. When our will, our intelligence, our sensibility act supernaturally, it is indeed they which remain at the beginning of these acts. In that way, the supernatural itself becomes really ours. And we might say similarly that if habitus gives us an increasing mastery over our activity, in the case of infused habitus, the latter is a cooperation with divine movement which enables us to act supernaturally. Likewise, in the natural order, habitus implies in the sensible affectivity, for example, a readiness to follow the commands of reason; our infused habitus are in us a capacity for easily cooperating with the divine movements we call actual graces. We must not forget, when we are speaking of infused virtue and of its increases, that habitus, if it makes us masters of our supernatural activities, does so first of all only by putting us in accord with the divine movement, which is creative in us of these new capacities.

6. THE DEVELOPING OF HABITUS

The possibility of the growth of habitus is one of the most important aspects of this doctrine. Habitus in its most complete meaning is the very reality of our spiritual progress. Result of an intense act, habitus disposes us to an act of the same quality, and releasing our energy through the mastery which it assures us, it allows for our

activity a spiritual intensity which increases our capacity for progress. Once more we see everything that distinguishes it from the
routine habit that is nothing more than a sterile mechanism of repetition.

With habitus we are in the domain of the life of the spirit: *se
habere,* to possess oneself. The living being is enriched by its own
activity, and the latter yields an immanent fruit which disposes us
to a more intense action, one less fettered, freer and at the same
time more spontaneous. Moreover, let us not forget the organic
aspect of our habitus. The living being that acquires habitus in
some way constructs itself. It gives to its activities in function of the
basic orientations which move it, an aspect of the whole. For a
spiritual being to grow at the same time that it gains greater possession of itself, is to be unified. Intellectual habitus appear as a growing capacity of synthesis. The moral habitus appear as a way of
organizing life better and better in conformity to the call for hier-
archizing the good. This is what makes of virtue itself, defined as
a habitus of good, a living inclination, a dynamism, the principle
of constant progress.

When Aristotelian-Thomistic philosophy attempts to explain the
nature of the growth of habitus, it discovers a double aspect: *extensive* and *intensive* growth. The former is realized when our activity
is rendered capable of being extended to new objects. This is the
case, for example, with intellectual habitus when they enrich our
knowledge with new ideas. But this progress would remain entirely
material did not our power of synthesis increase at the same time.
Again, genuine progress of habitus is this "intensive increase" which
renders an activity more and more sure of itself: an essentially
qualitative growth according to the very nature of habitus, a progressive actuation of the power. It is always in the area of intellectual habitus that we perceive the whole difference between knowing
more or less of things and being able to use more or less of this
knowledge. To know really is not only to be able to state a larger
or smaller number of conclusions, but also to be able to give an
account of them by connecting them with their principles.

How is this growth of habitus realized? Just as at the beginning
of habitus there is the influence of an especially energetic act, so
it is the *intense* acts, more than the habitual state itself, which
makes them grow. These more intense acts are themselves prepared
by certain activities in which habitus simply gives its normal meas-

ure. The growth of habitus here follows the rhythm of life. We cannot always be in a state of tension. It is a normal rhythm of the kind which permits certain periods of rest in which life, as it were, pulls itself together before launching upon some new enterprise. We do not always fully use our habitual capacities for action. There are what are called *actus remissi*, "remitting acts" in which our energy seems to be relaxed. We shall see how these can contribute to the degradation of habitus. But normally, acts on par with habitual capacity, and even in a certain measure the "remitting acts," prepare for the more intense act which is the immediate condition of progress.

In studying the growth of supernatural virtues we shall discover the special case of the infused habitus. Here let us merely note that acquired habits, just as they can grow, can also weaken and disappear. When the relaxed acts become too frequent, this psychological let-down gives way to the removal of the elements foreign to the orientation which the habitus has favored. Above all, we are always capable of inclining ourselves in a different direction, of acquiring contrary habitus, and of suppressing those which had been previously acquired. The struggle against vice, for example, is efficaciously realized through the acquisition of virtuous habitus. But it is likewise to be feared that insufficient exercise of virtuous habitus little by little allows them to be weakened, and if there is question of infused virtues, culminates in their sudden loss through a single act of sin which, separating us from God, deprives us at the same time of His Grace and of the infused habits which proceed from it.

7. THE MORALITY OF HABITUS: VICES AND VIRTUES

Habits are necessarily good or bad. Aristotle defined habit as a disposition relative to the nature of the subject: *Dispositio subiecti secundum naturam*. This reference to nature implies a value judgment, which presupposes a qualification of good or bad according as the natural finality of being is respected or not. Especially, we have seen the role of rational and voluntary activity in the formation of our habitus. They are an aspect of the mastery which we possess over ourselves and, through it, they inevitably require a moral qualification.

Good habitus bear the name of virtue. Bad habitus that of vice.

It is important to remark that vices properly so-called are themselves habitus, i.e. realities of an order deeply spiritual. There is in vice, such as St. Thomas Aquinas understands it, something besides a simple perverse habit in the current meaning of the word. The veritably "vicious" person puts more and more of mind and will into the bad utilization which he makes of his powers of action. He does not merely loose the reins of his passions. In a sense he governs them. They lend themselves to all the refinements of his bad will. However paradoxical that may seem, there is in vice a sort of spiritualization in reverse. Moreover, the *peccatum ex habitu* is one of the most characteristic forms of the sin of malice, again quite different from the passive habit which diminishes liberty.

The virtues assure good action, not only by favoring the success of a more decided human act, more freely voluntary, but also by making it an act *morally* successful. We shall see what is their role in this regard. Note that at present the name *virtue* is reserved for moral virtues, the virtues of pure intelligence (science, wisdom, art) being only virtues improperly so-called, not being good habitus except relative to a particular good which can also remain indifferent to the total human good. These intellectual virtues themselves can still be used well or ill. Virtues in the proper sense are moral habitus which concur directly in the realization of the good. Moral virtues cannot be used badly. Certainly one can act independently of these habitus, but if they come into play, it cannot but be in the direction of the good.

II. The Moral Virtues

1. ROLE OF THE MORAL VIRTUES: THEIR NECESSITY

The very demands of a prudent action require this virtuous habituation.

What is necessary in order that an action be morally well performed? First of all, it is necessary to have a sense of the finalities which impose themselves on us: rational discernment of the end to be realized joined to the understanding of the concrete situations in the circumstances in which we must act. Then, to know how to decide correctly, and this implies not only a grasp of concrete situations but also exactness in the choice of means, and the will to persevere. This implies that really opportune means are insisted upon and especially that the action be commanded with vigor and carried out with promptness. This is the general plan of the human act, with its intentional and executive phases. An habituation of the "practical reason" on the virtuous level insures, in function of the perspicacious discernment of moral ends, the rectitude and the precision of the choices, especially the vigor of command (*imperium*).

But it is clear at once that in the psychological complexity of human action, no prudence could be set up into an habitual state except by means of the accustoming of all our powers to the pursuit of moral ends, which is the point of departure for the prudent exercise of the practical reason.

Thus moral virtue appears as an essentially elective habitus, a principle of orientation, of discernment of choices according to which prudence governs the details of our practical life. In reality, no virtue is exercised except by means of the exercise of prudence, to which belongs the concrete discernment of the action to be realized and the employment of the executive phase. In our powers of sensible affectivity, in our will itself, in what concerns justice, our virtues, fruit of the exercise of moral life, are then first of all certain inclinations toward moral ends of which they furnish us with quasi instinctive discernment. This is an essential point of the doctrine that habitus *connaturalizes* us with its object and, through it, allows us to recognize it, as it were, by instinct. The virtuous inclinations in us are the principle of the moral sense which prudence utilizes in the rectitude of its discernment. Not only does habitus give this sense of the realities which concern it, but it is also, as we have said, an inclination to act, a propulsion of power toward its act. The firmness of prudential decisions, the force of the imperium which is the principle act of prudence, depends largely on the virtuous habituations which make the whole man cooperate in the least of his moral realizations. Through the establishment of virtues, the will to good ceases to be a theoretical inclination counterbalanced by the diverse spontaneities of our powers. It becomes concrete and efficacious. More particularly, the role of virtuous habitus in our sensible affectivity is to assist in the clear discernment of the good, through an enlightenment of the emotive impulses whose eruption might disturb the lucidity of the moral judgment. This pacification of emotiveness is necessary to the intentional phase of the prudential action, in which the principal thing is to judge well. Moreover, so long as virtue is not yet solidly established in sufficient control over sensibility, there is necessary what our moral theology calls *con-*

tinentia, i.e. a voluntary restraint preventing the invasion of the emotional disturbance. It follows then that the virtuous ideal is not simply to restrain our passions, but also to rationalize and spiritualize them. This is what St. Thomas calls the state of *temperatus,* in opposition to that of simple *continens.* It is then that, in the prudential discernment, virtue plays not only a pacifying role but, as we have seen, itself becomes an instinct for good, a moral spontaneity contributing as an interior principle to the concrete perception of the ideal to be realized.

As for the executive phase of the action, moral virtue contributes to it not only by strengthening our will to good, but by making the powers subject to it yield themselves readily to the injunctions of the rational will. The ideal then is one of emotivity no longer merely rationalized and pacified, but sufficiently well possessed so that its impetuosity can be utilized for a better purpose. It can thus be virtuous to release violent passions, even though they verge on the destructive. If virtue is really acquired, the virtuous person will be able to take in hand and retain all his calm when the necessities of moral deliberation require it.

From all this, at any rate, springs what we have already pointed out in speaking of habitus in general. We see in habit a phenomenon of living organization, a synthetic capacity of action. The moral virtues are bound up with one another. They are connected, we would say, and this connection is established relative to prudence, the first and most essential of the moral virtues. No one is able to exercise it habitually and pleasantly unless a whole virtuous organism accompanies it. The virtuous person tends more and more to be unified himself in an increasing mastery of self.

2. DISTINCTION OF VIRTUES

In this organized whole, we distinguish the moral virtues from one another; St. Thomas, for example, builds the whole plan of his special moral theology on the classification of the virtues grouped around the four cardinal virtues of prudence, justice, fortitude and temperance. It is important, we believe, to grasp the exact meaning of these distinctions which, in this theological context, do not proceed merely from a dialectical trick of the mind or from a desire to follow the traditional classification of the virtues.

We comprehend the meaning of this distinction between different virtues by recalling above all that at the point of departure of the development of our habitus, there is the reasonable control of our-selves. It is the rational order that serves as a norm for our moral life which our habitus reflect in our very inclinations. It is a plan of action transposed into living tendencies. Then too, they are diversified according to their different moral objectives which we propose to ourselves. It is then, the whole diversity of moral ends, themselves graduated, which are transplanted into the diversity of the objects of virtue.

But we must carefully note that the moral objects which thus serve to distinguish the multiplicity of our moral virtues, are in reality related to the acquisition and the development of the habitus in which virtue precisely consists. Not everything has been said when we have theoretically distinguished the diverse finalities which impose themselves on us. What is important is precisely the manner in which we educate ourselves in function of the divers aspects of the moral good. The "object" of a habitus is not an abstract reality. It is defined in terms of divers difficulties which we meet with in the education of ourselves, in the different ways in which we have to take ourselves in hand according to the moral matters in ques-tion: *secundum diversam habitudinem ad rationem.* Where a special difficulty presents itself in the realization of the moral good, and where, consequently, we will have to educate ourselves specially for this purpose, a distinct habitus is required. And the diversity consists in this that we take ourselves differently according to the diversity of cases. We cannot, for instance, develop the virtue of fortitude exactly in the same fashion as we would temperance. It is in full psychological reality then that this distinction which appears so theoretical, takes root among the different moral virtues.

3. ASPECTS OF THE DISTINCTION OF VIRTUES

A first great principle of distinction is taken from the moral material itself, which needs to be ordered quite differently according as it touches on our external life or on the personal government of our affective life.

It is the principle of "measure," that serves as a norm of moral conduct, which is here quite different. The definition of virtue bor-rowed from Aristotle appeals to this notion of the reasonable rule, the principle of balance to be introduced into our actions: *Virtus est habitus electivus in medietate existens.* This is the conception of the virtuous "middle way," which in no sense is a mediocrity, but a summit, a measure which the whole of moral art tries to find and realize.

(a) *The Medium Rei*

When it is a question of the external relations of our lives, the measure is essentially objective. Such is the case with the virtue of justice and the virtues dependent on it. It is to the real, such as it imposes itself on us from without, that we must here conform. That is why we speak in this case of the *middle way*. It means that the norm of the good to be accomplished is here independent of our personal impressions, of our feelings and of the manner in which we are affected. It is an equilibrium of rights which should be established between the persons concerned, and relatively to external realities which make up the object of our relations. I must give what is due, just as it is, measured independently of my instinctive feelings, contrary perhaps to the spontaneous claims of my egoism or to the delays which the weakness of my will might bring to it.

This is really the difficulty, one which presupposes a virtuous habituation. And no doubt there are at first other moral virtues which, by enabling us to dominate our passions suitably, favor the exercise of justice. We discover here, at the same time that we make clear the distinction between virtues, the need for their connection. The just man, inasmuch as he must force himself to see things objectively, and serenely render to each his due, must first pacify in himself all the disordered or violent feelings which might disturb the impartiality of his judgment.

But the virtue of justice, in order to arrive at the impartiality which the rights of others demand, itself presupposes an habituation of the will relative to the grand object which is to render to each his due. But, as we have already remarked in speaking of the will as the seat of habitus, if it is reasonable to render to our neighbor all that we owe him, it is not entirely natural for us if we keep in mind the state of fallen nature. Original justice lost, the will follows its immediate instinct which is the search for its own good. In order to prefer the good of others to our own immediate and apparent advantage, not merely ideally, but by tending toward it efficaciously, a complete self-education is necessary, no matter how apparently innate the understanding of and the taste for justice may be. This is the virtue of justice. Indeed, because this virtue is characterized not only by disinterested objectivity, but also by a prompt and active will for realization—*facere bonum, vitare malum* —the will has here again to be protected against its instinctive and lazy tendency to let things slide. The domain of justice is one of those in which it is easiest to sin by omission.

It is the province of special Moral Theology to study all the virtues which resembling justice, in the area of the middle way, are nevertheless specifically distinguished from the most typical virtue in this matter, that is, justice of exchange or commutative justice. The divers motives for incurring debt and the objective diversity of the relations which are established with persons whose right we must recognize, provide occasion for variations of action sufficiently different to justify speaking of a specific distinction of virtues. Different from commutative justice, which sets up strict equality between individuals, is social justice, which regulates the relations of the individual with the community, and which has for its principal object common welfare. It is a virtue which not only presupposes the personal moral virtues that, as we have said, assure to virtues in every situation the objectivity of justice which is their ideal, but also the virtue which gives to the exercise of other virtues positive orientation toward the good of all.

Similarly, how can we avoid distinguishing from the virtue of commutative justice the different virtues which rectify our attitude with regard to those who are our superiors and exercise over us some authority? The virtue which regulates our duties toward our parents—filial piety—is different from the one which subjects us fittingly to our governments. Especially distinct is the great virtue which, inclining us to render to God whatever is His due, bears the name of religion.

(b) *The Medium Rationis*

Let us now see how that ensemble of virtues which do not accustom us to order our relational life, but to govern ourselves and to introduce order into our affective life, is presented. *Medium rationis,* we say, in opposition to *medium rei* which characterizes justice. Not that there is no longer a question of reality, but the reality here is ourselves, our individual temperament, our more or less vehement and disordered passions, the framework of our life, our personal ideal. The *reasonable* here is essentially something *personal*. This is why the virtue of prudence takes on more than ever the appearance of the master virtue, inseparable not only from the exercise of the other moral virtues, but also from their very acquisition.

Moral education of itself remains essentially individual, even though it retains the common general lines, because in each one of us human nature is similar. Rather than speak of the distinction of special virtues one might speak of the individual distinction of virtuous people; for each one a personal balance is to be found. In this sense nothing is more concrete, nothing more individually diversified than virtue. In this connection, we note that if the virtue of justice, through the entirely objective character of the rule which is its own, can provide the occasion for the founding of a rather detailed casuistry, it is no longer the same for the moral virtues by which we control our sensible affectivity. Moral science, certainly, apart from the elements common with human psychology, traces out the great lines of a program of self-education. This is exactly the specific distinction of virtues which St. Thomas set up with such care. But the concrete standard of action is always a living standard of prudence. We indicated earlier what our moral virtues represented with regard to the exercise of the virtue of prudence.

4. COURAGEOUS VIRTUES AND TEMPERATE VIRTUES

If now we must trace the broad lines of the distinction of the virtues relative to this ideal of reasonable self-government we see diversity assert itself, not in the material sense of the distinction of the eleven passions, which the Thomistic psychology of emotions enumerates, but in the different aspects which characterize the diversity in its relation with rational activity. The "passions" themselves are distinguished in terms of the instinctive spontaneities that arise in us, whereas the virtues reflect the whole complexity of self-education. One and the same virtue is able to give to different passions a unique reasonable order, or on the contrary, in one and the same emotional domain different spiritual reactions are able to arouse distinct virtues. For example, the virtue of temperance has to moderate both our joy and our sorrow, and often correct the one by the other. Sorrow itself, for example, is material for certain virtues as diverse as temperance which restrains it, as patience which makes us bear with it, as mercy for which sorrow is compassion at sight of the misery of our neighbor, as penitence which enters into contrition to the point of evoking sorrow for our faults.

In its broad lines, however, we may say that the double aspect which Thomistic psychology recognizes in our emotional life, by distinguishing the irascible and the concupiscible passions, is able to make place for two broad categories of virtues, the temperate and the courageous virtues. Already on the instinctive level itself, this distinction of the simple passions of covetousness—love, desire, joy and their opposites, disgust, flight, sorrow—and of the irascible passions—hope and despair, courage and fear, anger—reflects a behavior somewhat different relative to rational activity. The passions of the "concupiscible" appetite are considered as elementary spontaneities, attractions and repulsions, concerning which there is question especially of holding them in check, of tempering their instinctive vehemence, concerning which there is a problem of complete rationalization. This is why, as a group, they give place to an attitude of temperance, i.e. of moderation.

While the passions of the "irascible" appetite, already more complex, seem to appeal in their instinctive spontaneity to a certain discernment of the possible and the difficult, they are controlled in a different way. These powers of aggression—courage, anger, etc.—each of which contributes positively toward the realization of an ideal of courageous strength, must be intellectually penetrated rather than dominated or utilized.

(a) *Temperate Virtues*

In the area of the passions of simple concupiscence which temperance controls, the distinction of virtues presents itself with special vehemence, the degree depending on the passion which we have to dominate. In this "political" dominance which we have over our emotivity, the manner of controlling ourselves is obviously not quite identical when we deal with powerful instincts to be vigorously mastered or with more delicate spontaneities which are more easily governed.

The strongest passions, those which are bound up with the preservation of the species or the individual, provide material for the virtue of temperance properly so-called which itself comprises diverse species. For the strong desires incident to the act of generation are not controlled in the same way as are those of eating and drinking. In the former case there is chastity, whose very name suggests an energetic mortifying character as requisite for this virtue. Abstinence and sobriety are distinguished with reference to eating and drinking. Here again it is clear that the norm can be sought in a psychology quite different.

To temperance is attached the whole problem of self-control and the general title of *modesty* expresses the ideal of balance, measure, self-possession to be brought into all of our sentiments.

The important thing then is to recall that if certain diverse habituations are to be acquired according to the particular difficulties experienced in mastering such or such a form of covetousness, the law of the connection of virtues continues here to operate more than ever. Before being divided up into species, temperance really seems at first to be the climate of the wise and harmonious whole, the taste for moderation in all things which is converted into the beautiful equilibrium of life. And perhaps it is well not to remain obsessed with its single aspect of chastity. The latter thrives the more, the more that there is an harmonious atmosphere in the whole of life.

(b) *Courageous Virtues*

An analogous principle, that of exerting our efforts against divers difficulties, provides a reason for the distinction of the different virtues attached to courage or fortitude. Under its most characteristic aspect courage faces the danger of death by mastering both our movements of fear and of audacious impulses. It is a complex virtue concerning which we should preserve a clear judgment in order to decide upon the correctness of the cause for which we might perhaps lay down our lives, and on the most suitable means to promote that cause. This is why in acts so diverse as toleration or attack the virtue of fortitude retains a profound unity, consisting in self-mastery, lucidity of mind and the reasonable employment of the passions of aggressiveness.

Here again it is the task of Moral Theology to treat in detail all the other forms of fortitude, such engaging virtues as magnanimity, virtues of tolerance, such as patience, and the other virtues which the various difficulties of daily life require—constancy, perseverance and long suffering.

5. THE CARDINAL VIRTUES

This rapid sketch of the whole field shows us that four broad orientations serve as buttresses for the virtuous life. Among the ancients as well as among Christian moralists, prudence, justice, fortitude, and temperance have been considered major virtues. Theological language has retained the term cardinal virtues to designate, according to the figure which the word suggests—*cardo* or hinge— the pivots of moral life. On these the human life in some way turns and is anchored, says St. Thomas, *quodammodo vertitur et fundatur*. We recommend to the reader the three excellent analyses of R. Bernard in vol. 2 of this commentary on St. Thomas' treatise on virtue (*op. cit.* p. 399 ff.). Here we merely retain the problem which medieval theologians raised on the subject: Do the cardinal virtues designate simply the general conditions which define virtue as such, or are they really special and distinct virtues?

St. Thomas explains himself very clearly on this point: "For some," he says, "they represent certain general conditions of the human soul which are found in all virtues. In this sense prudence would be only a certain rectitude of discernment in a given act or material; justice, the rectitude of soul which leads us to do what we should on every occasion; temperance, a disposition of soul imposing on our patience as on our works the moderation which restrains it from going beyond what is proper; fortitude, a firmness in following reason whatever may be the assaults of our passions or the difficulties of action." In this sense, our author continues, these four qualities would express the very conditions of every moral virtue: firmness of the habitus which stabilizes us, rectitude of the good habitus which should incline us toward what is due, the reasonable moderation which causes us to act temperately in the proper milieu. Only prudence, the virtue of practical judgment, would be distinguished from this group of virtuous conditions of a rectified affectivity. For himself, St. Thomas prefers, and we have seen why, to hold that these are specifically distinct virtues. But once again it is necessary to distinguish in order to unite. The theme regarding the connection of virtues, their tie-up with prudence, is reinforced by all these considerations on the general conditions of virtue. If there are distinct virtues, there is only one virtuous person who tends to unify his life by organizing it entirely according to the great tendencies which the cardinal virtues designate.

III. The Supernatural Organism of Virtues and of Gifts

1. INFUSED VIRTUES

"If the virtue of man is ordained to a good which is measured by the rule of human reason, it can be caused by human acts, inasmuch as these acts proceed from reason, under the power and the rule of which the contemplated good is realized. But when virtue ordains man to a good which is measured by the divine law, and no longer by human reason, it cannot be caused by human acts whose principle is reason, rather it is caused in us exclusively by divine operation" (Ia IIae, q. 63, art. 2).

Such is the infused virtue whose nature we must now study.

Obviously we have here particularly a question of finality. Because our final destiny surpasses our natural powers, and because at the same time we cannot attain it except by means of personal acts, the grace which destines us to it produces in all of us an organism of infused virtues which enables us to perform activities meritorious for eternal life. The supernatural order is thus modeled on the structure of the natural order. Sanctifying grace, an entitative habitus, becomes itself the radical principle of this super-elevation of our powers enabling them to produce supernatural acts. R. Bernard writes (*op. cit.* vol. II, p. 446), "Just as from the essence of being there flow the powers which are the principle of human activity, so likewise from this habitual grace in the depths of the soul flow, through the powers, the virtues which permit them to undertake works in keeping with the state of grace. The virtues which man acquires by his own activity are certain dispositions by which he places his powers in harmony with his nature, in what it has of the truly human. The infused virtues are dispositions through which the powers of man are made to harmonize with this borrowed divine nature which grace installs in the depths of the soul. Beyond acquired virtues, there is the light of reason: it is in this atmosphere that such virtues are formed and developed, and their role is most precisely to dispose man to walk according to the natural light of reason. Similarly, beyond infused virtues, we must always see the light of grace . . . ; the existence in us of infused virtues is not clear, and we run the risk of misunderstanding their true nature unless we take care always to attach them to the order of grace.

They form a part of the astounding transformation which the state of grace produces in us. They are given with grace; they increase with it; they are lost for us if it is also lost, except for certain cases in which God designs to allow faith and hope to persist in souls without love. The infused virtues are installed in our powers because of sanctifying grace and, as it were, under the influence of this grace. They are translated into acts by the aid of actual grace. Whatever they may be, they have no reason for existence except to accustom us to the divine intimacy. . . . They humanize us, true, but in a special way, more accurately they divinize us."

2. THEOLOGICAL VIRTUES

This order of infused virtues thus bound up with the life of grace, reveals itself first through the reality of the theological virtues of faith, hope, and charity. In order to understand their place in the infused spiritual organism, we must recall that every order of our moral activity is connected with the great inclinations which basically incline us toward our final end.

The moral virtues assure the reasonable control of our life by rectifying our choices and by making us execute as we should the acts relative to our end. Their material is our human activities which must be co-ordinated, our sensible activity which must be spiritualized and utilized, our acts relative to our neighbor which must be adjusted to his rights. Virtue itself is inclination, tendency to the realization of a moral objective which thus takes on the appearance of finality. But here the object pursued is the ordering of our activities, which an astute prudence can discern and impose by way of the virtuous rectification of our tendencies.

But these virtues, according to the plane of nature, suppose as their principle, certain natural lights and a corresponding natural inclination of the will toward human good. St. Thomas, when he explains this subject, sees at the beginning of the acquisition and the development of moral virtues a natural habitus analogous to what is for the speculative reason the habit of first principles, the point of departure of all intellectual habitus which are organized and developed in their light. Likewise, when moral life awakens, the first principles of practical activity are affirmed, in which the injunctions of natural law—the course of moral consciousness, and of the acquisition of virtues: *seminalia virtutum*—are spontaneously expressed. It is the habitus of practical reason—to which corresponds on the level of tendencies the natural inclination of the will toward the good in general—which enables us to discover that the good must be sought for.

It is on this level, at this depth, in this transposition of our human activities toward a supernatural end—the normal culmination of the most basic need of a spiritual nature—that the theological virtues are set up.

Their object is not, as in the case of the moral virtues, the ordering of our concrete activities. Their object is the final end, the principle of wise government, of which prudence is in charge. Hence, since they assure the profound orientation of our life in the light of love toward God, our last end, the theological virtues are the principle of every new order of infused moral virtues, and they are measured by this supreme finality.

Returning now to our immediate task which is to situate the theological virtues in the spiritual organism infused by grace, we first evaluate the necessity of this super-elevation of our natural inclinations. We admit that nature is unable to give us adequate knowledge of the existence of a supernatural happiness. We realize especially that the natural inclination toward the good, which provides the basis for our willing, is feeble and radically wrong. Feeble in the state of fallen nature, it leaves a constant temptation to egotism from the normal tendency to seek our personal good; it also leaves us at the mercy of the impetuous play of the passions. Radically insufficient, especially, because the efficacious love of God above all things and for His own sake surpasses the capacity of our nature.

Seeing then in our theological life this elevation of our most basic inclinations toward our final divine end, we realize that first of all we should know what this end is. Such is the role of faith. It is not idle to remark that its object is God insofar as He is our final end. It is not given us merely to satisfy our taste for knowing, but to direct our life and to guide our action. No doubt, giving us a glimpse of our beatitude which is the vision of God, it inaugurates in us an understanding of the contemplative life. But the pale lights which traverse its obscurity are made to teach us what is necessary for our salvation, not simply to satisfy a curiosity for knowledge. Christian wisdom here reverses somewhat the order of Greek wisdom. It shows us that our thirst for seeing God can be satisfied only in the next life. In this, the important thing is first to know how to orient ourselves toward it as we should—and for that to love it. The whole meaning of faith is to enable us to conduct our life in love. The gifts of faith—understanding, knowledge, wisdom—the movement of charity which it directs, they are practical as well as speculative. The articles of faith express essentially what it is necessary to know in order to be saved, i.e. in order to order oneself properly to beatitude. And it is because salvation is offered to all that the revelation of the faith universalizes for the use of all the knowledge of the true God. This introduction to the blessed life motivates also the mode of knowledge which is that of faith: a divine pedagogy in which God is presented as a teacher whom we must believe before possessing all truth, which is seeing Him as He is in Himself.

On the level, not only of the light which guides us, but of tendencies which, correlatively, move us toward our final end, this supernatural elevation gives place to a double virtue.

First of all, love is necessary. The end, as such, moves us by making us love it. And this is why, if one may say so, charity is the most theological of all the theological virtues. God is there quite uniquely envisaged under His aspect of final end, i.e. the object of love, principle of attraction soliciting the whole movement of the will by the seduction which it exercises over it. Here is the whole mystery of love which we must now analyze.

To love God as He is in Himself, in the attractiveness of His supreme good, is in some sense the most fundamental inclination of being supernaturalized by grace: *pondus naturae, pondus amoris*. Grace is a supernature. All of nature reveals itself in a basic inclination toward its own good. And here is the marvel: we become by grace participants of the divine nature, it is no longer we who are for ourselves the essential good that moves us, it is God who is our most personal good. God is my good. Such is the movement of charity which prefers Him to all things and to itself in an affection which is a love of choice, in a friendship which makes us discover ourselves in the share of the total divine good become our own.

Such is henceforth the principle of effective orientation, the moving principle of the whole of moral life. To the *seminalia virtutum* of the natural order corresponds the "charity, mother and form of virtues," *mater et forma virtutum*.

A third theological virtue, hope, comes to take its place beside the other two. It is the virtue of the way.

What is its role?

On the natural level the inclination of the will toward the good corresponds to an objective which is connatural to it, i.e. to the measure of nature and its powers. No doubt a slow and laborious acquisition of the moral virtues is necessary in order that this natural tendency to the reasonable good may bear its fruit. But it itself does not need to tend toward an ideal which surpasses its human powers.

Quite differently, on the supernatural level, the divine good to which we basically tend, this beatitude which is offered to us, infinitely surpasses us. Obtained at the end of our meritorious activity, it nevertheless remains a gift of God, more than the fruit of our efforts. What is necessary then is tension of our whole *intentio* toward this arduous end—the psychology of hope is made up first of the enthusiasm which portrays the grandeur of the end to be obtained, this conquering ardor which difficulty provokes (St. Thomas tells us that the object of hope is the divine majesty)—but at the same time a confident expectation on God's part of these eternal goods which we cannot acquire by ourselves, for our very merits have their source in grace.

Supernatural hope thus mingles in an admirable balance the tension of the will and the docile submission to grace. Virtue of the way, it unites in a single movement of the soul the conquering ardor and filial appeal made to God from whom it expects everything. Inspirer of prayer as much as of effort, hope makes us realize beyond all asceticisms and quietisms the harmony between the active personality and the docility of grace. Putting us in accord with divine providence it introduces into our lives more than a psychology of simple resignation: an attitude of cooperation at once active and dependent. We add that the psychology of hope, more than charity which is before all else divine preference, appears directly as a legitimate movement of self-love. But it pertains to special Moral Theology to treat of this delicate problem of disinterested love and of the apparent interest which implies hope. Let it suffice to say that there is no problem here of opposition and that this appeal to satisfaction in God of all our legitimate desires merely manifests the implanting of our supernatural life in the deepest aspirations of our nature.

3. GOD, THE OBJECT OF THEOLOGICAL VIRTUES

In calling them theological we mean to say that these three virtues have no other object than God Himself. That their role was to direct us toward our final supernatural end has been shown earlier. But it is important here to explain briefly what is understood by this motivation by the object in the case of theological virtues.

The Scholastics distinguish here what they call material and formal object. The material object means that to which our activity is applied. The formal object, the special aspect under which it is considered.

It is thus for example that a moral virtue has for its material object the passions which it should govern, as formal object the order of reason which is to be put there and the proper manner in which we arrive at this domain of self-possession.

In the case of theological virtues, God is at once the material and formal object of our activity. Faith considers in God the truth that we possess at the end of our assent, but He Himself is, through His revelation, the principle of this knowledge which we have of Him and of the certitude of our faith. Charity in its love of God has no other motive for loving Him than He Himself in the attractiveness of His supreme good. Hope expects God from God Himself. Thus it is God Himself who is inserted into our lives, who motivates by the trustworthy authority of His word the assent of our faith, arouses by the reality of His goodness our love, provides a basis for our hope by the fidelity of His beneficent wisdom.

Several important corollaries depend upon this doctrine.

We understand first of all that the habitus which dispose our mind and will to such acts bear par excellence the name of virtues: *dispositio ad actum perfectum* . . . On the human level, belief can never proceed from a virtue so long as some uncertainty remains in the assent of faith which we give to another man. But no assent is stronger than that which we give to God. Divine faith derives from its very object this quality which brings it about that making use of this habitus we cannot err. Likewise hope bears the name of virtue only by relying on God. But then its assurance is as total as the certainty of faith.

Another consequence of the divine motivation of theological virtues: while the ideal of moral virtue is moderation—the middle way which a prudent reason approves of—there is no question of excess in the theological virtue, at least insofar as the relation of our act to what is essential in its object is concerned. We cannot believe in God or hope in Him or love Him too much. We are dealing with the infinite. The measure of theological virtues is to have no measure. Certainly, great discernment is required when the question of incarnating this great current of divine life in a human psychology arises. There may be in it some faulty ways of believing, a presumptuous fashion of trusting God, a disordered means of proving His love. But in such cases we are departing from what is essential in the virtue.

Finally, it is clear that such virtues can have their origin only in the divine. They cannot be, in anything that they are, other than infused virtues. We have noted, however, in speaking of habitus in general that they are not new powers simply added to our powers, but a modification of the latter. If we are discussing an infused habitus, the habitus remains—a determination of the undetermined potentiality of the power to certain acts. In the case of infused habitus there is no longer question of the determination of a natural potentiality, but of an elevation of our faculties to acts superior to nature. The divine action is founded in this case on what we call obediential potentiality which causes the creature to lend itself to what God wishes to draw from it over and above its natural capacities. It follows that it is our human powers which are thus elevated and that the acts to which our infused virtues dispose us are indeed our own, made entirely of that human paste which we lend to the great current that inclines us toward God. The divine life which we share is thus realized in acts fully human. Habitus as such renders us capable of exercising them: *quo quis utitur cum voluerit.* The power, by lending to habitus its whole psychological texture, explains why, on the one hand, all the human which it contains is integrated in an activity substantially supernatural, and also why this divine life in us takes on human form. It is this modest act of obscure assent, expressing itself in propositions of conceptual form, which is a great act entirely divine in its depths, through which we possess on earth the divine truth. Just so can the whole divine fullness of charity be incarnated in the humblest act of almsgiving, or in the cup of cold water given to the poor.

4. INFUSED MORAL VIRTUES

God provides for us in the order of Grace as well as in the order of nature. To the natural lights and inclinations which incline us toward our human end, there corresponds, as we have just seen, on the supernatural plane, the order of the theological virtues which incline us toward the God of beatitude, our real last end. This movement of the divine life which is thus inserted into our human powers of knowledge and of will continue radiating into whatever is human in us. It is all our acts, governed in daily detail by a concrete prudence that we must make proportionate to this upsurge of life which henceforth is that of the Son of God. Moreover, a whole order of infused virtues corresponds to this orientation of theological life putting our whole moral life in line with our supernatural destiny.

Let us recall here that our moral virtues are not just isolated dispositions, independent of each other, but an adaptation of our instinctive powers to the rational order which must control them, a conformity of inclination to the moral ideal which rules us. Now this moral ideal is an order of the whole. Our virtues must contribute, each in turn, to the realization of a synthesis of action. We have explained their connection in prudence. But the latter, on the supernatural plane, finds an axis which gives a new meaning to its choices: charity, the love of God, tending to the perfect realization of intimacy with Him in the eternal vision.

The infused moral virtues are then distinguished from what would be acquired natural virtues, above all by the *norm* which is given to our moral ideal relative to the divine ends which henceforth are also our own.

The ideal of Aristotelian morality, for example, was that of a human balance required by the horizons of a social life compelling itself to realize the conditions of a relative earthly happiness. The horizons of the City of God change all the proportions, without however destroying the concrete conditions according to which the life of man here below is lived. The same duties remain, which are those of governing our own life and of realizing among men a friendly and just order. The nature itself of our moral virtues is not changed; it is necessary that we lend ourselves, through habitual good dispositions, to a reasonable order. It is the same passions which have to be mastered by assuring the primacy of the life of reason over instinct. It is always our human relations which we have to regulate according to the demands of the common good and of what is due to each one. But there is, as Fr. Gardeil says somewhere, "a lift at each commandment." And it would be well to reread here the pages of Bergson in *Les deux Sources* on the "unfolding of the soul." A new ideal penetrates the whole human texture of our moral life: a demand for perfection which comes from this that by one leap the soul transcends the conditions of a merely human ideal in order to seek to become like the Father who is in heaven; a moral delicacy, a spiritual refinement which depends upon the greater interiority of a morality in which the intentions are themselves so deeply drawn toward divine intimacy; a primacy of the spiritual, which assures by the moderation of desires a gentle felicity, but which tends to favor contemplative activities through which is inaugurated in us the blessed life; similarly in external activity, a primacy of the devotedness of charity which transfigures the relations of simple justice by endowing them with a fraternal feeling. The "golden mean" remains the rule for moral virtue, but the adjustment is not entirely the same. Infused temperance proceeds from an ideal higher than is the natural moderation of the passions. It recognizes acts that are proper to a Christian, e.g., virginity and mortification. A Christian courage has other dimensions than a merely human virtue of fortitude, for to lay down one's life takes on a new meaning when death terminates in eternal life, and patience among the infused virtues becomes one of the most immediate manifestations of a great charity.

Not only are the infused moral virtues distinguished from the natural moral virtues by this new regulation which modifies the norm of the reasonable good, but also by the disposition in which they put us to lend ourselves to the active influence of charity. The latter not only "informs" our moral virtues—*caritas forma virtutum* —it also engenders them by the moving influence which it exercises: *mater et motor virtutum*. It is love which moves us to act. Infused moral virtue prepares us with pleasant ease for the commands of which divine charity becomes the principle. The motive of the love of God here takes the primacy. If our moral virtues are normally docile to the commands of reason, the latter is not the mover except through the will which penetrates it. The infused moral virtues are docile to a reason which not only, in the rule which it follows, conforms itself to the demands of charity, but orders, in the proper sense, commands, under the influence of a living love of God.

5. WHAT SORT OF CAPACITY FOR ACTION DO THE INFUSED VIRTUES BRING US?

It is in the light of these reflections which we have just made that we are going to try to see what capacity for action the infused virtues bring us. For the traditional comparison which is here made between acquired natural virtue and infused virtue does not seem to be in favor of the latter, so long at least as long exercise has not yet developed the potentialities of the habitus. And yet as soon as infused virtue exists in the soul, even before it has been exercised, it bears the name of virtue, while the natural virtue is the fruit of a laborious acquisition, of a spiritualization which culminates perhaps only at the end of life. Are we at this point transformed by Grace?

Experience it is true does not at first seem to confirm it. Natural virtue being habitus acquired at the end of long exercise has a stability, an ease, a pleasure in action—in short all the traits which characterize a habitus—which the infused virtue does not possess so long as it itself has not been exercised for a long time. There is no joy in acting frequently, so much resistance on the part of nature still going contrary to the ideal. It is certainly not yet the state of the *temperatus,* but of the *continens,* in which passions must he coldly restrained, instead of allowed to be drawn by a genuine virtuous spontaneity. And how fragile from then on is this infused virtue—the whole virtuous organism can be lost by one stroke!

And yet we speak of virtue. It is no doubt at first by reason of the quality of the acts that our infused dispositions permit us to function: *Virtus est dispositio subiecti ad actum perfectum.* This objective perfection of a moral ideal measured by our destiny as children of God can be sufficient to allow us to qualify as virtue the habitus which leads us into it.

And yet it is necessary at least that we discover, in the powers thus accustomed to such acts, the reality which defines habitus: not indeed in a theoretical or ideal situation but to see how this power is transformed into a capacity for action which is a certain turn of mind, a certain propensity of the tendency.

Now, it really seems that this influence of charity which we have seen at the source of our whole infused moral organism, should reverberate deeply enough in our human psychology in order that something be changed there.

It is in fact a new attitude of mind which is given to the Christian who enters and remains in the grace of God. Divine friendship is of such a price, if the Christian becomes conscious of it, that his principle of evaluation for everything must be changed by it; and it is changed, apparently, on many points. Is this divine norm which is henceforth imposed on our activities perceptible to one not in the state of Grace? I know that in many Christians this capacity for supernatural evaluation is very mediocre or quite dormant. But is it not ready to be awakened on the day on which his heart is touched with the disire for loving God? Infused prudence certainly does not of itself give us any natural qualities which are really necessary for the concrete conduct of life. But putting our practical reason in accord with charity, it surely gives us, if we make use of it, an understanding of duties that do not occur to an honest pagan. And if the natural qualities which make up good counsel, good judgment, always need to be developed, infused virtue, through the climate of dependence with regard to God in which it flourishes, favors a sane and humble distrust of self which perhaps restrains from imprudent action.

The deep psychological reality of infused virtue is perhaps better noticed from the side of the motive: docility, we said, to the injunctions of love. And not of any kind of love. It is our last end itself which appears to us as immediate, under the very personal traits of a God loved, of a Father and a friend, on all the turnings of the way. It is the proper role of infused moral virtue to make us heed these appeals of a living charity. A divine preference can be affirmed despite the fragile nature of the habitus still badly exercised by the vehemence of contrary currents. In its more essential reality, infused moral virtue appears mutually related to the interior appeal of charity as a possibility of victory over ourselves.

Let us not forget either that on the most direct ontological level, one which reunites this psychological reality of life in us with charity, the infused virtues depend in their exercise on actual graces. These we must welcome as well as cooperate with. To become aware of them is to introduce into our moral psychology an attitude of confident dependence on God, of appeal to His helpful beneficence which corrects in virtue insufficiently exercised what it might have of the fragile and the unstable. The great current of supernatural hope here comes to strengthen our whole moral life. God Himself does not change, and this conviction forearms us against our own changeableness.

6. ACQUIRED AND INFUSED VIRTUES IN MORAL PROGRESS

From these considerations some rather important consequences follow in what concerns the development of our infused virtues and the moral progress which results from it.

It is the reality of every habitus, as we have previously pointed out, to constitute the very essence of our spiritual progress. This reality is on the natural level the fruit of an intensely spiritual act; its whole role consists of preparing a still more intense activity which itself disposes us to growth.

This is no less applicable to infused virtues. They were given to us as the principle of this interior growth which permits us progressively to arrive *ad plenitudinem aetatis Christi.*

The nature of their growth may be defined simply in terms of dependence upon their divine origin. Infused in its establishment, a supernatural virtue remains established in each of its developments. It follows that this growth of a divine gift is that of a habitus, of which we have said that it is not simply added to our powers, but represents a determination of them relative to the acts which they should produce. The development of an infused virtue then follows the general law of all growth in habitus. A more intense and fervent act is its condition—that is, the divine gift which grows. The more intense act does not directly cause growth, it simply makes the power lend itself to the reception of a better gift.

Our actions then in the development of an essentially supernatural virtue play only a disposing role—the whole efficacy belongs to God. The idea of *merit* expresses this relation of our human activity to the influence of God, the source of a life which shares in divine nature.

But we must be on our guard, at this point, lest we conceive of merit in its purely juridical form. Certain theologians have sometimes translated the meritorious conditions of progress into a rather disconcerting arithmetic. All this accounting is wholly foreign to the thought of St. Thomas Aquinas for whom things remain on the level of life. It is in the measure of a more fervent act that habitus will grow: the "remitting" acts or those simply equal to the habitual capacity merely prepare for a more intense act and it is in this way that their own merit contributes to progress. We keep on the plane of life which is that of habitus. The idea of merit simply emphasizes the character of a divine gift which retains the supernatural from one end to the other. It no doubt implies the idea of justice, but justice does not consist in some kind of business deal between ourselves and God, who owes us nothing. It pertains to the logic itself of the divine work, to the laws of life such as eternal Providence establishes them. As on the plane of nature the germ is developed and the plant bears its fruit in virtue of an eternal law of growth, so on the supernatural plane everything grows according to a rhythm of life.

This implies that infused virtue is developed in a twofold way: on the one hand, acquired, on the other, infused. Not indeed that there is established alongside of our infused virtues an order of acquired virtues which would be in some sense at their service. Certainly, a number of theologians admit the existence of acquired virtues which are subordinated to infused virtues and supernaturalized by this subordination. But does this concept really show respect to the basic unity of the virtuous life and to the ideal of habitus which is to integrate all the elements that concur in the success of the action into a constructive synthesis? Charity, *mater virtutum,* polarizes the whole psychology of virtue.

It follows that just as in the case of the acquisition of a habitus through practice, the infused moral virtue develops this increasing mastery of ourselves, this spiritualization of the affectivity which makes our powers yield themselves to the control of reason. That is part of its nature. And so long as this is not acquired, the infused virtue runs the risk of retaining this fragility, this lack of ease which we pointed out earlier. We must become masters of our infused virtues, and that is a long and difficult process.

Neither should we forget what characterizes it most formally as an infused virtue and what we have analyzed above as a disposition to yield ourselves to the appeals and the commands of the love of God. It is there that the progress of infused virtues is most formally achieved—in this greater and greater emphasis on the motive of love, in this more and more spontaneous disposition, at the very center of our moral struggles, to yield to its demands. And that is precisely what contributes most in our psychology to this process of being rooted; through the experience of an acquired habitus, all the solidity is realized which defines the true virtue. For if the latter is not made firm except through its being implanted in an increasing mastery of ourselves, this mastery is the result of the impulse given by infused virtue to yield ourselves without hesitation to the appeals of charity. Thus we comprehend that the whole supernatural organism is assured by the activity of some supernatural virtue or other. The Augustinian idea of virtue, order of love, *virtus ordo amoris,* finds in this doctrine its full meaning.

7. MORAL CONDITIONS OF PROGRESS

The whole supernatural organism thus grows simultaneously, inasmuch as it is an entire order of love radiating into our behavior patterns from the rule and the motive of divine charity. To the profit of this growth in love which in the last analysis is the whole supernatural meaning of our progress, our virtues have to be rooted in a growing mastery of ourselves. However, certain related motives, relying upon the healthiest spontaneity of our nature, come, on the psychological level, to lend their support. It is for that reason that we discover in the infused moral virtues this distinction and this order which we discerned in speaking of moral virtues, abstraction having been made from the supernatural order. They really retain, if I may say so, their whole human consistence. But their greater or lesser value is appreciated in function of their capacity to more or less direct our activity toward the beloved God, and of the greater or lesser intensity which their own motive communicates to the fervor of our will. Later we shall speak of the greater or lesser merit of such and such virtues. This simply designates the twofold condition of which we have just spoken.

In this order, with its aspect of moral government of ourselves, the four cardinal virtues no doubt continue to appear as the great psychological pivots of morality. But, relative to spiritual progress, certain virtues emerge whose role appears important, by the orientation which they give to the rest of morality as well as by the intensity of will which they provoke. It is thus that the virtue of religion, developing in us a sense of the rights of God, contributes by its own motive to the right direction of our life and especially to the reinforcing and stabilizing of our will in love. Likewise, building on these powerful human instincts which are, for example, yearning for greatness and a sense of honor, a virtue such as "magnanimity" retains, in the order of infused virtues, by placing itself at the service of supernatural ideal, the great role which early morality gave to it and which St. Thomas continues to recognize in it, together with the specifically Christian virtues, humility and patience. It is the whole order of our moral virtues relative to spiritual progress that must be described here, a whole hierarchy of values conceived not in the abstract, but in their psychological connections in which the human and the divine so closely concur. Let this brief statement of principles suffice.

8. THE GIFTS OF THE HOLY SPIRIT

The infused spiritual organism born of grace is not complete unless we find a place in it for the gifts of the Holy Spirit. But what place precisely can we make for them? In what way are they distinguished from the infused virtues and what is their role?

We have recourse to the teaching of St. Thomas Aquinas, who was convinced throughout the whole course of his theological teaching, though not without certain variations in details, that he should attach this reality of the gifts to the body of his moral synthesis.

The concept of habitus aids once more in the elaboration of this doctrine.

Habitus, we have said, is a docility in our powers which makes us yield to the regulating and motor influence of the directive principle of action. Thus moral virtue makes our affectivity yield to the commands of practical reason. The gifts are certain habits which make us docile to a divine movement.

But in what precisely are they distinguished from infused virtues? The latter being infused habitus, do they not already look to the motion of actual grace with which we cooperate when we exercise them? We then say that the gift disposes us to receive in a connatural way a special movement of God, a divine "instinct," which takes the form of an operative grace in which we have only to permit ourselves to be moved to an operation which transcends, in a certain sense, the whole human mechanism of deliberation and of choice which virtue, even infused virtue, implies. The divine movement is vitally received, thanks to the reality of habitus, but the latter stays before all else passive to the divine influence at the very moment in which we act.

Let us explain.

Is there simply a question of disposing us ontologically to receive a divine movement? It seems not. On the ontological level there

is no need of any such *habitus*. God holds in His hand every creature and can move it as He pleases. If a special *habitus* is necessary,
it is because on the psychological plane itself, in the play of our
powers, divine inspiration implies a particular "turn of mind." In
us there is a question of yielding to this manner of acting which
here implies a transcendence of the "human mode" of acting and a
wholly divine regulation of action.

It is by distinguishing the "supra-human mode" of the gifts from
the "human mode" of the virtues that St. Thomas, in his first teaching, felt justified in differentiating one from the other. In the *Summa
Theologiae,* he sets out, it is true, from a quite different point of
view, that of a special divine movement to which the gift subjects
us. But the two points of view should not, we think, be opposed to
each other. We note first of all the meaning of the word *modus* in
this theological language: *modus a mensura dicitur.* There is question of a new regulation of the action which is measured no longer
by simple rational conduct, but directly by God with whom charity
unites us. This means basically that, in the case of the gifts, we
direct ourselves by the sentiment of love, by the impulse of charity
which is found finally only in God Himself. It is a rule adequate
even to His divine inspiration. Does the "special movement" of God
which the gifts prepare us to receive really have another meaning?

We must recall here that the *motio gratiae* by which God draws
us to our final destiny—to see Him face to face—is translated in
us first by the movement of charity. On this plane, and relative
to the fundamental inclination of charity, we are radically *moved.*
Thus it is that on the level of essences, from the first movement
which God impresses on every creature in creating it, He profoundly
moves it toward its connatural end. But we also know that it is
proper to rational nature that it take over, so to speak, on its own
account, this movement which is impressed upon it. It *moves itself.*
Note, however, that ontologically this self-determination still depends upon the first cause. But we distinguish in our activities the
level on which we are moved purely and simply from that on which
we move ourselves. Here grace is modeled upon nature. Charity is
the "pondus naturae" of nature elevated by grace. Its impulse toward eternal life is in us entirely from God who attracts us to Himself by making us love Him. But it is still within our power to
freely respond to this appeal and, beginning with the love for God
aroused in us, to choose our way. The infused virtues, with pru-

dence at their head, permit us to take in hand our supernatural life, to direct and to command our action in function of the fundamental inclination of charity. Such is really the human condition of our divine life. But a hiatus quickly appears. This supernatural movement which God impresses upon us by making us love Him surpasses by the eminence of its object the normal conditions of our human understanding. We are not in full possession of a supernatural life which is only shared in. Charity, by way of a rule which is its own and which transcends our own means, is the principle regulator of our conduct.

It is charity which demands our going beyond rational means in the conduct of our life.

If then God Himself takes us in hand (through these movements which theologians call "operantes" to signify that there is something more in our act than we can put there ourselves), we are able nevertheless, on the psychological plane, to explain these "instincts" of the Holy Spirit as species of "coups du coeur" in which our supernatural love comes to fashion our action according to a completely divine measure which is its own. The heart has its reasons. The normal psychology of all love here becomes more than normal —in some sense necessary.

Let us not forget, at any rate, that, cooperative or operative movement, God moves us vitally in the order of grace only by means of this first movement in us which is that of charity. In attributing to the Holy Spirit these divine "instincts" to which the gifts correspond, we relate them to Him to whom is attributed in us the movement of love. The whole psychology of the gifts of the Holy Spirit, such especially as the great commentators on St. Thomas have analyzed, reflect this intrusion, in some sense direct, of charity in our life. The seven gifts themselves then appear as the moments when a Christian psychology should give itself over to a single possible solution in order to surmount antinomies and hesitations—that which consists in love. They then take the form of instincts, of spontaneities of an affective origin. In our spiritual psychology, they are like the grand "passions," which unlike our sensible passions, no longer have to be controlled by us, but which govern us. God Himself and His love arouses them: *Pati divina*.

We then notice that if a special divine movement is here required as a theological explanation of these spontaneities which are the acts of the gifts, it is still, and perhaps especially, because such spon-

taneities should have not only a moving but a regulatory principle.
If the divine instinct puts us in harmony with what, in the movement
of charity, surpasses our rational means of imitating the divine life,
it is in God that it finds its rule. These reasons of the heart, which
here transcend our reason proper, reside in God Himself. Moreover, there is no illuminism in all this. We follow this intimate appeal without anxiety—certainly it is this movement which God controls, and which He communicates to us along with the supernatural
love which He awakens in us.

9. EVANGELICAL BEATITUDES AND FRUITS OF THE HOLY SPIRIT

Here is a last problem: does this theological systematization
whose coherence we have especially wanted to grasp, really have
a place in the total scheme? Faith, hope, charity have found their
place in it under the caption of theological virtues. Around the
four great cardinal virtues, natural pivots of morality, good Christian behavior patterns have come to be ordered. The concept of
infused habitus has permitted us to show the part which God and
especially grace plays in us. It is from this supernature that all the
infused virtues arise like a sort of coherent organism which renders
us supple to the movement of grace. A deeper analysis of this *motio
gratiae* permits us also to find a place for the traditional group of
seven gifts of the Holy Spirit—habitus distinct from virtue, but
which succeed in giving to our Christian life a turn which is in keeping with the love which should inspire it.

But what place shall we make for the great call of Christ issuing
from the Sermon on the Mount: "Blessed are the poor in spirit . . . ,
blessed are the meek . . . , blessed are they who mourn . . ." and
the other "Beatitudes"? Likewise what place is there for the "fruits"
of the Holy Spirit mentioned by St. Paul? Are these not great sum-
mits which give to the virtuous life, to the spiritual life, its properly
Christian quality? Does not the proclamation of the Beatitudes
indicate what ought to be, in the conversion of the heart, the dominant inclinations of the Christian life as well as its great aspirations?

The theological traits which terminate in the systematization by
St. Thomas could not fail to place these great attitudes of the Christian soul in relation with the virtuous life and the exercise of the
gifts:

The theologians and the Fathers joined the Beatitudes to the gifts of the Holy Spirit and the virtues. Why that? No doubt because they considered less the happiness and reward which each one of them expresses, than the conduct, the manner of acting for which the reward is promised. . . . Poverty of spirit, meekness, tears, ardent desire for justice: so many dispositions of the heart, recommended by the Saviour as a means for obtaining a place in his kingdom. So many virtues, the Fathers seem to say to whom St. Thomas refers. Not, however, any kind of virtues, not ordinary virtues, certain theologians have corrected. The solemnity, the insistence of the exhortations of Jesus, the very particular and unexpected enumeration which he proposes, the close bond established between these states of soul and celestial happiness—all that makes one think that there is a question here of perfections higher than virtues, higher even than the gifts of the Holy Spirit. According to this opinion, from virtues to gifts, from gifts to beatitudes, there would be a difference of degree, if not of kind, a progression from the less perfect to the more perfect.[6]

But in a theology in which the notion of *habitus* has served to define virtue, the Beatitudes are formally considered on the plane of *acts*. Not indeed as new virtues and of a superior quality, but as more perfect activities in which, when the gifts of the Holy Spirit give to it its full measure, is fulfilled the virtuous life. The Aristotelian idea of happiness conceived as "an operation in which perfect virtue is achieved" serves as middle term in this explanation of the theologian. Here we are on the level of the loftiest acts, i.e. of finalities which incline toward the very exercise of virtues. Blessed finality of eternal life in the end; but it is already begun and gives us a foretaste of itself in the spiritual attitude which leads to it. In the formulation of the Beatitudes we shall distinguish a *praemium* and *meritum*. But the *praemium,* the reward, is not only eternal. This aspiration for eternal life which moves from within the Christian soul transformed by grace, finds a prior guarantee and an anticipation of hope in the great meritorious acts which very legitimately bear the name, Beatitudes. . . . A whole plan of Christian perfection is here traced out, at the same time that the happiness of the Christian is described.

As for the *fruits* of the Holy Spirit mentioned by St. Paul in the Epistle to the Galatians (5:22-23), a text of St. Ambrose cited by St. Thomas shows well under what caption our theologians should give them a place: "The works of the virtues are called fruits because they procure for their possessors the procurement of a holy

[6] M. D. Roland-Gosselin, *Le sermon sur la montagne et la théologie thomiste,* in *Rev. des sc. philos. et théol.,* 1928, pp. 203-204.

and sincere joy." It is the savor of life according to the spirit, in opposition to the misery of the "works of the flesh," which is here implied.

REFLECTIONS AND PERSPECTIVES

Habitus and Habits

Retain the difference between habitus and habits. Habit is a sort of *material* fold or crease which we have contracted; it aids us, like a tool long since brought to a point, but it also conditions us. We are slaves of the creases we have contracted. Habitus, on the contrary, is a *spiritual* quality; its characteristic is that we can always use it when we choose to do so (*quo quis utitur quando vult*).

In this respect, note the difference between training and education. Training can form habits; it does not develop habitus. Education, on the contrary, has as its end to guide, to strengthen, to supply the necessary helps to the growth of habitus. This does not mean that education can always get along without training, or habitus without some habits, but training remains at the service of education. Theology of education. Show the qualities of a true educator. Role of discipline, of rewards, of punishments, of regulations (cf. Prov. 13:24, etc.), and of what is external to education. Can a man have influence on the "habitus" of another, even though but a child? Ways in which he can influence the will of another. The role of love in education. Role of example. Limits of education: on the part of the educator—just how far can one exercise influence? On the part of the educated—does not the best education received involve some risk? Can a man recover from having received a bad education?

The Virtues in Theology

The principles and the definitions given above uncover as much as possible the truth about our *nature* and its active *qualities*. It is in this sense that our whole moral life is theological. It is an effort to see, as God sees, our nature, the end for which it was created, the principles of action which have been given to it, and to try to set forth—always in the light of reason enlightened by faith—a few certain rules of action. Not indeed some external rules which would have no reference to nature, but on the contrary, some rules which would be like laws of nature (of the nature which God has made and of which man, friend of God, little by little becomes aware), that is, like divine laws. The first principle of morality then is this: God is our Father; He created us "in His image," and His image consists in this: that we are essentially spirits or intelligences like Him.

Being spirits, intelligences, beings endowed with reason, our whole perfection consists in acting "according to right reason," in imitation of Him who is inaccessible light and has engendered us children of light. The principle of all our acts is reason, a derivation in us of eternal wisdom. The rule for all our acts is the eternal law. That is good which is conformed to right reason (which the Christian understands as reason enlightened by faith and caught up in the movement of charity which proceeds from the will), what is bad is everything contrary to it. So much for the acts.

As for the virtues, they have no other role than to furnish wherever possible the *bonum rationis,* the good of reason (or the *ordo rationis,* the order of reason). This order of reason, we find first of all in the practical intellect which discerns what there is to do—and that constitutes the virtue of prudence which is at the heart of our whole morality. We find it in acts and exterior operations— such is the work of the virtue of justice; we find it in the passions— either the virtue represses a whole movement which is opposed to reason—temperance—or the virtue conducts to the very end a reasonable enterprise which passion fears—the work of fortitude. Thus prudence is found to be "of the reasonable by essence," the three other cardinal virtues, "of the reasonable by participation": participation of the will in the order of reason (virtue of justice), participation of the concupiscible and the irascible in the order of reason (virtues of temperance and of fortitude). The dignity of each of these virtues is quite naturally determined by the divers degrees of this participation: first comes prudence, then justice, then fortitude, then temperance. (We have already said that the irascible, because it supposes a certain "judgment," an appreciation of the "cogitative" or particular reason, was nearer to reason than the concupiscible. Its participation in reason is greater; the virtue which the order of reason disposes in it can more deeply penetrate into it and is, by that fact, nobler.)

"Inferiority complexes." Show that every "complex" comes from a lack of regulation by reason, that every maturity, every adolescence, consists essentially in an emancipation and in a liberation of

reason faced by everything that is instinctive, forbidden, taboo. A man's maturity—insofar as it can be acquired in this life, for it is always to be acquired—coincides with his taking on of power, and the greater and greater impregnation of reason in all of his powers (see the chapters on human act, on the passions).

The "reasonable" man and the moral man. Could we not however draw a caricature of the morally good man with what we have just said about the role of reason in moral conduct? Show the possible deformations of this doctrine (Stoicism, "moralism" which is annoying and inhuman, etc.). Show that human reason is not only a faculty of calculation and of organization, but that it can also be "according to reason" a faculty of calculated risk. (Role and place of *risk* in human life and morality; of *surrender, confidence, faith, hope.* Place and role of reason in *love.* Function of reason in relation to *sentiment, intuition,* human *instinct.* Place and limits of the irrational in the "order of reason.")

Show that the most beautiful charity consists in applying the will to action "according to reason." Reason, safeguard of a love which desires to be spiritual.

Compare the morality of the good, or of reason, or of virtue, with the moralities of commandment, or of honor, or of grandeur of soul, etc.

Beauty in morality. Can beauty (of sentiment, of thought, of act, of deed) be a rule of morality?

PRINCIPLES AND DEFINITIONS

We here set forth the principles and classical definitions which control the argumentation of the theologian in this treatise.

Habitus and Nature

The concept of habitus becomes clear if it is compared with that of power, operation, disposition and nature. Here are certain simple principles:

A disposition is what is easily changeable (or changing); habitus is what is changed with difficulty.

Between habitus and operation there is the same relation as between power and act. Habitus renders a man capable of acting (it puts in him a power of acting), and of acting easily according to his nature.

Habitus occupies the medium state between pure potency and perfect act.

Virtue. Some sayings anent the notion of virtue.

The term virtue designates a certain perfection of a power.

Virtue is defined by the final point which a power can attain (if anyone, for example, can carry 100 pounds and no more, his "virtue" is measured by 100 pounds). This is why the virtue of anything is measured by its relation to good (evil comprising a certain defect, the *ultimate* point of a power is good).

Virtue is the habitus which makes one act well.

Virtue is that which makes the goodness of him who possesses it and of the works which he performs.

Intellectual, Moral and Theological Virtues

Every virtue properly so-called depends in some way on the will; this does not prevent one from having intellectual virtues which may be real virtues; this is the case of *faith* (for the will has a part in it: *nullus credit nisi volens;* intelligence adheres to the Truth only under the influence of love); it is also the case of prudence, *recta ratio agibilium,* "right reason is the realm of action" (the principles of this "reason" are the human ends to which man can adapt himself only by rectifying his will: As each one is, so the end appears to him).

An intellectual habitus in which the will does not intervene is not fully a virtue, except in an accommodated sense, for it does not perfect man purely and simply, but only the power in which it resides. Nothing however prevents one from making use of these habits through charity. The ancients counted three "intellectual virtues":

Science, *recta ratio speculabilium,* "right reason in the area of speculation."

Art, *recta ratio factibilium,* "rectitude and cleverness of reason in doing."

Prudence, *recta ratio agibilium,* "rectitude of reason in acting."

Only prudence is a true virtue, for the reason that we have given. The subject of prudence is in reason, but it presupposes, as an indispensable principle, a rectified will.

The truth of the speculative intellect (knowledge) is taken from the conformity of the intellect with reality; the truth of the practical intellect (art and prudence) is taken from conformity to the will.

No moral virtue can exist without either intelligence or prudence. Moral virtue perfects the affective part of the soul by adapting it to reasonable good.

Omnis virtuosus delectatur in actu virtutis et tristatur in contrario: Every virtuous being finds its joy in the act of virtue and is made sad by the contrary (there is no perfect virtue, no true virtue except that which renders agreeable and pleasant the acts which one performs. To say that you do something "through virtue," in the sense that you do it because of "duty" and without loving it, is to say precisely what is lacking to the virtue necessary in order to do it. On this subject, compare once more the morality of the good with the morals of duty or those of precept. It will be seen that *continence* has no claim to the title of true virtue, because the continent person is in some way a chaste person despite himself; the acts of chastity are not yet agreeable and pleasant for him; continence is only a half-virtue).

Distinction of moral virtues: things which make up the object of our appetites are constituted in divers species according to the manner in which they are present to reason (our appetites in fact do not all receive the influence of reason in the same way, never being more than reasonable through borrowing, and not reasonable by essence).

The demands of *justice* are those of reality itself; virtue which is in the irascible appetite (fortitude) or in the concupiscible (temperance) is nothing else than a habitual conformity of its powers to reason: *nihil aliud quam quaedam habitualis conformitas istarum potentiarum ad rationem.*

Per virtutes theologicas homo ordinatur ad beatitudinem supernaturalem. By theological virtues man is ordered to supernatural happiness.

The object of the theological virtues is God Himself inasmuch as He transcends the knowledge of our reason.

The "Mean" of Virtue

The good of moral virtue consists in adapting the act to the measure of reason. (This adaptation is the golden mean between a defect and an excess.)

It is the business of prudence to establish the mean. It is prudence that rules and measures, not being anything else than intelligence (rectified) of what it is necessary to do. The other virtues are measured and ruled by it.

The mean of the moral virtues is determined by the intellectual virtue of prudence; the measure of intellectual virtues on the contrary is determined by reality itself. (Every word and every thought conforming to reality is true.) The measure and the rule of a theological virtue is God Himself.

Connection of Virtues

Prudentia sicut ex principiis procedit ex finibus agibilium ad quos aliquis recte se habet per virtutes morales: The principles from which prudence proceeds are the ends of human action and man adjusts himself to these ends by the moral virtues.

All of the intellectual virtues depend on the understanding of certain principles, just as prudence depends on the moral virtues.

The terms of the inclinations which engender in man the moral virtues take the place of principles for prudence.

The rectitude of prudence requires that man be suitably disposed face to face with the final end and ordained to it (something that is done by charity), and this ordination counts more for prudence than for an ordination to other ends (something that is done by the moral virtues).

With charity all the moral virtues are infused together. The virtue which is referred to the end is principal and moving in relation to those which are referred to the means or circumstances.

Ratio connexionis virtutum moralium accipitur ex parte prudentiae et ex parte charitatis quantum ad virtutes infusas: The connection of the moral virtues is made by prudence, and by charity if they are infused.

BIBLIOGRAPHIE

En dehors des ouvrages généraux et des dictionnaires, on lira, au sujet des "habitus":

Les commentaires du traité de saint Thomas dans la Somme théologique, de R. Bernard, *La vertu,* tome 1 er, Coll. *Somme théologique,* publiée par les Éd. de la R. des J., Paris, 1933, et de Fr. Satolli, *De habitibus,* Doctrina sancti Thomæ Aquinatis in 1a 2ae qq. 49-70 Summæ theologicæ, Rome, Prop. de la foi.

Dom Placide de Roton, *Les habitudes,* Desclée de Br.
B. Roland-Gosselin, *L'habitude,* Paris, Beauchesne, 1920.

J. Chevalier, *L'habitude*. Essai de métaphysique scientifique. Paris, Boivin, 1929.

Au sujet des vertus:

J.-M. Parent, *Les vertus morales infuses dans la vie chrétienne*, in *Théologie*, cah. 2-3, Ottawa-Montréal, Éd. du Lévrier, 1944.

O. Lottin, *Les premières définitions et classifications des vertus au Moyen-âge*, dans Rev. des sc. phil. et théol. XVIII, 1929, pp. 369-407.

Signalons aussi pour son importance ici l'article *Vertu* de A. Michel, paru en 1948 dans le *Dict. de théol. cath.*, 15 II, col. 2739-2799.

Au sujet des dons du Saint-Esprit:

Raïssa Maritain, *Les dons du Saint-Esprit*, Éd. du Cerf, Juvisy, 1930.

J. de Guibert, S.J., *Études de théologie mystique*, Toulouse, 1930.

A. Gardeil, O.P., *Le Saint-Esprit dans la vie chrétienne*, Éd. du Cerf, Paris, 1934.

BIBLIOGRAPHY

BOOKS

Connell, Francis J., C.SS.R., *Outlines of Moral Theology*, pp. 57-64. Milwaukee: The Bruce Publishing Company, 1953.

Farrell, Walter, O.P., *A Companion to the Summa*, Vol. II. New York: Sheed and Ward, 1940.

——, *Swift Victory*. New York: Sheed and Ward, 1955.

Gardeil, Ambrose, O.P., *The Holy Spirit in Christian Life*. London: Blackfriars Publications, 1953.

Kane, John A., *The School of Virtues*. New York: The Pageant Press, 1954.

MacGillivray, G. J., *Christian Virtues*. New York: Kenedy & Sons, 1934.

McHugh, John A., O.P., and Callan, Charles J., O.P., *Moral Theology, A Complete Course*, Vol. I, pp. 46-89. New York: Joseph Wagner, Inc., 1929.

Pierce, Garrett, *Virtues and Vices*. Milwaukee: The Bruce Publishing Company, 1935.

Sheedy, Charles E., C.S.C., *The Christian Virtues*. Notre Dame, Ind.: University of Notre Dame Press, 1949.

Von Hildebrand, Dietrich, *Fundamental Moral Attitudes*. New York: Longmans, Green & Co., 1950.

Wallen, C., *The Twelve Fruits*. New York: Joseph Wagner, Inc., 1950.

ARTICLES

"Grace and the Virtues," *Theological Studies*, 2: 113-116 (Feb., 1941).

Mageean, R., "Notes on the Christian Virtues," *Irish Ecclesiastical Record*, 42: 225-234 (Sept., 1933).

"Notes on the Connection of the Virtues," *Thomist*, 11: 218-240 (April, 1948).

CHAPTER V

SIN

by V. Vergriete, O.P.

I. INTRODUCTION
  1. Affirmation of sin in the Bible
  2. Human liberty, condition of sin

II. NATURE OF SIN
  1. Sin is a disordered human act
  2. Sin is an offense against God

III. KINDS OF SINS
  1. The different kinds of sin
  2. The number of sins

IV. UNEQUAL GRAVITY OF SINS
  1. The gravity of sins varies according to their objects
  2. The gravity of sins varies according to circumstances
  3. The gravity of sins varies according to their willfulness

V. THE SEAT OF SIN
  1. The will
  2. The intelligence
  3. Sensuality

VI. THE CAUSES OF SIN
  1. Internal:
      (a) Ignorance
      (b) Passion
      (c) Malice
  2. External:
      (a) God is not the cause of sin
      (b) The devil
      (c) Man

Chapter V

SIN

I. Introduction

1. AFFIRMATION OF SIN IN THE BIBLE

That there is evil in the world all men agree. It is a truth of experience. Suffering, injustice, multiple forms of misery, sickness and, above all, death are manifestations of evil which are immediately perceptible to the senses. But there is no man with any sincerity in him who is content to dwell exclusively on the evil of pain. We acknowledge ourselves as more or less the accomplices of this evil, and then we rise to the conception of genuine evil which is *sin,* and of which the other evils which weigh on the world are only the consequences, although it is not always possible for a mind not informed by Christian truth to discern the relation of cause and effect which unites these two realities.

The true evil of the world is sin, and all men are culpable. If we open the Bible we find in it the affirmation of sin on every page, accompanied by calls to do penance. The faults of humanity are constantly recalled in the accounts of Genesis and the historical books, in the warnings and the threats of the prophets, in the complaints and the prayers of the psalmist, in the disenchanted considerations of Ecclesiastes and the sapiential books, down to the terrible analyses of St. Paul and St. John: "We know that the whole world is plunged in evil." The words of Psalm 13 can sum up the view of the Bible: "The Lord looks down from heaven upon the children of men. . . . All gone astray and have surrendered to evil: there is none who does good, no not even one."

The idea of culpability is inseparable from the idea of liberty. When a man is aware of his sin, he is aware at the same time that he was free not to commit it. It is a human liberty which explains the possibility of sin.

2. HUMAN LIBERTY, CONDITION OF SIN

"God made man from the beginning, and left him in the hand of his own counsel . . . If thou wilt keep the commandments and perform acceptable fidelity forever, they shall preserve thee. He hath set water and fire before thee: stretch forth thy hand to which thou wilt. Before man is life and death, good and evil, that which he shall choose shall be given him" (Ecclus. 15:14-17).

Man is a free being. He is really master of his judgments and of his actions. It is in his power to decide his history and his destiny. Admirable privilege, a condition of his communion with God, but an autonomy also which constitutes his great temptation, his possibility of falling and of turning away from his last end. If a man walks in the direction toward which the deep desire of his nature made for God inclines him, if he accepts his condition of dependence, if he welcomes the call of God and corresponds to it with all the fervor of his soul, he will fulfill in himself the image of God and will share in the happiness of the sons of God. But if he makes bad use of his liberty, does not correspond to his vocation, if he pretends to be self-sufficient and walks in the ways of disharmony and of "dissimilitude," then he cuts himself off from God, he misses his end and dedicates himself to damnation. This tragic refusal is sin. The Bible constantly represents sinners as men who abandon the right ways in order to follow dark and crooked paths, and who finally fall into their own traps.

Sin does not always have the metaphysical breadth of a revolt of the creature who says no to his creator. Such a degree of pure malice has perhaps existed only in the angels. The ways of man are sinuous, often obscure. Man himself sometimes succeeds in doubting his own attitude. His activity is fragmentary. A multitude of acts compose the history of a human life. These acts are nevertheless inscribed in a fundamental option which takes place in the heart of man, at the very center of his spiritual life, and renders him "worthy of love or of hate."

II. Nature of Sin

1. SIN IS A DISORDERED HUMAN ACT

Sin may be considered in its cosmic dimension. It then acquires a sort of personality, it becomes an entity that plays a role in the world. St. Paul considers it in this way: "By one man sin entered the world. . . ." Thus considered, sin represents the sum total of evil forces which militate against God and bring disorder into the plan of creation.

We shall, however, leave the cosmic plane and descend to the level of man. Between the two camps which between them divide the scene of the world, that of good and that of evil, man takes a personal part. He chooses the one or the other. He collaborates more or less with one or the other. The sin of man is to participate in the evil which is in the world, and to be an accomplice of the sin of the world. Sin is then also in man. It is a human act, the affirmation of the free being that we are. Sin is included among human realities; it is, alas, within our reach. Not every act of man, however, may be called human. Human action requires freedom. There can be no sin where neither intelligence nor will intervene. The fool deprived of his intelligence is not responsible for his actions; he commits no formal sins. Neither is a man constrained by the physical force of some external agent to commit an action, responsible for it. Where voluntariness is wholly lacking there can be no sin. In her official documents, the Church, on many occasions, has affirmed the voluntary character of sin (Denz. 410, 771, 1046, 1068, 1292). She merely makes explicit a doctrine of the faith already in Scripture.

Sin takes its place then among human acts. We thus indicate the species of reality to which it belongs. Further explanation is necessary if one would understand in what way sin is distinguished from good acts and how it is opposed to them. Do not think that they are divided into two groups by an arbitrary judgment; the distinction is based on the nature of things. That act is good to which nothing is wanting; it is bad and sinful if something is wanting to it. Its malice comes from the fact that it is deprived of some due perfection. Now the perfection requisite for a human action is that it be conformed to the rule of reason which presides over the development and the full flowering of this spiritual and reasonable being which is man. Man must act in accordance with his nature under pain of forfeit. He should conduct his life in an orderly way in the direction of his vocation as a man, and should respond to the superior ends which attract him. It is the part of reason to measure the object, the end and the circumstances of action. If these elements are in conformity with the rule of reason, the human act receives from them its moral goodness. If they are not conformed to it, the human action is no longer good. It no longer respects its rule. It constitutes a disorder. It is a sin. Sin therefore is something irrational. The Bible calls it a folly, and presents the sinner as senseless.

Still not everything is bad in sin. One cannot will privation as such. The sinner seeks a genuine good, but he finds that this good is not suitable and is contrary to a greater good. In turning toward a lesser good, the sinner, consequently, turns away from a higher good which it would be reasonable to pursue. "To sin," writes St. Augustine, "is to attach oneself to temporal realities and to neglect eternal realities" (*In I Lib. Arb.* ch. 11). "Sin," he says again, "is not a desire for bad things, but a renunciation of better things" (*De natura boni,* xxxiv). "Sin," as a recent author has defined it, "is a preference shown to some created value by those who have no other purpose than to recognize God" (*Jeunesse de l'Église,* No. 6, p. 155).

This is really the tragedy of sin. The sinner does not desire evil as such, which would be impossible, for the will can seek only the good. But in willing a given good which is not fitting, the sinner commits evil. He departs from rectitude, he despises his true end and deprives himself of true happiness.

2. SIN IS AN OFFENSE AGAINST GOD

Sin is something more than a derogation of the natural law. By remaining on the moral plane, we could not grasp the whole greatness of sin. Sin is also an attack on the law of God. The law of God overlaps the natural law, for God is the creator of natures and the universe is governed by him. It is He who has dictated the natural law. It is an element of the order desired by God. When a person is lacking toward himself, his neighbor, his state of life, to society, it is against God that he sins. It is this religious dimension of sin which the books of the Bible have especially set forth, and it is the principal one, for it reveals the monstrosity of sin, which is an offense against God whose law has been despised: "We have sinned against the Lord our God, we and our fathers" (Jer. 3:25). "Against thee alone have I sinned and what is evil in thy sight I have done" (Ps. 50:6).

The human will opposes itself to the will of God. Sin is a refusal of submission, an injury to the sovereignty of God. There is in every sin something of the satanic, a revolt of the creature who does not wish to serve and claims to be self-sufficient: by sin, the sinner rebels against God (Ps. 5). "Your iniquities have set up a division between you and your God" (Is. 59:2).

The Bible also defines the sinner as a man of violence; sin, as a work of violence.

And that is not all. Not only is sin an attack on the rights of God over us, an infraction of justice, it is also disdain for His love. The law of God is a law of love. What He wants is our friendship. By sin we do not deprive Him of any of His rights over us, we entirely withdraw His love from ourselves. Sin is an ingratitude, an infidelity, a betrayal: "I have brought up children, and exalted them, but they have despised me. The ox knoweth his owner, and the ass his master's crib, but Israel hath not known me, and my people hath not understood" (Is. 1:2-3).

Only Christianity, which has an exact understanding of God and which knows what the redemption cost, can have an exact understanding of sin, a grasp of its supernatural religious dimension; and among Christians, only the saints, who call their least faults monstrous crimes, have glimpsed the unfathomable depths of sin. Those to whom there has been revealed in a transient intuition the whole malice of sin, say that they thought they were going to die.

It is one of the tragic marks of our time to have lost the sense of sin. The moral sense comes in a period of crisis and we all breathe more or less the air of the century. Not only has the religious sense of sin as an offense against God become dormant, but even the most elementary moral sense has also been lost. The distinction between moral good and evil appears as something arbitrary. We have passed "beyond good and evil," and amoralism has become for some a legitimate rule of conduct. Sin no longer exists. Everything is permitted. It is the inevitable consequence of loss of faith in a transcendent God and the attempt to deify man.

Yet, inversely, we must still recognize that the collective feeling of human misery seems particularly acute in our day. The whole movement of the liberation of the workingman is a result of it. The shock of horror at the sight of the war crimes comes to us as a living witness that the moral sense is not extinct and that events can reawaken it. Perhaps in the presence of the misery of the world which strangles us, we will also feel that we ourselves are in part responsible for this misery, and that "we are in the camp of the assassins." Perhaps the more acute perception of evil experienced by man will aid us to discover the moral origins of this evil. We will acknowledge that the evil experienced, which is the result of sin, has a cause in our own heart: sin.

III. Kinds of Sins

1. THE DIFFERENT KINDS OF SINS

All sins are ill regulated acts, but they introduce a disturbance into different points of order. They are diversified according to the different objects desired by the sinner. To steal is not the same thing as to fornicate. We already find in the Bible all the forms which evil can take on when it germinates in the heart of man.

Idolatry:

"This people hath sinned a heinous sin, and they have made to themselves gods of gold" (Ex. 32:31).

Pride:

"Woe to you that are wise in your own eyes, and prudent in your own conceits" (Is. 5:21).

Vanity:

"Because the daughters of Sion are haughty and have walked with stretched out necks, and wanton glances of their eyes, and made a noise as they walked with their feet . . . the Lord will make bald the crown of the daughters of Sion." (Is. 3:16-17).

Intemperance:

"Woe to you that are mighty to drink wine, and stout men at drunkenness!" (Is. 5:22).

Corruption and injustice:

"Woe to you that justify the wicked for gifts, and take away the justice of the just from him" (Is. 5:23).

The lie and hypocrisy:

"Woe to you that call evil good and good evil; that put darkness for light and light for darkness; that put bitter for sweet and sweet for bitter" (Is. 5:20).

We could multiply texts and cite other sins. This list provides some examples, and does not claim to be exhaustive.

Sins are not diversified only by reason of the different objects on which the action bears. The end and the circumstances of the action also change the nature of the sin. To steal in order to be able to indulge in a debauchery constitutes a sin of injustice, theft, but also of debauchery because of the end pursued. To steal a chalice consecrated to worship constitutes a theft, and in addition a sacrilege, by reason of the aggravating circumstances connected with the action.

It may be useful, in view of the examination of conscience or of the accusation of sins in confession, to possess a method of classifying sins. The Bible suggests to us that of the Decalog (Ex. 20:1-17; Deut. 5:7-18). Another division passed into usage, also excellent, is that which divides sins into sins against God, against our neighbor and against ourselves.

2. THE NUMBER OF SINS

The Church, on several official occasions, at the Council of Trent, e.g., has prescribed the confession of all mortal sins. The prophet Ezechiel had already said: "Be converted and do penance for all your iniquities" (18-30). It is therefore obligatory for the sinner to declare all his grievous sins, according to their kinds and number, and the confessor, in certain cases, is bound to ask, in order to insure the integrity of confession.

To aid in the numerical distinction of sins, theologians propose certain rules: sins that are specifically distinct are also numerically distinct, even though they may be committed in one and the same physical act. Thus he who steals a consecrated chalice commits two sins, one sin against justice (theft), and one against religion (sacrilege).

If there is question of sins of the same kind, it may be said that there are as many sins as there are morally interrupted acts. The interruption of a voluntary act takes place when it is expressly revoked, by reason of a new act of the will opposing it, or virtually, when certain external circumstances happen to interrupt it, as, e.g., sleep, or an occupation somewhat prolonged. In the latter case, if it is an external action of which one desires that there should be an interruption, the fulfillment of the action after this interruption would not constitute a new sin, for there would be question of only one sin; there is a connection between desire and its satisfaction. But if the question is of a purely internal act, a salacious thought, for example, to return to it after a notable interruption constitutes a new sin.

Always having in mind sins of the same species, we can find another basis for the multiplication of sins. There are several sins, even though there is only one physical act, when several objects of morality are attained at the same time. Thus to kill two men with a single shot constitutes two homicides.

These few rules will not always be enough for those of more delicate perceptions, but good sense will always guide a loyal and upright conscience.

IV. Unequal Gravity of Sins

Our Christian people need to be enlightened on this point. There is too great a tendency among them not to make any comparison of sins except between mortal and venial, a distinction, as we shall see, based on the effects of sin. They are inclined to think that on either side of this line of demarcation sins are equal. Or, indeed, it is in the ordering that they are deceived. It is not rare, for example, to meet with the opinion that sins of the flesh are the worst of all.

The evil with which sins are affected comes to them from their lack of agreement with reason. The gravity of sins will then be based on the greater or lesser departure which they show from the order of reason; just as a malady is more or less grave according as it deviates more or less from good health. In order to measure this departure, the object of the sin, its circumstances and the amount of voluntariness put into it must be considered.

1. THE GRAVITY OF SINS VARIES ACCORDING TO THEIR OBJECTS

A sickness is by so much the more grave as the equilibrium is disturbed on some vital point. Likewise sin is by so much the more grave as it carries disorder into a more important principle of the reasonable order. Among the objects of human action, it is clear that the highest, that which constitutes the first principles of the rational order, is God. Then comes man, and finally external goods. The sin that directly attacks God is graver than one which attacks man, and the sin which attacks the very substance of man, homicide for instance, is graver than one which attacks an exterior good, theft, for example.

2. THE GRAVITY OF SINS VARIES ACCORDING TO CIRCUMSTANCES

There are circumstances which change the nature of sin. Fornication consists in having carnal relations with a woman not one's wife. If the circumstance is added that she is the wife of another man, there is committed in addition a sin of injustice. This is what makes adultery a more grievous sin than fornication.

There are circumstances also which do not change the nature of a sin, but which nevertheless increase the gravity of the same sin. To steal $100, e.g. is a graver sin than to steal 10 cents. The condition of the person offended is likewise a circumstance which affects the gravity of the sin. For a man to strike his father is a more grievous sin than to strike a companion. The personal dignity of the sinner also modifies the gravity of the sin. In cases of deliberate sins, a person habitually virtuous and instructed is more culpable, for he is better armed against temptation, and his sin manifests greater ingratitude, for he has received more graces. When we are dealing with sins of surprise, on the contrary, he is less blameworthy, for such sins, from which human weakness does not escape, come more frequently to one of a natural temperament than to one voluntarily negligent in the correction of his defects.

3. THE GRAVITY OF SINS VARIES ACCORDING TO THEIR WILLFULNESS

So far, the examinations of the causes of the variation of the gravity of sin bore on objective elements, more easily subject to analysis and evaluation. With internal consent we are in the realm of the subjective. The secrets of human conscience are known only to God, and he alone can measure the degree of culpability of the sinner. We may say however that whatever tends to weaken voluntariness by tempting the will outside its free movement, passion, violence, fear, diminishes as a general rule the culpability of the sinner. In extreme cases, a complete ignorance, a physical constraint to which no consent is given, certain pathological deficiencies which totally suppress voluntariness, also suppress sin.

V. The Seat of Sin

For the Greeks, sin was either ignorance or error, consequently something foreign to the intimacy of the soul. In many religions which have remained quite formalistic, sin is confused with ritual impurity, awkwardness or an accident irritating the taboo. The Bible on the contrary does not consider sin as a simple external transgression. Its conception is far from being as material as that.

Sin has its origin in the depths of the human heart. It is a spiritual evil, a stain upon the soul. To have access to the mountain of Yahweh, or, in other words, conversation with God, it is not enough to have hands that are innocent, but also a heart that is pure (Ps. 23:4). The culpability of a man is not measured by his acts but by his hidden intentions. It is impossible for anyone but God to judge of it: God alone fathoms the loins and the hearts, penetrates even to the depths of the soul. The seat of sin is the heart (will) and one may sin even though nothing is apparent exteriorly. Appearance is often deceiving: "Drag me not away with sinners and those who commit crimes, who speak of peace with their neighbors, but have evil in their minds" (Ps. 27:3).

1. THE WILL

The seat of sin is therefore the human soul. But the soul acts only through the instrumentality of its powers. What are these sinful powers? The will, which in the first place is par excellence our power of action and which is the origin of all the activity of our liberty. Man sins because his will is bad. Sin can remain at the interior of the will (sin of desire), but it can also be transmitted outwardly and pass into our external acts. Because the will is a faculty of command, it moves to a certain degree our other faculties and also directs our exterior activities. When voluntariness ceases, sin ceases.

2. THE INTELLIGENCE

The function of intelligence is to know. It can be the seat of sin to the degree in which the will moves it. Ignorance or error which have their seat in the intelligence are culpable to the degree in which they are voluntary. He commits a sin of ignorance who is ignorant of what he can and should do, whether it be that he directly wills to be ignorant of what it is necessary for him to know, or whether he neglects the acquisition of the requisite knowledge. Likewise, he commits a sin of error who is deceived through culpable negligence.

3. SENSUALITY

The intelligence and the will belong only to the spiritual part of the soul. But there also exists in the soul a group of faculties which are bound up with bodily life. This is the area of sensibility.

Insofar as this domain is subject to the will, it is clear that it can also be the seat of sin.

Now there exist certain disordered movements of sensibility (of "sensuality," as in this case St. Thomas calls them) which are produced by surprise before any control of the will. Every virtuous man knows of such weaknesses: a sudden burst of anger, an excess of strong desire. The just man falls seven times a day, says the Bible. These weaknesses seem to be inevitable. Can we still speak of them as sins? St. Thomas holds for the affirmative. Sensibility is made to remain subject to reason. Moreover its closeness to the higher faculties makes of it a moral power capable of sin. Let us note, however, that these sins of surprise, not attaining to the perfection of the voluntary act, can only be venial.

VI. The Causes of Sin

1. INTERNAL

It is the will which is the immediate and universal cause of sin; there can be sin only where a disorder of the will is introduced. But there are nevertheless certain movements which precede this act of the will and which lead the sinner to commit his sin. What takes place in the psychology of him who is going to commit a sin? What are the origins of this act? The interior sources of sin can be reduced to three: ignorance, passion, malice.

(a) *Ignorance*

There is an ignorance which causes the act of sin by depriving one of the knowledge which would have prevented the act. This is said to cause sin accidentally.

There is also an ignorance which simply accompanies the action which is done. One would have acted in the same way, even if he had known. This second ignorance is not in question for the moment, since it in no way causes the sin committed.

We speak of the ignorance which causes sin. It can itself be a sin or not. To be ignorant of what one cannot know (invincible ignorance) or to be ignorant of what one is not bound to know is not a sin. Such ignorance is not culpable and it excuses the fault of which it is the cause since it renders it entirely involuntary.

But to be ignorant through negligence of what one is bound to know is a sin. In this case ignorance does not excuse the fault of which it is the cause. If this ignorance is directly willed in order to sin more freely, it indicates a strong will to sin and in no way excuses the sins of which it is the cause, but quite the contrary. But if the ignorance is only indirectly and accidentally willed, as happens to him who is ignorant on account of not having willed to work during his school days, or to him who no longer knows what he is doing on account of having had too many intoxicants, then this ignorance diminishes what there is of voluntariness in the act of which it is the cause and partially excuses the sin committed.

(b) *Passion*

A great number of sins originate in passion. A sensible good is presented and passion is inflamed at the sight of it and draws the will into the disorder. He who is in the grip of passion is aware that what he is going to do is a sin. Ordinarily he would not commit it, for his will is not bad. But passion urges him, and despite a moment of interior struggle between his will which desires to remain faithful to the moral law which it knows and esteems, and his passion, he finishes by giving in. The reasons for passion have been the stronger. It has presented a concrete sensible good to be grasped at once, while the moral good has appeared suddenly very abstract and distant, for one effect of passion is to concentrate attention on its object and to turn aside consideration of what is contrary to it. Drawn by passion, the will has given its consent to sin. It has agreed to no longer consider the claims of morality and no longer wishes to consider anything but its immediate satisfaction.

This struggle between the solicitations of passion and conscience is the struggle between the flesh and the spirit so often described by St. Paul: "For when we were in the flesh the sinful passions, which were aroused by the law, were at work in our members that brought forth fruit unto death" (Rom. 7:5). And by St. James: "But everyone is tempted by being drawn away and enticed by his own passion. Then when passion has conceived it brings forth sin; but when sin has matured it begets death" (Jas. 1:14-15).

What is the gravity of a sin of passion? It can happen that passion, by its unusual violence, may produce such a physiological disturbance that the use of reason is found to be totally suspended and voluntariness suppressed. In this extreme case no one is responsible for the sin committed, unless the moment of passionate folly had no previous responsible causes. It might have been sought directly or indirectly, and one might have done nothing to avoid the occasions and the outburst. These extreme cases are rare and we are not judges of them. We can say however that as a general rule, if passion does not suppress a fault, it nevertheless diminishes its gravity, to the degree in which it diminishes the voluntary character of it. Passion brings pressure upon the will and removes in parts its spontaneity. "Sins of weakness," as we commonly say apropos of sins of passion, is an expression which indicates a shade of indulgence. But this does not prevent sins of passion from being mortal sins. "The passions were at work in our members so that they brought forth fruit unto death" (Rom. 7:5).

(c) *Malice*

Even without any appeal to ignorance and to passion, the will can of itself take the initiative to sin. In such a case we have to do with sins of malice. The sinner commits them knowingly and deliberately. He is not enticed by passion. This time the sinner knows the evil and chooses it. He does not want evil for its own sake, something which is impossible, for the will can never be inclined toward anything but a real or apparent good. But he does not fear to reject his real good in order to choose a more immediate one and one which he knows to be forbidden.

This category of sinners takes in a large number of different cases. First there are certain abnormal people who have inherited from birth a certain number of perverse tendencies which give them a taste for evil. Here we are at the frontiers of pathology. There are also normal individuals who through temperament have a propensity for certain sins. Endocrinology discovered some years ago the importance of bodily conditionings.

There are especially the habitual sinners, those who through habit fall back into the same sin. Habit is like a second nature which creates new needs. Those who have contracted a vicious habit return to their sin and they commit it without the disturbance accompanying passion, through malice. "They walk after the perversity of their most wicked heart" (Jer. 3:17).

Finally, independently of all habit or perverse disposition, there are those who sin through malice because there is no longer anything which restrains them on the slope of evil, neither hope of eternal life nor fear of punishment.

In the Middle Ages, when temperaments were, it seems, more vigorous than today, and the passions stronger, more sins of passion were committed. In our day of disbelief in which the notion of good and evil is dangerously glossed over and in which there is not much faith in the punishments of the future life, it is the sin of malice which is most frequently committed.

The sin of malice is graver than the sin of passion because in the former the will is in no way disturbed in its proper activity and is inclined of itself to evil.

It would be fitting to approach here the question of the sin against the Holy Ghost (cf. Mk. 3:20-30). But on its nature there is no agreement. Each theologian, each exegete sets forth his own particular solution. According to the majority of the Fathers it would be blasphemy against the Holy Spirit or the Holy Trinity. According to St. Augustine it would be final impenitence. St. Thomas Aquinas is inclined to identify it with the sin of malice.[1] In the course of an excellent article, Father Bouyer suggests an interpretation of the unforgivable sin against the Holy Ghost which seems to us to be better.[2] To sin against the Holy Ghost is to refuse to recognize in the works which Christ accomplished among us the triumph of the divine spirit over the evil spirit. It is the voluntary rejection of the Light coming into the world, a preference given to the darkness, a culpable blindness which refuses to seize the occasion which is presented of escaping the slavery of Satan.

2. EXTERNAL

(a) *God Is Not the Cause of Sin*

Man can be the cause of sin, of his own and of others, in two ways. In a direct manner, if he inclines his will or the will of others to do evil. In an indirect way, when in certain cases he does not restrain others from the way of sin: "If, when I say to the wicked, thou shalt surely die: thou declare it not to him, nor speak to him, that he may be converted from his wicked ways of living . . . I will require his blood at thy hands" (Ez. 3:18). But God cannot be the cause of sin either by Himself or by another. For every sin is committed by a departure from the order which has God for its

---

[1] On the meaning of the Gospel versicles, cf. Lagrange, *Évangile de saint Matthieu*, Paris, Gabalda, 1923, pp. 244-245.

[2] L. Bouyer, *Le problème du mal dans le Christianisme antique*, in *Dieu vivant*, no. 6, p. 36.

end. Now God, on the contrary, inclines and leads everything to Himself as to an ultimate end. It is therefore impossible that He be, for Himself or for others, the cause of departure from an order which is wholly orientated to Himself. He cannot therefore be in any way the cause of sin. That would be absolutely contradictory. It would cause injury to the wisdom and the goodness of God to believe that He could be an instrument of derivation from an order which He Himself wishes and which is the expression of His very nature.

(b) *The Devil*

The devil is the worst enemy of God. He is the "adversary." He wishes to withdraw as many adorers as possible and he deploys all his astuteness to lead others into sin which separates them from God. In other days, for Christians, evil and the devil were the same, and the *deliver us from evil* was translated: deliver us from the *Evil One.* Our epoch, in which faith in the supernatural world has largely disappeared, no longer believes in the devil. Christians themselves being influenced by the times, willingly bear witness to a certain skepticism when one speaks to them of the activities of the Evil One. They know, however, the text of St. Peter which makes up the brief lesson of Compline. "For your adversary the devil, as a roaring lion, goes about seeking someone to devour" (I Pet. 5:8). Faith in the malificent activity of the devil was very vivid in the Middle Ages, as the imagery of our churches and cathedrals bears witness.

The devil has no direct power over the will of man who remains the only genuine author of his sin. He exercises nevertheless a power of suggestion and of persuasion; he possesses the art of proposing a thing as desirable. He seeks also to obscure the intelligence through the play of imagination and the excitation of the sensible appetite. Finally he can produce certain material effects perceptible to the senses. The disagreeable tricks which the evil spirit played on the Curé of Ars are well known.[3]

It remains true however that "God is faithful and will not permit you to be tempted beyond your strength" (I Cor. 10:13). Man remains free and responsible for his sin, but it will be necessary

---

[3] The reader will find, in humorous form, but not without seriousness, a fine analysis of the practices employed by the devil in C. S. Lewis, *Screwtape Letters,* 1945.

for him perhaps to struggle against Satan in a spiritual combat "more bloody than the battles of men."

(c) *Man*

One man can be the cause of sin for another man by suggesting it to him from the exterior, just as the devil does. There is besides a special manner of bringing sin into the lives of others which is to transmit it to them originally. Here the question of original sin is opened. It is an important subject and will occupy our attention for several pages.

VII. The Doctrine of Original Sin

The doctrine on original sin and on the state of the fall which followed it is one of the sources of the Christian explanation of the problem of human misery. Sin is an event which changed the face of the world. No history can be written, not even a cosmology, without taking it into account. Without recourse to this primitive fault which has brought disorder everywhere, which marks the entrance of sin into the world and which was followed by the spread of evil, the existence of our wretched condition would remain an enigma which would do injury to the goodness and the justice of the Creator. "The Creator," says St. Bonaventure, "could not have placed man in the lamentable condition in which he is born today; moreover, the thought would be a sign of great impiety." [4] If our faith did not teach us the existence of an original fault and of its disastrous consequences, the simple awareness of our wretchedness would invite us to set up such an hypothesis. "Since God is provident, he rewards the good and punishes evil," writes St. Thomas Aquinas. "At sight of the sufferings we are able to imagine the fault. Now the human race, as a whole, suffers a great many kinds of punishments, corporal as well as spiritual. Distresses of the body, of which the principle one is death, toward which all the others tend and lead us: hunger, thirst . . . Distresses of the soul, of which the principal one is the weakness of reason, which appears in the difficulty man has of arriving at the knowledge of the truth, in the ease with which he falls into error and allows himself to be dominated and to a degree bestialized by his lower appetites." [5]

[4] In II *Sent.,* dist. 30, a. I, vol. 2, p. 716. Cited by Gaudel, art. *Péché originel* in D. T. C., col. 464.

[5] *Contra Gentiles,* book IV, ch. 52, cited by Gaudel, art. cit., col. 473.

If there had been no sin, then our condition would be incomprehensible. The disorder of the world would not have a cause which could furnish a valid explanation of it and render it intelligible. It would be necessary to agree with the pessimism of numerous existentialist philosophers. Such is not the Christian solution. From the book of Genesis down to our own day, passing through St. Paul, St. Augustine, St. Thomas Aquinas, sin is presented by all the doctors and theologians in the Catholic tradition and by the Church in her official documents, in a remarkable continuity of teaching, as the universal cause of human wretchedness.

1. THE TRANSMISSION OF ORIGINAL SIN IS A DOCTRINE OF FAITH

(a) *Genesis 2:8 to 3:24*

The doctrine concerning the fall of the first human couple already appears in the first of the books of the Bible. The essential text (Gen. 2:8; 3:24) has for its manifest purpose the explanation, through the recital of the temptation and the fall, of the origin of the evils which afflict humanity—which has since remained in a fallen condition. After the description of the primitive happiness of man there follows the recital of the trial presented under the form of a commandment which God gave to man: "Of every tree of Paradise thou shalt eat: but of the tree of knowledge of good and evil thou shalt not eat. For in what day soever thou shalt eat of it, thou shalt die the death" (Gen. 2:15). The devil, appearing under the form of a serpent, is the author of the temptation which he addresses to the craving of man for knowledge: "No, you shall not die the death. For God doth know that in what day soever you shall eat thereof, your eyes shall be opened, and you shall be as gods, knowing good and evil" (Gen. 3:4-5). The woman succumbs and draws Adam into the fall. The consequences of this fall follow immediately: the awakening of concupiscence: "They perceived themselves to be naked" (Gen. 3:7); punishment of the guilty. The woman shall bear children in sorrow, and man will henceforth have a life in which work will be difficult, in which he will know suffering and finally death. The happiness of Eden is definitively lost for man; Adam and Eve are driven out and will live thereafter in an inferior condition which will make them regret their former state of innocence.

The time is past when exegetes and theologians claimed to preserve the literalness of all the details of the account in Genesis. It
has been recognized, in studying the question of literary forms, that
there was a question of a popular and concrete account. Knowing
better the modes of expression of the early Orientals, it is no longer
imagined today that God really took some mud in order to fashion
the body of man, that the woman really came forth from the side
of Adam, that the temptation was presented under the appearance
of a fruit to be eaten, that the tempter had actually taken the form
of a serpent. It nevertheless remains true that this account explains
a profound historical truth and that it furnishes an authentic religious teaching resting on facts. It is not a bit of mythology. We
have here a clear affirmation of an important event in the religious
history of mankind: the existence of a primitive fault which placed
man in a lowered condition with respect to his prior state of innocence and happiness. Not less clearly affirmed is the spiritual nature
of this sin. It is the resemblance to God which man pursued. On
the other hand, what has not yet appeared clearly is the "transmission of the guilt of Adam to all his descendants. The guilt does
not appear as a source of sin, but as a source of an unhappy state,
of a ruin into which he draws his whole family" (Gaudel, art. cit.,
col. 286). It is necessary to wait for St. Paul in order that the
moral solidarity of all men in Adam, the source of sin for his race,
be revealed.

(b) *Other Texts of the Old Testament*

The idea of the original fall of Adam and of the transmission of
its consequences to his descendants does not appear in the other
books of the Bible. But the consciousness of the universality of sin,
of the wickedness of men and of their tendency toward evil goes
on spreading, especially in the psalmists, the prophets and the sages
like Job; the authors moreover are not seeking an explanation of
this universal corruption. They witness to a fact but they do not
refer it to any primitive fault.

Certain interesting indications appear in books whose redaction
is near the Christian era. "From the woman came the beginning of
sin and by her we all die," we read in Ecclesiasticus 25:33. And
in the book of Solomon: "For God created man incorruptible, and
to the image of his own likeness he made him. But by the envy of

the devil, death came into the world, and they follow him that are at his side" (Wis. 2:23-25). We find here an affirmation similar to that of Genesis. God had created man in a state of justice and of happiness, and the miserable state in which man now finds himself is the consequence of a fault of our first parents. The idea of a transmission of original sin does not yet appear. "At the moment in which Christ appears, Jewish thought does not yet know that Adam transmitted sin to us, with death and the pains of the body" (*ibid.* col. 305).

(c) *Saint Paul*

The Gospel remains silent on the question of original sin. Jesus announces that He has not come to save the just, but sinners (Mk. 2:17). He announces that His blood will be shed for many unto the remission of sins (Mt. 26:28). He decrees that He has come to destroy the empire of the devil, but nowhere in the Gospel does He distinguish between original sin and actual sin. It is St. Paul who has elaborated in the most explicit way the doctrine concerning original sin. Wishing to show the universality of the redemption through Christ, St. Paul takes as an example the universality of the consequences of the fall of Adam. A parallelism is established by him between the two heads of humanity. "Therefore as through one man sin entered the world and through sin death, thus death has passed unto all men because all have sinned . . ." (Rom. 5:12). Only the first member of the parallelism is expressed. The word sin has led St. Paul to pass on to another idea which in his thought is always connected with it, the idea of death. But a few lines further on, he resumes and completes his thought: "But where the offense has abounded grace has abounded more; so that as sin has reigned unto death, so also grace may reign by justice unto life everlasting" (Rom. 5:21). "The idea of an original sin common to Adam and to all humanity is contained under the form: because all have sinned" (Gaudel, art. cit., col. 309). St. Paul affirms the universality of human culpability. From the deed of Adam, not only have all men died, but they all have sinned. All have been constituted sinners. "The universality of sin is absolute because it derives from a condition inherent in our existence; the fact which constitutes us men and sons of Adam also constitutes us sinners." [6]

[6] Prat, L. A., *Théologie de saint Paul,* Vol. 2, p. 261.

(d) *The Fathers of the Church*

Following St. Paul, the whole patristic tradition affirms the existence of original sin and the necessity of baptism in order to be saved; yet we must recognize that the Greek Fathers, preoccupied in combating the dualist heresy affirming the existence of two principles at the beginning of things—the one good and the other evil—, and moreover little inclined toward introspection (which might have brought experimental awareness of the wretchedness of man the sinner), they readily show themselves optimistic in what concerns human nature and have never insisted on the transmission of the sin of Adam.

It is St. Augustine, who, after St. Paul, was the great teacher of the doctrine of original sin. The acute sense which he had of sin and of the misery of man led him to affirm energetically our state of decadence and to have recourse in order to explain it to an original disorder. The richness of the Augustinian experience imposed the doctrine of original sin with the force of an undeniable fact. It is this Augustinian contribution which ran through the centuries and which appears in Pascal when he speaks of the mystery of original sin: "Man is more inconceivable to himself without this mystery than the mystery is inconceivable to man" (*Pensées,* Edit. Brunschvicg, 434).

But there are in St. Augustine several inaccuracies on the plane of theological systematization. Does he not confuse the essence of original sin with concupiscence? Does he not make the libido which accompanies carnal union the cause of the transmission of original sin? It is in St. Thomas Aquinas that we find, conceptually, the most balanced teaching and the most enlightened attempt to justify this doctrine and to render it intelligible. St. Thomas modifies considerably the Augustinian conception of experimental proofs for original sin. For St. Thomas, human misery, the mortality of man, suffering, the discord between body and soul can be rigorously explained because man is a complex being and because, through his body, he belongs to the material world. Now according to Aristotelian principles which St. Thomas has adopted, matter is subject to disintegration. "We might say that our miseries, corporal as well as spiritual, are natural phenomena and have no penal character" (*Cont. Gent.* bk. 4, ch. 52). We cannot therefore give an apodictic proof of original sin from the experience of human wretchedness alone, as St. Augustine, and after him all the Augustinians, thought (Peter Lombard, St. Bonaventure). "Nevertheless," adds St. Thomas, "if one takes the point of view of Providence which gives to each being the perfections suitable to it, he is able to say with probability that God, by uniting a superior nature to an inferior one (soul to body), willed that the domination of the first over the second should be perfect, and that he had to remove, by means of a special and supernatural gift, the obstacles which these defects of nature could raise to this empire" (*ibid.*). "St. Thomas, replacing the world on the providential plane of a just and wise and good God, is disturbed then at the view of the miseries of man; he recognizes that these miseries make us perceive that they are a punishment, that they allow us to guess at a fault, that they make us suspect that God did not create the world in the state in which it is today; but it is in the explanations provided in the teaching of faith, that he finds the genuine proof" (*Gaudel,* art. cit., col. 474).

(e) *The Councils*

After such explicit texts from St. Paul, the Church on numerous occasions, in particular the Council of Carthage in 418, at the 2nd Council of Orange in 529, at the Council of Quiersy in 853, at the Council of Sens in 1140, at the Council of Trent in its 5th session in 1546, and more recently in the person of Pius IX in 1854, has returned to this doctrine of original sin in order to affirm that it was necessary to baptize infants and that the expression "for the remission of sins" should be understood in its true sense (*Denz.* 102, 791). Not only the death of the body, that is to say, the punishment for sin, but also the death of the soul, sin, has passed from a single man to the whole human race (*Denz.* 175, 376, 789). There is little doctrine of the faith which has received so many and so frequent confirmations as this one.

2. LOSS OF ORIGINAL JUSTICE

This doctrine of the transmission of an hereditary fault and of the culpability of all men from the fact of their descendance from Adam, does not come without shock to our sense of individual autonomy. How explain the insertion of an original fault in the bosom of a nature endowed with liberty? How can man be born guilty even before having performed his first free act? Theologians have tried to make this fact intelligible. St. Thomas Aquinas, as we have just said, furnished perhaps the most coherent and the most complete explanation.

In order to understand the doctrine of original sin, it is necessary to join it with that of original justice of which the sin of Adam deprived us. The world which left the hands of God could not but be good. The splendor of the universe at its origin is described in the second chapter of Genesis. The essential element of order, the key to the arch, was the submission of man to God. Man lived in the perfect accord of submission to God, and there followed from it a complete domination of the soul over the body. It is this original state which the sin of Adam destroyed. This sin was possible because man remained free. He could misuse this privilege reserved for spirits. The occasion of it was a commandment which God had given him. By refusing to obey his Creator, man pretended to be self-sufficient. He sought a "resemblance by imitation" to God. "You will be like gods," the devil had said. It is his state of dependence, inherent in the condition of creature, which man rejected.

The effect was immediate. The union of man with his Creator was broken. The order of the universe was attacked, the key to the arch gave way. Man was deprived of this state of original justice which had placed him in relation with his end and assured him of beatitude in the future. His human condition was changed. What was tragic about it for him, was that he was able to destroy the primitive order, but that he was not able to restore it. The road which he had followed was irreversible. Man was irremediably deprived of his privileges. He had fallen into a state of decadence with regard to his first state.

Although this revolt against God, on the part of man, was spiritual, in his soul, it entailed a disturbance in the other elements of his being. Once discord and disorder are introduced into an essential organ, they propagate themselves into the rest of the organism. The body was no longer under the perfect control of the soul. It, in part, escaped this control. It had dedicated itself to dissociation and to death, according to its natural condition. This was the consequence of sin. It was no longer protected from the attack of the enemies of its integrity and it became acquainted with suffering. And especially, the body was no longer an instrument faithfully subject to the soul. It opposed its heaviness and material opaqueness to the exercise of thought; and in the domain of appetite, it opposed the disorder of its instincts to the spiritual mastery henceforth impossible. The soul being radically wounded in its relation with God, the body was wounded in its turn and became for the soul "a perverted instrument, a trial rather than an aid." [7]

3. TRANSMISSION OF ORIGINAL SIN

The consequences of original sin struck not only its author, but all of his heirs. Fallen man could transmit to his descendants only his state of decadence. Original justice was not for Adam a purely personal gift, but a property of human nature. Adam also transmitted this state of original justice to his descendants, in the way that properties are transmitted in generation along with the nature. He could no longer transmit anything but the nature, such as he had rendered it by his sin, i.e. deprived of original justice. One can only give what one has. The descendants of Adam are not implicated in his personal act which pertains to him alone, but they are placed at birth in the state of decadence which derives from him. By receiving human nature through generation, the descendants of Adam receive it soiled with the contamination in which he left it.

But it must still be shown how, without the descendants of Adam participating in his personal act, the state subsequent to this act can be culpable in them. "There is the great mystery: the tiny infant which is born is already *guilty,* a son of wrath. It participates in the first sin of humanity at the same time that it participates in human nature." [8] The reason which St. Thomas gives for it is that through the fact of generation a profound physical community is established at the heart of humanity. All men, descendants from Adam, in some way make a single body with him by reason of the common nature which they have received from him. The generating influence has communicated to them this same life, constituting them as so many members of one and the same body. There is a single source of life, it is the same movement which is propagated and transmitted to the different members by generation. Remaining in vital dependence upon their head in humanity, man also shares in his culpability. The example of an individual body will make us understand it: "In the body, if the act of any member, let us say, of the hand, is voluntary, it is not through the will of the hand itself, but by that of the soul which is the first to give movement

[7] Mouroux, *Sens chrétien de l'homme,* Aubier, p. 71.
[8] Nicholas, *Le mal qui est en nous,* in V. S., Oct. 1, 1941, p. 297.

to any member. This is why the homicide which a hand commits would not be imputed to it as a sin unless one looked upon it and regarded it as separated from the body, while it is imputed to it inasmuch as it is something belonging to man and receives the movement from what in man is the first moving principle. It is then in this way that the disorder which is found engendered in this individual by Adam is voluntary not by his will, as sin of Adam, but by that of his first parent, who impresses the movement in the order of generation upon all those of his race, just as the will of the soul does on all the members of the body in the order of action. Thus this sin is called original which flows from the first parents to posterity, as is called actual the sin which flows from the soul into the members of the body. . . . Original sin is not the sin of any person in particular, except in so far as it receives its nature from the first parent; and it is called for that reason, sin of nature, in the sense in which the apostle says that we are by nature sons of wrath" (*Sum. Theol.,* Ia IIae, q. 81, a. 1).

The notion therefore of *human solidarity* that we must form for ourselves if we would obtain some light on the possibility of an overflowing of responsibility from the head of humanity unto all his descendants is very realistic. In our daily experience we find other manifestations of human solidarity. "Man was not made to live alone, and whatever may be the force of his personality, his individual destiny is connected with the great collective destiny from dependence on which he can never completely withdraw himself." [9] The doctrine of original sin clashes no doubt with a limited conception of personal responsibility but we may ask ourselves if our times, still very much impregnated with individualism, a heritage of several centuries, have not lost their sense of certain collective realities which the Hebrews understood very well. They firmly believed that Yahweh punished the children for the sins of their fathers: "I am the Lord thy God, mighty, jealous, visiting the iniquity of the fathers upon the children unto the third and fourth generation of them that hate me" (Ex. 20:5). We are not going so far, and we are reserving the case of Adam as a unique case. The Hebrews recall for us, however, certain lost realities. Let us be thankful moreover that we are perhaps on the way to discovering them. The accent placed today on communal values disposes us to understand better that in the domain of sin, as in other domains,

[9] Nicholas, art. cited in V. S., Oct. 1, 1941, p. 298.

the law of solidarity can take effect, without any injury being done
for that matter to the autonomy of the individual.

The analogy of the human body, employed by theologians, does
not claim to remove all obscurity from the transmission of original
sin. But by invoking the mysterious bonds which unite the different
elements of an organism it makes the mystery more acceptable to
our reason.

4. THE NATURE OF ORIGINAL SIN IN US

Faith asserts firmly the transmission of original sin, but it does
not pronounce upon the nature of this sin. The decision is that of
the theologians.

⌜Original sin was an actual sin in Adam who committed it. But
the descendants of Adam received it with nature. They inherited
it from him at birth, prior to any positive act on their part. In
them, original sin is not an act, but a culpable state in which they
find themselves placed from the fact of their descendance from
Adam. Original sin is the state in which the fault of Adam has
placed human nature. It is a situation of decadence, for this human
nature was originally crowned by grace and wholly orientated toward
God. That was its vocation, its state of health. ⌜After the sin of
Adam, nature is deprived of original justice,⌟ "left to itself," in a
state of languor and of sickness. This unfortunate state is defined
by comparison with the harmonious state in which it existed in the
first instance.⌟ In consequence of this privation, nature, no longer
having the "great spiritual bond which so marvelously contained it"
(St. Thomas, *De Malo*, q. 4, a. 2), becomes a sin of disorder. The
spiritual creature, not being any longer in a state of submission to
God, born in dependence, is in rebellion. The powers of nature are
left to themselves, "and we are exposed to everything, like a generous wine which flows in all directions or like a spirited horse which
is not controlled" (*ibid*). The darkening of intelligence, the wound-
ing of the mind, the tendency of the will to evil, the wound of
malice, the lack of courage in overcoming obstacles, the wound of
weakness, the disordered appetite for pleasures, the wound of concupiscence, are the consequences of this "languor of nature," the
manifestations of the "seat of sin" which henceforth multiplies in
the bosom of wounded nature. ⌜Original sin is defined then formally
as the privation of original justice, materially as concupiscence.
Through original sin we have in us from birth till death a root of

all sins. No theologian has described the wretchedness of our condition of decadence, consequent upon original sin, better than St.
Augustine.

5. ORIGINAL SIN AND SIN OF THE WORLD

We have just exploited, especially for our exposition, the doctrine of original sin developed by St. Thomas. It represents on this
point Augustinian tradition. It may be asked whether the Greek
Fathers, very discreet in what concerns primitive justice, almost
never speaking of the transmission of original sin, did not supply
us with other doctrinal riches, completing the Augustinian contribution and opening up new perspectives on the content of revelation. It would be enough, without forgetting the sin of Adam, to
think of the fact that a whole series of crimes has intervened and
aggravated the efforts of the first sin in order that human decadence should not only be perceived as a consequence of the fault
of a single man, but also as the result of a universal complicity in
evil. Adam is the head of all humanity, but even so the whole of
human behavior was prefigured in him. Original sin must not be
too isolated from the sin of the world, from the sin of the whole
human race. No doubt it is the first. It opened up a source of evil
in the world. It had by that fact a capital importance since it consummated a rupture with God and marked a radical change from
the prior situation which was a state of innocence; but we cannot
forget that all men subsequently have committed evil in their turn.

No doubt before the fall, Adam was in a privileged situation.
What exactly was it? Must it be conceived of as a state of intellectual perfection, except in the sense of a basic uprightness of
intelligence not as yet exercised? It is more and more agreed to
recognize as valid the results of the science of evolution, estimating
that the human species progressed slowly after the appearance of
the mind. "Must we represent Adam to ourselves as a superhuman
being, endowed with extraordinary knowledge, or on the contrary
as a man still an infant who, however privileged he might have
been, was only at the beginning of the long rise which led toward
Christ the men descended from him?" [10] In short, "the Catholic
Church is very much more preoccupied with calling us sinners, with

[10] H. Rondet, *Les origines humaines et la théologie* in *Cité nouvelle*,
June 10, 1943, p. 976.

recalling the necessity of the grace of Christ, than of telling us in detail the manner in which sin entered the world" (*ibid.*, p. 979).

Sins, Causes of Other Sins

The study of man, the cause of sin, led us to open up the whole study of original sin. Let us return to our original plan and bring to completion a list of the causes of sin.

Actual sins which the sinner commits can become the inspiration, the occasion for other sins. They also, in their own way, are causes. Among them it is proper to put in the first place those which Christian tradition calls "capital sins." Capital, not necessarily because they are grave: gluttony or anger, for example, are not of themselves mortal sins. Capital because they involve others. They are the heads of the list. Capital comes from "caput" which means head or source.

We cannot mention them all. Each one of them would deserve a special study—and such a project could allow for some interesting psychological analyses. We are satisfied simply to list them according to the traditional order adopted by moral theology and religious art. There are seven: pride or vainglory, avarice, gluttony, lust, envy, anger and sloth. St. Paul had already said that "cupidity is the root of all vice" (I Tim. 1:10), and in Ecclesiasticus, we read that "Every sin begins with pride" (Ecclus. 10:15). Let us add apropos of sloth, included in the modern list, that the old authors understood it to mean spiritual sloth, a kind of lassitude with regard to divine things.

VIII. The Effects of Sin

What are the miseries which sin entails? Sin, which is a human action, passes away, but it leaves traces which endure. We can group these under three headings: sin has for effect a general lowering of the goods of nature, a stain which obscures the soul, a certain number of penalties or punishments to be undergone either in this world or the next.

1. CORRUPTION OF THE GOODS OF NATURE

Among the goods of nature we can place: the constitutive principles of the nature of man and the properties which flow from them, the natural inclination to virtue, the gift of original justice which had been granted to the first man and which was to have been transmitted by him to all humanity.

This third good, original justice, has been completely lost by the sin of Adam—for him and for his descendants.

On the contrary, the first good, which concerns the essential constitution of nature, was neither removed nor diminished by sin. Catholic teaching has not varied on this point and has never shared the pessimism of the Protestants and of the Jansenists, who say that the goodness of nature has been effected in its root by original sin and that the essential principles of nature were corrupted. Despite the ravages caused by original sin and by the actual sins which have followed, we must retain a certain optimism and hold that the constitution of nature was not touched. Man remains a man, endowed with intelligence and free will, made for the good.

It is the second good cited, the inclination to virtue, which, among the goods of nature, is found diminished by sin. Human acts engender certain tendencies which are inscribed in the being and push it to act again in the same way. The man who sins finds himself inclined to sin again. Sin which is repeated gives rise to a vice which becomes a kind of second nature. Nevertheless, since the root has not been touched, a straightening out is always possible.

It is especially in connection with original sin that we speak of the wounds left by sin. By depriving nature of its harmonious inclination toward God, original sin has brought disorder among the powers of man. Man is wounded in his intelligence, he does not as easily direct himself toward the truth, his reason is as it were stupefied, made dull, particularly in its practical function. This is the wound of ignorance. The will also is wounded. Hardened with regard to the good, it manifests a certain propensity for evil. "And God saw that the wickedness of men was great on the earth and that all the thought of their heart was bent upon evil at all times . . ." (Gen. 6:5). This is the wound of malice. Our vigor for overcoming obstacles is likewise diminished. An extreme lassitude sometimes seizes us in face of the difficulties of life and of the good to be accomplished. This is the wound of weakness. Finally our desires often seek, with ill-regulated impetuosity, sensible goods. This is the wound of concupiscence. These wounds, which are in the first place consequences of original sin, are emphasized by the fact of our personal sins.

There are other miseries which are consequences of sin, particu-

larly suffering and death. That death is a consequence of original
sin is a doctrine of faith. The Old Testament affirms it repeatedly
and St. Paul said without hesitation that "therefore as through one
man sin entered into the world and through sin, death . . ." (Rom.
5:7). Let us note, however, that according to St. Thomas suffering
and death are accidental effects of sin, in the sense that sin is not
the direct, but only the indirect, cause of it. By suppressing original
justice, sin left the body of man to its material nature and delivered
it to the powers of disintegration of matter.

2. THE STAIN LEFT BY ORIGINAL SIN ON THE SOUL

In addition to a diminution of natural good, sin leaves on the
most spiritual part of the soul a stain which alienates it from God.
It is difficult to define the nature of this stain otherwise than by
means of an image. A spot or stain is opposed to the brilliance of
a thing. By attaching itself in a disordered way to lower goods, the
soul soils itself with this contact and loses the brilliance which it
had by adhering to God. Henceforth there is a shady spot between
it and the divine Son, a spot which lasts as long as the soul remains
in the state of sin. A distance which the soul has placed by its sin
between the light and itself, and which deprives it of its spiritual
brilliance, an obstacle which makes a shadow by inserting itself between the soul and the light—such are the images which permit us
to grasp the spiritual effect which sin leaves after it. Scripture often
speaks of this disastrous effect of sin by which "thou hast stained
thy glory" (Ecclus. 47:22).

3. OBLIGATION OF THE PENALTY

(a) *The Disruption of Order*

Sin is a disorder which necessarily provokes the reaction of injured order. This law of retaliation has a universal character and is
already verified in the natural order. Every organism reacts vitally
at the very point at which it is wounded and seeks to reestablish
the disrupted equilibrium. Numerous illustrations of this law can be
found. For example, the phenomenon of the healing of wounds, manifesting an activity of reparation and a cellular proliferation at the
very point at which the tissues have been damaged. Sin does not
escape from this general law. And this reparation is the penalty.

"Woe to the wicked unto evil: for the reward of his hands shall be given him" (Is. 3:11).

The punishment will be the wages of the evil works: "Give them according to their works, and according to the wickedness of their inventions. According to the works of their hands give thou to them; render to them their reward" (Ps. 27:4).

Men being subject to three orders—the order of reason, the order of human society, the order of divine government—undergo, when they sin, a penalty from these three orders. The remorse of conscience is the revenge of the order of reason; a temporal punishment, that of society when it has been injured by sin; a temporal or eternal punishment, that of the divine order.

Let us distinguish clearly between the idea of penalty and of reparation. Reparation springs from penitence and from satisfaction. The sinner makes reparation by entering into the ways of repentance and by returning to God through penance freely accepted. It is a liquidation of sin that leads to reparation. The idea of penalty suggests the image of two contraries which are made to balance. Penalty is essentially opposed to the will of the sinner. It places an obstacle to it and reestablishes the order of the world. Besides penalty can have a medicinal or atoning effect, but these are later consequences which do not define penalty in its essence. Likewise it is not quite exact to say that the just suffer the penalties due to the sins of others. "These tribulations of the just should rather be called 'medicines' than 'penalties,' for medicines inflict pain, in view of their giving the sovereign good of health to those who take them." [11] They are not real penalties; for they do not correspond to any personal fault.

(b) *The Eternity of Hell*

The pain inflicted upon the sinner by the divine order can be either temporal or eternal, temporal if the sin is only venial, eternal if the sin is mortal and if the sinner dies without repentance. The existence of hell is a doctrine of faith.[12] Hell is the eternal punishment incurred by him who sins against the order of charity and breaks all bonds with God.

[11] Deman, art. *Péché,* in D.T.C., vol. 12, col. 224.

[12] Text of the Gospel: "Depart from me ye cursed into everlasting fire" (Mt. 25:41). Profession of faith of Michel Paléologue at the second Council of Lyons in 1274; cf. Denz. 464. Decree for the Greeks at the Council of Florence, 1438-1445; cf. Denz. 693.

Is there not disproportion between mortal sin, a passing and limited action, and hell which is an eternal punishment? It is necessary, if we wish to understand that this disproportion is only apparent, to see clearly that the sentence of condemnation merely sanctions a situation in which the sinner has voluntarily placed himself and in which he has kept himself through his obstinacy. By mortal sin the sinner has turned himself away from God, he has refused divine friendship. He has committed an act which, by reason of its importance, surpasses the measure of time. We must consider this act, not in its material content, but in its spiritual signification. Mortal sin is a total rupture with God. The punishment of loss, by which the sinner is eternally deprived of the vision of God, is not therefore the fruit of an arbitrary sentence on the part of the sovereign judge, but the inevitable conclusion of a situation in which the sinner has placed himself. It is the sinner who condemns himself. By sinning mortally he freely chooses his eternity. He chooses to be separated from God. Hell is the unbearable consciousness of a lost heaven. Hell therefore does not come from God, but from an opposition to God on the part of the sinner. As the Bible tells us, the sinner digs his own pit, the ditch in which he himself falls: "His wickedness will revert upon his own head: and his violence will return on his crown" (Ps. 7:17).

Hell is eternal and it cannot be otherwise, for God would be wanting in justice if one day he welcomed the sinner who has obstinately rejected his friendship. God cannot but have the last word. The sinner is a deliberate obstacle to the will of God. In sin, the sinner wins out, for his will is squarely opposed to that of God. Here below the sinner gains the victory. But this victory can only be provisional and must be followed by a definitive defeat. Justice thus reclaims him. If the sinner could count one day on entering into beatitude while remaining in his sin, he would be right as against God. The Bible describes the arrogance of the unpunished sinner: "Why does the wicked man spurn God, and say in his heart: 'He will not punish'?" (Ps. 9B:13).

This situation cannot last. Man cannot deny God indefinitely. The sense of justice demands that man not triumph: "Arise, O Lord, let not man prevail; let the nations be judged in thy sight. . . . Let the nations know that they are but men" (Ps. 9A:20-21).

The pain of loss which corresponds to the departure from God in sin is infinite, just as this departure itself which is the rejection of an infinite good. It does not admit of more or less. The break is complete.

The pain of sense, on the contrary, which is the second pain that the damned will suffer, corresponds to the disordered attachment which they have had for perishable goods—a limited and more or less susceptible attachment. This pain, the revenge of damaged order demanding compensation, will be limited and unequal just as was the culpable attachment with which it strikes a balance.

(c) *Venial Sin and Mortal Sin*

In conclusion we must explain the classical distinction between mortal sin and venial sin, a distinction which is based on the duration of the punishment. Mortal sin, as its name suggests, entails the death of the soul and it is rewarded by an eternal punishment: venial sin is rewarded by a temporal punishment. It is therefore apropos of punishments that we must study these two kinds of sin. Evidently, if these sins imply this difference of punishment, it is because anteriorly their gravity is different. Mortal sin attacks the very principle of supernatural life, which is union with God through charity. "As sin," writes St. Thomas Aquinas, "is a malady of the soul, we say that the sin is mortal in the same way that we say that a sickness of the body is mortal from the fact that by attacking a vital principle it introduces into the organism an irreparable harm. Now the principle of spiritual life, when it is developed according to virtue, is the understanding of the last end" (Ia IIae, q. 88, a. 1). Through mortal sin the will renounces God and puts its last end in a creature. Certain mortal sins are such by reason of their object. There are some objects of sin which are of themselves incompatible with a final inclination toward God. "When the will is borne toward a thing which, of itself, is repugnant to the charity by which one is orientated toward the last end, the sin, by its very object, has the wherewithal for being mortal. It belongs consequently to the genus mortal; whether it be against the love of God as blasphemy or perjury and other sins of this nature, or against the love of one's neighbor, as homicide, adultery, and other similar crimes" (Ia, IIae, q. 88, a. 2).

But it can happen that one may sin mortally even though the object of the sin is not of a nature to turn one away from God. This happens when one considers an object which excludes charity and when one is related to it as a final end.

On the contrary, an object which by reason of one's matter, involves of itself a mortal sin, can give place only to a venial sin when there is a lack of knowledge of the gravity of this matter or when there is defect of consent.

Venial sin itself does not have the scope of mortal sin. It does not involve an undertaking directly concerned with our last end. It does not attain, for that reason, to the full definition of sin, which comprises an opposition to the divine law. Venial sin does not separate from God. It constitutes, no doubt, a disorder, for the creature is loved apart from the divine order, but there is not sufficient consistence to bring about a rupture. It is in a way something illogical on the part of the sinner, who remains basically attached to God, but who nevertheless actually posits an action which is not ordained to Him.

The angel is too intelligent to fail to seek his ultimate end in all his acts. But man, the lowest of intelligent beings, does not always seek this last end in everything he does. He can orient himself toward the means without subordinating them in the order of the end to which he remains attached.

That there are mortal sins as well as venial sins is a doctrine of faith.[13] Pius V condemned this proposition of Baius: "No sin is of its nature venial; but every sin deserves eternal punishment" (Denz. 1020).

Do not therefore believe that venial sins are without a disastrous influence, especially those which it is agreed to call deliberate, because they are fully voluntary, in opposition to the sins of surprise, which are only partly voluntary. Venial sins prevent the growth of charity and dispose one to mortal sin. They lead to lukewarmness and deprive the soul of its strength on the day on which a stronger temptation presents itself. An upright soul will seek to exclude from its life even the least of deliberate venial sins which holds it back from union with God. The deliberate venial sin is the greatest obstacle to progress in the spiritual life.

(d) *Venial Sin Cannot Coexist with Original Sin*

This thesis which St. Thomas has always defended is interesting because it is connected with his doctrine on the beginning of moral life in man. There comes a moment in the history of every individual

[13] Cf. Council of Trent, Sess. VI, can. 11 and can. 23, 25, 27. Denz. 804, 833, 835, 837.

in which for the first time a conscious moral choice becomes necessary. This takes place at the age which is commonly called the age of reason or discretion. The child who has not yet reached this age of discretion is not capable of discerning that there exists a rule of morality which binds him in conscience. He is in the pre-normal stage. His faculties of intelligence and of judgment are not yet sufficiently developed to permit him a genuinely free act. When he attains the age of discretion—it would be idle to try to make that age precise, for it varies according to individuals—the moral world is opened to him. Becoming suddenly aware of the responsibility for his actions, he experiences himself drawn by the necessity of a choice of which, however, he is the master. It is he who must choose either for the good or against the good. On this important moment depends in great part the whole direction of his life, for at that instant in which a personal event is produced in his moral life, there is in fact the totality of an attitude at stake. In a dramatic intuition the last end of man is proposed. Even if the nature of this last end is only confusedly perceived, the gravity of the choice permits no doubt that it is implicitly present. This is why St. Thomas affirms that the decision taken at this moment is so grave that it provides occasion either for the justification of him who, not yet baptized, chooses the way of the good, or for a mortal sin for him who turns away from it. There can be no middle way. A position taken in regard to the last end does not belong to that area of a simple venial sin. Thus before reaching the age of discretion, original sin exists in the non-baptized person, but there is no actual mortal sin, and a fortiori no venial sin, since the individual is not capable of a free act; when moral life begins, the initial choice is such that it involves an entrance into the life of grace, and therefore the remission of original sin, or a mortal sin of omission bearing upon the final end proposed and rejected.

Clearly, the early education of the child is important since it lays down the concrete conditions in which the child will find himself when the first free choice, which orients his whole life, will be demanded of him.

REFLECTIONS AND PERSPECTIVES

Throughout this study of sin, we have followed a didactic plan. It was necessary for this reason to try to be complete and classical. But our desire for being complete obliged us, conversely, to be succinct and to give to the parts only the importance claimed by the balance of the whole. Moreover, in wanting to set forth the classical doctrine, we neglected whole sectors of research. These terminal reflections are intended to remedy in part these gaps, at least by indicating in the doctrinal order and in the pastoral order certain points on which the thought of research students can still be exercised. In the doctrinal order, the question of original sin certainly demands most attention and also some very delicate clarifications. The discoveries of paleontology have already raised the question of polygenism. This is a risky hypothesis for the scientists; it is also quite dangerous for theologians. The encyclical *Humani generis* (1950) has recently issued some doctrinal directives on this subject. On this question, the reader may consult the first chapter of the work of Father A. M. Dubarle, *Les sages d'Israël*. We recommend also the study of Father H. Rondet, *Le péché originel et l'état primitif de l'homme*, announced in the collection "Théologie" (Aubier), to be published. A study of the Greek tradition and especially of St. Irenaeus would be very useful here; and it would enrich and shape our conception of the state of primitive justice.

In the pastoral order, we cannot remain totally ignorant of the works of contemporary psychology, especially of characterology and psychoanalysis. They can often be quite helpful if we would understand the psychology of the sinner somewhat less abstractly. The same is true of the arrival of the critical age in which the first free choice is made, and of all of the conditionings which surround sin. Psychology may teach us that perhaps a considerable number of human beings is found who never reach the use of reason, and that, even among those who do, the moments of lucidity and of genuine autonomy are not very frequent. That should prompt us, in addition to the supernatural reasons which we have already given, to show ourselves more merciful and not to multiply beyond measure the number of mortal sins which are committed in the world.

Finally, we will remember that a genuine knowledge of sin is impossible apart from the redemptive plan of God. We will understand better the whole broad tragedy of sin when we see the infinite goodness of God who is offended by them and the astonishing decisions to which His will was led to save sinful man: the Incarnation of His well-beloved Son, His suffering and death on the cross. In the presence of the cross of the Savior, we will acquire the horror which sin should inspire in every Christian living by faith and loving God. We will be thrown into confusion at the sight of our own transgressions, we will understand the necessity of introducing penance into our lives, and the benefit of the sacrament in which the blood of Christ cleanses us of our stains.

(V. Vergriete, O.P.)

Plans for Work

Sin being defined *aversio a Deo, conversio ad bonum commutabile* (turning away from God, and a turning to a perishable good), show how psychologically this twofold movement takes place in the heart of the sinner. May we speak of a first movement and then a second? Can they exist separately? Can there be an adherence to the perishable good without any turning away from God, and consequently without sin, the "aversion" being what formally constitutes the sin? Can we judge of the gravity of the turning away from God by the simple consideration of the attachment of the sinner to perishable goods? Degrees and causes of responsibility of the sinner in his attachment to perishable goods? Are there "conversions to a perishable good" such that the aversion from God would be absolute and the sin necessarily mortal?

Original Sin and the "Age of Reason" of the Non-Baptized

If it is impossible that original sin should coincide with a simple venial sin in the soul, if it is necessary that the first "human act" of man be a free act (the fruit of grace) or a mortal sin, try to analyze theologically and psychologically the first human act of the non-baptized. The place of faith, of baptism, of the Church in such an economy of grace; theology of "salvation of infidels." Psychology of the "age of reason." Sins and imperfections. Can we speak of simple imperfections? Is it not just a manner of speaking, without real meaning?

Original Sin and Earthly Paradise

Analyze theologically the first sin of man (what it was, its causes, its end). And psychologically. Analyze temptation. The scientific idea of an "evolution" which would leave no place for an earthly paradise in history. Is this compatible with the doctrine of original sin? Can we admit that material creation was already "subjected to vanity" before the sin of man, because of the sin of the angels and the existence of demons? And that man will enter a world already badly conditioned?

Sin and Concupiscence of the Flesh

Is concupiscence of the flesh the fruit of sin? Show what is the part of nature (and what had existed in paradise) and what can be the part of sin, in the sexual instinct, carnal concupiscence, the "will of the flesh." Can we say what marriage, the carnal act, procreation would have been in the state of original justice? Try to show how they would have been harmoniously organized, in "justice," i.e. the concupiscence of the flesh with a rule of infallible reason. The error of every doctrine which finishes by making the difference between the senses and their mutual attraction, a fruit of original sin.

Sin and Ignorance

Show how the fact of being ignorant of God (what kind of ignorance?) is a sin. Comment on Rom. 1:20-21. Explain Osee 6:6 and the numerous texts of the Old Testament relative to this "knowledge of God" which God desires before all else. Show along this same line how eternal life is a knowledge. Dialectic of "knowledge," on the one hand, of ignorance, of darkness, on the other, in the Old Testament. Dialectic of light and darkness, of sons of light and sons of darkness in St. John. The ignorance in every sin; show how sin, of whatever kind, involves some ignorance. Causes and responsibility for this ignorance. Vincible and invincible ignorance. Degrees of culpability. Ignorance, cause of new sins. The theologian, because he ignores nothing, is forearmed against sin, and, inversely, the simple man, because he is ignorant of "moral theology," would seem to be liable to sin more frequently and more gravely. Is this true? Necessity and limits of knowledge in moral education.

The Punishments of Sin. Hell

Revelation and theology on hell. What must we believe about hell? Explain theologically the eternity of punishment. False representations of hell (cf. on this subject *L'enfer*, Éd. de la Revue des J., 1950, especially the chapter of M. Carrouges). How can the love and mercy of God be discovered in the teaching on hell? How does mercy triumph over justice? *Purgatory:* Revelation, theology, history of doctrine. The affirmations of faith. Aid to the souls in purgatory; basis of this doctrine; theological significance. *Indulgences:* Origins, theology and history. *Limbo:* Can it be considered as a "punishment"? Origin and history of this doctrine. What is of faith? *Punishments in this life:* Can sin involve a temporal punishment here below? Danger of this doctrine. The Book of Job. Sin, or at least *the cause (or one cause) of a present sin*—can it be punishment for a past sin? How understand that sickness, suffering, the thorns and the thistles, the resistance of nature to work, are all punishments for sin?

BIBLIOGRAPHIE

- Celui qui voudra se livrer à une étude approfondie du péché se reportera aux articles du T. Deman, O.P. et de M. Gaudel dans le *Dictionnaire de Théologie catholique,* tome XII. L'article "Péché," colonnes 140-275, du T. Deman, article fort consciencieux et très complet, reste difficile cependant et un peu abstrait. L'excellent article "Péché originel," colonnes 275-606, de M. Gaudel, qui comporte une bonne étude historique de la question, est plus abordable, mais il est fort long et ne porte que sur le péché originel.
- Les deux volumes des Éditions de la Revue des Jeunes: S. Thomas d'Aquin, *Somme Théologique,* "Le péché," traduction et notes par le R. P. R. Bernard, O.P., fourniront peut-être le meilleur instrument de travail.
- On pourra se servir aussi de l'ouvrage du R. P. H.-D. Noble, *La vie pécheresse,* Lethielleux, 1937, qui donne un ensemble clair et bien ordonné de la doctrine thomiste sur le péché.
A signaler encore:
J.-B. Kors, *La justice primitive et le péché originel d'après saint Thomas,* Les Sources, La doctrine. *Bibl. thom.,* Le Saulchoir, 1922. (Ce livre n'est pas à utiliser sans précaution, car il présente une exégèse de saint Thomas qui est souvent discutable.)
Paul Claudel, *Positions et propositions.* Tome 2. (Quelques pages sur le péché originel et l'éternité des peines de l'enfer.)
Fr. Mauriac, R. P. Ducatillon, R. P. Maydieu, etc., *L'homme et le péché.* Collection "Présences," Plon, 1938.
J. Mouroux, *Sens chrétien de l'homme,* Aubier, 1945.

BIBLIOGRAPHY

BOOKS

Davis, Henry, S.J., *Moral and Pastoral Theology,* Vol. I, pp. 203-250. London: Sheed and Ward, 1941.
Manning, Henry E. Card., *Sin and Its Consequences.* London: Burns and Oates, 1878.
Mahoney, E. J., S.J., *Sin and Repentance.* New York: The Macmillan Company, 1928.
McHugh, John A., O.P., and Callan, Charles J., O.P., *Moral Theology, A Complete Course,* Vol. I, pp. 59-90. New York: Joseph Wagner, Inc., 1929.
Mouroux, J., *The Meaning of Man.* New York: Sheed and Ward, 1948.
——, *The Christian Experience.* New York: Sheed and Ward, 1954.

Slater, Thomas, S.J., *Manual of Moral Theology,* Vol. I, pp. 133-165. New York: Benziger Bros., 1908.

Walsh, Aloysius, *Scholastic Teaching Concerning the Specific Distinction of Sins in the Light of Current Moral Theology.* Washington: Catholic University Press, 1942.

ARTICLES

Grabowski, S.J., "Sinners and the Mystical Body of Christ," *Theological Studies,* 8: 614-667 (Dec., 1947) and 9: 47-84 (March, 1948).

Kelly, Gerald, S.J., "Subjective Sin," *Review for Religious,* 6: 114-120 (March 15, 1947).

Magrath, O., O.P., "St. Thomas' Theory of Original Sin," *Thomist,* 16: 161-189 (April, 1953).

Muntsch, A., "Root of Social Evils," *Social Justice Review,* 40: 124ff (July, 1947).

Renard, Henri, S.J., "Introduction to the Philosophy of the Existential Moral Act," *New Scholasticism,* 28: 145-169 (April, 1954).

Roberts, J., O.S.B., "Injustice of Sin," *Downside Review,* 71: 233-242 (Summer, 1953).

Chapter VI

LAWS

by V. Grégoire, O.P.

INTRODUCTION

I. LAW IN SCRIPTURE

    1. Old Testament
        (a) The Mosaic law: the law of the Covenant
        (b) Other laws: the Eternal Law
    2. New Testament
        (a) The Gospel
        (b) The Acts of the Apostles
        (c) St. Paul

II. THE CONTRIBUTION OF ANCIENT THOUGHT

    (a) The Philosophers
    (b) The Jurists

III. THE GENERAL NOTION OF LAW

    1. Law is an ordinance of reason
    2. In view of the common welfare
    3. Established by him who is in charge of the community
    4. And promulgated
    5. Means of action for law

IV. THE ETERNAL LAW

V. THE NATURAL LAW

    1. Definition of the natural law
    2. Content of the natural law
    3. Scope of the natural law

271

Chapter VI

LAWS

Introduction

We are creatures of God. He is our final end. We are destined to the beatitude of the Kingdom of God, which will consist in the possession of our God in vision and in love. This beatitude is acquired by meritorious acts that should shape the course of our lives, and we know that these acts are not accomplished easily, spontaneously and joyfully, without deep virtuous dispositions to which the vices that incline us to sin are opposed. These virtues which deeply affect us are then personal interior resources of action which leads to beatitude.

The study of the human act and of sin, corroborating daily experience, has made us somewhat aware of our weakness in order that we might understand our need of assistance from a superior being. What would the virtues themselves which we cultivate be and what might they be for beatitude if we were not first enlightened on the direction in which our effort should carry us, on the object consequently of beatitude and on the way which leads to it—and if, on the other hand, we did not receive unexpected powers to attain it, since God is infinitely above every creature?

It is what the Church makes us say so often, especially in the large number of prayers of the missal: ". . . that we may learn from your authority what we have to do and that we may accomplish it by your action" (Prayer of Tuesday of the second week of Lent), ". . . what we seek because you suggest it to us, that we may obtain it because you make a gift of it to us" (Third prayer of the Saturday of Ember week in September).

There is reason then for now studying these great lights which, after all, come to us from God and which are called *laws*, before studying the supernatural power, called *Grace*, which permits us to fulfill what the laws prescribe for us.

I. Law in Scripture

In Scripture (Old and New Testaments), the Law is designated by numerous terms and they imply shades of meaning that are rather appreciable. Most frequently, however, the Law is a divine teaching revealed to men by the instrumentality of certain spiritual leaders of the people of God. But, expressed or not by terms which designate the Law understood in the first sense, other kinds of laws affecting moral life figure also in Scripture.

1. OLD TESTAMENT

(a) *The Mosaic Law: The Law of the Covenant*

In the Old Testament, the Law can be defined as the charter of the Covenant concluded between God and His people, or again as the body of clauses of the testament of which God made His people the beneficiary. Concluded with Abraham and renewed with his descendants, Isaac and Jacob, the Covenant is definitively sealed after the revelation of the proper name of God: Yahweh, in the course of the theophanies of Sinai, during the great purification of the forty years in the desert, in which the people of Israel, the people of Yahweh, is constituted under the direction of Moses. It is this Moses who is the inspired Mediator of the Covenant, but he does not go up on Mt. Sinai to discuss the clauses of it with Yahweh in the name of the people, but in order to receive them, to hear them dictated to him, for the Covenant is not properly a contract. God no doubt proposes it to those whom He wishes to make His People, but to reject it or to discuss it would be a major offense, for the Covenant, on the part of Yahweh, is a merciful gift, not a "business transaction." This is also why the charter of this Covenant is not a treaty, but a Law for the People who as such are bound to receive it with meekness, respect and submission, and at the same time with gratitude.

Its content. This law, which will commonly be called Mosaic, but which is also a Law par excellence, comprises essentially: 1) moral precepts condensed into the commandments of the Decalogue (Ex. 20: 1-17); it is to them that Yahweh makes allusion when He says to Moses: "This commandment that I command thee this day, is not above thee nor far off from thee . . . But the word is very near unto thee, in thy mouth and in thy heart, that thou mayst do it" (Deut.

30:11, 14); 2) ritual precepts, detailed in what the author himself
calls "the book of the Covenant" (Ex. 20:22; cf. 24:7) and completed
or explained throughout the remainder of the Book of Exodus and
the books of Leviticus and Deuteronomy; 3) finally, closely united
to the ritual precepts, the precepts of civil and penal law or even of
public right; for the temple of God is organized into a theocrat, the
most rigorous that has ever existed, and the whole of private and
public life is directly inspired by the concern for observing the Law
of God and of celebrating His worship.

The Law in the history of the people of Yahweh. The history of
the people of Yahweh after its establishment in the land of Canaan
can be summarized in the history of its infidelities to the law, then of
its return to the observances of its precepts, notably the moral and
ritual. The prosperity of Israel, the gift of Yahweh, is always tied in
with its fidelity to monotheism, to its zeal for the observance of worship, center of the national life. The Law remains the soul of the
people, for it is the charter of the Covenant and the Covenant with
Yahweh is the only reason for being and the sole guarantee of con-
tinuance for this little nation in the midst of its enemies, nomadic
tribes or great empires, which surround and menace it. Judges, Kings,
prophets themselves are not raised up by Yahweh to replace the Law,
but on the contrary to revive it with all its authority, according to a
renewed and a more vital understanding of its precepts.

The Law and Judaism. This attachment to the divine law will be
more exclusive than ever on the day on which, during and after the
exile, the political autonomy shall no longer exist. More than ever,
the Law is then the unique bond of national unity; the strict observance of its precepts and of its rites is the great common activity. Judaism properly so-called is constituted at the beginning of the
new promulgation of the Law by Esdras (Neh. 8:9). With it comes
the grave threat of legalism into which it will fall every time the
doctors of the Law trespass on the priesthood, and every time the
rubrics of worship seem more important than the precepts of the Decalogue, that is, more important than the spirit with which worship is
accomplished.

The grandeur of the Law. Despite all the deformations in practice, the Law is always first a teaching of truth, a source of high moral
light. Following the perspectives, it is imposed on the will or it solicits
it gently; but it is in any case beneficent and life giving, for it is holy
and no one can grow weary of chanting its praises (Ps. 119). The

anointing of the Lord, the servant of Yahweh Himself fills a mission which Israel describes in terms which evoke the Covenant and the Law (Is. 42:3-4, 6).

Attempts at renewal. For if the law is unalterable, if it is forever that Israel must be faithful to it, the prophets left the impression to those who were friendly to them, that the Covenant had not yet revealed its full content, that the Law had not yet been fully accomplished according to all of its potentialities. If legalism makes progress after the return from exile, it is easy to recall the appeals of an Isaias or a Jeremias to a more interior fidelity (characteristic of the new times), and an eternal alliance: "But this shall be the covenant that I will make with the house of Israel, after these days, saith the Lord. I will give my law in their bowels and I will write it in their heart, and I will be their God and they will be my people (Jer. 30:33; cf. 11: 4-5; 50:5 . . .).

Toward Universalism. To this interiorization of the Law corresponds also a universalism which is clearly affirmed after the exile. Already in Micheas the perspective had opened up (4:1-3) and the Deutero-Isaias proclaims it with all desirable clarity. The reign of God will extend over all men for the Servant of Yahweh will have received a mission of universal salvation (Is. 42:6) and all nations will put themselves on the march toward the new Jerusalem (Is. 60: 1-15; 68:19). There is question here of a general conversion, and consequently of a new triumph of the unchangeable Law, however transfigured it may be in this definitive order of things.

It is then on the expectation of a higher accomplishment of the Mosaic law, in the renewal of the Covenant, that the Old Testament comes to a close.

(b) *Other Laws: The Eternal Law*

God gave His Law only to the people of Israel; only this people then is entitled to call itself the people of God. But this does not mean that God limits His sovereign action to the beneficiaries of His law. Nothing that exists escapes His power; consequently, neither does anything escape the legislation of His wisdom. This legislative wisdom of God shines forth in the harmony which reigns in creation. Everything is good, very good, as it leaves the hands of God. Each creature and all together are good, and not only in themselves, but also in their development, their growth, their life (cf. Gen. 1). In the same way, the power of God and His activity as legislator are at work in the government of all the peoples of the earth. It is Yahweh who judges them, who imparts movements to them, who arouses their warlike passions to make of them the executioners of His designs, and who in His wisdom, rules over their enterprises and sets limits to their destructive work (Is. 47:6; Jer. 4:6; 5:10). Thus, without being expressly designated, another law appears in the great prophets, more universal than the Mosaic law and moreover implying it no doubt by special title. This is what will appear even more clearly from the post-exile idea of the wisdom of God such as it is described in the Sapiential Books (Prov. 8; Job 39; Wis. 7:8; Ecclus. 24), poetically personified, as a presentiment of the revelation of the Word. The wisdom of God governs the whole universe for all eternity: "I was with him forming all things" (Prov. 8:30). His kingdom extends from end to end of the earth and it rules all things sweetly (Wis. 8:1). This wisdom, legislator and sovereign law, is manifested especially in Israel in the gift of the Law, the Book of the Covenant (Ecclus. 24:7-22), but is not limited to it. It is this wisdom which communicates of its intelligence to everything which preserves a trace of it on the earth (Wis. 7:23, 27); it is therefore on the laws of this divine wisdom that all human legislation should be based under penalty of being fundamentally invalid: "By me kings reign and lawgivers decree just things, by me princes rule, and the mighty decree justice" (Prov. 8:15-16).

Human laws. And, at the same stroke, alongside the Mosaic Law and the eternal law of divine wisdom, the work of human legislators exists also, and is founded on God, for if the leaders of Israel did not hesitate to promulgate laws, these, by reason of the theocratic constitution of the People of God, always shared somewhat in the sacred character of the Law. Thus the legislation of all earthly authorities, even of pagan princes, is not only sanctioned by God but also attached to the eternal law.

2. NEW TESTAMENT

With the Christian revelation a new regime begins. According to the expression of St. Paul, the old, the "outworn" is rejected, a new life springs up in the heart of those who have heard and received the message of Jesus Christ, who have received Him and have thus become children of God. What is to be understood by the "old man" which the Christian has put off in order to put on Christ? Does the Law of the Covenant constitute a part of it? Is the Christian dispensed from observing it? And, if such is the case, would there no longer be any law to guide him in his new life, to regulate his actions and to propose to him an end to be attained?

(a) *The Gospel*

"Until John came, there were the Law and the Prophets, since then the Kingdom of God is being preached, and everyone is forcing his way into it" (Lk. 16:16). This is the first evangelical theme which seems really to include the Law, and even the message of the prophets in the service of the law, together with outdated elements of the Jewish religion. The old order is abolished, there is a new preaching, that of the Kingdom of God, at once eschatological and current, which should inspire the life of the disciple of Jesus. Moreover, Scribes and Pharisees are the most rigorously faithful of all the Jews in the integral observance of the law, and now Christ categorically opposes their justice to that which He wishes for His own (Mt. 5:20); then developing this opposition (Mt. 5:21-48), it is to the very words of the Law that he opposes His new precepts: "You have heard that it has been said . . . but I say to you. . . ."

The Law shall not pass. One might really understand it as a pure and simple rejection of the Law, if this whole passage were not introduced by an affirmation equally solemn about the permanence of the Law and the Prophets: "Do not think that I have come to destroy the Law or the Prophets. I have not come to destroy but to fulfill. For amen I say to you, till heaven and earth pass away, not one jot or one tittle shall be lost from the Law till all things have been accomplished" (Mt. 5:17-18). And the expression is still more emphatic in St. Luke: "Yet it is easier for heaven and earth to pass away than for one tittle of the Law to fail" (16:17); thus it seems to attach the Law to a higher will of God than all the rest of creation, to the immutable divine essence. Moreover, it is on this complete fidelity to the Law that the position of each one in the kingdom of heaven will be determined (Mt. 5:19), and consequently the justice which gives access to it cannot be opposed to that of the Law, even though it be that of the Scribes and the Pharisees.

The Law must be perfect. The key to this apparent difficulty is furnished by the explanation of our Lord: "I have not come to destroy, but to fulfill . . ." (Mt. 5:17) and by the motive, which He first explained, for His condemnation of the Scribes and the Pharisees: "You are they who declare themselves just in the sight of men, but

God knows your heart; for that which is exalted in the sight of men is an abomination before God" (Lk. 16:15). The justice of the Law is not bad, it is merely insufficient, but the Law is open to the complement which Christ brings and which corresponds to His secret expectation, to the expectation which the prophets had preached more and more clearly as the ancient economy unfolded itself. On the day of the Transfiguration the Law is there in the person of Moses, who with the prophets in the person of Elias, renders homage to Christ (Lk. 24:44-7).

The interiorization of the demands of the Law. There is question then of perfecting the Law itself, by surpassing it yet maintaining its proper line, by an interiorization of its demands in the heart of man ("God knows your hearts . . ."), touching the very intentions and giving at the same time such a vigor and such a radiance that its final ideal is the imitation of the perfection of the heavenly Father Himself (Mt. 5:48). Thus the fundamental commandment, of which all the others are only particular applications, is the double and unique commandment of love, love of God and of neighbor: "On these two commandments depend the whole Law and the Prophets" (Mt. 22:40).

Love efficacious and unlimited: "All that you wish men to do to you, even so do you also to them; for this is the Law and the Prophets" (Mt. 7:12); love which is worth more than holocausts and sacrifices, even though the latter are prescribed by the Law. This gradation, wisely recognized by the Scribe, makes him deserve to be heard when he says, as if it defined the justice of the kingdom: "Thou art not far from the kingdom of God" (Mk. 12:34). This is also what the attitude of Jesus before the problem of the young man or of the sabbath expresses (Lk. 5:33-6; Mk. 2:18—3:5; Mt. 9:14-17): "The sabbath is made for man, and not man for the sabbath . . ." (Mk. 2: 27), a fact which does not condemn the sabbath, but subordinates the external observance to the spirit which inspires it. The fault of the Pharisees consists precisely in being satisfied with the external work and consequently in stopping short of any surpassing of their justice; this is why their justice is condemned but not that of the Law, even though they materially coincide. The first should be surpassed and the second made perfect.

Thus the Law remains and is fulfilled, but this very accomplishment transfigures it so well that Christ can still say: "A new commandment I give you . . ." (Jn. 13:34), and St. John can compare the work of Christ with that of Moses in terms which seem to set them in opposition to each other: "For the Law was given through Moses; grace and truth came through Jesus Christ" (Jn. 1:17). But the new Law neither abrogates nor repeats the old, any more than the new Covenant (Mt. 25:28; Mk. 14:24) does not suppress, properly speaking, the old of which it is on the contrary the definitive renewal.

The new Law is at once mild and demanding: The counsels. Finally this new Law, this law renewed and promulgated notably in the sermon on the mount (Mt. 5:1-7, 27; Lk. 6:20-49), being a law of love, is for the disciple of Christ an easy yoke and a light burden (Mt. 11:30) in comparison with the excessive and fatiguing requirements of the ancient material observance.

Nevertheless, at the heart of the Law of Christ, we are invited by His own words to distinguish as it were two levels, that of the common obligation which is expressed in the commandments that are addressed to all those who hear Him, and that of the more special appeals which He makes personally to certain ones, those particularly who constitute His immediate company—the small group of disciples (Jn. 1:43; Mk. 1:17-20; Mk. 4:19-22) to whom it was given to know the mysteries of the kingdom of God (Lk. 8:10) and the rich young man whom Jesus loved (Mt. 10:17-21). The invitation to leave everything in order to follow him, certainly constitutes a particular vocation—Peter is very conscious of this (Mt. 19:27)—always moreover in view of the unique Kingdom of Heaven, but it seems that the complete conquest of it would be difficult for him who, thus called, did not accept the personal invitation of Christ (Mk. 10:22-23).

The eternal law. Quite as much as the Old Testament, the gospels —apart from the Law par excellence that Christ renews and perfects— recognizes also, even if a proper term does not appear to designate it, an eternal and universal law according to which God sovereignly reigns over the whole living order of creation. No sparrow falls to the earth without the consent of God and the very hairs of our heads are numbered (Mt. 10:29-31; Lk. 12:6-7); and it is in conformity with the divine plan that the lilies of the field are clothed and the birds of the air are nourished (Mt. 6:26-30; Lk. 12:24-28).

Human Laws. Likewise, human laws are not ignored. The fiscal legislation of the emperor deserves to be respected, it is necessary to pay the tribute, even though Caesar be a pagan: "Render therefore to Caesar the things that are Caesar's, and to God the things that are God's" (Mt. 22:21; Mk. 12:17; Lk. 20:25). And if Jesus pays only through compliance, this condescension shows sufficiently that the common run of human beings must fulfill this duty (Mt. 17:24-27). Moreover, the accusation attached to this theme by the Jews before Pilate, will hang fire (Lk. 23:2), and Jesus affirms his royalty in terms which in no way weaken the value of earthly royalties (Jn. 18:33-38).

The law and the Church. As for the legislative authority which Christ Himself conferred on His disciples, upon the Apostles and their successors, it is clearly implied at the same time as the power of order, whether with regard to St. Peter, after the famous "confession" of the latter (Mt. 16:18-19), or after the resurrection: "Feed my sheep" (Jn. 21:15-17), or whether with regard to the Twelve (Mt. 18:18; cf. 10:40; 28:20). In a more general way, the justice of Christ, whose new commandment is grace and truth and therefore a completely interior justice, perfects the old Law; but nevertheless describes itself in the community of the disciples as kingdom or vine. Thus is Christ's justice the object of a new alliance at once personal and collective. It supposes quite normally that the necessary organs for all social life begin with a legislative power.

(b) *The Acts of the Apostles*

The teaching of the Gospel on the Law and laws, accepted by the disciples and fully understood in the light of Pentecost, immediately inspired the acts of the first Christian community. Before hearing the echo of it in the Epistles of St. Paul, we must see it at work in Jerusalem.

The first martyr of the gospel, the deacon Stephen, was pursued and condemned for having "proffered certain words against the holy place and against the Law," for he had taught, it was said, that Jesus would change the institutions established by Moses (Acts 6:13-14). He himself terminates his discourse before the Sanhedrin with the pathetic reproach addressed to his accusers of not having observed the Law received from the angels and by the affirmation that the Most-High is not limited to the walls of the temple built by the hands of men (Acts 7:49-53).

Two or three years later, a decisive stage is marked by the conversion of Cornelius the Centurion with whom St. Peter lodged and ate, even though he was a Gentile; a sign from heaven revealed to the head of the apostles that the material observances of the law have had their day, and that now the Spirit has come (Acts 10:1-18). After several years, the apostolic Council of Jerusalem settles definitively the controversies raised with regard to the problem of the circumcision of the Gentiles and the observance of the Law of Moses, and it is St. Peter who makes the decision. The Holy Spirit has purified by faith the heart of the Gentiles as well as of the Jews, let there then be no further question of imposing upon the disciples "a yoke which neither our fathers nor we ourselves have been able to carry" (Acts 15).

The letter of the law is then rescinded, but spiritual obedience to the commandments of God is more necessary than ever. No human precept holds against this first necessity: "We must obey God rather than man" (Acts 5:29).

(c) *St. Paul*

St. Paul had been a Pharisee, reared in the study of the Law, zealous for its complete observance. More than any other apostle, he should know in himself the drama of the opposition between the Old Law and the message of Christ; his letters in fact often speak of it, particularly the Epistles to the Romans and to the Galatians, on the occasion of the great difficulties raised in the communities by the contrary attitudes of the Christians coming from Judaism and those who had been converted from paganism.

The curse of the Law. The law does not justify: such is the essential and categorical affirmation which St. Paul never tires of repeating (Rom. 2:16; 3:5; 3:20; 4:16; Gal. 2:21; 3:11, etc.); justification is the work only of grace and of faith. Also it seems illusory that the law itself should be the cause of internal disorder and of sin: "Now the sting of death is sin and the power of sin is the law" (I Cor. 15:56), and we can even speak of the "curse of the Law" (Gal. 3:13), "an act cancelling the decree against us, which was hostile to us. Indeed, it has taken it completely away, nailing it to the cross" (Col. 2:14). The Law is the old regime of the letter, opposed by the new regime of the Spirit (Rom. 7:6).

The Law is holy. Still it was by a singular privilege that the Jews received the Mosaic Law, in the same manner as they received the adoption, the Covenant, the Patriarchs, etc. (Rom. 9:4); and the interior man, who lives according to "law of the mind" (Rom. 7:23), perfects himself in the Law of God (7:22); likewise the Gentiles who have not received the Law, have nevertheless in their heart a law of their own, in virtue of which they spontaneously fulfill the prescriptions of the Law. Is it therefore true without doubt that the Law is good, in spite of its familiar contacts with sin?

Yes, the Law is good, and St. Paul also knows how to proclaim it. It is not sin (Rom. 7:7); it is holy, just, good (7:12), spiritual (7:14); it is from God (7:22). It is a lofty teaching for him who receives it and if the Jews glorify it vainly, that does not detract in any way from the praise which St. Paul makes of the light which it diffuses on those who know it (Rom. 2:17-20). Moreover the expression "those who are under the Law" is laudatory, at least by contrast with the "nations without the law" (I Cor. 9:20-21).

It seems that the Law justifies those who observe it integrally, if not those who are content merely to receive it (Rom. 2:13), and St. Paul cites Lev. 18:5: "The man who does that justice which is of the Law, shall live by it" (Rom. 10:5; Gal. 3:12)—this "justice of my own which is from the Law" (Phil. 3:9), justice of works, which moreover is vain because it is impossible.

It is impossible to fulfill the Law. It is here in fact that the drama of the Law resides: it is impossible to fulfill it. For if there is in man the "law of the mind," it is not the latter which triumphs in him, but another law which chains it to the Law of sin, which is in his members (Rom. 7:23)—unregulated desire which insures the reign of sin and makes him commit it, even when he would prefer to obey the Law: "Your wish is within my power, but I do not find the strength to accomplish what is good" (Rom. 7:18).

The providential mission of the Law. Inevitable failure of the Law; but this failure is also in the intention of God, the legislator, and consequently corresponds, paradoxically, to the end of the Law! For the Law is a new obligation imposed on man without the new assistance which would be necessary in order that he might observe it; it therefore reveals to him his weakness as a sinner. Finally, man by having taken occasion to sin knowingly takes also occasion to make an appeal to Him who alone can justify the sinner: "Now the Law intervened that the offense might abound" (Rom. 5:20; 7:7-11); and thus it is that it finally leads to Christ, in the faith in which every man, Jew or Gentile finds the justice of God (i.e. conferred by God) (Rom. 10:3), for whom the Law will have prepared humanity, ". . . therefore the Law has been our tutor unto Christ that we might be justified by faith" (Gal. 3:24).

We are delivered by the Law. Although the Law is good in itself, we are simultaneously freed from sin and the Law by Christ. Dead to sin and dead to the Law through the body of Christ crucified (Rom. 7:4-6), we have reached our majority and become heirs in Christ who has conferred upon us adoption and consequently delivered us from the authority of tutors and regents, from servitude under the rudiments of the world, i.e. from the Law (Gal. 4:1-5). And since this adoption is the sending into our hearts of the Spirit of the Son, St. Paul adds: "But if you are led by the Spirit, you are not under the Law . . . Against such things (of the Spirit) there is no Law" (Gal. 5:18, 24).

The genuine opposition between the Law and the regime of Christ. There is then a real opposition between the old Law and the regime of Christ, but an opposition that can be defined as that of the imperfect to the perfect, and which is resolved in the aspiration which the kingdom of the faith brings to the regime of the Law, in conformity with the hidden demands of the latter, even though in contradiction with its letter which is definitively surpassed: "For Christ is the consummation of the Law unto justice for everyone who believes" (Rom. 10:4). While leading to Christ, the Law prepared itself for its own disappearance, which is its being surpassed: "For I through the Law have died to the Law that I may live to God" (Gal. 2:19). And the Epistle to the Hebrews underlines this preparation of Christ by positing the principle that everything in the old Law was a figure of the Christ to come. The Law was the shadow of future goods (Heb. 10:1).

Love, spirit of the Law. St. Paul also only apparently contradicts himself when he affirms by means of the faith, that we do not destroy the Law but strengthen it (Rom. 3:31) or again, that the justice of the Law is fulfilled in us who walk not according to the flesh, but according to the spirit (Rom. 8:4). For the spirit of the Law is love; on this ground it subsists completely and St. Paul recalls it again to his correspondents: "By charity serve one another. For the whole Law is fulfilled in one word: Thou shalt love thy neighbor as thyself" (Gal. 5:13-14). Law of love, secretly contained in the old letter and revealed by Christ, in such wise that it also could be called the "law of Christ" (Gal. 6:2).

No more than our Lord in the Gospel, does the teaching of St. Paul ignore the fact that alongside the Law of God under its ancient form and then under its more spiritual form, there exist other laws, other commandments, which are addressed to men, even to the faithful of Christ, to the disciples of the law of love, and are sealed on their very consciences.

The eternal Law. That the whole universe of creatures, and not only man, is under the government of God, is an idea evidently underlying the impressive outline which the Apostle traces of the kingdom of Christ, delegated in some way to the exercise of this universal government, and so a contributor, if one can say so, to the infinite legislative power of God: ". . . to reestablish all things in Christ, both those in the heavens and those on the earth" (Eph. 1:10; cf. Col. 1:15-20).

The law of the Church. But alongside the eternal law of God, or more exactly, under the law, men themselves participate in the legislative power. And first within the Church of Christ, St. Paul points out, among different charisms which he enumerates, the existence of the charism of ruling (I Cor. 12:18) or the gift of governing (Rom. 12:8)—a special grace which comes from Christ, for it is He who has appointed the pastors and the doctors (Eph. 4:11). But the charisms are certain exceptional gifts which might not suffice to found a regularly organized hierarchy. But the latter also exists, moreover it is often animated by the charisms and is superior to them since it controls their origin and exercise (I Cor. 12:14). The Epistles called pastoral are entirely consecrated to the definitions of these rights and also the duties of these pastors who particularly have to legislate for the spiritual welfare of those confided to their care: "Command and teach these things . . ." (I Tim. 4:11). St. Paul himself gives the example. He legislates with authority, not only through reminding them of the commandments of Jesus Christ, but by determining henceforth what will be the attitude of the Church to which he speaks in such or such a domain where the Lord had Himself not prescribed anything (cf. e.g. II Tim. 5:2-16: legislation concerning widows); he speaks of the "instructions which I have given you" (I Cor. 11:2). These instructions he often grounds on the general custom of the Church which has the value of a holy rule: "But if anyone is disposed to be contentious—we have no such custom, neither have the churches of God" (I Cor. 11:16; cf. 14-33); but after all, the legislative power rests on a mission received from Christ: the commandments of the Apostles are then the commandments of the Lord (I Cor. 14:37); he is fully aware of that and will not hesitate to penalize rigorously the failure to carry them out (I Cor. 4:21; II Cor. 10:5-11).

Civil laws. In the state itself, there exists an authentic legislative power, authentic because it also comes from God: "For there exists no authority except from God and those who exist have been appointed by God" (Rom. 13:1) in order to be ministers of God for the benefit of their subjects. These, therefore, for their own good and through obedience to God himself, obey the magistrates, not only because of the sword which they brandish even as ministers of God, but also "for conscience sake" (Rom. 13:5); the fiscal law itself deserves this respect, for those who promulgate it are "ministers of God" (Rom. 13:6-7). The Christian, a good citizen, should therefore obey the authorities (Tit. 3:1) and pray for them, "for kings and for all in high positions" (I Tim. 2:2), i.e. in actual fact for the emperor Nero who at that time launched the persecution in which St. Paul was to find martyrdom. And St. Peter, also recognizing the divine origin of all power in it, echoes this teaching: "Be subject to every human creature for God's sake, whether to the king as supreme, or to governors as sent through him . . ." (I Pet. 2:13-14).

II. The Contribution of Ancient Thought

The Christian of the first centuries, nourished by Holy Scripture, saw also in the "Law" the work of Moses. It was, in fact, the gift of God to His people, transfigured by the spiritual message of the Messias, and summed up in the basic commandment of love. But, like Holy Scripture itself, he did not ignore other uses of the word "Law" which revelation placed in more or less direct and definite relation to the Law of God.

The Christian life developed in the historical milieu of the pagan Roman empire, which had already a tradition of broad and varied thought on this matter. No doubt the pagans were unaware even of the existence of the Law of Moses; they gave little thought to the possibility of a law of practical use given by a God properly so called to humanity or to a particular group of men. But they had laws, they had at length and profoundly meditated on the idea of law, and, at least in principle, the laws were held in great respect. Very quickly Christian thinkers, often themselves formed in a completely pagan atmosphere, were led to experience the value of the philosophy of laws which were the product of Greco-Roman thought and, quite spontaneously, to assimilate the best of it; they introduced the major part of it into their own synthesis, except that they modified the perspectives and sometimes even the spirit of the work of their predecessors.

Two classes of thinkers raised the problem of laws: philosophers, mostly Greek, and jurists, all Roman.

(a) *The Philosophers*

Among the philosophers may be cited Heraclitus who taught the existence of a reason immanent in the world, a sort of law which governs it—Logos-God, a secret harmony resulting from the opposition of contraries, a basis on which all human laws must rest; but this organizing thought, which permeates the universe is without consciousness of its own intelligence.

The Stoics. The Stoics, especially, exploited these ideas and spread them throughout the world in which Revelation had been announced. From Zeno to Marcus Aurelius, passing through Epictetus and Cicero, with many variations, the Stoic School asserted that the world is penetrated by an impersonal reason, a common law for the common nature, readily called Logos, which is not the efficient cause or the external model of the world, but the internal rule. All that exists, and primarily the universe taken as a whole, is according to this conception highly reasonable. For man, who is free by autonomous reason, morality consists then in regulating his behavior according to the reasonable demands of nature. To follow nature is the last word in wisdom, and it would be folly to expect a line of conduct from any god external to the universe and to man, because this would be something supernatural; nature, which is reason, alone counts.

The Stoics were very far from Christian thought. But the latter strong in its power of assimilation, and very much alive, knew how to seek its own good. It retained the necessary subordination of human laws and of the individual conscience to the superior rule of a reasonable nature, it extended its radiation through all the beings of the entire universe—for it seemed to recognize in the Logos of the Stoics a work of expectation, a presentiment of the revelation of the divine wisdom of the Word (Logos) to which is attributed the Law dictated by God to the universe which He created. And on the other hand, between this eternal Law of God and the free determinations of the human conscience is there not, in the depths of this conscience a mysterious command, an expression in us of the law of God, the law of those who did not have any law and to which St. Paul made allusion apropos of the pagans (Rom. 2:14)? The Stoics were right in speaking of a reason internal to the world; their error, largely corrected by Christian thought, was in being content with it alone and in omitting from it any connection with the superior divine Law.

In restoring this connection, Christian thought, wholly impregnated with faith in God the Creator, and in His Son made man for us, was able, without abandoning any of the authentic riches discovered by the Stoics, to make of virtue not a resigned submission to a blind though reasonable natural order, but an ardent conformity to the personal thought of the God of love. It made of the natural law not merely the echo in us of the order of the world, but an intimate decree of the benevolent providence of the Father. At the same time, the supernatural gift made first to the chosen people, then to the universe through Christ, this gift of the divine law, namely the Mosaic Law, and the evangelical Law is perfectly possible if it pleases God to make it and to harmonize it with the eternal law and the natural law which He has placed in us.

(b) *The Jurists*

With often important distinctions, the Roman jurists, deeply affected by Stoic doctrines, had been led to admit, beyond "civil" law (that which is given for each people, its legislatures freely established) the existence of a zone of law much more stable, more necessary, common to all the peoples of the earth, which is no longer the law of this or that state, but the common human law, which they call "jus gentium," "the law of nations," i.e., of all men to whatever nation they may belong, a law which is most natural, most purely reasonable (since reason is common to all men and to them alone). Finally, a good number of the jurists admitted a still larger zone of law, the "jus naturale" which Ulpian, one of the most distinguished of them, defined as "that which nature has taught to all animals"—a law entirely unchangeable, universal, the most profound necessity in every living being.

In these distinctions, Christian thinkers were able to find the elements for an hierarchical organization of the different kinds of laws. St. Isidore of Seville (about 560–636) transmitted to the scholars of the Middle Ages the materials worked up by the Roman jurists, not without having somewhat retouched them; particularly, he abandoned the conception of a law common to men and animals.

Elaboration of the treatise on law. Christian thought, nourished above all on Scripture, never forgets that the Law for men is, first of all, the Decalogue and the great commandment of love. But, because it holds on to this supreme truth, it does not fear to assume everything that human nature has been able to discover of truth, except that it purifies and completes the partial conquest of the pagan world. In the matter of laws, to submit to the light by which the revealed Law clarifies our Christian conscience, is not to deprive ourselves of rules of action which natural reason or social authorities dictate to us, but rather to subordinate these rules of action to their proper place. This implies the discovery and explanation of the harmonious hierarchy of the different kinds of law.

To this task the great masters of mediaeval scholasticism set themselves. There are few treatises which they made as great an effort to synthesize. Courageously they gathered together the divers materials supplied by the Roman jurists and statesmen, the Greek philosophers, the depositaries of the Judeo-Christian revelation, and built up an imposing structure in which each of the classes of law, according to its proper nature and its more or less imperious demands with regard to the human conscience, comes to find its proper place in correct relation to all others.

Moreover, there is no question in such a treatise on laws of furnishing a complete documentation on the content of the laws themselves. It is apropos of each of the particular domains of the moral activity of man that such research must be made. At best, the problem was to make manifest to the moral conscience, desirous of acting well, i.e. of tending toward the true beatitude of the sons of God, the sources of the light from which it must seek to be enlightened in its movements and informed in its decisions in order that they might be correct and meritorious of this beatitude. And since these sources are divers—Scripture itself bears witness—one of the most urgent questions to which these great treatises must reply is that of the mode, more or less direct, according to which each one nourishes himself with the supreme light that is called the eternal light.

III. The General Notion of Law

A multiplicity of laws is imposed on our attention and calls for our respect. These are quite different from one another, and yet all are designated by the same term "law." The language here indicates to us that there exists among them a relationship sufficiently close so that we can risk a general definition of "law," which would be valid respectively for each species.

We shall adopt the following classical definition, except that we explain it and justify it point by point: "law is an ordinance of reason established and promulgated for the common good by whoever is in charge of the community."

1. LAW IS AN ORDINANCE OF REASON

It might seem at first sight that law springs more from the will than from reason. Does not making laws involve command, and so an act of the will compelling the will of the subject to submit? There is no question of denying the voluntary aspect of every law, but it is not the will which is the primary characteristic of man as a moral being in the midst of other creatures; it is reason which permits us, created as we are in the image of God, to go out in some way from ourselves, to judge our action in the light of great principles, to reject or to give in to the solicitations which are offered to us, to make our own life conformable or not to the appeal of beatitude in us, in short, to be free and responsible for ourselves.

Law is precisely such a dictate of reason capable of directing our acts, of regulating and measuring them in order that they may be meritorious for beatitude. There is in fact a question of proportioning certain actions to a result to be attained, of discriminating among different means which claim to lead to this end. There is in this a task of comparison, of adjustment, of ordering, which is exclusively the work of reason; for reason alone can simultaneously lay hold of several objects, isolate what they have in common and verify their relations.

Insufficiency of Will

The will which is as it were the weight of reason, is an inclination in us which by a single impulse inclines to a good known by reason; but by itself alone it would be only a blind power and so inert, susceptible of being used for all ends, the best and the worst. To attribute to it the legislative work is to set up caprice as a principle, even though there be a question of a "general will;" or a fortiori if it is a question of the dream of a leader; and instinct alone, being inclined toward a particular sensible good without being capable of dominating or judging it, has no greater value. Moreover, what could the sole will of a legislator do, even supposing that it could be exercised independently of his reason? The will of the subject, like every human will, cannot be directly bent by anybody, unless it be God, its author. Man is free. He can be constrained in his body, totally perturbed in his sensibility by suffering or even by fear. Such means of violence can more or less completely paralyze in him, his spiritual faculties—but no one can ever, contrary to his choice, obtain from the exterior the consent of his will which belongs to him alone. This would be a contradiction in terms. It is only by way of reason that he can determine his deliberate and free consent.

Therefore from reason, which conceives it, the law receives its value as a guide of human action, and when it is said that the law is a command (of reason), we first understand by this that it is an ordering, a rational ordering, a creator of harmony and of justice in the action in which the good will would not suffice, unless there had previously been a correct judgment and so a higher light. This is what there was of truth in the intellectualist morality of Socrates and Plato or in the Stoic exaltation of universal reason.

The Role of the Will in the Practical Reason

There is no intention of saying by this that the will has nothing to do in the formation and the application of law. Law is not a "disinterested" proposition of an intellect which would be satisfied to be right; it is not the work of a speculative mind, but of the "practical reason." The legislator does not announce what is, but what ought to be. His object is truth—and this is why he does a work of reason—but the truth of action. The truth is that by it his will is committed, just as that of the subject to whom he is speaking; there is no question of pure thought, but of engaged, executive and efficacious thought. Consequently, in its whole enterprise the reason of the legislator must be inspired, dominated by concern for the good toward which he must effectively direct the subjects of law. It must be true, if it is going to be just. It must be in some way intimately penetrated, saturated, borne by the love of the good, in other words, by the moral virtue of which this good is the object. One must oneself be just, must *love* justice, in order to *judge* and ordain in matters of justice.

Bound to the principle of the law, the will is also bound to its term, i.e. in its application. For the law is not merely a proposition which is made to a subject, it is not a counsel which is suggested to him or a prayer which is addressed to him, still less an announcement of a speculative truth which is presented to him, it is an *order,* in the imperative sense of the term this time, which is imposed upon him. It is an *obligation* for him.

Obligation and Constraint

What shall we say? We must carefully distinguish between obligation and constraint. Constraint is a pressure of the physical order which is exercised without any appeal to the liberty of the subject and under which he is passive; he submits to it, consequently, even though this constraint releases in him some movement. It is still more true to say that he is moved rather than that he moves himself. On the contrary, obligation is characteristic of reasonable beings whose will cannot be compelled from the exterior, but who because they are intelligent and because it is necessary for them, can be placed by their superior in a situation to recognize and to realize the good for which they are made, to act in a manner that their superior by his law has determined and made known.

Obligation and Liberty

This presupposes that the subject, just as the legislator, has love for the good. In this situation, he is obliged—and not constrained—by the very activity of his will and his practical reason to prolong in some way the will and practical reason of his superior. Thus obliged, he remains basically free and autonomous, since the intimation of the superior has only helped him to explain and determine his deep desire for the good and the understanding which he has of it.

Law Is Only for Reasonable Beings

This means that strictly speaking there are no laws for animals who do not know and do not will their good except by a knowledge and a love that is sensible, who are incapable of being inwardly impressed by the setting up of a relationship between means and end, incapable of being obliged. And likewise we do not legislate for idiots, insane people, or for all those who seem to have lost the light of practical reason. Likewise he escapes the domination of law as a work of reason who through the voluntary blindness in which sin plunges its author places himself to that degree among the animals and the demented.

He, on the contrary, who loves the good and who makes full and good use of his reason, deserves the benefit of law—benefit, since law comes to enrich his practical reason in the service of the good which he loves and which he wants to realize, since it comes to help him accomplish it by instructing him in his duty, i.e., in his profound and personal necessities which, left to himself, he could not fully make clear. To welcome laws and to feel oneself obligated is a sign of nobility; it requires intelligence and love of the good, it is a guarantee of human development and of happiness, since through the more informed mind of the ruler the subject is enriched and so better disposed for the happiness which the ruler and the subject both have in view.

It is understood that we have here an ideal which not every law measures up to, but that is the fault of the legislator or the subject. It remains true that, of itself, law is the great light of moral life, the high and indispensable directive of the realization of a good act.

Generality of Law; Its Unifying Action

Finally we observe that law is *general,* for otherwise we would speak of precept [1] or of a particular order. When one legislates it is for a group of analogous cases and not for a determined action which will be performed only once. It even seems that the majesty of the law and the respect that we have for it should follow this condition, namely, that one should obey more readily a rule of considerable extension than an order which is valid only for certain isolated cases. It is because as spiritual beings, we have, more or less explicitly, but always really, the desire of acting only with the highest motives, and of putting the greatest possible unity into our whole life. But we are really forced to particularize each of

---

[1] In current language, "precepts" will also be often understood not as certain particular orders but different articles in which a true law is organized. It is thus that here even we do not scruple to speak for example of "diverse precepts" of the natural law.

our actions according to the multitude of concrete circumstances which determine it and which are never absolutely the same; thus we would be in some fashion dispersed, scattered in our acts, if we did not have precisely these very general directives which are laws valid for all cases which, without being absolutely identical, have a sufficiently close relationship to one another; thus man subject to laws can, by attaching himself to them, give to very particular actions all the breadth of which they would be deprived by themselves; thus he can, more and more closely, place in the unfolding of his life a unity which, at its best, is achieved in the convergence of all his enterprises toward his Sovereign Good, in the light of the highest law, the law of love of which Christ Himself is the author.

2. IN VIEW OF THE COMMON WELFARE

Law is defined as the rational rule for human acts. And since activity properly human, i.e., reasonable, always tends toward a conscious and willed result, toward an end, we must also say what the end in question is in order to know exactly what law is. It is understood that each particular law has its particular end, according to the special domain of human activity which it has a mission to put in order; but even in a general study of law, there is doubtless place for important explanations of the end of all law.

Law and Beatitude

Now the activity of man is explained definitively only by the search for a supreme good, and a final end, that which satisfies all the needs of man conformably to his spiritual nature; and so long as man has not attained this end, he remains restless and his restlessness inclines him toward new goods; he will find peace and happiness only in the supreme act which will place him in possession of the Sovereign Good. If such is the end which directly or indirectly arouses all human activity, it is also necessary that every law tend toward it directly or indirectly under penalty of badly fulfilling its role of rule, of *disordering* the activity which it should rather *order* toward the true end. Thus beatitude is the end of all authentic law.

Beatitude and Hierarchy of Laws

Consequently, without misunderstanding the legitimacy of laws which do not claim to tend toward it except indirectly—as is the case, for example, with civil laws with respect to supernatural beatitude—we must admit that that one deserves more the name of law in which the definition is more perfectly realized, which has directly for its end this supreme conquest of the divine good. *The law par excellence, is evidently the law of Christ.* This law is also the one which possesses the greatest imperative value, which engenders the most exacting obligation, an obligation really absolute, since it orders directly toward what is the end pure and simple of our activity, corresponding to what there is deepest in us and most divine in the image of God which we are.

To this law which is made for us, all other laws are subordinated and placed in hierarchical order according as they rule more or less directly activity concerning the beatitude to be acquired; the different kinds of law are not then in any sense juxtaposed and truly independent, but organized into a system. This system comprises some very different levels (what apparent relation is there between our civil laws and the Law of Sinai?), but one and the same intention gives to them deep unity and explains the relations which exist necessarily among them.

Law and the Common Good

But this good, which the law has for its end and which in the last analysis is the good of perfect beatitude, is a *common good.* Language apprises us of it, for it is not said that anyone makes a *law* when he addresses an order to a particular person, even when this order is to regulate a large part of his activity and so possesses the characteristic of generality which is indispensable to the law though insufficient to define it; the Law of Sinai was not given to Moses for himself alone, but for the people of Israel, the Law of Christ was confided to the apostles, but in order to be addressed to the universal Church, the Body of Christ, to innumerable members, and we feel that no one uses strict language when he says "I am a law unto myself . . ."

It is because isolated man is contrary to nature and, to speak truly, exists nowhere; for human nature is a social nature. This means that each man can be considered as a member of a body in which he finds the conditions for a development, and outside of which he is mutilated in the most natural demands of his being. For the moment, the exact determination of these required societies through which each individual man becomes fully himself matters little; it is a very general fact that the a-social individual cannot remain outside the conditions of humanity. Thus the good of man is necessarily a *common* good, and that the ordinances of reason which govern his activity, that is to say laws, necessarily have this common good for their end.

Law and Society

Thus law is the rule of integration for individuals in society, of parts within a whole, in which these parts moreover find their personal fulfilment, *their* greater good. The common good, though by definition it can exist only in society and as a good of society, is not however external to the persons who compose it; it does not exist outside of these persons who, as spiritual beings capable of interiorizing the common good in what is best in them, are the real beneficiaries of the social life to which they belong. Thus there is in the social nature of man a need for overcoming himself in order that he may find himself finally enlarged by his participating in a common life; and it is for that reason that the rules of human action are not certain particular orders, but laws. What appears in them at first sight is the sacrifice that they demand of each one's isolation, but more profoundly we must also see in them, for those who conform themselves to them, the guarantee of a full human development of which the isolated individual is radically incapable. It would not be otherwise unless the law tended toward a false common good, toward the private good of the ruler, who is then a tyrant, or of a group of profiteers to the detriment of the real good of the social body and its members; but such a law would no longer be a law since it would have lost the reason for its existence—the tendency toward the common welfare.

Law and Subordinate Rules of Action

Since it is the law which establishes in moral life the fundamental order toward the common good, and so its essential rectitude, every other possible rule will have to attach itself to law, be inspired by it, be regulated by it in order to be conformed to the demands of the best human good. This will have to be the case, for example, of regulations drawn up by the industrialist in his industry, of statutes dictated for a welfare association, of commands given by a father to his children, even of decisions which an individual makes for himself.

Law and "Perfect" Society

These examples indicate moreover that not every common good confers the qualifications of "law" upon the rational rule which ordains to it. We do not ordinarily speak of law except with regard to those societies whose common good corresponds to the profound needs of human nature and which can, for this reason, be considered wholly complete and perfect. It is only by using loose language that we speak of laws interior to a family or a factory, or even a municipality, even though the custom or the regulation, or the command which one has in mind is to regulate for a long time the diverse activities of a rather large number of persons. In order to find the "perfect" common good, the "perfect" society, and therefore also law in the proper sense, we must rise to that political institution which is today the state, tomorrow perhaps humanity, or to that most perfect society which is the Church.

We have admitted that all of moral life is regulated by laws; we know now what that means. All of moral life is in a certain sense *social;* not that there is not also an individual morality and, alongside it, a morality properly called social. But all human actions, even the most private, are acts of persons who by nature are members of societies and cannot arrive elsewhere than at their final end; even the most personal activities will therefore be absolutely correct only if they have been measured, at least indirectly by the common welfare. This is why for these activities the rules are laws; and it is the reason, too, whatever may be the particular virtue directly involved in a given act: fortitude, humility, temperance, etc., why another virtue will always have its word to say, the one precisely which has for its object the common good—the justice called general or social, but which is also called *legal,* because to incline the will of the just man to serve the common good or to incline it to confirm itself to law means the same thing.

3. ESTABLISHED BY WHOEVER IS IN CHARGE OF THE COMMUNITY

We know now what a law is: a reasonable rule for our moral life in view of our greater good, which is a common good. It remains for us to find out who is qualified to make laws, in order to give with authority directives to our conscience in quest of beatitude. This is the hot problem of authority, of its foundation, of its limits. Moreover, there is no question of resolving here all the problems raised by political authority, but of defining all legislative authority in the general way in which we have defined law and the common good.

Definition of Authority

Not every man is in a position to make laws. That is evident. The concern for the good of our neighbor and for the common good can impel each one of us to give good advice, i.e., positive encouragement, but there is no bond in it which obliges the interested party, whether individual or community.

Since there is an obligation of conscience from the moment and in the exact measure in which there is a necessary bond between prescribed acts and the common good—a bond which is defined by law—, since therefore it is from the demands of the common good that obligation flows, it is also from the common good that authority flows; those who are qualified to define the common good, to recognize the conditions of it, to measure its demands, are also qualified to make laws. We might define legislative authority—and at the same time authority in general—as follows: "competency in view of the common good."

Can we also determine who is the holder of this authority? No one person as such, especially not one in deliberate opposition to the community as a whole, but, given the great diversity of kinds of laws, all further explanation could only emphasize the great diversity among the types of legislative authorities.

The Legislative Authority of God

The first one who is competent to provide wisely for our common good, and therefore to promulgate, is God. In fact God is our cause, as he is the cause of everything that exists outside Himself, the cause particularly of our spiritual soul which He created in His own image, making persons of us in the midst of a universe of material creatures. These creatures and we, ourselves, are not abandoned by God after creation; for, being entirely dependent on Him, we would cease to exist if we were not at every moment supported by Him. And neither would we act if He did not constantly give us our action and therefore also rules for this action, that is to say, laws according to which we are governed by Him, but also delivered to our autonomous government of free and reasonable creatures. God is our first legislator, because as Creator, it is He who not only knows, but also determines our common good or rather our participation in the common good of the universe, which is no other than Himself.

These divine laws which order us with sovereign competency to our good, to our beatitude, are called "eternal law," "natural law," "divine positive laws"—distinctions with which Holy Scripture has already acquainted us, even though it may have been under other names, but which are only graduated expressions of the same divine plan progressively revealed.

The Secondary Legislative Authorities

This legislative authority of God over us is absolute because He is our author. But though absolute, it is not exclusive, for if God is not a stranger to anything which is and which moves toward a greater perfection, He has nevertheless willed to associate with Himself collaborators who work, under His movement and under His direction, at the task of their development and that of the universe. This is true to a certain extent of every creature, for every creature has its own action, but especially true of the rational creature. The rational creature then, under the light of the divine laws, must order itself to its good, and order itself toward it socially, since its nature is social and since its good is a *common good;* human society is obliged to give itself laws, to have over itself legislative authority measured by divine legislation. Here is the solid foundation of authority. It imposes itself on our conscience in the commands which it gives because they set up an order toward the common good, because it legislates for the common good and in this exact measure, because the social authority of the community over us is an intimate personal need of the social human nature in each of us.

What in short confers on this authority its obligatory value, what even gives to its laws a quasi-sacred character when they tend toward the common good, is that it forms a part of the plan of God, of the order thought out, willed and realized in creatures by God, the sole sovereign authority. Human legislative authority is therefore of divine right, because God Himself has allowed man-in-society to collaborate in the fulfilment of His plan. St. Paul has informed us of it: "All power comes from God."

The Holder of Legislative Authority

But the question immediately arises: who in the community will exercise this authority; who will dictate the law? That depends first of all on what human society we have in mind; there are some in which the competency with regard to the common good, and consequently the legislative authority, pertains to certain persons by a designation which does not depend on human liberty, or at least must be attributed according to rules not subject to this liberty and leaving to it only the choice of a titulary or titularies. In the Church of Christ, the Papacy is of divine institution, the Sacred College elects the Pope—, in the family the paternal power (which moreover is not properly legislative) corresponds to a demand of nature, the wife chooses freely the holder of it, but it is imposed on the children—, inversely, Scripture tells us how the Israelites chose a monarchical regime, but they demanded of God to make them the beneficiaries of it (I Kgs. 8, 9: 15-17; 16:1, 12-13).

. . . in the State

In political society except for the case of Saul and David, the indetermination is much greater. No man has of himself a superiority which permits him to dictate the conduct of his neighbor, by obliging him in conscience or by fixing with authority what the common good is, for the common good by definition is not the good of each individual as such, but only of all individuals as an associated body. It is then the community, which alone is naturally the depositary of authority over itself, which most naturally possesses the power to make laws in keeping with the divine laws, to dictate to its members certain common rules of conduct in view of the common welfare and, even if indirectly, in view of beatitude.

But that does not allow us to conclude that a democratic regime follows of natural right! For the question is not settled just through knowing how the community will exercise this legislative authority; it can do it itself, it can put it in the hands of representatives to whom it can confide itself entirely or whose competency it can, on the contrary, more or less determine. All this lies in the free area of political opportunities. What must always remain inviolate is the major principle that he alone who has charge of the community, hence, of the higher good of each of those on whom he then imposes these laws with authority, is qualified to make laws. Every other legislator would be no less than a tyrant.

4. . . . AND PROMULGATED

When the legislator, whoever he may be, has estimated the needs of the common good and determined the conduct which the community will have to observe in order to attain it, conformable to its nature and its possibilities, when he has thus proclaimed the rational order which is law, the latter is perfect; it is the constituted rule, but it does not begin to play its role so long as it has not been communicated to the members of the community (Church, nation, etc.). In the same way the plan which the artisan works out to organize his enterprise is already perfect as a plan as soon as it is conceived in the mind of its author, but it is not efficacious until it is applied to his tools and raw materials by the movements to which he subjects them, by the transformations which he will cause them to undergo.

But there is yet a considerable difference; it is that the legislator does not address himself to inert matter, but to living, reasonable beings; neither do we properly speak of motion, but of promulgation; [2] to promulgate a law is to bring it to the knowledge of those who are bound to observe it, who will not be moved by it before having received it into their minds, before having in some fashion relived in their mind the deliberation, the judgment, the decision of their ruler in the fullest measure possible, before having, in a word, assimilated the law, made it their own, accepted its obligation, but as reasonable beings, so that finally their acts which, though bearing the imprint of docility, will nonetheless be wholly personal. Here we verify once again that law is, of itself, an instructor made to raise up those who receive it to the level of enlightened reason and upright will, to the level of the morality of the legislator.

We have thus verified the proposed definition: "Law is an ordinance of reason in view of the common good, established and promulgated by him who is in charge of the community"; without ever forgetting that, in order to be fully correct on the plane on which we are of Christian morality, i.e. of the only complete moral-

----

[2] The term *promulgation,* as employed here, i.e. in the sense of the moralists, corresponds to what in constitutional law is called the *publication* of laws and not to what is there called *promulgation* (by the head of the state) which succeeds in setting up a law by giving it its executory character, but does not yet render it applicable.

ity, this definition has to be taken in the broadest acceptation of each one of its terms.

Law, Promotor of Virtue

Law is then—it is thus that it was presented to us from the first—the rule of action which, closely or from afar, leads us to beatitude, the rule of life ultimately beatifying, i.e. the full Christian life. Now we know that such acts, such a life, presuppose that we possess, on the level of the deepest dispositions within us, the whole cortege of beautiful and solid virtues, acquired and infused. It is on this condition that the moral life is assured, spontaneous and joyful. Consequently, the acts whose regulation is a function of law are not only acts good in themselves, but also acts normally emanating from a similar center of virtue, from virtuous acts, which amounts to saying that law is made to conduct us to virtue, however astonishing that may at first seem if we think only of human laws, forgetting that the common political good which they serve is itself a human good ultimately ordered to the eternal beatitude of the citizens.

How can law go as far as such a result?

5. MEANS OF ACTION FOR LAW

Affirmative and Negative Laws

We can say that law acts, even though in itself it is only a rational formula; for it is a formula of action, a commandment, a commandment to do the good acts or to abstain from the bad ones which it defines. It is a prescription and an interdiction, which at bottom are the same thing, corresponding to a single intention; for all moral development takes place between these two terms, the good and the bad. To choose the good is to withdraw from the bad; to neglect the good is to slip toward the bad, and the interdiction might also be analyzed into a prescription under a negative form.

Permissive Laws

It also happens that the law may permit one only to do this or not to do that; but we must not be deceived by that. These laws, called "permissive," are not of an essentially different type than the preceding ones; to permit entails no obligation for the beneficiaries of the permission. The case is not the same for the third parties

who are the ones really obligated by the law, obligated to not find
it evil that one profit by the permission, nor for judges and holders
of power who are obliged not to disturb but to protect the exercise
of the liberty granted.

But in prescribing and interdicting, does law attain the *virtuous*
result which should be its normal goal? Yes, no doubt, but differently for different categories of law:

Interior and Exterior Laws

There are laws for which the virtuous rectitude of the acts which
they govern is directly possible. These laws act from the interior
and are, by definition, in correspondence with a movement of the
will, with an effective inclination of their subjects in the direction
which they prescribe, toward the good which they help to accomplish. This is the normal case of the natural law which commands
only acts toward which nature herself inclines, and the evangelical
law which prescribes the same things that interior Grace, a new
nature, tends to accomplish; partially for the first, totally for the
second, we can with more or less culpability paralyze, turn aside
or destroy these inclinations and as a consequence reduce the natural law and the law of love to a condition less perfect than that
of other laws.

The latter, which are human laws or of the human type (divine
laws of the old Covenant), act only from the exterior, and so they
can prescribe directly only certain exterior attitudes commanding
the performance of good acts, forbidding evil ones, without being
able to put forth the claim of immediately regulating interior dispositions—the development of virtues. Still even in this latter domain
they are not entirely inefficacious, for acts repeated often enough
end up by forming corresponding virtues. Still there is no question
but of an indirect action of the law—one which, by definition, can
never terminate except in acquired virtues, and not in those infused
virtues which are the only source of acts meritorious for eternal
beatitude and the gifts of God who places the law interiorly in our
hearts.

But how can laws so infirm obtain from subjects many of whom
are not yet virtuous, nor inclined to be good, the accomplishment of
the good acts prescribed? This would in fact be impossible, and
there would be no recourse except to physical constraint, if the
legislator did not have the right to take a stand despite everything

on the minimum of upright reason which always subsists in every man possessing at least a modicum of sanity, and which always leaves him a disposition, however feeble it may be, to welcome, as a reasonable being, the imperative, rational lights of the law.

The Sanctions of Law

A final means of action for law can always be, and is, employed largely by human laws or laws of the human type: the threat of punishment. No doubt to punish does not constitute an essential act of law, but, in the service of a prescription or an interdiction, it can be an efficacious instrument through the exterior bond—which the legislator establishes without the nature of things demanding it—between the bad act which he interdicts or the omission of a good act which he prescribes on the one hand, and, on the other hand, a physical evil (in the broad sense), the fear of which will prevail over the attraction of the bad act or the repugnance in accomplishing the good act. Moreover, the law can also be given the benefit of a means of action equally indirect, but inverse: compensation. But this latter is not reserved to the legislator, for a particular individual can freely offer something of his own good to another individual, while only the holder of authority is qualified to deprive the guilty, without injustice, of one of his rights.

At any rate, the sanction of law (punishment or reward) is only a complementary and accidental element which adds nothing to its substance. Consequently a law without a foreseen sanction, a "purely moral" law, according to the canonists, an "imperfect" law, according to the secularists, is already a complete law. It deserves to be heard, respected and obeyed, because it is already a qualified regulation of the acts of the subject for the virtuous life in view of the common good, which is his true personal good and, finally, his beatitude or a condition of his beatitude.

IV. The Eternal Law

The first of all laws is evidently that which the Sapiential Books praise apropos the eternal Wisdom associated with God in the work of creation and government of the universe. It is by this law that we must begin the study of each of the species of laws if we would reach an understanding conformable to their nature and to their proper role.

God Creates . . .

God is the Creator of the universe; and, if the latter exists only in time, from all eternity God has conceived it. He has carried the conception in Himself, in His intelligence which is not subject to the laws of becoming. It is the model of which we are really compelled in virtue of the convenience of thought and of language to speak as though it were really distinct from God and His wisdom; but we know that these distinctions, imposed on the weakness of our mind, in no way divide the simplicity of God, even while expressing its richness.

. . . and Governs . . .

Now God is not only the creator of the being of things and of beings, it is He also who gives them the order to their end, their movement and their life. Also, in the same way must we speak of models or ideas of creatures in the divine intelligence; we are likewise assured that there is in Him a world of thoughts, of rules which imperatively define the development and orientation of each of these creatures, that is, its end and the steps it will take in order to attain it—so many partial plans, if you wish, which preside over the divine government of beings, the destiny of none of which, we know, is a matter of indifference to the Providence of the Father.

. . . the Universe . . .

But the world which God has created is not an immense and fortuitous assembly of creatures. It is a universe, i.e. an organized whole, bearing the seal of its author and particularly of the unity of the Creator—a unity absolutely simple in God, which is found in the order which reigns among the manifold creatures. And it is first of all a static order resulting from the hierarchy of creatures arranged in series—an order which our mind never stops discovering, but which, through the little that is discernible, imposes upon the mind the conviction of an admirably arranged plan. And then there is also a dynamic order which reigns in the universe, an order made up of the multiple active relations which are established among creatures and of the convergence of all their efforts toward one and the same transcendent end, and which, as a consequence, is a common good which God has established for them and which cannot be anything else than Himself, the principle and terminus of everything that is.

. . . According to a Plan . . .

This unique dynamic order for the whole universe possesses, as necessarily as the order of each created life, its exemplar in God; and since this plan is the norm of activity of the greatest community that is, in view of the most extensive common good, no name can better express it than that of *Law:* supreme law—"summa ratio," said St. Augustine after Cicero—whose particular plan for each creature is only a detail which gets its whole meaning only in the integrated whole, just as the formula which expresses the activity of the wheels is not understood except in the function of the whole machine.

. . . Appropriated to the Word

The Fathers of the Church readily appropriated this law to the person of the Word—although it is the common patrimony of the Three—because the Word proceeds from the Father in the manner in which every idea, and therefore law also, proceeds from intelligence. They have seen in it also the figure in that book of Life of which Scripture speaks (Ps. 39:8; 138:16; Dan. 10:21; Heb. 10:7) in which God inscribes what leads to life, i.e. to beatitude, and what also remains to be accomplished. Moreover that book of Life is itself ordinarily appropriated to the Word.

Eternal Law and Promulgation

The divine law which regulates the divine government of the universe is eternal, for God is eternal in everything that He does; but its promulgation is evidently not, since to promulgate is to apply the law to reasonable creatures. It is then only in the depths of created time that God works this promulgation: promulgation improperly so called, yet an authentic application of the eternal law to material creatures in the impression on them of this ordered activity which the legislator has thought of eternally, and through promulgation to reasonable creatures in the progressive gift of the natural law and of revealed laws.

Eternal Law and Love

Since everything which we distinguish is really one in the eminent simplicity of the being of God, He is at once the legislator of the eternal law, the common good to which it ordains the universe, and this law itself; thus God Himself is really the rule of life for His creatures, their transcendent model, exactly as He is their Creator and their end. And as God is love, as St. John testifies (I Jn. 4:8,16), and inspired in all His works by the eternal love of Himself, the law which He gives to His creatures is itself a fruit and a guarantee of His love for Himself and for us; and in this love we ourselves are associated through the eternal law, since it constitutes there our common good, the object of our love. Work of divine love, gratuitous love, universal and intensively personal love, the eternal law can be appropriated to the Spirit of Love at the same time as to the Wisdom of the Word.

Eternal Law and Stoic Reason

Despite verbal similarities, we are here very far from the Pantheistic ideas of the Stoics; there is no question of a law immanent in the universe, impersonal and cold, subjecting all things to a blind fatalism in a necessarily inexorable and highly rational unfolding; for God is not the unconscious soul of the world, but, in his infinite Wisdom, its creator and its transcendent legislator—luminous Rule inaccessible to every created intelligence, who mercifully imprints Himself through the laws which derive from Him in lights within our reach.

Every Other Law Is Subordinated to the Eternal Law

"Summa ratio," supreme ordinance of reason, means that the eternal law is not itself subordinated to any other and at the same time that all others, each in turn, must be regulated by it under pain of not being valid. Everything that is depends upon God; and the very weaknesses of all things manifest their essential subordination.

Everything Is Subject to the Eternal Law

Everything in the created universe is then subject to the regulation of the eternal law, for nothing escapes from the order of God. The failures which frequently take place in the order of creatures toward their ends stem from themselves; considered in isolation they no doubt constitute an obstacle to the orientation inscribed in the nature of the being which they affect, but we must raise our gaze higher, even to the universe of which every creature is only a part; then the apparent conflicts are harmonized in the order of the whole of which the eternal law is the rule. Free beings, whose liberty might at first seem contrary to the universal authority of the eternal law, are themselves subjected to it, for God is not a legislator who controls free wills by an external decision, the source of constraint, but He is at the very center of reasonable creatures, the author of the free mode of their acts. And in beatitude itself the eternal law will remain the rule of our life of vision and of love, the measure of our adherence to the divine good possessed as it actually is in our pursuit of this hoped for good.

Eternal Law and Liberty

Since God rules the movement and the life of His creatures from the interior, He does so without doing any violence to them, but rather with that gentleness with which the Book of Wisdom speaks, by an interior movement with which free man is invited to make himself a genuine cooperator by receiving as a beneficent light what God reveals to him of the eternal law. Moreover, should he refuse it, he will not by so doing escape from the law whose light he rejects only to undergo its restraint. Here once more we can verify that submission to the law of God is the condition of liberty.

Knowledge of the Eternal Law

The eternal law, sovereign thought of God on the order of the universe to its end, cannot be directly known in itself by any created intelligence; it cannot therefore be directly our rule of life. Still it is so in the indirect and partial knowledge that we can have of it, in the measure in which it is already fulfilled, if we know how to recognize the universal order of the world which God has set up in order that we might find in it some trace of the thoughts of its creator; it is especially so on two levels: first, in the reflection which God has made of it, in ourselves this time, in the depths of our consciousness, under the form of an inner dictate of the natural law; secondly, in surpassing the natural law, in the revealed commandments of the old and of the new Laws. But all that God has thus made known to us of His eternal law concerns only our salvation as Christians, the conquest of our beatitude. The thoughts of God reveal on every side what He communicates to us. It is only in the face to face vision of heaven that we will know even as we are known but without ever exhausting the mystery of God, the marvels of His law.

V. The Natural Law

1. DEFINITION OF THE NATURAL LAW

As the very name suggests, we understand by the *natural law* that law, true law, dictated by practical reason, which is not the measure of any free elaboration of any human legislator but which is imposed on men at the same time as their nature.

Natural Law and Eternal Law

For as we already know, the natural law is nothing else but the eternal law impressed upon our intelligence, the light which is detached from it in order to come and illuminate our soul and the reflection in us of the light of God, as St. Augustine says; or again, according to the usual Scholastic expression, the initial spark which is to kindle the luminous fire in our soul. Promulgation or participation in us of the eternal law, to the degree in which we should understand it in order to direct ourselves toward our end—at least in the order of nature—the natural law is not really *another* law; yet, although it adds no more to the eternal law than creation adds to the creator, it has exactly as much distinct reality as the creature with respect to the creator. Whereas for the Pantheistic Stoics for whom God is not really distinguished from nature, the eternal and natural laws were also confused. Being in us without being of us, having only God as author, the natural law, better than any human law, can be said to be of divine right.

Natural Law, Expression of Nature

The natural law is then an ordinance of reason which emanates from nature. Our human reason, even though autonomous, is none the less first of all the reason of a definite nature. For us this is a datum of which we can change nothing. In a way, God has given it to us; according to the expression of Ecclesiasticus: "God . . . left him in the hand of his own counsel" (Ecclus. 15:14) by creating us rational and free, masters of our choices, regulators of our activity. But this liberty is the liberty of a creature which, like everything else, has already certain basic inclinations, a certain structure which corresponds as it were to an original web on which liberty can amplify but which is an indispensable support for it. Consequently reason (in its twofold function, speculative and practical) begins at first by translating the needs of the first structure of man. In a first practical knowledge—to keep to the moral sphere—it expresses the order to the end of its nature and the principal means of attaining it; it reveals imperatively the practical needs at the depth of a being and traces out the broad lines of what should be its free action in order to conform to this nature, and so in order to be good and beatifying. The natural law is nature in its dynamism expressing itself rationally. It is therefore the pivot of the two orders, physical (or natural) and moral. It is also, from another point of view, the pivot of the divine order and the human order.

The Natural Law Is Innate at Least in Its Principle

It is not the laborious term of reason as is all other human knowledge; it is a proposition which is presented to our mind and is imposed on it with an evidence more or less weighty depending upon its different articles, but always true, while the certitude of a conclusion is borrowed from its premises. It is the object of a simple glance of the mind in which human reason participates in something of the angelic intuition. No doubt it is not known and cannot be expressed by the practical reason except on the occasion of some sensible experience, for that is the condition of every human intellectual activity, though, precisely, this is not only a condition, for such a dictate completely transcends the sensible world. It is really a light from on high. It cannot therefore be acquired. It is a gift to rational nature by the author of this nature, an innate gift—if not under its consciously expressed form, at least as a natural disposition in the reason of man; it is what the Scholastics call the innate habit of *Synderesis.* Then comes the awakening of reason, at an age which varies according to persons, "the age of reason," when the practical reason, naturally enabled by Synderesis formulates for itself as something obligatory the moral principle which must dominate the whole of life. The eternal law is reflected in the human mind, it is thenceforth promulgated in it and so applicable, even though this mind does not know how to make the connection between these two lights which are only one.

The Natural Law and Liberty

Moreover reason, thus instructed in its natural duty, can refuse to hear the dictate of the natural law to conform itself to the activity which it commands, but that would be to deny its nature, to deny itself in what there is in it of the most profound, of the most divine;

it would be to deny its Creator and the love which inspired Him in His work, without however suppressing this nature and this law or escaping from the power of the legislator.

Universality of the Natural Law

An imperative formula of the needs of our nature, the natural law is expressed in universal terms and not in exclusively personal terms; each one hears in it a dictate valid not only for himself but also for all those who share the same nature with him. It becomes then the rule of his activity, but also the rule which will be his inspiration for others and which he will have to apply to them first to the degree in which he will be called upon to direct them.

2. THE CONTENT OF NATURAL LAW

Is it possible to explain the content of natural law? If it must be our first rule of life, if it has universal value and is applicable in social relations, this content cannot be purely subjective, but must be capable of being explained.

"The Good Must Be Done"

The natural law expresses what is most fundamental in man, the essential demands of his nature which constitute the principles of all his rational activity. Its first precept is then necessarily that we must seek the good of nature, or rational nature, the good in general, such as reason defines it and which the spiritual appetite in us desires, and not at first any particular sensible good which would correspond only to the demands of purely sensible natures, such as those of the animals. "The good must be done." Here is what the law interior to our nature demands first of us, for it is to the good, in all its breadth, without restrictive qualification, that rational being is by nature proportioned, and we must add at once: "Evil must be avoided." That is nothing but the negative expression of the same precept since, as we know, to prescribe and to forbid differ basically only in form. It is this precept which the practical reason formulates for itself from its first awakening, no doubt more or less confusedly, but with an imperious certainty which radiates over the whole of moral life.

Every other article of the natural law is merely a determination of it to the broad natural directions of human activity. It is then the heart of rational life, the inspirer of all ulterior demands.

The Other Articles of Natural Law

But can we go further in the analysis of the natural law? Yes, especially if we take account of the means of investigation which the knowledge of our natural inclinations furnishes us; for, running parallel to the natural dictates of practical reason, there are also in our appetites (will and sensible appetites) certain absolutely natural tendencies which it suffices to observe in order to recognize the essential demands of nature and consequently in order to take advantage of them to discern the content of the natural law.

The Law of Conservation

It seems that we can then distinguish as it were three zones in us. The first corresponds to what we have in common with all creatures, whatever may be the kingdom to which they belong; on this ground, like every being, each one of us has an inclination of nature toward the conservation of what he is. He is then subject to the law—natural —to the degree in which it depends on him to preserve himself, i.e. to do everything reasonable to accomplish that end. The interdiction of suicide, of mutilation, of unreasonable risks to one's health, the legitimate right of self defense, are direct translations of this first natural demand.

The Law of Fecundity

Then we can circumscribe a second zone characterized by everything in us that we have in common with the animal world and with it alone. Here the fundamental inclination of nature is that which urges us to the multiplication of the species according to the means designed to assure it in the best possible conditions conformable to nature; marriage is therefore a natural institution, from which the natural law forbids the exclusion of anyone who has not forfeited his right to it by some proportionate moral fault. This is for example the motive which condemns the sterilization of the innocent, likewise the law of nature condemns the selfish bachelor, the forms of sexuality and of marriage which contradict their natural function, the abandonment of infants (in this case we speak of the "unnatural" mother), the denial of the primary, because natural, right of the parents over the education of their children, etc.

The Duty of Being a Man

Finally a third zone in human nature is measured by what there is in us of the specifically human. We alone among the creatures of this earth are reasonable beings. And since this is a trait of nature, there corresponds to it in us basic inclinations which are also natural, even while being rational, and which are therefore also the object of special articles of the natural law. This is notably the inclination, which is also a duty, of pursuing knowledge; this general natural obligation is obviously diversified according to circumstances but bears very specially on the knowledge which is necessary to attain the final end of man, beatitude considered at last as a demand of the nature in us. For this reason there is a capital precept of the natural law to tend, according to the capacities of reason, toward the knowledge of Him who is the supreme explanation, the final answer to all the Whys, the only object proportionate to the human desire for knowing.

But reasonable, open to the universal, man by nature loves to be with others; he is not only gregarious, like many animals, he is social. He is made not only for conjugal society, but for the larger society, in short, for the universal society of all men. He is therefore subject to the natural law of universal human brotherhood which condemns all exclusive particularism, a fortiori the misanthropism which would turn the individual back upon himself.

Unity of the Natural Law

This multiplicity of the articles of natural law, these three progressive zones, do not prevent the natural law from being also one with the nature to which it dictates its demands. Human nature is one; there is only one soul in man, but this unique soul is rich in diverse powers, vegetative, sensible, spiritual. Man has only one end for his unique nature, but many means to employ, simultaneously as well as hierarchically, to attain it. Thus the natural law which shows the obligatory relation of nature to its end is basically one, but with a complex unity. It is summed up in the fundamental precept of doing good, but it is expanded into diverse precepts which explain how this fundamental precept must be fulfilled in the great areas of moral life. Here we verify, in this striking case, that the law, a general formula of practical reason, establishes unity in the multitude of actions in which, without this common inspiration, our effort would be irremediably scattered.

3. THE SCOPE OF THE NATURAL LAW

A detailed study would no doubt enable us to add to this sketch certain complements and precisions; but it is necessary, in this field, to be on guard against the temptation of finding in the natural moral law precepts which are readily admitted by contemporaries in our civilization to correspond to the demands of custom—called a "second nature"—but which do not translate the inclinations of common human nature and cannot therefore be qualified as genuinely natural. It is into an exaggeration of this kind that many jurists and philosophers of the 18th century have fallen and it has brought into disrepute with too many thinkers the very concepts of law and of natural right.

Primary and Secondary Precepts

Moreover, within the natural law itself we must recognize the existence of two classes of precepts. The first are immediate data of consciousness that impose themselves with an evidence and a rigor such that to infringe upon them would be to compromise irremediably the attainment of the end to which our nature tends. This is the case for example of the duty which our nature imposes on us to exercise domination over the material world which surrounds us in order to insure our survival; to refuse to recognize this duty would be suicide. Then there are other precepts, still natural, but which presuppose a minimum of reason: natural precepts, for every man having the use of reason formulates them for himself so easily, so spontaneously that they are as it were immediate commands of practical reason, but precepts called "secondary," in opposition to the first which are called "primary," because they are already conclusions, however close they may be to their premises; this is the case for example of the duty of organizing a certain personal appropriation of material goods the better to insure natural personal ends. To infringe these precepts is to gravely endanger the attainment of the end; it is certainly to condemn oneself to a partial failure, though not necessarily to a complete failure.

The Natural Law Is Unchangeable and Indelible

With this reservation it is true that the natural law is unchangeable and indelible in the heart of man, exactly as nature is. The variations or the obliterations that can be pointed out among savage peoples, or simply among the contemporary barbarians of our civilized western world, can bear, and sometimes heavily, on "secondary" precepts, and it is moreover properly a regression below the human level. But, in its first demands, the natural law could disappear only with reason itself; it is impossible to completely ignore it; its unchangeable dictate always makes itself heard in the depths of the conscience through unrest and remorse.

No One Can Dispense from the Natural Law

From what has been said, it is clear that there is no possible dispensation from the natural law, neither by God who cannot will evil and proscribe the good, nor a fortiori by any human power, even though it were that of the Church of God, since man has no power over himself except in the service of God and since to the living person human reason, in which liberty is rooted, is determined by nature *before* being free in order the better to serve nature.

In short, the natural law is in the practical reason of man a participation in the eternal law of God, a reflection of the divine reason; it is in us the fundamental light of our rational activity. It is therefore also the source of all other lights which we can give ourselves to illuminate our march toward the good.

But, interiorly present in every reasonable decision, it is not by itself alone the complete guide of our life. For, differing from the animal world in which everything is determined, in which the urges of nature command every action even in its most concrete circumstances, man is master of the ordering of his own life aside from a general direction given by nature or more exactly by the author of his nature. Certain principles are imposed upon him. We know now what their demands are; it is for him to draw from them many and variable conclusions which alone will be sufficiently circumstanced and enriched with free choices in order to be fully efficacious rules of his conduct. It is at this level that we are going to meet human laws.

VI. Human Laws

1. NECESSITY AND BASIS FOR HUMAN LAWS

The natural law, divine in its origin, human through its subject, makes us participants in the intuitive mode of angelic knowledge by supplying us with the supreme principles of our conduct, by dictating to us our natural end and the essential means for attaining it. There natural moral knowledge stops.

It remains for us to make use of these clear lights, to reduce these universal principles to principles of conduct closer to our particular actions which they are to regulate. And this supposes the intervention of reason extending the intuition, i.e. a laborious use of the natural dictate: it is here that the human legislator intervenes.[3]

No doubt each one of us has in himself the ability to reflect upon the obligations which are his by reason of the natural law, and each of us can, by himself, draw certain necessary consequences concerning his conduct. But we are social beings by nature and practically it is in the social framework through laws, in function of the common good of the perfect societies of which we are members, that in as far as possible, this rational utilization of the natural law must be made.

Human Law Governs Only External Actions

We say, in as far as it is possible human law governs only external actions, because the human legislator has direct competency only over external acts; it is by these that we enter into relations with one another and that society is constructed. It is therefore the area of natural justice, and it alone, which lends itself to a complement of collective human regulation. No doubt many other demands of the natural law are assumed in our laws, but only from the angle of visible acts in which they are expressed, i.e. in the strict measure in which they concern justice which is the virtue that regulates relationships in life. The legislator who would go beyond and directly rule the interior life of his subjects could not help but use odious and moreover inefficacious means of constraint against the inner liberty of conscience.

Necessity of Human Laws

The outlines of human law being thus explained, it remains for us to show that its intervention is necessary and helpful.

Human law is a guarantee against the current deficiencies of judgment, thus compensated for through a pooling of common experiences and through the appeal to better informed personalities. By the very general nature of laws, it is a security against the errors which would not fail to result from passions if we should have to lay down a rule apropos of each particular case. It is the best possible guarantee for

[3] Here we use the term "law" in the philosophical sense defined earlier and which may or may not coincide with the word "law" in the legal sense.

planning the future since future activity is defined in advance in its broad lines. It serves to reinforce the prestige of the ruler and to endow him with the means of eventual constraint which public authority alone can employ.

The Human Law and the Natural Law

Between the eternal law and the natural law there is no gap because the latter is only the partial reflection of the former; the distance is greater between the human law and the natural law and consequently the eternal law. There is not however lack of continuity; in legislating, the human legislator does not set up a structure *alongside* of and in full independence of the demands of nature, even though he respects them by not encroaching on what they may have already determined. He applies the natural law in two quite different ways, although they almost always go together.

First, he confirms the natural law. He does so by making it explicit according as the common good and the latest social demands require it, by drawing all the *conclusions* from it which are contained in it, but not yet formulated in poorly awakened consciences. It is thus that he decrees for example the monogamous form of marriage; we are yet on the frontiers of the natural law, in that zone which the ancients called "law of nations," recognized, but not without important exceptions, by the ensemble of human nations.

But especially the human legislator makes the natural law clear by bringing to it certain *determinations* which the nature itself of things did not define but which are necessary in order to satisfy the needs of action. Then he is really a creator and is not content with recognizing what is; he finds ways and means of facilitating the complete fulfillment of natural precepts; he lays down something new which was not "given," but which he "constructed"; we shall therefore speak of "positive" laws.

Diversity and Likeness Concerning the Same Object

This condition of human laws explains sufficiently their endless variety apropos of the same object, according to various epochs and countries; since there is a large area for free choice, we will be able to find examples of very different types of legal attitudes toward marriage in different countries. Human nature lays down certain broad directives, but neither the separation of goods, nor the dowry system, nor the community form any part of these directives.

Still human law must not "posit" anything outside of the course laid down by the natural law. It determines it but it does not substitute itself for it; for reason, even though free, is the reason of a definite nature, and its very liberty is at the service of nature and of its ends. Moreover, we ought to be able to find, in the most diverse positive legislation apropos of the same object a common inspiration and so an analogy, or, if you wish, a proportionate equality.

If this were not so, human law would have lost its foundation and its soul. To claim to govern human activity independently of the natural law of this activity, whose first requirement is to be the keystone of moral life, would be in contradiction with this law and consequently also with the eternal law; it would have lost all justice, it would no longer be a law except in appearance. The case would be the same if, without opposing the natural law, human law should set itself in contradiction to the other reflections of the eternal law which are called divine positive laws.

Thus human law itself, through the mediation of the natural law which inspires it, comes to be inserted into the universal order which the provident wisdom of God eternally defines; unlike the natural law it is really different from the law of God but not a stranger to it.

2. NECESSARY QUALITIES AND LIMITATIONS OF HUMAN LAW

Conformity to the natural law is the most general condition of validity and the first quality of human law. Still it is necessary that it correspond to the common definition of law and notably that it assure the pursuit of the true common good. That goes without saying; but we must insist on another of its qualities: human law must be *possible*.

Human Law Must Be "Possible"

Its mission is to set up a rule of activity as a means for attaining the end; it is therefore at the service of the end. But the end of a being, the end of the subject of law, is not only a good which one thinks of with satisfaction, an ideal which he caresses from afar and which arouses at most a certain velleity for realizing; it is a goal which we really try to achieve effectively because of the efficacious means we have for fulfilling this firm and clear objective. If then the law determines means which are practically impossible for the social body to put to use, it deserts the end which it should procure, it does not accept the task which is incumbent upon it. It is bad. As we know, this problem is not raised for the "inner" laws, natural and evangelical law, because they express duties to which effective inclinations already correspond, while a gap can exist, even a considerable one, between the objective requirements of the human legislator and the subjective resources of the subject, because the prescriptions of the former can exercise no direct influence over the interior life of the latter.

These possibilities of the social body of which the law must take account are of many diverse kinds: personal possibilities first of all, level of morality, education received, habits contracted, age, etc., but they are also conditionally social: density and distribution of population, established customs, history; external conditions of climate, of natural riches, in a word, everything that weighs heavily on human conduct, even if liberty is only conditioned and not suppressed.

This is to say that human law must not be thought of in the abstract. But we do not wish to say by this that we are resigned to make imperfect laws, even if intelligent submission to the possibilities in question are to lead to a lowering of the ideal that was first dreamed of; for perfection is defined as a rule of action in view of the end to be obtained. The perfect law is one which is applicable and which effectively brings about the accomplishment, through those to whom it is addressed, of the acts which it commands, and which therefore makes possible the attainment of the end pursued. To say that the law must be possible is therefore to express an essential condition of the *perfection* itself of law.

Limitations of Human Law

Moreover it follows from this that human law cannot claim to forbid every bad act, nor to prescribe every virtuous act, even while keeping to the domain of external acts—those through which we enter into physical communication with one another and are under the authority of our legislators. For there is always question of the common good. Having to consider the factual possibilities which the community as a whole offers, it will no doubt be necessary to tolerate certain abuses, to not be too exacting in this or that matter, under pain of succeeding only in indirectly encouraging evasion of the law, social hypocrisy, if not open disobedience, all of which are results often worse than the mediocrity to which one closes his eyes.

Human Law Obliges in Conscience

The efficacy of human law has therefore limitations; but this does not prevent this law from placing under obligation those whom it effectively ordains to their end. It cannot directly regulate any but appreciable social activity, and external behavior and intentions only inasmuch as they are necessarily bound up with the acts which are visibly performed. But it follows that, if it is just, if it is really law, ordained to the common good and established by qualified authority, it also derives, in its own way, from the eternal law; it is wholly charged with the potential deposited in it by the natural law which it prolongs and which underlies it, it corresponds to the demands of social nature, which are imposed upon our conscience as a duty of divine origin.[4]

There is therefore no gap between the external official order and the interior life, between the domain of parliament, of judges and policemen and that of the tribunal of conscience, for the external order satisfies an imperious need of the nature of man in the very service of the interior life.

The Case of Unjust Laws

It could be otherwise only if the law were unjust, not satisfying this or that requirement of the definition which we have analyzed. If it go against the common good, if it be dictated by a pseudo-authority or if, being unreasonable, it fall gravely short of the higher rules of justice in the distribution of social burdens and advantages, then of itself it would no longer have what is necessary to impose obligation, for it would no longer be truly a law.

We must distinguish two hypotheses: for the injustice of law can come either from the fact that it demands of the subject an attitude which it should not demand of him, but which in itself is not bad, or from the fact that it claims to impose upon him a behavior which not only goes beyond his power, but is even in itself bad by nature. In

---

[4] Here we only mention the theory of "purely penal laws" according to which certain human laws did not directly oblige in conscience the fulfilment of what they apparently prescribe, but only in case of being caught, to accept the punishment provided for violation. A generalization of a rule proper to the conditions of certain Religious Orders, this theory which is easily explained in the case of the evangelical counsels, generally invaded the moral theology of the 19th century. At that time certain abusive applications were made of it and these abuses themselves seem to have provoked a lively reaction which today is exerting itself in a beneficial way.

the second case, the unjust law directly contravenes the law of
God, a divine interdiction or prescription (revealed or natural); there
can be no possible doubt: rejection is obligatory, for it is better to
obey God than men. In the first case, that the legislator is culpable
is certain, and that his law is unjust, and so invalid, is also certain,
for there is no right against the liberty which God has given to each
man when the common good does not demand submission to those
responsible for the common good. But although the law be in itself
invalid, it can happen and it frequently will happen that for some
other reason the common good may demand or even require that we
sacrifice some of our right in order to avoid giving scandal to those
who would not understand the apparent disobedience or in order not
to disturb seriously the social order: a question of charity and of
social justice. If one is moved to obey, nevertheless, he does not atten-
uate in so doing the fault of the legislator but neither does he collaborate with him in his contempt for divine law, because this law is
interpreted in this event as a permission which obliges the legislator
to respect the liberty of his subjects but which precisely leaves to
them the duty of making the reasonable use of it which they may
desire. We cannot yield any of the rights of God, but if there is question of social peace it is often our duty to yield many of our own.

Human Law Supposes Also a Personal Effort

Except for the case of basic injustice in human law, we must not
forget that it is condemned to be only a *general* formula of action.
This is its grandeur, but this is also its weakness, for unlike the divine
legislator, the human legislator is incapable of embracing at once the
whole group of cases which the same law must be concerned with
and the particular circumstances of each of these cases.

This means that the human law remains in some respects midway
between the really universal commands of the natural law and the
final determinations of particular decisions. Now we must go so far
in order to act, for one does not act in general but always in a particular way; we never posit an action-type, but a concrete action which
is never realized except in a fashion more or less close to the theoretical cases envisaged by the legislator. There remains then, even under
the law, a margin of determination which supposes on the part of the
subject of the law a personal reflection, an effort of intelligence to
understand the law, to judge of its particular situation, to bring about
a union between the two, in a word, to verify the conditions of appli-

cation of the law and finally to accept it reasonably as a reasonable being and therefore, in a sense, free even in docility and obedience to authority. The law, as we know, is instructive.

The Spirit and Letter of the Law

This necessary examination will sometimes result in the verification that to apply the law, even a just one, is, in a given case, to compromise the common good which the law has in view. The hypothesis is not chimerical, since the legislator legislates according to what ordinarily takes place and cannot—for lack of a reason vast and penetrating enough, for lack also of means of expression sufficiently supple —foresee all the exceptional cases which can rise. In such a circumstance, the legislator himself should interpret his law, determine its application to new circumstances; but if it were impossible to appeal to him and if the case were gravely urgent and evident, the intention of the law, i.e. the promotion of the common welfare, would certainly prevail over the incomplete and clumsy letter of it; this would not be revolt, but only intelligent obedience.

3. LEGISLATIVE EVOLUTION

The Materials of Law Evolve

Unlike the natural law, human law is not and cannot be unchangeable. The first is the impression on human nature of the law of God who does not change; it controls human activity from on high by taking account on the one hand of what is our unchangeable nature and on the other of the not less unchangeable end of this nature. On the contrary, human law, within its broad and permanent directives, explains what human actions ought to be in order to lead finally to beatitude by taking account both of the particular determinations of human nature and of the demands, in the service of beatitude, of this more immediate end which is the common good of such or such a particular society.

It is therefore normal and even necessary that it follow the transformations of its material, i.e. the changes which occur in the society for which it is promulgated: modifications of national temperament, of average morality, of the economic situation, of the political regime (itself a work of human law), etc.

The Reason of the Legislator Also Undergoes Changes

It is not only society which evolves, the reason of the legislator does also, not indeed in its fundamental dictates which are articles of the natural law but in the means at its disposal for making positive application of this natural law to a given society. Indeed, experience of earlier attempts, of failures and successes, can give to minds open to the lessons of the past, sharpness of discernment, a security of judgment, a clearness of decision which previously would have been more difficult. In principle then, this consideration works in favor of a progressive evolution of human law; but we know well enough that experience is not always attended to and that the gravest regressions are also possible.

It Is Necessary that Laws Change

At any rate, it is certain that human positive law is never valid except for a given milieu and a more or less lengthy duration, but always in fact limited. And its very change has no other purpose than to make better known the unchangeable demands of the natural law. There is then reason for pursuing legislative progress by adapting laws to new conditions or by ameliorating the law for unchanged, but better understood, conditions.

But One Respects More the Law to Which He Is Accustomed

Nevertheless, we must not forget either that, practically, the average of humanity, that is, its great mass, respects law in proportion to its duration much more than to its rational value. Most men think, at least in a confused way, that what exists for a long time, what has always existed in the memory of man, cannot enjoy such longevity unless by virtue of an exceptional intrinsic quality; what is always done is then more easily esteemed than that which *ought* to be done. This sentiment corresponds to a deep need of stability which very strongly subsists even in the greatest innovations. We should not neglect to place it in the service of human law to the greatest possible extent and to permit society to become accustomed for a long time to the laws which are given it.

If therefore we misuse legislative modifications we run the risk of rapidly reaching a state of disrespect for law. We will quickly judge that the preceding law was not as good as had been thought, since it has become necessary to change it, and of the new, precisely because it is new, we will believe with difficulty that it deserves greater respect; and we shall not be slow in accepting the well known formula: in such a situation we will not hesitate when an order is given to await a counter-order.

Law and Custom

There is then a very real opposition between necessary legislative progress and the not less necessary becoming accustomed to laws. This opposition can be largely reduced through the influence of custom which little by little modifies the old law and prepares minds for the dispositions which will be new only in their official promulgation. The preceding law, at first perfectly adapted to needs, had met with individual cases, more and more numerous, in which the circumstances were such that it was necessary to have recourse to a respectful interpretation of the spirit to the detriment of the letter. For these manifold cases, exceptional measures are installed in some way in the law, and the day comes on which we can without inconvenience set them up in a new law to which the masses are already accustomed, since they themselves have prepared for it by their behavior. Moreover, authority also plays a role in this evolution, for it is to it that recourse is had for reasonable dispensations—advance signs, perhaps of future legislation and precedents which are the creators of custom—or at least for the toleration of derogations or modifications to which new circumstances little by little rise.

4. CIVIL LAW AND ECCLESIASTICAL LAW

Without going into detail on the different types of human laws which spring from right more than morality, it is necessary to point out the division of laws into ecclesiastical and civil. The law of the Church constitutes a positive human right; it is a true law, because the Church is, in her order, a perfect society just like the state in its order; it is a human law affected therefore by an irreducible coefficient of relativity, since there is question of a large area of positive determinations by a human legislator, as in the case of civil law.

Ecclesiastical law is at the service of the common spiritual good to which it ordains the exterior activity of Christians, while the function of the civil law is to promote the temporal common good. Moreover, although their means may be analogous and although they both constitute human laws, they are inspired by different principles. The civil law is a determination of the natural law in social matters, the ecclesiastical law does not ignore, certainly, the requirements of the natural law which are universal, but besides, and especially, it extends another law, the law of grace which gives it its wholly particular physiognomy and its eminent place among human laws.

Insufficiency of the Natural and Human Laws

Everything is not said with the treatment of human positive laws. For these laws extend the natural law, which is itself a communication to the rational creature, and so of what concerns it according to reason in the eternal law of God. Thus do they not complete a complex but harmonious legislative aparatus which furnishes us with all the directives that we need in order to act well?

To answer this question would be to enter the domain of hypotheses and suppositions, which would have only a problematical value unless there were finally verified and, to begin with, suggested by the facts themselves.

With this reservation, we must first of all recall the uncertainties of human reason, especially in the practical field which is that of law; as we know besides, human law governs only external actions and only by taking account of the limited possibilities of the majority of subjects. Would that the supreme legislator could intervene to assist the incurable weakness of man!

On the other hand, we have considered so far the conditions of human activity only by abstracting from historical facts. Now the whole history of humanity is dominated by two facts which, without destroying the order of nature, have profoundly modified its equilibrium and have therefore also overturned the economy of salvation. These two facts are the call to *supernatural* beatitude and the sin of man.

Original sin had as a consequence a weakening of the moral powers, even outside the area of grace, which manifests itself in what concerns the law in a progressive obscuring of the natural law. We have verified it, apropos of secondary precepts, without yet connecting it with this cause. Even in full knowledge of all the requirements of the natural law, we must add to it the disposition to actual sin particularly heavy with consequences for the legislator. Here again there is in man a misery which expects, without however being able to demand it, a merciful intervention of the divine legislator to promulgate anew the law which is in us, but which we find more and more difficult to recognize.

More basic still is the transformation introduced into the conditions of moral life by this other fact, historically prior, which is the supernatural vocation to a higher than natural beatitude, the vocation properly supernatural and absolutely unhoped for by nature, though in perfect harmony with it. Only a new legislation can be proportioned to supernatural beatitude which God effectively proposes to us: legislation which can only have God for its author, a new communication to the rational creature of a part of the eternal law which still concerns it but which could not find its expression in natural law.

Recognizing this distress, realizing this vocation, God effectively has given us the divine positive law.

VII. The Divine Positive Law

Let us recall the teachings of Scripture. We have learned there that the law of God is twofold, the Old and the New, and we know that no expression seems too strong for St. Paul to show the opposition between them; he himself does not hesitate to render to the Law—the Old Law—a deep respect. For, if there are two laws, there is only one God and only one beatitude which is proposed to us, supernatural beatitude. The apparent and also very real opposition between the two laws, as we are going to explain, is finally resolved in the harmony of the two successive moments of a providential development. The Old Law is preparation and prefiguration and announcement. The New Law is fulfilment and presence and arrival of the same reality expected and then possessed. The New Law is perfection, and consequently the Old Law is still the imperfect state, but the imperfection itself is a good for him who is not satisfied with it, since it points out to him the road to the perfect.

1. THE OLD LAW

The Old Law Was Imperfect

The Old Law was then imperfect. It directed the faithful toward the unique beatitude, whose object is God in His inner mystery, but it was not yet able to be more than a distant orientation. Of itself and directly, it led to the temporal success of the enterprises of the people of Israel and to the common good on earth of this theocratic community, even though this good had no meaning except in view of the higher good.

. . . Of Human Type . . .

The Old Law also is divine, but it is of human type—God directing His people somewhat like a great contemporary legislator might do it. The activity of which the Law constitutes the rule is exterior activity, the sum total of the acts of the social life of the people; the means that it can employ in order to succeed in its application are especially the accessible means of threat and constraint or of promise.

. . . Incapable of Complete Fulfilment . . .

Perfect in its kind, perfect as law in a political community, perfect if we abstract from its secret intention, it remains true nevertheless that it gives us a glimpse of the end which it leaves inaccessible; moreover, human weakness is too great for it to be able to obtain, even on the political level, the complete success of its design. It is in this sense that St. Paul could call it the occasion of the fall, the cause of death, a law impossible to fulfill.

. . . But Still a Gift of the Goodness of God . . .

But for all that it was beneficent, since it prepared for a better law which would not be anything but its own development. It demanded much and gave little, but by this very demand it aroused desires which the New Law comes to satisfy. Cut off from its extension, it would have been bad: the letter (to understand without the spirit) kills, but the spirit of the Old Law is the very cause of its imperfection and the expectation of being surpassed. Creating this expectation and disposing minds and hearts for its being surpassed, it was the marvelous and divine teacher of the chosen people and, through it, of humanity. It is a gift of the goodness of God, although in it this divine goodness has not yet yielded all its treasures.

There is no reason for being astonished or scandalized at this imperfection of divine law. God has, in creating man, created a perfectible being, a being who was not given to himself in his full perfection from the day of his birth, but who attains his adult age only by a slow and patient progressive course through the crises of growth. And what is true of the individual nature of each one of us is true also of all humanity, which also is subjected, considered in its totality, to the laws of time and of growth. God governs each creature, God Himself determines its laws in conformity with the nature which he has given to it. The Old Law, in its very imperfection is an effect of the condescension of God who, in His legislative intervention, subjects Himself, even before the Incarnation, to the humility of our condition.

The Content of the Old Law: the Decalogue . . .

The Old Law was addressed only to the people of Israel, the people of God. It was the charter of the Covenant and the constitution of this political community set aside for the service of Yahweh. Still the pagan nations could not entirely ignore it, for the essential element of this law, aside from its profound intention, is the Decalogue, and the Decalogue is nothing else but the natural law common to all men; its ten articles merely promulgated anew by a solemn publication on the tablets of stone on Sinai what all men have engraven on their hearts and hear or should normally hear dictated by their conscience; only the prescription of the Sabbath rest is a positive determination; all the rest is a rule common to humanity. This is why the Decalogue cannot, any more than the natural law, be the object of dispensations and why, as Christians who live under the regime of the New Law, it is still our law.

Moreover the Decalogue, although it is the fundamental element of a divine law of human type, not only prescribes external acts, but also and directly interior attitudes of mind and heart. It comprises not only natural social morality, but even all natural morality (in its secondary precepts, for the primary indelible precepts have no need of this recall). Also it can be provided with sanctions only for a part of its articles, those regulating the relations of justice.

The Liturgical and Social Precepts

The Old Law also contained many precepts which can be grouped into two classes: the precepts of liturgical order and the precepts of social order. Both together constitute a legislation no more foreign to the Decalogue than positive human laws with regard to the natural law. They are essentially the determinations of the Ten Commandments, with regard to God for the first ones, and with regard to our neighbor for the second ones. Both moreover pertain to a law secretly and entirely pointed toward something beyond itself. They have a scope which infinitely surpasses the immediate worship to be instituted and the people to be organized. Or, more exactly, the worship and political life regulated by these principles received from it a mission more vast than their immediate utility: "Now all these things happen to them as a type" (I Cor. 10:11). Everything in the life of the old Covenant is figure and preparation of Christ to come: it is true of its structure and of its social life, it is still more true of its worship. Also this whole ancient order—unlike the Decalogue—is to disappear when Christ comes, because the imperfect is fulfilled.

2. THE NEW LAW

New Law, Interior Law

And now there is the New Law. The imperfect regime in which God commanded the impossible, since by His law He directed it toward a supernatural life, comes to an end. Not that the final requirements are different, there is at bottom only one law of God; but now it points directly to the end which immediately explains all enterprises, namely the supernatural beatitude, this beatitude which consists in participation in the mystery of the life of the Trinity. And this renovating of the law is possible because it makes its dictates heard, no longer principally from the exterior, as in the Sinaitic promulgation, but in the interior of hearts, in the depth of the Christian conscience as the inner expression of the effective inclination which is placed in us, and assures us of the possibility of fulfilling what is thus prescribed for us with, however, the grace of God, since this effective inclination itself is a gratuitous gift.

In every man there is a certain nature which is at once a principle, in the appetite, of an inner inclination to the good of this nature (to its natural end), and principle, in the practical reason, of the imperative dictate of a natural law. The latter is only the expression of the needs and the effective inclinations of nature and is always accompanied by the power of fulfilling them. In the same way, in everyone faithful to the New Law there is a certain new nature (supernatural or grace), which is at once a principle in the appetite of the effective inclinations of charity and of the other infused moral virtues to the good of this supernature (to the supernatural end), and a principle in the practical reason of the imperative dictate of an inner law of supernature or grace. This law, being only the expression of the needs and the effective inclinations of supernature, is always accompanied by power to fulfill them. In the New Law as in the natural law what must be done is exactly that which one is inclined to do, whether by virtue of nature or by virtue of grace. The Old Law was engraved on tables of stone; but the New Law, just as the natural law, is engraved on the hearts of men although it is also called positive, unlike the natural law, because it was freely given by God over and above the requirements of nature.

Thus the law of God, under its new form, is fully efficacious and justifying of this justice which consists, through the grace of God, in the union of faith and love in the Triune God.

Christ, Legislator of the New Law

The legislator of this Law is the Incarnate Word, Christ. It is in the Word that the Father decrees the eternal Law of the universe; it is to Him that this law is appropriated. It is He, incarnate, who is constituted head of humanity; it is He who is the manifestation to us, and the Third Person is His spirit, the Spirit of Jesus. He gives His Law to His people, the new Israel, which knows no frontiers in either space or time. It is the definitive participation by us in everything which in the eternal law concerns our salvation in view of the common good of redeemed humanity. And this common good of the New Law, of the eternal law, of the law of the new and eternal Covenant, is God known and loved as He knows and loves Himself, it is the participation in the life of Christ, God with us, head of the Mystical Body, source of life for all those for whom He is the inner legislator.

New Law, Grace and Faith

How is this salutary attachment to Christ effected? How consequently is the promulgation of the New Law effected? Through the infusion of grace; but this grace itself has its beginning by faith. Thus the New Law is subject to the same conditions as the faith. Like the content of the faith, it is offered to us with a certitude borrowed from the infallibility of God Himself, but at the same time in an obscurity which will be dissipated only in the future life, despite all the evangelical formulations and explanations. In the New Law the Christian is assured of his end and of his way, for Christ is the way and the life, but he is moved interiorly by a Spirit of whom it is not known whence He comes or whither He goes, even while being assured that He comes from God and that He goes to God.

The Possible Legislation of the New Law

The object of faith, the ministry of God, the common good of the New Law, is too obscurely grasped to be imposed on our choice, to captivate necessarily our love, and so we are able to refuse its dictate in ourselves. But as through our insubordination we lose the grace of which the New Law is the interior dictate, the latter no longer makes itself heard except from the exterior: it is imposed on us, but it is no longer for us a law of love, a law of life; it becomes for us, through the fault of our rejection, a law of death which continues to prescribe for us what we are no longer capable of accomplishing until the mercy of God restores to us Life and therefore replaces His Law in our hearts.

Interior and Exterior Precepts of the New Law

Like the faith, the interior knowledge of the New Law, in its spirit which is the Spirit, surpasses every formula, every conceptual expression, but, like the faith, it nevertheless supposes a minimum of explanation, of secondary elements of this law, necessary dispositions in order to benefit by it and necessary information in order to use it to the best advantage; it is thus that Christ taught us in the Sermon on the Mount. The apostles have extended this instruction, and the Church ever since has not ceased to do so; she recalls the lessons of the divine legislator and, in the service of the New Law, takes the measures which seem to her indispensable to aid us in the fulfillment of the essentially interior commandments of the Lord. We discuss here these human ecclesiastical laws because their external form suggests similarity to the civil laws, but their spirit, their intention is directly drawn from the evangelical Law.

Promulgation of the New Law

As for the promulgation of the New Law, it is not so much in the discourses of Christ that we must look for it as in His works. Since the New Law is a moral dictate in our conscience which comes directly from the life of Christ in us, it is in giving us His life, it is in giving Himself to us, it is therefore in His death and His resurrection, and it is for each one of us in our association with His death and His resurrection, that is, fundamentally, in baptism, the sacrament of faith, that Christ promulgates His law; and it is finally in the Eucharist, the sacrament of love, in which we announce His death (I Cor. 11:26) in order to receive life (Jn. 6:51), that the Law of love makes us hear His most imperious command.

Law of Love and of Liberty

It is the Law of love, since its model is the requirement of the love of Christ for His Father, since its origin is the salutary death of Christ through love for us, since it is in ourselves the expression of the requirements of the love which the Spirit of love, the Spirit of Jesus, has placed in our hearts. It is the Law of liberty, since it has enabled us to accomplish the acts which it commands through an interior impulse of grace, i.e., without any constraint; law which finds its supreme expression in the counsels which the legislator, become friend, makes us understand through the very desires which it arouses for a higher perfection in which not only interior liberty entirely remains, but in which also, more than anywhere else, it is the condition of success for the Law.

In the New Law the opposition or at least the distinction which was at first imposed on us of light and help, of the instructions expected of God in order to know the way toward happiness and of the powers necessary on His part to accomplish these instructions is transcended. It is a law which is at the same time a power because it is the law of love, the law of grace, a law which consequently is under the transcendent light of the eternal law, is the point of convergence of all others, a law also whose study must be pursued through that of the grace which it expresses and of the whole of Christian morality of which it is the rule.

REFLECTIONS AND PERSPECTIVES

Some simple principles to be kept in mind. Law is a work of reason (on this account it obliges in conscience) and it ordains for the happiness of man. Every command which is unreasonable is undeserving of the name of law.

Since law is linked up with reason, it is not pure exteriority, it guarantees our liberty, rather than, fundamentally, running contrary to it. Law sets up order in the city or in the state or in ourselves, just as the reason of man introduces order among his acts and his passions.

Projects for Study

Education and law. Explain the saying: law is a rule for action for the good, a restraining force for the bad. The role of law in the education of citizens. The role of rules in the education of the young. Abuse of legalism. Education without laws (justification and limits of "boys town"). Legal constraint in education.

The end of law. Happiness: the common good (temporal, cultural, spiritual?); the education of citizens. Relations among these things.

The life of laws, custom. Who is the creator of the right? Right itself? Customs? Is custom a proper interpreter of law? Where custom, little by little, substitutes itself for law, does this law cease by that much to oblige in conscience? How can it be right to introduce a custom which runs counter to law? Can a law not only be abrogated by custom, or replaced by another, but also of itself evolve, by itself, in the midst of unforeseen circumstances? Can one law engender another law? Can one go backward from law to law, or forward from law to law, by way of induction or deduction? Compare (and contrast) the evolution of laws with the evolution of dogmas.

Law and politics. Is law the only way of assuring political order? Does law derive its power from government? Does government derive its legitimacy from laws? Are good laws sufficient to make a good society? Do bad laws necessarily make a mediocre society? The moral scope of laws in a society.

Should one always judge according to the laws? Who can pass judgment on the justice of the laws themselves? Who can determine the justice of a political regime or of a government? Ought one admit that the regime is the supreme rule to which practically he must always submit?

Is the political education of citizens useful for the good conduct of the political regime? Should it necessarily be in conformity with the existing regime? Where should it be given? By what teachers? Does not education according to the regime run the risk of stifling liberty? What are some of the possible remedies for this?

Law and revolution. Is it ever permissible to reverse the laws, to change the regime? In what circumstances? Is there any virtue or any sin in retaining obsolete laws, and any virtue or any sin in reversing them? Elements of moral risk taken by the revolutionary.

Should the Christian, who puts his confidence in the Holy Spirit and in persons more than in institutions, reject laws and institutions in certain cases? Analyze two typical cases: St. Paul and the institution of slavery and St. Paul and the institution of the Synagogue.

Old and New Law

Law in the Old Testament. Origin, development. Details of law; end of laws. Symbolism of laws. Role (political, educational, religious) of Law. The Law and Wisdom of God in the Old Testament. The Old law in the New Testament (especially the Synoptics and St. Paul). The morality of the Old Testament according to the Law; religion, social, family and conjugal relations, justice, according to the Law. Commentary on the commandments of the decalogue.

The New Law. Pronouncement, foreshadowing, origins, promulgation. In what does it consist? Its author, end, role. Its perfection, content. To what does it oblige? Precepts and "counsels." Role of the counsels, scope, constraining power over the body of Christians and for a Christian by whom they are "understood." The New Law and the inspired "books." A comparison of the Old Law with the New. Law and Grace. Law and the Holy Spirit. The New Law and laws. Are laws still possible, useful, and necessary in the Church? Role, end, scope of the laws of the Church. Origin, development. Obligatory power. Who can promulgate the laws of the Church, who can change them?

Laws of the Church and Religious Constitutions. Legitimacy of Religious Constitutions. Origin, authors. How judge the value of Religious Constitutions? Diverse constraining powers of Religious Constitutions. Sin against the Constitution. Does the Constitution multiply sins, aggravate them? Benefits of the Constitution (Study, e.g., the Rule of St. Benedict). See Vol. IV, Chap. 12.

Particular or "interior" regulations. If the Constitution finds its justification in its social character, what basis is there for particular regulations? May one man give to another an "account of his conscience" and the latter ask it of the former? Value of particular regulations and revelations of conscience in the Christian regime.

Law and virtue. Place of law in theology. Exact role of law in Christian morality. Can the Christian still live under a regime of the Synagogue by applying the laws of the Church? Can the devout

Israelite live under a regime of the Church by conforming his life to the commandments of the Thora?

Prolong these reflections and perspectives by those which follow Chapters 4 (Prudence) and 5 (Justice), Vol. IV.

BIBLIOGRAPHIE

Sur les lois dans l'Écriture, outre les passages du texte même, dont on trouvera les références dans la première partie, on pourra lire:

De Vaux, O.P., *La religion de l'ancien Testament,* dans Robert et Tricot, *Initiation biblique,* Paris, Desclée et Cie, 1938, pp. 667-691.

Robert, P.S.S., *Le sens du mot Loi dans le Psaume* 119, dans *Revue Biblique,* 1937, pp. 182-206.

Lemonnyer, O.P., *Théologie du nouveau Testament,* Paris, Bloud et Gay, 1928.

Prat, S.J., *La théologie de saint Paul,* 2 vols., Paris, Beauchesne, 1929.

Sur l'ensemble du traité et sur la loi en général:

Saint Thomas d'Aquin, *La loi.* Trad. et notes de M.-J. Laversin, O.P., Paris, Desclée et Cie, 1935. (Premier tome du traité des lois de la Somme Théologique; le second, comprenant Loi ancienne et Loi nouvelle, n'est pas encore paru).

Sertillanges, O.P., *La Philosophie des Lois.* Paris, Alsatia, 1946, 124 p. (magistrale synthèse de tout le traité).

Janvier, O.P., *La loi* (Carême de Notre-Dame, 1909). Paris, Lethielleux.

Sertillanges, O.P., *La philosophie morale de saint Thomas,* Paris, Aubier. (Chap. V: *La loi morale,* sur la loi en général et la loi naturelle).

A. Molien, art. *Lois,* dans *Diction. de Théol. cath.,* t. IX[1], col. 871-910.

Sur la loi humaine en particulier:

G. Renard, *La valeur de la loi,* Paris, Sirey, 1928.

Sur la Loi nouvelle, spécialement comme loi de liberté:

J. Tonneau, O.P., *L'Église parle,* dans *La Vie intellectuelle,* 1937, t. 2, pp. 165-186, 325-347.

L'histoire médiévale du traité des lois a été étudiée par Dom Lottin, O.S.B., dans une série d'articles très éclairants:

La définition classique de la loi, dans *Revue néo-scolastique de philosophie,* 1925, pp. 129-145, 244-273.

Le droit naturel chez saint Thomas et ses prédécesseurs, dans *Ephemerides theologicæ lovanienses,* 1924, pp. 369-388; 1925, pp. 32-53, 345-366.

Les premiers exposés scolastiques sur la loi éternelle, ibid., 1937, pp. 287-301.

Tous les traités de Théologie morale comportent un chapitre, souvent beaucoup trop réduit, sur les lois; cf. par exemple:

Merkelbach, O.P., *Summa theologiæ moralis,* Paris, Desclée De Brouwer, 1931, t. I, pp. 204-344.

Vittrand, S.J., *Théologie morale,* Paris, Beauchesne, 1942, pp. 27-48.

Van Hove, *De legibus ecclesiasticis* (*Comm. in Cod. Jur. Can., t. II*). Malines, Dessain, 1932 (abondantes notions sur la loi en général).

(On pourra se reporter à un semblable traité pour tous les renseignements d'ordre très pratique que nous avons systématiquement écartés ici).

Sur le problème particulier des lois purement pénales, qui a donné lieu à une assez abondante littérature:
G. Renard, *La théorie des "leges mere pœnales,"* Paris, Sirey, 1929.
Il existe enfin, dans la littérature, de nombreux ouvrages sur les lois dans les différents sens du terme; citons, simplement à titre d'exemples:
L'*Antigone* de Sophocle, la plus célèbre mise en scène de l'opposition entre les lois iniques de la cité et la loi naturelle, le dialogue de Platon intitulé *Les Lois*, mais surtout son *Criton* qui contient les admirables déclarations de Socrate condamné à mort et refusant de s'évader par respect pour les lois de la cité;
Le *De legibus* de Cicéron,
L'Esprit des lois de Montesquieu,
Le Contrat Social de J.-J. Rousseau, spécialement livre II, chap. 6 (*De la loi*) et 7 (*Du législateur*), etc., etc.

BIBLIOGRAPHY

BOOKS

Davis, Henry, S.J., *Moral and Pastoral Theology,* Vol. I, pp. 117-200. London: Sheed and Ward, 1941.

Kreilkamp, Karl, *The Metaphysical Foundation of Thomistic Jurisprudence.* Washington: C. U. Press, 1938.

McHugh, John A., O.P., and Callan, Charles J., O.P., *Moral Theology, A Complete Course,* Vol. I, pp. 90-148. New York: Joseph Wagner, Inc., 1929.

Natural Law Institute Proceedings, 5 vols. Notre Dame, Ind.: University of Notre Dame Press, 1949.

Prat, Fernand, S.J., *The Theology of St. Paul,* 2 vols. Westminster, Md.: The Newman Press, 1952.

Pound, Roscoe, and Lyne, Daniel, *Jubilee Law Lectures.* Washington: C. U. Press, 1939.

Rommen, Heinrich A., *The Natural Law* (trans. Thomas R. Hanley, O.S.B.). St. Louis: B. Herder Book Co., 1947.

Rooney, Miriam T., *Lawlessness, Law, Sanction.* Washington: C. U. Press, 1937.

Slater, Thomas, S.J., *Manual of Moral Theology,* Vol. I, pp. 81-133. New York: Benziger Bros., 1908.

ARTICLES

Brown, B. F., "Natural Law, Bases of Juridical Institutions in the Anglo-Saxon Legal System," *Catholic University Law Review,* 4: 81-94 (May, 1954).

Pius XII, "Nobility of Law," *Catholic Mind,* 50: 632-637 (Oct., 1952).

———, "Private Law and Its Coordination," *Catholic Mind,* 48: 754-756 (Dec., 1950).

Chapter VII

GRACE

by Sister Jeanne d'Arc, A. M. Henry, O.P. and M. Menu, O.P.

FIRST PART: Stages in the Revelation of Grace
(Sister Jeanne d'Arc)
1. The Old Testament
2. The Covenant of Grace
   The Synoptics and the Acts of the Apostles
   Saint Paul
   Saint John
   Convergencies

SECOND PART: Conciliary data (A.M.H.)

THIRD PART: The Theology of Grace

I. GRACE OUTSIDE THE TREATISE ON GRACE
1. Treatise on God:
   (a) The presence of God in us
   (b) The beatific vision
   (c) Providence and predestination
2. Theology of the Holy Trinity
   (a) The appropriations
   (b) The missions
   (c) The habitation
3. Theology of the angels, of man, of divine government
   (a) Relations between the natural and the super-
       natural
   (b) The image of God
   (c) The divine idea of freedom
4. Moral Theology: beatitude
5. The economy of salvation
   (a) Capital Grace and Grace by adoption
   (b) Sacramental Graces
6. Grace, "exterior" helps

337

II. THEOLOGY OF GRACE CONSIDERED AS ASSISTANCE

1. Our miseries and our necessities (M.M.)
    (a) Possibilities of man without grace
        Knowledge
        Will
    (b) Miseries of man without Grace
        Explanations furnished on the occasion of the Pelagian error
        On the occasion of the error of semi-Pelagianism
        1. The case of the sinner
        2. The case of the just
2. The nature of Grace (M.M.)
    (a) The realism of Grace
    (b) The status of Grace in the soul
3. The divers forms of Grace (A.M.H.)
    (a) Sanctifying and charismatic Grace
    (b) Habitual Grace and actual Grace
    (c) Operative and cooperative Grace
    (d) Other divisions
4. Whence comes Grace (A.M.H.)
    (a) God the sole, efficient cause of Grace
    (b) Role of free will in the reception of Grace
        Is it in inertia that Grace seizes us?
        Is Grace given with certainty to him who is disposed?
    (c) Corollaries
        Is Grace equal in everyone?
        Can one know that he has Grace?
5. The effects of Grace (A.M.H.)
    (a) Justification
        Definition
        The components of justification
            The part of God
            The part of man
        Synthetic grouping
            Time in justification
            The order of nature
        Justification evalued among the works of God

Chapter VII

GRACE

First Part

STAGES IN THE REVELATION OF GRACE

The word Grace in Greek has several different meanings, (*kharis,* χάϱις) from a root which signifies joy, light, to shine.

Beginning with this root the derivation is clear. We can easily reduce all meanings to four principal ones.

The first meaning of χάϱις is "grace," that gay and free form of beauty—a meaning to which corresponds the adjective gracious and which finds no place in theological language.

This grace in a being normally attracts to him the "good graces" of others, whence the second meaning: favor, good reception, benevolence, generosity.

That which manifests itself through "graces," is the third meaning: gifts, presents, benefits, which the obligated person receives and which effectively become his own.

He "gives thanks" for them, the fourth meaning: gratitude, recognition, *thanksgiving*. The last meaning has passed over onto the religious plane only in the compounds, of which the principal one is the Eucharist, εὐ-χαϱις-τια.

The first and the fourth being eliminated, there remain for our consideration the two in which this word is the bearer of eternal truth: on the one hand the favor, the divine benevolence, and on the other, the gift which God makes to man. These two meanings are often difficult to distinguish. Certain texts are clear in the one meaning or the other, but most frequently they imply both inseparably, and we must take them with all their fulness of meaning. We can almost say that the task of the New Testament is to make clear the second meaning, of revealing that this divine benevolence betrays itself through an effective gift which surpasses everything that has happened to the heart of man.

340

1. THE OLD TESTAMENT

In the Old Testament, how was this Revelation prepared and presented? What are the terms which correspond to it?

First, there is *hen,* from a root which means to lean out, to incline—whence the meaning of favor, benevolence—a very general term, little enough characterized, which generally serves in the common formula: "That I may *find grace* in thy eyes." There are however certain texts in which its religious value clearly appears: "To the meek he will give his grace." [1] "The Lord grants grace and glory" (Ps. 83:12). And especially the mysterious promise of Zacharias (12:10) in which the messianic times are thus characterized: "And I will pour out upon the House of David . . . the spirit of grace and of prayers." No doubt one should not read these texts by projecting into the terms conceptions elaborated through twenty centuries of theology; it remains true, nevertheless, that these formulas (in which *hen* is always rendered by χάρις) are remarkable; the word grace is there ready to express a higher truth.

A richer word by itself in its religious and moral capacity, is *hesed,* "pity, piety, goodness, love," [2] the word type of the prophet Osee. Unlike the purely gratuitous benevolence *hen* expresses, *hesed* is a duty, the attitude which is imposed with regard to persons to whom one is united by a bond: relationship, friendship, pact, gratitude. Between God and Israel this bond is the Covenant by which God deigned to be attached to this people. All this comprises an effective behavior, and it is what is signified by *hesed,* on the part of man as well as on the part of God.[3] The word takes on its full religious richness in the last case when it is associated with others which clarify the cause, for example, in the beautiful text of Jeremias: "Yea I have loved thee with an everlasting love ('ahabah); therefore have I drawn thee, taking pity on thee (*hesed*)" (31:3).

It would be necessary here to translate in terms of *fidelity,* that is, loyalty of God in observing this covenant, fidelity which has its

[1] Prov. 3:34. The text will be cited by St. Peter (I Pet. 5:5) and St. James (4:6).

[2] Osty (Bible de Jérusalem) does not hesitate to translate it in terms of charity (Osee 4:1).

[3] Osee never applies the word except to man and preferably to men: 2:21; 4:1; 6:4-6. . . . On the contrary, when Jeremias speaks of *hesed* it is always to God that he attributes it, except in 2:2.

source in eternal love, and which contrasts so much with the infidelity of this changeable people. Not that there is ever any question
of testing, of feeling the *hesed,* but almost always of "doing *hesed"*
and often with the association of *'emet* ("to do good and truth");
this formula so full of meaning and so untranslatable is the one
which St. John evokes when he speaks of the Word "full of grace
and truth" (1:14) and also St. Paul: "rather are we to practice the
truth in love" (Eph. 4:15). The Greek translation, ἔλεος, mercy,
which is an approved sentiment, has distorted a little the effective
and realistic perspective of *hesed* by confusing it with *rahamim,*
this other word which resembles grace.

Rahamim completes *hesed,* by expressing the whole richness of
the emotion and of the sentiment: [4] it is tenderness, maternal love,
the pity which stirs your heart. And that singularly brings us close
to the perspective in which the tenderness of God will appear.

Certain texts in which all these words are found united constitute
the most striking stepping stones to Christian grace. And first this
solemn declaration which is already like "the charity of grace," and
at once the place at which God has best expressed His nature:

Yahweh pronounced the name of Yahweh.

"To pronounce the name," in good Hebrew, is to indicate the
nature of a being. What does God say of the nature of God?

"I, the Lord, the Lord God, merciful (R. *rahamin*) and gracious,
patient and of much compassion, (*hesed*) and true (*'emet*), who
keepeth mercy (*hesed*) unto thousands . . ." (Ex. 34:6-7).

All of these notes are assembled, the different shades of meaning
which proclaim the definitive revelation: at the other extremity of
the New Testament, St. John has only to recompose the prism in
order to give us in a single word, which includes everything, the
total light: "God is love" (I Jn. 4:16). It is remarkable that this
revelation of grace should have been made on the mountain of the
Law. That permits us perhaps to understand more profoundly the
old Dispensation. It is correct to compare with St. John (1:17) and
St. Paul (Rom. 6:14-15), the Law and Grace. We must not forget
either that it is to the same man, this Moses to whom He spoke "As
a man is wont to speak to his friend" (Ex. 33:11), and on the same
Sinai, that Yahweh delivered at the same time as the Law, this
formula which enables us to enter perhaps further into the revelation

---

[4] The Greek often renders it by οἰχτιρμός. On the value of all these words,
cf. Guillet, *Thèmes bibliques,* to whom we owe a great deal.

of the mystery of His name, and into the depths of His personal life. This is to suggest that the Law itself was a grace. It is in line with the future dialectic of St. Paul: "For the law indeed is holy and the commandment holy and just and good" (Rom. 7:12).

Another text also brings together all these concepts preparatory for grace in a still richer group, not indeed from the point of view of God, but from the point of view of His gifts to man. This is the great promise of the espousal in which Osee expressed the whole hope of Israel, all the conditions of the true knowledge of God, in the language of love and under the image of a wedding: "And I will espouse thee to me forever. And I will espouse thee to me in justice and judgment (*hesed*) and in mercy (*rahamim*) and in commiserations. And I will espouse thee to me in faith (*'emet*); and thou shalt know that I am the Lord" (Osee 2:19-20).

Presently it was after the most shameless prevarication of Israel that God had pronounced the most profound words on His goodness and His mercy. Now again, it is to the adulterer and the unfaithful that are addressed these declarations full of tenderness as to an espousal: the love of God is creative of good, He will fill her with spiritual gifts, all the riches of the spouse are her presents; she cannot know fully either God or the secret of His promised gifts, but she can await in the faith this *grace* of which the prophets have given to her an obscure vision: the effusion of the Spirit (Joel 3:1), a new covenant (Jer. 3:31), eternal love (Jer. 31:3).

2. THE COVENANT OF GRACE

Finally in the fullness of time "the grace of God our Saviour has appeared to all men" (Tit. 2:11; I Jn. 3:15), but this appearance itself has been a progressive development. The epiphany has known stages.

The Incarnation remained a secret. "For while all things were in quiet silence" (Wis. 18:4), Mary alone had received the confidence. This first descent of the Holy Spirit has been for her alone and "in order to cover her with his shadow."

Grace was there, but no one knew it except the Virgin plunged into the mystery.

Nine months later, "she brought forth her first-born son." The manifestation becomes visible but only slightly so. And the Word remains concealed for thirty years in the secret of Nazareth.

The baptism is a more striking epiphany. The Spirit descends on

Christ, visibly this time. It is the inauguration of a new stage, that of His public ministry (Lk. 3:21-23) and the opening up of the current of grace which having come from the Father, through Jesus will be spread throughout the world.

Christ was "filled with the Spirit" (Lk. 4:1), "led by the Spirit" (Mt. 4:1); but to the disciples "the Spirit had not yet been given, since Jesus had not yet been glorified (Jn. 7:39). This is why the Master said to them, "It is expedient for you that I depart. For if I do not go, the Advocate will not come to you; but if I go, I will send him to you" (Jn. 16:7). Jesus "exalted by the right hand of God, and receiving from the Father the promise of the Holy Spirit has poured forth this spirit . . ." (Acts 2:33).

Thus it is Pentecost, the coming of the Spirit, the baptism in fire, inauguration of the new and definitive economy through the appearance of grace.

"They were all filled with the Holy Spirit" (Acts 2:4); and the Church ever since lives in this fullness and spreads it abroad, "for the earth is filled with the knowledge of the Lord, as the covering waters of the sea" (Is. 11:9).

One of the notable means by which this diffusion is effected and this knowledge assured is the small circumstantial writings, edited by the disciples under the movement and with the special assistance of the Holy Spirit, whose collection form the New Testament.

In this very diverse group of writings, scattered over a half century, we must seek to grasp how revelation formulated the gift of grace, how the notion is elaborated and how it formed its outlines and its stability.

First we should remark that the word by which this new reality is expressed, χάρις, is precisely the least rich in religious value among all those which we have gathered in the Old Testament. God has chosen what was weak in order to confound what was strong. Is this also true in the linguistic domain . . .? There was in it "mercy" and "tenderness" and "goodness" and "love" . . . The first Christians (among them perhaps St. Paul himself) took the vague and rather secular word of "favor," "grace." There are two intelligible reasons for this. Quite rightly, it was less precise, less reminiscent of the values of the Old Testament, and so more apt to translate a reality which was experienced as something entirely new. For some readers of the Septuagint who gave to the Greek the complex value which these words take in translation, χάρις had undergone the attraction of *hen,* and so in its most frequent meaning it should imply, unlike a pure Greek word, charm which draws favor at first and then benefits, but like the Hebrew word, it emphasizes especially the gratuity, the absolute liberty of the sovereign who distributes his favors as he pleases. In that way it rendered marvelously this impression which the Acts so strongly give us, this dizziness before the gratuitous Gift, this sensation of being plunged into the superabundance of infinite divine generosity.

The Synoptics and the Acts of the Apostles

It is in fact a reflexive theological concept. It was necessary to search to find this novelty of which they became conscious and which Jesus had not named. He had only spoken of the Kingdom, this complex reality at once future and present, social and personal, exterior and immanent: this last meaning was close to grace, for example when Jesus says, "Whoever does not accept the Kingdom of God as a little child, will not enter into it" (Mk. 10:15). It is necessary also to point out the equivalence between "kingdom" and "life" or "eternal life," for example in Mt. 19:16: "What good work shall I do to have eternal life"; Verse 18: "If thou wilt enter into life . . ."; Verse 23: "Enter the kingdom of heaven." But the word grace is not found in the Synoptics—except four times in St. Luke under the form of the usual Greek turn: "What manner of greeting might this be . . ."; there are also a few interesting uses in the gospel of infancy in which the influence of the Septuagint is so manifest. These are the old formulas: "Thou hast found grace with God," "The grace of God rested on him." But when they are applied to Jesus or to her who is called full of grace, they are charged with an unknown obscurity (Lk. 1:28-30; 2:40). We should not forget either that St. Luke, before writing, had been the disciple of St. Paul, whom he had heard throughout long journeys and nights (Acts 20:7-11) proclaim "the gospel of the grace of God" (Acts 20:24). It is not surprising therefore that from then on a little of the word grace infiltrated into his own message.

But, more than these uses of the word, there is an aspect of this gospel—the place which the Holy Spirit holds in it—which directly concerns the revelation of grace.[5] Luke loves to give prominence to

[5] Jn. 1:15. Elizabeth 1:41. Zachary 1:67. And particularly Jesus 4:1. This last text, in close parallel with Mt. 4:1, is particularly significant because this incidental phrase is proper only to Luke. And later in the Acts: the disciples, 2:3; Peter: 4:8; Paul: 9:17; Stephen: 6:3; Barnabas: 11:24.

the role of the Spirit. Jesus returns from the desert with the "power of the Spirit" (4:14); He trembles with joy "under the action of the Spirit" (10:21). It is the Spirit who "comes upon Mary and overshadows her with his Spirit" (Lk. 1:35). It is the Spirit who "reveals to Simeon . . ." (2:26), this Spirit which "reposed on him" (2:25). Here the parallel is particularly interesting between this expression and that which we recalled a moment ago: A few lines further on it is said of the infant Jesus: "And the grace of God rested on him" (2:40). ἦνέ π'αὐτόν is the same formula; it even seems that the expressions "the grace of God" and "the Holy Spirit" are here almost interchangeable.

The whole gospel of Luke is thus pointed toward the Acts, which are inseparably "the gospel of the Holy Spirit" and the book of the expansion of Christian grace. They begin with Pentecost which is at once the effusion of the Spirit and the gift of grace, and they show the irresistible dynamism of this grace which invades the universe. The word "grace," moreover, in the Acts often has a note of force or of very special power (cf. Acts 4:33; 6:8; 11:23), along with the meanings entirely Paulinian (15:11) and others which one would call restored to the level of the Septuagint (2:47). This renders difficult for our subject, the utilization of this complex book which gives an account of the earliest beginnings, but with a perspective of thirty years, which transmits to us the primitive catechesis, but already developed, in which we hear Peter [6] and Paul speak but through the summaries of Luke. Grace is everywhere present in it, but all the currents converge in such a way that it is hardly discernible, and it seems difficult to establish any points of direction.

The great current which dominates everything is the *gift of the Spirit*. The expression is proper to the Acts (2:38; 10:45; 11:17), and it completes all the formulas in which it is said that the Holy Spirit "fell" (10:14), "descended" (1:8), "came" (19:6), "was received" (8:17), etc. The historian, which Luke is, notes especially the facts, this series of successive little pentecosts which succeeded the first, the charisms, the transitory and visible aspect of grace. But with the "gift of the spirit" the fullest theological expression is at-

[6] Moreover it is remarkable that, in the Acts, it should be Peter who has the most Paulinian formula (15:9-11).

tained. The Holy Spirit Himself is given to us [7] and this is the foundation of the whole doctrine of grace.

Saint Paul

Peter, John, Luke, and the other apostles and disciples from the beginning are of the *anawim,* of the poor and humble Israelites who awaited the Messias by living according to the spirit of the prophets and the psalmists. They knew Jesus and they slowly became aware of his quality of Messias. The transition from the old Covenant to the new was made insensibly, in contact with the Master, who "did not come to destroy but to fulfill." They do not have the impression of any sudden break, but of that accomplishment which is a fulfillment. Jesus is He who has realized the promises, and their catechesis is greatly concerned to emphasize this continuity (Acts 2:16-36; 3:22-26; I Pet. 1:10-11). St. Peter avows that "neither our fathers nor we have been able to bear the yoke of the law" (Acts 15:10); but for James, who does not seem to have found this yoke so heavy, Christianity is itself a law: "perfect law" (1:25), "royal law" (2:8), "law of liberty" (2:12); the most beautiful epithets are used to defend the law, but it remains a law: he does not find a word more dear to his heart.

Paul, on the contrary, is a "Pharisee, the son of a Pharisee" (Acts 23:6). He belongs to a sect which tends to harden man in his self-sufficiency, to procure for him a justice through the minute and proud fulfillment of infinite details of a law surcharged by the Scribes and the doctors. He knew the intolerable weight of this law, and at the same time this mentality so supremely hostile to the spirit of the gospel. The frightful words of Christ [8] alone can give us an idea of this absolute opposition. And without any transition, without any preliminary evolution, at the height of his rage, Saul is converted by the Lord of Glory. He experiences the irresistible empire of grace, the radical incompatibility of this regime in which everything is a gift, in which everything comes from God, with the attitude which hereto-

[7] We notice that Holy Scripture never speaks of the "grace of the Holy Spirit." It speaks of the grace of God, of God the Father, of our Lord Jesus Christ—but not of the Holy Spirit. The Father and the Word send the Spirit; the Spirit Himself is given to us and this gift in us is a source of grace.

[8] Hypocrites (Mt. 6:2), whited sepulchers (Mt. 23:27), race of vipers (Mt. 12:34), perverse and adulterous generation (Mt. 12:39), blind guides (Mt. 15:14), etc.

fore had stiffened him in this justice which he himself produced. His whole doctrine is affected by this unique experience; it is concerned no longer with continuity and fulfillment, but with rupture and opposition. Christ is not for him principally the Messias of the Jews who fulfills the prophecies, but rather the Lord who "came into the world to save sinners, of whom I am the chief" (I Tim. 1:15). The regime of grace is offered to the whole world by the "unique mediator" (I Tim. 2:5).

From his conversion, his doctrine is in all essentials complete: "How that by revelation was made known to me the mystery" (Eph. 3:3); and it is entirely centered on grace. The word, which is characteristic in him, comprises the two meanings which we have noted: of divine benevolence and of a gift which God makes to man, sometimes distinct, but most often confused, and without there having been the least discernible evolution of the thought of the Apostle on the subject.

Still, there is an explanation, a more and more clear formulation, a synthesis which is organized under a more profound interior light— these revelations of which he speaks on several occasions—and at the same time under the pressure of circumstances—the questions which are raised and the needs of the Church.

In the first discourses which the Acts relate, the word χάρις does not appear. At Antioch, for example (Acts 13), eight or ten years after his conversion, he finds the means of setting forth the whole new doctrine without pronouncing the word "grace" (it is certain that he would be incapable of doing that later!). But the reality of grace is so present that when there is question, on the following day, of summing up in a few words this teaching, Luke tells us that he exhorts "to remain faithful to the grace of God" (13:43). Evidently, we can use these arguments based on vocabulary only with great reserve when the text of the discourse reaches us in summary, introduced into a subsequent narration. We must not be narrow, but the index can be revealing: who would be able to sum up even briefly the letter to the Romans without introducing into it the word *grace?*

A dozen years later, about 56, St. Luke tells us of the sad farewells with the Elders of Ephesus (Acts 20:17-38). He was present at this moving scene, and with all the tenderness of his heart he knew how to fix upon the details of it in such a way that even now it touches us deeply. He retained the very expressions of the apostle, and we can believe that he relates them to us in their exact context: ". . . that I may bear witness to the gospel of the grace of God . . . And now I commend you to God and to the word of his grace" (Acts 20:24, 32). The whole gospel is summed up in this grace from which it issues and which it manifests. God acts through His word which is grace. If these formulas so complete rise spontaneously to the lips of Paul it is because he has just written his great epistles; this profound elaboration has marked a stage in his thought, it furnishes him with summaries very rich in meaning.

With his own writings, we are on safer ground to set up a comparison by following the chronological order, at least through the series of his epistles.

The two short *Letters to the Thessalonians,* about 51 or 52, correspond to his preoccupations on the subject of the second coming and of the eschatology which troubled his recent converts. The subject does not lend itself to the developments on grace. But we make a twofold verification: first, his doctrine is essentially complete. Certain scattered words constantly suppose it: "God loves us" and "gives us through his grace eternal consolation" (II Thess. 2:16); "He also called you by our preaching to gain the glory of our Lord Jesus Christ" (II Thess. 2:14); "He sanctifies us" (I Thess. 5:23), "by giving us his Spirit" (I Thess. 4:8), "whose action is sanctifying" (II Thess. 2:13); "may the Lord strengthen your hearts, blameless in holiness before God our Father" (I Thess. 3:13; II Thess. 3:5). The initial greeting unites as in the succeeding letters, the Greek wish of χάρις and the old Semitic wish of peace (I Thess. 1:1; II Thess. 1:2).

Already more complete explanations had appeared. This grace is at once "from God and from the Lord Jesus Christ" (II Thess. 1:2, 12; 2:16); "the Lord died . . . in order that we might live in union with him" (I Thess. 5:9-10). The reality appears everywhere but underlying rather than expressed. One gets the impression that St. Paul lacks turning points, that he lets escape certain occasions which would furnish him later on with his beautiful developments. The synthesis is not made; the place of grace, at least in so far as the expression goes, is not yet what it is going to become, i.e., central.

The *Epistles to the Corinthians* correspond also to precise questions, to accidental circumstances and are found in the same perspective of the salvation to be brought to the pagans. Already a word (II Cor. 3:6-11) contrasts the letter with the spirit, the ministry of the letter with that of the Spirit. It is the first sketch of an antinomy which is going to be the dominant preoccupation of Paul and make him state precisely his personal synthesis: the comparison of the law with grace which fills the *Epistles to the Romans* and the *Galatians*.

Faced with the problem of the judaizers in the Church, and of the mystery of Israel, the apostle strongly emphasizes the gratuity of the divine gift and he goes back to its uncreated source, the free design of God. The radical impotence of sinful man without grace, and the impotence of the law to bring him assistance, the necessity of redemption common to all, the justice which comes from faith and faith which is itself a pure grace, the adoptive filiation, the triumph of Christ over death—all these great themes merely construct the synthesis of the regime of grace in the powerful ensemble which is the essential theological locus of the treatises on grace.

Other difficulties arise from the first contacts with the oriental philosophies, the errors which tend to denature the role of Christ: in the *Epistles of the Captivity,* whose climax is the first part of the *Epistle to the Ephesians,* St. Paul sets up his Christology with a magnificent sweep. Christ is placed in a perspective no longer merely soteriological, but cosmic: He is the very bosom of God, "image of the Father," "principle," "head of the whole creation" (Col. 1:15-18) and the universal source of grace. And the doctrine of grace here gains a new scope. It is no longer that which dominates the history of humanity, as in the *Epistle to the Romans,* but that which fills the eternal design of God, which deploys "the riches of his grace," from eternity to eternity, "in order that the splendor of his grace may be praised" (Eph. 1:6).

The *Pastoral letters* correspond to the immediate needs of the new heads of the churches. There is question of "guarding the deposit" (II Tim. 1:14), of organizing the hierarchy, of preserving orthodoxy, of giving to each one his place in the Church. These wholly practical perspectives do not lend themselves to great doctrinal developments. And yet it is there that we find these powerful summaries in which St. Paul gathers together his doctrine on grace in formulas so rich, so close that there is no better summary in his whole thought: "For the grace of God our Savior has appeared to all men, instructing us, in order that, rejecting ungodliness and worldly lusts, we may live temperately and justly and piously in this world; looking for the blessed hope and glorious coming of our great God and Savior, Jesus Christ, who gave himself for us that he might redeem us from all iniquity and cleanse for himself an acceptable people, pursuing good works. Thus speak, and exhort, and rebuke, with all authority. Let no one despise thee" (Tit. 2:11-14). "But when the goodness and kindness of God our Savior appeared, then not by reason of good works that we did ourselves, but according to his mercy, he saved us through the bath of regeneration and renewal by the Holy Spirit; whom he has abundantly poured out upon us through Jesus Christ our Savior, in order that, justified by his grace, we may be heirs in the hope of life everlasting" (Tit. 3:4-7).

Thus to take in at one glance, however schematic it may be, the development of the thought of the apostle, one is struck by seeing how it is built up with the aid of successive oppositions and errors; thus the Church proceeds when she carefully explains dogma on the occasion of heresies, and theology when it is applied to the points of controversy.

And that should make us careful to confront each progressive thought, as well as each development of dogma, with the occasion which gave it birth, in such a way as to distinguish the periphery from what lies at the heart. Because of controversies the frontiers are disputed, but the most essential vital center is not there. Particularly in dealing with the occasional or polemic writings, as well as most of the letters of St. Paul, it is necessary never to lose sight of this perspective and to be constantly on guard lest a doctrine be placed out of context.

Saint John

With St. John we are at the center. Even if his gospel is born on the occasion of errors and contemporary quarrels, it does not retain any tone of controversy. It gives us pure light received into a heart which loves and has ripened throughout a long life of contemplation with the aid of her whom the dying Jesus had given to him as mother —who is at the same time the mother of divine grace.

One fact strikes us from the first: except in the prologue, St. John does not speak of grace. The prologue gives the doctrinal key to the fourth Gospel. In these essential texts—"full of grace and of truth," "and of his fullness we have all received, grace for grace," "for the law was given through Moses; grace and truth came through Jesus Christ" (1:14, 16, 17)—he affirms the place of grace in his doctrine, then speaks no more of it. The word χάρις is not found in his work— if we except the stereotyped form of salutation in one epistle and in the letters of the Apocalypse. Why? St. John comes after St. Paul, and was acquainted with his letters, but psychologically he is nearer the Synoptics. He did not know the break either of returning, or the sudden and irresistible domination of a new reality which it was necessary to name, to locate intellectually. He had lived close to the Master and Friend, and after Pentecost he understood better his words, better and better according as his own life progressed; he understood that he lived by the life of Jesus, and that this new life in him was already eternal life.

One point worthy of remark is that the possession of eternal life is habitually expressed in the present tense: "He who believes in the Son *has* everlasting life" (Jn. 3:36), "He who eats my flesh and drinks my blood *has* everlasting life" (6:55), etc. The texts are quite numerous in which this affirmation is repeated.[9] Clearly, in St. John there is the consciousness that eternal life has already begun and that this reality in us is what we call grace. One text even employs the precise word as we would say "grace" in the sense of "state of grace": "No murderer has eternal life abiding in him" (I Jn. 3:15). And the whole gospel is constructed on this theme of life: baptismal life after the water: dialogue with Nicodemus (Ch. 3), then with the Samaritan woman (Ch. 4), "The water that I will give him shall become in him a fountain of waters, springing up unto life everlasting"; Eucharistic life after the bread, "the bread of life" (Ch. 6). And since "the life was the light of man," here is the teaching on light: "I am the light of the world. He who follows me does not walk in darkness, but will have the light of life" (8:12). And, as a sign, he leads the blind man to the light (Ch. 9). The good Pastor has come "in order that his sheep may have life in abundance," he "lays down his life for them" (Ch. 10). And the rest of the gospel shows us the gift of His life in the passion as a march toward the Life in definitive exaltation, "in order that we may live by him" (I Jn. 4:9).

And this eternal life is love: "Let us therefore love, because God first loved us" (I Jn. 4:19). "We know that we have passed from death to life, because we love the brethren" (I Jn. 3:14). Equivalently: "He who loves . . . remains in the light" (I Jn. 2:10).

A longer explanation is given, which allows us to go to the depths of the doctrine: "He who abides in love abides in God and God in him" (I Jn. 4:16). This is the meaning of the conversation after the Last Supper, in which this word *abide* is constantly repeated: "Abide in my love" (15:9); "Abide in me, and I will abide in you" (15:4); and in the plural we can perceive the whole Trinity: "We will come

---

[9] Cf. Jn. 3:14; 5:24; 6:40, 47; 10:28. Cf. also 8:51; 11:25.

to him and make our abode with him" (14:23). And this phrase, which shows us the child of God plunged into the very bosom of Trinitarian life: "I have made known to them thy name . . . in order that the love with which thou hast loved me may be in them, and I in them" (17:26). Other texts will explain to us the name of this love by which the Father loves the Son: the Paraclete, Spirit of Truth (14:16-17).

The *Gift of God* is nothing less than this (4:10): "And the glory thou hast given me I have given to them" (17:22), the glory of which grace is only the inchoative name. Like a true contemplative, St. John does not stop at the present stage. His whole message speaks to us only of grace but under its definitive form of glory, of light, of eternal life already begun in love, in faith, in this real abode in us of Jesus, of His Father and of the Holy Spirit.

In short, for St. John, grace is—he dares write quite simply this extraordinary word—σπέρμα θεοῦ, a "seed of God" (I Jn. 3:9).

Convergencies

It is very easy from this point of view to compare, as is commonly done, St. John with St. Paul, "the doctor of sanctifying grace and divinization, with the doctor of actual grace who delivers the sinner and leads him to Christ." Let us not forget that it is on St. John (Jn. 15:5) that the dogmatic definition of actual grace is based: "Without me you can do nothing" (Council of Carthage, can. 5).

Paul is the doctor par excellence of the life of the soul sanctified by grace and inhabited by the Holy Spirit: "You are the temple of God, and the Spirit of God dwells in you" (I Cor. 3:16). "The charity of God is poured forth in our hearts by the Holy Spirit, who has been given to us" (Rom. 5:5): ". . . that you may be filled unto all the fullness of God" (Eph. 5:19). And the condition of this fullness is faith by which "Christ dwells in our hearts"; it is charity in which one must be "rooted and grounded" (Eph. 3:17). All that is "the work of the Lord": "But we all with faces unveiled, reflecting as in a mirror the glory of the Lord, are being transformed into his very image from glory to glory . . ." (II Cor. 3:18). In keeping before ourselves constantly the Glory of the Lord, the image of God recovers the resemblance which it had lost from the beginning. . . . If everything is the work of the Lord, why ask of Him to work it in us? "We do not know what we should pray for as we ought, but the Spirit himself pleads for us with unutterable groanings" (Rom. 8:26). "God

has sent the Spirit of his Son into our hearts, crying, 'Abba,' Father"
(Gal. 4:6). "For whoever are led by the Spirit of God are the sons of
God" (Rom. 8:14).

An ancient dream of salvation and of becoming like God has
haunted the human spirit. "For we are also his offspring," said the
Greek poets (Acts 17:28). The pagans sought to realize it by impure
or facile means, against which the slow and severe education of the
Old Testament struggled. There was question of separating it from
Israel at any price. At the same time, a marvelous pedagogy introduced the chosen people to the knowledge of the true God, strongly
inculcated into them the sense of his incommunicable transcendence.
But on account of being transcendent, God became inaccessible. Other
texts began to reveal his proximity, love, grace.

One day the antinomy is resolved, "Goodness has appeared," and
at the same time the unconscious aspiration of the pagans for divinization, and the better expectation of the Jewish people are both found
realized—but in a way how worthy of God! This grace which He
offers us is a participation in His very nature.

. . . Γένησθε θείας κοινωνοὶ θύσεως

The second epistle of St. Peter (1:4), utilizing, as later theology
will, its *handmaid*, Greek philosophy, reached this magnificent formula, so strong, so clear and so technically perfect, which opens the
way for all Christian centuries to the reflection of faith seeking to
penetrate the mystery of grace: "You shall become sharers in the
divine nature."

Second Part

CONCILIARY DATA

After having considered the Biblical texts, let us examine briefly
the positions which the Church has been led to take in the course of
her history against heretical and erroneous interpretations with regard
to grace.

As we shall frequently have to return to this subject in the course
of the treatise, we shall here give only a sketch destined to assist the
mind. We shall group our conciliary references around four major
errors: those of the Pelagians; of the group in Provence in the fifth
century; of the Protestants in the 16th century; of Baius and of Jansen.

(a) *The Pelagians*

Pelagius was born in Great Britain toward the end of the fourth century. He became a monk, came to Rome, and was formed by the reading of the Greek Fathers, especially of Origen. Of an extraordinary mind, he quickly gained influence, composed several works, notably a commentary on St. Paul in which was expressed a dangerous doctrine. According to Pelagius there is no original sin; Adam had been created mortal and subject to concupiscence even before his sin, but man can always by himself do good. The willing and doing of man are integral, i.e., without "wound." Henceforth baptism is not necessary in order to cleanse the soul from original sin, it effaces only the actual sins of those who have committed them and it is an ornament instituted by Christ, an obligatory title in order to enter the Church.

Pelagius and his disciples did not directly deny the reality of grace but they equated grace with natural goods, notably free will, given by God. They saw also in the *Law* and the *doctrine* taught by God a kind of grace. Finally they recognized certain graces of illumination, for the intelligence alone, which did not affect the free will. Some, however, not all, conceded that "grace" could be accorded to the will, not in order to fulfill precepts purely and simply, but in order to fulfill them better.

At the time of the capture of Rome by Alaric (410), Pelagius like many others fled with Celestius, an Italian lawyer whom he had won over to his ideas. Both propagated their doctrine in Sicily, then at Carthage where Pelagius left Celestius and embarked for Palestine.

The separation of the two protagonists did not arrest the diffusion of their doctrine. One of their first disciples, Julian, later Bishop of Eclane (near Beneventum in southern Italy), at first supported by St. Augustine who for a time drew him to Africa, turned vigorously against the latter. A powerful dialectician and adversary, Julian became the doctrinaire of the Pelagian heresy. Deposed, then exiled, he finished by dying in misery in 454.

The broadsides which were given him by Augustine, especially in his *De gratia et concupiscentia* and his last unfinished work, *Contra Julianum*, did not help to raise Pelagianism up from its ruins. Still, he had exercised a certain influence in Great Britain, the country of Pelagius, to which Pope Celestine sent St. Germain of Auxere to combat it.

Let us recall these two canons of the Council of Carthage (418). Canon 4. If anyone says that grace aids us to avoid sin in this sense alone that it reveals to us and makes us understand the precepts in such a way that we may know what we should do and avoid, and not in the sense that it enables us to love and to do what we have learned should be done, let him be anathema. Since the apostle has said (I Cor. 8:1): "Knowledge puffs up but charity edifies," it is impious to think that grace is given us in view of what puffs up and not in view of what edifies, when the gift of God is not only that we might know what we should do but also what we are born to do by love; really constructive charity prevents all knowledge which would puff us up. Likewise it is said that God is he who "gives knowledge to man" (Ps. 92:10). It is also written that *charity is of God* (I Jn. 4:7).

Canon 5. If anyone says that the grace of justification is granted to us in order that what we are commanded to do by our free will, we might be able to do more easily by grace, as if, by supposing that grace is not given to us, we might be able to fulfill without it, although not so easily, the divine precepts, let him be anathema. The Lord did not say without me you can act with difficulty, but "without me you can do nothing" (Jn. 15:5).

(b) *The 5th Century Ascetics of Provence*

The vigorous anti-Pelagian reaction of Augustine aroused among the ascetics of Provence a new effort in favor of a Pelagianism which the theologians called mitigated, and at the end of the 16th century and especially the 17th century, "semi-Pelagianism." The authors of it were especially Cassian, a monk of Marseilles, founder of two monasteries, one for men and the other for women, and St. Honoratus, founder of the Abbey of Lerins. The Provencians admitted original sin and the necessity of grace, but they rejected the Augustinian doctrine of predestination which made salvation depend entirely on the will of God, not seeing that this not only worked no prejudice to the liberty of man but actually helped it. Making a plea for free will and the efficacy of ascetic acts, the Provencians felt that at least the beginning of salvation should come from the obedience of man and not from grace, and that man would be able to *will* the good even though he would not be able to *do* it without grace.

The Council of Orange condemned their error in 529. We cite Canons 3 and 4:

Canon 3. If anyone says that grace can be conferred at the request of man and that grace itself does not enable man to call on God, he contradicts the Prophet Isaias and the Apostle who says: "I was found by those who did not seek me; I appeared openly to those who made no inquiry of me" (Rom. 10:20; cf. Is. 65:10).

Canon 4. If anyone contends that to cleanse us from sin God awaits our will, and does not believe that, even in order that we might wish to be cleansed, our will is formed by the infusion and the operation of the Holy Spirit, he resists the Holy Spirit himself who says by the sacred writer: "Thy will is prepared by the Lord" (Prov. 8:30-5), and the apostle who declares: "For it is God who of his good pleasure works in you both the will and the performance" (Phil. 2:13).

(c) *Protestants of the 16th Century*

It is impossible to sum up a doctrine like that of Luther or Calvin or of the Council of Trent, which in condemning the errors of the reformers stated the Catholic faith. Let us recall simply that the Council affirmed the existence, even after original sin, of free will in man (Sess. 6, Ch. 1); it affirmed also that man could give his consent and freely cooperate with divine grace (Ch. 5). Among the Canons on the doctrine of justification which ended the session, Canon 4 says: "If anyone says that the free will of man stirred and moved by God can in no way cooperate by its assent with God who touches and calls it in such a way that he could not dispose himself or prepare himself to obtain the grace of justification, and that this same free will can no longer detach itself even if it wants to, but that it acts in the manner of the inanimate thing not being able to do anything of itself, and that it behaves in a purely passive way, let him be anathema.

(d) *Jansenism*

The Protestants exaggerated the misery of man before God. Baius exaggerated the native goodness of man, a fact which winds up in the same practical pessimism.

For Baius, grace is never different from moral rectitude. For him, the gifts of integrity, of original "justice," which the first man received, were not freely granted by God, since without them man could not have been anything but bad. God was not able not to grant them since He cannot be the author of evil. Original integrity was a condition of nature, not a gratuitous gift.

In this regard Jansen differs little from Baius. Jansen thinks that the gifts of integrity were not due of right to the creature, but that God owed them to His wisdom and to the natural order which He set up.

In the 4th and 5th centuries, the Church had to struggle in order to vindicate the primacy of grace against an irreligious naturalism. In the 16th century, she had to affirm vigorously that our liberty is not diminished, and still less annihilated, but preserved by grace.

Elements of biography:

Luther, born in Saxony in 1483, was the son of a minor craftsman. After having finished his early education in Erfurt, he joined the Augustinians. Having become a professor at Wittenberg, he was sent to Rome to represent his Order; he there defended with zeal the authority of the Pope and of the Church. Back in Saxony, he turned violently against Catholic principles, notably on the occasion of the preaching of indulgences. Denounced at the court of Rome, he finished by being excommunicated by the Pope in 1520. The secularization of the property of the clergy made easier, or even possibly permitted, the reform of Luther. Having married, he organized, with Melanchthon, his church, which after a fashion was given its charter in the diet of Augsburg in 1530. Luther died in 1546.

Calvin, born at Noyes in 1509, died in 1564 at Geneva where he had established "a Christian republic." Less mystical and more rationalistic than Luther, he pushed to further extremes than the latter the logic of the "Reform." He suppressed ceremonies, reduced the sacraments to baptism and the Last Supper, and despised Tradition. He is the author of *L'Institution Chrétienne*.

Baius, born in Hainaut in 1513, died in 1589 and was, during his whole career, professor at Louvain.

Jansen, 1585–1638, was Dutch. His life was passed in Holland, at Louvain and in Paris where he joined up with the Abbé of Saint-Cyran with whom he was later to develop his doctrine at Bayonne, and then at Ypres of which he became bishop. He had scarcely finished his work, *Augustinus*, when he died of the plague which he had contracted by touching infected archives.

Third Part

THE THEOLOGY OF GRACE

I. Grace Outside of the Treatise on Grace

In the manuals which divide theology into Dogma and Moral and oppose one to the other, the "tract on grace" which is found in Dogma occupies ordinarily a prominent place. But a large part of the matter thus considered is found to be studied elsewhere in our theological organization. To direct minds and to familiarize them with our plan, and also to show how the two different parts are integrated, we are going to review rapidly the different aspects of grace which have already been studied, or which should be in the following chapters, and which are, from many points of view, the principal ones. This sketch will have the further advantage of introducing our treatise and of making clear its object.

1. TREATISE ON GOD

(a) *The Presence of God in Us*

A consideration of Divine immensity has led us to see that God is everywhere, in all things, and in all the ways that we say one thing or one person is in another thing. If we reflect on our manner of speaking, we say of a king, for example, that he is in his whole kingdom by his authority, for nothing escapes his power; that he is in his room by his presence, because everything is open to his view; because he is in himself by his own essence. Thus God is in every created being by His *power* because everything is subject to Him; by His *presence* because all things are uncovered and naked before His eyes; by His *essence* because He is there Himself indivisibly in everything that exists.

God is in all His creatures in three ways; but in His spiritual creatures He can be present in a fourth way. He can be present in these creatures in a way that a thing known is in him who knows it or that a thing willed is in him who wills it. God can be known and loved by those to whom He gives His grace. This manner of being in creatures as direct object of knowledge and love is characteristic of what we call the presence of grace.

(b) *The Beatific Vision*

The consideration of God raises once more the question of the beatific vision: how can a creature see God face to face, *sicuti est* (I Jn. 3:2), such as He is in Himself? The theologian explains the gift of faith by developing the properties of grace in the soul when it in some way attains its full measure which is the light of glory. For we know that by grace we are made "similar to God" (I Jn. 3:2), "sharers in the divine nature" (II Pet. 1:4).

(c) *Providence and Predestination*

The study of the "virtues" of God, or at least of what this word, coined for the spiritual organism of man, implies when applied to God, has made us discover the prudence (or the providence) of God, by which God orders and governs all things. And since the elect reach the kingdom only by a gratuitous help of God which we call grace, we shall speak of a special providence for the elect, which we call predestination. It is the fruit of a love of predilection.

2. THEOLOGY OF THE HOLY TRINITY

(a) *The Appropriations*

We have already asked (Volume II, Chap. III) how the texts of the New Testament in which certain determined acts are attributed to a given divine Person and not to another are to be interpreted. Why is the gift of grace attributed to the Holy Spirit rather than to the Father and to the Son since the Father and the Son are also at work in our sanctification? The theologian is thus led to coin the word *appropriation*. Essential attributes are appropriated to a certain Person, i.e. those which are suitable to the divine essence as such, Scripture attributes by preference to one given Person rather than to another.

Under the pretext that these attributes are only appropriations, let us be on our guard not to minimize their scope. Thanks to the appropriated, i.e. in some way reserved attributes, God allows us to enter here on earth into the particular knowledge of and familiarity with each of the three Persons. Not having yet seen Them, He permits us to know Them somewhat, through the quite special affinity of each Person with the attribute which is appropriated to Him by Scripture.

We should also piously follow the teaching of Scripture when it attributes to the Holy Spirit the gift of grace and of sanctification of our souls. It is the Holy Spirit who spreads grace in our souls and it is because of the role of sanctifier which is attributed to Him that the Fathers have established His divinity. Although we know that grace is always the effect of a divine act in which the three Persons are at work, we shall prefer to attribute it to "the gift of the Holy Spirit" because this manner of speaking is that of Holy Scripture and because it is capable of introducing us to the knowledge proper to the third Person. We shall return later on to this point apropos of *adoption.*

(b) *The Missions*

Scripture teaches us not only about the "physiognomy" of the Divine Persons, but it also teaches us about Their origins and Their active relations. The Son is said to be sent by the Father (Jn. 5:16); the Holy Spirit, He who gives charity, is proclaimed as a gift of the Father and the Son for the sanctification of our souls (Rom. 8:5). There is also mention of habitation, of the indwelling in us of the divine Persons.

Theology is thus led to consider the scriptural terms of "mission," of "sending," of "habitation," of "indwelling."

It is not necessary, in order that there be mission that the person sent be inferior to the one who sends (cf. on this subject Vol. II, Chap. III). It suffices that he depend on him, by taking from him, for example, his origin. Neither is it necessary that the person sent be displaced—a bishop can be named legate in his own diocese—but it is necessary that there be verified between him and the person who receives a new relation. Thus it suffices that there be established between a divine Person and the creature to whom He is sent a new relation. This new thing does not affect the divine Person, who is unchangeable, but the creature.

The irrational creature cannot enter into a special relation of knowledge and of love with God. It is touched by God at the terminus of His creative and conservative influence, but God is not present to it. Whereas the spiritual creature can meet Him. The mission of a divine Person consists in making Himself known and loved by giving the power to do it, that is by giving the grace or the particular assistance (actual grace).

(c) *Habitation*

Since the divine Persons do not change it is necessary that it be we who are changed when there is a sending and coming of a divine

Person. The divine Persons ennoble our soul, illumine our intelligence, warm our heart, in a word, impress on us Their own likeness and make us sons of God. To those who have received Him, says St. John, He has given the "power of becoming sons of God" (Jn. 1:12). By receiving Them we enter into participation of Their nature (II Pet. 1:4) and, if one dare say so, of Their Personality. Through the presence of the Father, our soul receives the authority, the mastery of self, the dignity by which it becomes capable of knowing by itself and of freely loving the God of glory. By the presence of the Son, our soul shares in the knowledge of the Word, not in any kind of knowledge, but in a living knowledge which "breathes" love. By the presence of the Spirit, our soul is warmed, consoled, filled with life and love.

God gives Himself to us, as He does to Himself, freely. Moreover we believe that no necessity impels Him to communicate Himself. The gift is gratuitous, the more so as it is freer. Love is so much greater according as it necessitated the sending and the suffering of the Son. The grace of God puts in our soul a special debt of gratitude with regard to each divine Person.

3. THEOLOGY OF THE ANGELS, OF MAN, OF DIVINE GOVERNMENT

(a) *Relations Between the Natural and the Supernatural*

The angels raise an important question in theology. How are creatures, perfect in themselves from their origin, perforce so poor in means with respect to their ultimate end that without a special help from God they cannot attain it? The whole question of the relations of the natural to the supernatural has already been considered apropos of the angels. We shall have occasion to return to it later.

(b) *Image of God*

The attribute of "image of God" given to man by Scripture and especially by Gen. 1:26 leads theology to distinguish three levels on which is found a certain image of God in man: the level of nature, the level of re-creation in grace, the level of the consummation of grace or of the beatific vision.

It is the custom of a certain tradition to speak of an "image of God" only where there is a gift of grace, or the possibility of a gift. In irrational creatures we shall speak only of *vestige,* rather than of image, of divinity.

(c) *The Divine Idea of Freedom*

The theology of divine government, finally, leads us to consider how God can love a free creature without contradicting his liberty, or, in better terms, how the free act under the influence of God must be conceived, knowing that without this influence there would be neither act nor liberty. It is clear that this symbiosis of the divine acts and of our free acts is found, on a higher level, in the activity of those who have received or who receive the gift of grace.

4. MORAL THEOLOGY: BEATITUDE

The question of the relations of the natural to the supernatural is raised again when theology confronts the mystery of human destiny: what is the end of man?

If we carefully consider what the mind is, its native aptitude to know everything that is, its infinite capacity, we are led directly to conclude that there is no rest for it, no perfect happiness short of the vision of God. And yet no mind can *see God* by its own powers. Here we have stated the paradox of man and of every spiritual being.

Man, by the end which is proposed to him and without which he could not be perfectly happy, is the worthiest of creatures. But man is at the same time the poorest of all creatures, for he does not possess in his nature the instruments of his perfection and of his happiness. He cannot attain by his own resources that for which he nevertheless has a natural desire, that is, to see God. Like a woman who has a desire for conception and who can effect it only with the cooperation of her husband, so in a similar way the soul cannot conceive God in its own mind unless God begins by giving Himself to it. Man, who is of himself *capax Dei,* capable of God, cannot by himself grasp that which alone can satisfy him. He needs the gift of grace and with it in the first place, the gift of faith through which are accomplished the espousals ("faith" and "espousals" have the same etymology and the same deep meaning) of God and the soul. Grace appears to us here as the dowry of God, the created effect which results in the soul from the fact that it is especially loved by God, "married" to Him.

5. THE ECONOMY OF SALVATION

(a) *Capital Grace and Grace by Adoption*

In the part of theology which we call the *Economy,* the problem of grace is placed in a new perspective.

It is really Christ, who by His passion, death and resurrection, has merited for us grace, and it is through the sacraments that He communicates it to us. There is no grace which is not a participation in His grace, that is to say, which is not "Christian."

Christ possesses the perfect grace which merits the hypostatic union for Him and it is of its fullness (capital grace) that we have all received. Through grace and through adoption—we say through the grace of adoption, and we really mean that this grace transforms us, modifies us in our very being—we have the power of calling God, Father, as the Son calls Him, and of being really His children, stamped with His likeness.

Although Christ has merited grace for us, there does not follow from it, as we have already said, that the Holy Spirit has no part in it. "Adoption springs from the entire Trinity," writes St. Thomas Aquinas. "It is however especially attributed to the Father as its author, to the Son as its exemplar, to the Holy Spirit as Him who impresses on us the likeness of this exemplar" (cf. *Summa Theol.* III, q. 33, a.2, ad. 3). The grace which the Holy Spirit gives us makes us like the Son and carries us with Him toward the Father.

(b) *Sacramental Graces*

The economy of grace is not changed by the fact that it is communicated to us through the sacraments. Although the different parts of our theology are closely knit together, it is the advantage of the plan of St. Thomas which we have adopted, to show the perfect independence of the concepts of grace and of sacrament. "The grace of God is not bound to the sacraments," that is to say, that God is not bound by the means which He has decided to make use of. Whether it be before or after Christ, and even before the institution of the sacraments of the old Law, justified man is justified by the same grace of God, in the name of the same merits of Christ. It must be said then that it does not follow that man is free to neglect the sacramental rites in which God intends for each one the possibility of receiving the grace of salvation.

But is grace found qualified in a special way by the different sacraments? Can we speak of a grace of baptism, of a grace of confirmation? Yes, if we understand by it that God intends to communicate it by means of each sacrament. No, if it is understood that the graces of baptism and of confirmation are not substantially of the same nature.

The theology of the sacraments opens up to us a final perspective on Christian grace. Grace is communicated in us in certain social rites by the ministers of the Church. That means that we are not alone concerned, that the grace of salvation renders us solidary with all others in the Body of Christ.

6. GRACE, "EXTERIOR" HELPS

We can sum up the doctrine on grace developed in the first part of our theology by saying this: as soon as there is a new relation of God to man, there is a creation or production in man of a new quality which provides a basis for the relation. To say that God becomes present to the soul and places Himself in it as the object of knowledge and of love, to say that God is seen by the elect face to face, that God predestines this one or that, that He sends His Spirit or that He gives Him, that He adopts a given creature and makes of him His child, that He communicates to him His own likeness and makes him in the image of Himself, is equivalent to saying that He communicates to the mind a new quality without which neither the presence, nor the vision, nor the sending, nor the divine habitation, nor predestination, nor adoption, nor the divine image would be verified. God does not change. If there is anything new in the relations between God and man it does not come from any change in God but from a change in man. God creates in man a new quality which affects him in a new way face to face with Him. This new quality, by which presence, mission, habitation, image are verified, is grace.

The perspective adopted in Moral Theology (excepting the theology of beatitude) is different. God is no longer considered in Himself or in His "exterior" activity of creation and of government, but as the end of human action. Instead of considering grace as the necessary effect of adoption by the Father, of the mission of the Holy Spirit, Moral Theology considers it as a means super-added to nature and placed gratuitously by God at the disposal of man in order that he might reach his end which is eternal life with the Three Persons. The whole problem for the moral theologian is to see how in our journey toward God, the "synergy" of our own natural acts and of the divine aids, always inseparably mingled with our activity, functions.

However long this preamble may be, at least it has shown us that there are really several ways of considering the divine life in our souls. In this regard, it is a veritable deformation of piety to replace, as is generally done today, the devotion to the Holy Spirit by the devotion to the "state of grace." The Holy Spirit, the sanctifier of souls, He who has been given to us and who dwells in us, He who gives us a filial spirit, has come to be forgotten and misunderstood. Today we speak of losing the state of grace, of recovering the state of grace, of being in the state of grace, where formerly, with a deeper religious sense, we spoke of losing or of saddening the Spirit, of receiving the Spirit, of being filled with the Holy Spirit. In fact, all these expressions are good; the misfortune is that some have been adopted to the exclusion of others. And it is noted that the egocentric devotion to the state of grace can here or there coincide with a certain loss of the understanding of God. The point of view of the moralist, who considers grace as a help and confronts it with the natural qualities and activities of man, is not the only, nor even the best or the principal one, for instructing us on grace.

II. Theology of Grace Considered as Assistance

1. OUR MISERIES AND OUR NECESSITIES

The convergence of a triple ray of light invites us to begin this tract on grace by an inquiry into its necessity.

Biblical light, first of all. For St. Paul, as for St. John, the help of God is the sole escape which is open to man to get out of the impasse into which sin has led him and to lead him to the sanctification to which he has constantly been invited. St. Paul never invokes "grace"—whether it be by this very term or by some equivalent term—except on the background of the picture of the weakness of man and of the impotence of the sinner.

Next, moral light. Considered from the point of view which we now take of man, grace appears as a help which God offers us. But he who mentions help evokes by so doing a need which before all else must be explained. First we think of the ravages caused by sin in the powers of man, but the problem is broader than that. The grace which the condition of man requires does not have merely a role of remedy, a medicinal function justified by the wounds of sin. It implies also positive dimensions according to which man, sanctified by it, is capable of attaining his supernatural beatitude. It is therefore necessary to establish the balance between our necessities and our miseries, and thus to explain the exact role of grace in our spiritual organism.

Finally, an historic light. Theology is tradition before being speculation; it cannot be drawn from the concrete condition which scans the development of doctrine in the course of the centuries. How can we speak of grace without invoking St. Augustine or the controversy *De auxiliis?* The explanations of the magisterium on the question of grace were given on the occasion of such an error and on the same points which raised the difficulty. Now the most important of these explanations concern the mystery of grace, a thorny question on which two extreme views claim to have the truth: the one exalts nature to the point of rendering grace superfluous (Pelagianism), the other so minimizes the natural powers that man without grace is only a monster dedicated to evil (Jansenism). It was necessary to clear a "via media" which would be something more than an eclectic compromise, a vision in depth in which the opposing theses might see their legitimate demands satisfied and their antinomies resolved.

The convergence of these reasons obliges us to give to the present question a considerable development. We force ourselves to conciliate the demands of logical expression with those of an historic perspective.

An explanation is demanded. Man in the course of history has passed through different *states:* state of an integral nature, state of fallen nature, state of redeemed nature. These changes have brought about in the needs and capacities of man certain more or less profound modifications. It is clear that the economy of divine help has been affected by way of reaction: it is impossible to begin at a precise point without bringing in the notion of "state."

Still it is necessary to situate the study of grace on a level which transcends accidental differences in order to attain to a valid notion for each of the historic types of grace. The theology of grace should not be limited to such or such a state; it is applied, with the variations which are imposed, to the grace of innocent Adam as to that of the Christian and to that of Jesus Christ Himself.

(a) *The Possibilities of Man Without Grace*

Under pretext of better manifesting the need that we have of a supernatural help, a current exaggerated pessimism misunderstood the possibilities of nature, even of fallen nature, in the domain of knowledge and of voluntary activity. It is therefore necessary to explain the extent as well as the limits of the natural powers of man.

Knowledge

Does the natural equipment of intelligence suffice to attain truth? Or has it need of an increase of power?

That some help is necessary in order that man assimilate the revelation of mysteries properly supernatural, goes without saying. The communion which all knowledge implies cannot be made when the object is absolutely disproportionate to the intelligence. It is necessary that an increase of power enable the intelligence to enter into communion with the divine object. This increase of power has a name: it is faith.

But what shall we say of the truths of the natural order? Those which include all the truths of the profane sciences, and also the knowledge of the first principles of morality, the natural law, the rational proofs of God's existence. Does not the admission that we cannot arrive at this knowledge by our natural powers amount to the ruin of the natural order?

If the sector of the profane sciences offers but little difficulty generally, there are men such as Baius, Quesnel, and the Fideists of the 19th century who affirm that it is impossible without grace to acquire notions of the moral order and of establishing certain proofs of God's existence.

The magisterium of the Church has reacted so as to safeguard the possibilities of nature. The Church does not deny, it should be said, the necessity of this transcendent motion of God which the theologians are wont to call the "natural concurrences." But that much admitted, she maintains that intelligence, even fallen intelligence, can attain by itself the truths of the natural order. If not, we would find ourselves in the presence of a natural power, powerless in the presence of its own object. And this would be equivalent to the very destruction of this nature and to the absolute necessity of grace in the natural order itself. How can what is gratuitous be of necessity for nature?

Is it to be said that the natural endowment of intelligence offers all the guarantees of security in the order of natural knowledge? The answer here varies according to the "states." Man is stamped with original sin whose ravages have not spared the intellect itself.

This is what the exaggerated Augustinianism of Baius and others have foreseen.

It is known that the moral function of practical intelligence, following the directives of prudence which is "recta ratio agibilium"—an exact expression of what should be done—presupposes the rectitude of the will. Man is personally "engaged" in this evaluation, and the uprightness of his judgment requires the basic uprightness of his will. It is then by rebound, because of the wound which directly attains the will, that practical knowledge is obscured by original sin. Grace is necessary as a remedy in the presence of this weakness.

Thus the intemperate man will need assistance from God in order to judge rightly on the legitimacy of a given pleasure which is offered to him. The sinner will need a grace in order to deduce from the first moral principles the kind of conclusion which condemns his attitude, and this aid will be so much the more necessary as the question considered will be more distinct from the evidence of the first principles. The personal coefficient in the judgment increases in the measure that the compelling clearness of the first concepts diminishes.

Will

If the wounds of original sin entail the necessity of a remedy in the order of knowledge itself, we can expect to find more pressing still the necessity of grace in the domain of the will. The will being the subject of sin is also its greatest victim.

In the state of integral nature, only the properly supernatural activity of man required the assistance of grace. That is clear. When sin steps in, the domain of grace is extended, to the degree of the misery of man, to everything which is weakened and wounded in him.

Is man then going to become totally incapable of any good? Luther and a certain extreme Augustinian view, such as that of Baius, have insisted with vigor and excess on the impotence and the radical perversion of the free will. Such propositions of Baius as: "All the works of infidels are sins and the virtues of philosophers are vices," or again: "Free will without the grace of God merely facilitates sin," for example, could not be accepted by the Church. The impossibility for the will of performing by itself a single good act means in fact the destruction of human nature and the absolute necessity of grace. The Augustinian extremists perceived this, and they deny the gratuitousness of the supernatural.

A condemned proposition of Quesnel characterizes this pessimistic tendency: "The will which grace does not predispose has no light except to go astray, no ardor except to throw itself down, no force except to wound itself, capable of all evil and incapable of any good."

(b) *The Miseries of Man Without Grace*

Without being unduly pessimistic, it remains true that the limits of our possibilities are quickly reached. For not having been willing to recognize this, the over-optimistic current which recognized as its chief the monk Pelagius, fell into a grave error: it misunderstood the necessity of grace to attain perfection.

Of more versatile tendency, the group of monks at Marseilles was compelled to enlarge as much as possible the field left to the natural powers of man, but it too restrained the necessity of grace.

These errors led the Fathers, then the Councils to explain little by little the limits and the possibilities of man.

Explanations Furnished on the Occasion of the Pelagian Error

Is the natural love of God above all things in the power of man?

The principle is known: God being analogically for man as the whole is to the part, man loves God *naturally* more than himself; this "natural" love can be compared to that of the hand which does not fear to expose itself in order to protect the life of the body. For this love no aid is required except the metaphysical notion of God, "Prime Mover," of which there has already been question and which cannot pass for a grace.

Does this law subsist after original sin? Are we not in the presence of the law of nature, expressing the very condition of the creature before God?

To reply affirmatively would be to forget that such love implies the free play of the natural inclinations of the will and that the wound of sin has precisely consisted in disturbing this play. Since then, man cannot succeed in divesting himself of a basic egoism which prevents him from going out of himself and elevating himself to the love of God above all things. The impotence of the will in this domain comes from the perversion of nature turned back in some way upon itself. That does not mean to say that man is incapable of putting aside even a little bit his own egotistic interests, but he is no longer in a condition to execute this flight toward the transcendent Absolute which would necessitate the love of God above all things. He has need of a medicinal grace which would restore to him the liberty of the natural impulse toward God.

The problem of the love of God, first of the commandments, leads naturally to that of the *integral fulfillment of the commandments.* Here we touch upon one of the crucial points of the Pelagian controversy.

The difficulty is great, we must admit. It is the dramatic situation of St. Paul: how can man be subjected to a law which he is obliged to observe and yet whose observation surpasses his powers?

And yet, as we have seen, each good act is in our power. Such is really the paradoxical situation of man since sin! Capable of performing certain good acts, man does not have in him the possibility of fulfilling *the whole law;* each act is in his power, the sum total of them is too much for him. The continuity and the stability which presupposes the constant exercise of virtue exceed his powers. The weakness of the will after sin explains this relative impotence, just as that of the convalescent explains why he is able to take one step and then another while remaining incapable of putting forth a continuous effort. Does not experience show that the success of a life perfectly integral on the natural level is an exploit which surpasses human powers?

Since sin, the divine assistance is written into the status of the natural condition of man. The latter has need of God in order to be faithful to his duties as a simple creature.

In order to perform *acts meritorious for eternal life,* acts meritorious in justice, grace is required for a still greater reason; not only a transient motion, but also a permanent increase in the manner of nature is needed if we are to be made capable of performing these acts in a personal and vital way.

The reason for this is simple. The plan of God implies that man should reach eternal life, his end, by means of acts proportionate to this life, even to the point of meriting it himself in justice. God has willed for man the honor of meriting eternal life by his own acts. This life remains supernatural, the acts which merit it must then be equally so. They cannot be accomplished by man without the addition of a grace which elevates his powers and enables them to produce proportionate acts.

Nothing can make us perceive better at what point we depend on God for the success of our human life than this *absolute* necessity of grace to obtain supernatural life. The latter, however supernatural it may be, is not for man such as God has made him, a luxury which he can get along without. If he does not obtain it with the assistance of God, he does not attain his end, he does not become "happy."

For man it is a sign of superiority over other beings to be capable of such a destiny, but for him also it is a supplementary title of attachment to God whose good will alone can grant him what is necessary for him.

On the Occasion of the Semi-Pelagian Error

The doctrinal benefit of controversies has here especially borne on the question of the preparation for grace and on that of perseverance in grace once received.

1. *The case of the sinner.* After the condemnation of the Pelagian error no one any longer denied that the attainment of eternal life was the work of grace. The problem which was raised from then on was different; it bore on the initial distribution of grace. Was grace an absolutely gratuitous gift, the fruit of unconditioned initiative on the part of God, or did it take account of the good dispositions of the subject for whom it came in some way as a recompense and a crown?

There were acute difficulties on both sides. To insist on the gratuitous initiative of God was to enter into the delicate problem, among others, of predestination; to see in grace a reward for the efforts of man, was to place man at the origin of the life of grace and to contradict the constant doctrine of St. Paul on the gratuity of the gift of God: "And if out of grace, then not in virtue of works; otherwise grace is no longer grace" (Rom. 11:6).

The solution of these difficulties requires that one examine minutely the divers possible types of preparation for grace. The sole preparation admissible is that which detracts in no way from the divine initiative nor the generous efforts of man.

Positive preparation. Why should acts morally good, performed by man before justification, not constitute for God a sort of obligation to confer grace on man thus disposed? The semi-Pelagians, obsessed by the concern of saving human liberty at any price, readily accepted this natural preparation which has received the names of "first step" and of "beginning of faith." But they made the mistake as soon as they believed it necessary, in order to preserve liberty, to give to man the *initiative* of salvation. The Church then took a very clear-cut position. Her doctrine is solidly based on revelation: "No one can come to me unless the Father who sent me draw him . . ." (Jn. 6:44), and: "Without me you can do nothing" (Jn. 15:5).

To open our mind to this truth, so paradoxical in appearance, that man has need of a grace in order to prepare for grace, it is necessary to appeal to the fundamental principle of the *correspondence between the order of ends and the order of "movers,"* i.e. of those who act in view of these ends. A determined end requires a mover proportionate to itself; it is thus that the return to God—final end—necessarily implies motion from God Himself—the Prime Mover, for God alone is an agent proportioned to this activity. There are, however, two ways of returning to God. If the contemplated return to God is situated on the natural plane, a divine motion of the natural order suffices. If, on the contrary, the contemplated return to God is situated on the supernatural and gratuitous plane of the beatific vision, a special motion is required, a motion of the supernatural order which is a *grace*.

This grace, which the theologians call "actual," plays on its level the role assumed in the natural divine government by the motion of God concerning which there was a question in a preceding chapter. Actual grace is presented with the characteristics of the natural motion of the first mover: like this motion, it is necessarily required in every activity of its order; it is not a permanent help but an intermittent aid, it intervenes only at the instant of action, it is finally diversified according to the types of activity which postulate it.

Grace is therefore indispensable in the preparation of man for grace. There is no vicious circle in this. Initial grace is an actual aid, a motion, and the grace conferred at the end of the preparation, a permanent gift, a second nature. Actual grace and habitual grace are then well distinguished.

The entire problem remains however: how to save the liberty and the responsibility of a man to whom belongs the initiative of conversion? The rejection of the semi-Pelagian solution does not suppress the problem which the theologians have tried to face. It is a delicate question, which touches at once on the mystery of predestination and on that of the efficacy of grace. St. Thomas replies to it in these lines: "Certainly," he says, "the conversion of man to God is made by his free will. Besides, man is commanded to convert himself to God. But free will cannot be converted to God unless God converts himself to it" (Ia IIae, q. 109, a. 6, ad. 1). The doctrine is simply affirmed. It presupposes, as we know, the explanations given in the tract on human acts (Ia IIae, q. 9 and 10).

The Thomistic solution is intelligible only within a metaphysical vision of the divine intervention in created action. If one leaves this plane, there is no longer any room except for more or less illustrated anthropomorphic compromises which, though more satisfying at first sight, are incapable of clarifying the essence of the problem. Appeal must be made to the quite special immanence of the divine movement in order to establish that this movement does no violence in any way to the secondary cause, but inserts itself into the normal play of this causality—moving it with necessity if there is question of a necessary cause but moving it according to its liberty, when there is question of a free cause. The whole mystery lies in these last words. It is necessary to add that for every other movement except that of God one would be in the presence of a pure verbalism, implying contradiction; it is uniquely the absolutely special manner of uncreated action which permits God to move with a sovereign efficacy without injuring the free cause in the least but, on the contrary, by rendering it such.

The application of this general doctrine to the present case is immediate. The grace of preparation conferred by God does not make vain the movement of liberty. But on the contrary, grace arouses it and joins with it in the unity of a vital act of conversion. Only metaphysical analysis would be able to distinguish the part of man from the part of God which is always first. The error would be to wish to recognize "psychologically" and to distinguish in the same way a divine part and a human part in our acts. This is unthinkable. The activity of the first cause in us and our activity do not make two distinguishable activities. The activity of a first cause is the very condition of our activity. We are commanded to convert ourselves to God because that is in our power, although we could not do so without the divine assistance.

Are we going to object that the divine assistance is given to the will of one and not that of another? In such a case we shall hold to the wise reservation of Augustine: "Why does he draw this one rather than that one? Do not seek to know if you do not wish to err."

We must maintain therefore the impossibility of any positive preparation by man which would take place without the divine assistance.

Negative preparation. What are we to think of a negative preparation, that which consists in giving up the sin in which the sinner has fallen or in avoiding falling back into it in the future?

Past sins. The case of the sinner who gives up his sin brings up once more the principle of the correspondence between the order of ends and that of agents. An act which looks to union with God, such as conversion, can come only from God. Besides, sin implies an offense whose pardon belongs only to the one offended. The sinner resembles a man who has thrown himself into a well. Once in the well, he cannot get out alone, it is not therefore in the power of man to reunite with God the bonds which he has broken, without the assistance of a special grace.

Future sins. Is the same impotence verified with regard to future sins? Could the sinner who remains in his state avoid at least falling into new mortal sins in the future? On account of a prior sin not forgiven which has turned him away and turns him away from God, his will is habitually inclined toward evil. This inclination will influence his subsequent acts the more successfully as these acts will be less deliberate. Some of these acts will follow the habitual inclination of the will, and as the latter is not turned toward God, it is inevitable that in a short time man will sink deeper into sin. Such is the case at least with the sinner, but what of the just?

2. *The case of the just.* His situation does not present the same characteristics. Habitual grace favors in him an inclination toward God and so renders easier resistance to grave sin. Is he therefore assured of not falling into sin and without the intervention of a supplementary grace? To affirm that would be to forget the backwater of a sensibility which retains from original sin, even when forgiven, a certain lack of equilibrium. These movements, always imperfectly controlled, predispose man to the transient deviations which are called venial sins. Although he is not unarmed against every temptation in particular, it is not possible for the just man, without an exceptional privilege, to surmount *all of them together.* Such is the balance sheet of the deficiencies of man faced with sin.

But the *condition of the just man,* which this inquiry has led us to consider, was to raise in the atmosphere of semi-Pelagianism another series of questions on the subject of perseverance. Here is the last revenge of the partisans of the autonomy of man with regard to the good.

Does the *daily life* of the just man require for its rectitude any special help distinct from sanctifying grace and from the natural movement of God on each of our acts? Some reserve this special help for difficult acts, those which require greater generosity and courage. But why reserve to exceptional circumstances the necessity of this actual grace? Just as the natural act implies, in more than one nature, a special movement of the Creator, so the supernatural act requires, in more than one habitual grace, which plays the role of a second nature, a special proportionate movement that is of the supernatural order. Moreover the weakness of man, even of justified man, seems really to require normally a special help from God in order to render him capable of persevering in grace. As for *final perseverance,* it brings us face to face with a mystery which makes us grasp, more vividly even than all the rest, the necessity of grace.

This perseverance signifies, at its term, the conjunction of grace with the instant of death. To imagine that man has it in his power to preserve grace indefinitely and therefore to confront death with assurance, is to forget that grave sin is always possible and that the conjunction of the moment of death with the state of grace is due only to the will of God. Looked at in this light, which is the true one, the problem of final perseverance links up with that of predestination. Moreover it is not surprising that the same absolute gratuitousness of the one and the other should manifest itself. No doubt it is difficult for us to admit that a given just man, who has lived for a long time in the friendship and the service of the Lord, should be surprised by death in a state of sin. Would not our difficulty come in part from the false security which we experience at the sight of a Christian life habitually faithful? Man never has a guarantee of salvation: "Work out your salvation with fear and trembling. For it is God who of his good pleasure works in you both the will and the performance" (Phil. 2:12-13). The continuity of the state of grace is certainly an index, and the least hazardous one, of predestination, but this continuity which is itself a good is not a guarantee of the future. And not to have any fear of being able to offend Him and of losing His friendship would clearly be unfaithful to the grace of God.

The balance which we have struck culminates in a twofold statement: on the one hand of the needs of man who is radically impotent with regard to the supernatural, extremely feeble even on the plane of natural activity; and on the other hand of the pure gratuity of the extra assistance of which man stands in need. Indigence and lack of necessity: such are the irreducible data of the problem. Man has need of another, and this Other is wholly free.

To sum up, man is called by God to the order of adoptive filiation. His only end and final fulfillment, comes from grace: necessary orientation, but inaccessible by human powers alone. Moreover, the increase of help which alone can raise to the level of the supernatural end depends only on the free and unforeseeable initiative of God, and that, before any consideration of sin.

The intervention of original sin extends the necessity of grace to the natural plane itself. No doubt man is still capable of some good, but his will is turned away from God when by right of nature it should be orientated toward Him. Whence this group of internal disorders whose constant eddyings escape most frequently the control of an anemic will. The necessary grace is here doubly gratuitous, for God is in no way obliged to repair what the perverse will of men has destroyed. If He does so, it will be by means of sanctifying grace which exercises with regard to the wounded natural powers a healing function.

But then the sanctification is instantaneous, the healing takes place little by little. Paradox of redeemed man, son of God and yet man imperfect in his very nature! Whence the necessity of special divine movements to sustain the endless weaknesses of the sons of God on earth.

To say that everything is grace, is to recognize that everything is dependence with regard to God. After that, we are unable to make any absolute pronouncement on the laws and conditions of individual salvation. The mystery of grace is a mystery of predestination and of good pleasure. Our liberty is not the fundamental datum, it appears and is developed in dependence on God.

Thus grace is *necessary,* we cannot get along without it; and an initial grace is necessary in order to obtain it, and one cannot give it to himself.

2. THE NATURE OF GRACE

(a) *The Realism of Grace*

The term grace is not peculiar to theological language. We have already run the gamut of its four meanings: beauty, favor, gift or benefit, gratitude.

Each of these acceptations in the Christian regime has known a corresponding excess. If the term grace more frequently calls to our mind the gift which has been made to us, we must not therefore forget that the first meaning remains that of favor, and more fundamentally still that of beauty, of charm, of sovereign freedom of movement.

Let us remark at once that "favors" are not elicited in the same way in human relations as in the relations between God and man. In human relations, a favor is solicited by "grace," the amiability of the person who presents himself. It is the constitutive law of the human will to be stirred by a good which exists independently of it. In God on the contrary favors are creative: creatures are good because God loves them and not inversely.

On the plane of human affection, God loves everything, that is, with a creative love. Here already it would not be unsuitable to speak of grace, since such a love springs from pure gratuity, creative of natures.

But we reserve the word on the level of special affection to signify the love according to which the creature is drawn by God above his natural condition. Revelation affirms the existence in God of this, in some sort, second love which creates in man a *real* gift and introduces him to the sphere of divine friendship. Grace in us is nothing else than the affection of God which takes form.

Here is the point for insertion of a development on the subject of *divine missions* which effects the junction between the two poles of grace: God who attracts to Himself His creature, and the gift which consecrates His favor; but we shall not insist upon it since we have already mentioned it. A remark is necessary on what we cannot too often return to: it is on the level of love and its largesses that we must situate, in order to understand them, the problem raised by grace. The necessity of the distribution of grace, for example, should be considered only in the light of the principle of predilection raised by St. Thomas in the treatise on God: "No created being would be better than another, if it were not loved more by God."

(b) *Status of Grace in the Soul*

The realism of grace, i.e. the existence in us of something which corresponds to the favor which God shows us, is verified of actual grace as well as habitual grace, i.e. of the transcendent divine movements as of the permanent gift which renders us sons of God. Moreover it was not necessary up to the present to analyze their distinction. That does not mean that both divine favors represent the same thing in the soul. There is question now of explaining the ontological status of these two graces.

We have verified, in the course of establishing the balance of our needs, the necessity of these special divine movements which play on the supernatural level the role which is recognized in the ordinary movements in natural divine government. These graces, destined to promote or realize certain precise *acts* of knowledge or of will—whence their name of actual *grace*—are only transitory aids, impulses of the moment which come to be exercised on the powers of the soul which acts and which cease with the end of the action.

Habitual grace corresponds to another necessity. The favor of which we are the object on the part of God transcends the level of the transient aids in order to introduce us into an habitual relation of friendship and of filiation with God. Scripture instructs us in express terms: "Behold what manner of love the Father has bestowed upon us that we should be called *children of God,* and such we are" (I Jn. 3:1); "What we have seen and have heard we announce to you, in order that you also may have *fellowship* with us, and that our fellowship may be with the Father and with the Son Jesus Christ" (I Jn. 1:3); "He has granted us very great and precious promises, so that through them you may become partakers of the divine nature" (II Pet. 1:4). Between God and the man to whom His favor is shown durable bonds are established which, based on a permanent gift, serve to seal in man this new situation.

The expression of the second epistle of St. Peter: "Participants of the divine nature," invites us to look beyond the ordinary level of friendship and lets us see the depth and the transformation effected in man by grace: there is no question of anything less than to accede—in a human way, it goes without saying—to the divine life, to become gods. Such is the essence of sanctifying grace—a gratuitous participation in the divine nature. Grace is inserted into the soul in the manner of a *nature*.

The ease and the "naturalness" which characterize the creature in the activities which are proper and proportionate to him are possible only through the presence in the creature of the principle of action which is his "nature." The latter confers on the acts of the creature this ease which we recognize in him. Each creature is born in order to posit acts which are suitable to its "nature." The immanence of sanctifying grace at the root of our supernatural activity confers on it this very vital and connatural character which a nature confers on the activity that depends on it. This character would be lacking to it if each of our acts proceeded solely from a transcendent movement of God. Grace is in us as a second nature.

How situate this new nature?

We do not profit here by the divine certitude which accompanies the gift of faith. If the Council of Trent affirms that grace is *ours* because it *inheres in us,* it did not pronounce on the nature of this inherence. It is for the theologian to explain this point with the reservation which should characterize his own reflections.

We have seen that grace was presented as a stable disposition in the manner of a nature which permits each one of us as a matter of course to be on the supernatural plane and to act with facility, pleasure and promptitude, in a word, in a way which is connatural to him. Now all of these traits recall the description of habit (*habitus*). This is why we say that this stable disposition which is grace is in us like a habitus.

Let us explain: does this disposition affect the essence of our soul or only its powers (intelligence and will)? If habitual grace strengthens the powers, how do we distinguish it from the infused virtues which have their seat in the same powers? The comparison is impossible. Still certain theologians have not recoiled before the difficulties; they have agreed to identify grace and virtue, in particular, grace and charity. The analogy with the natural order permits us to throw some light on the debate. The virtues which dispose the intelligence and will with regard to this or that object presuppose a nature, the radical principle and end of all activity. Does not grace present itself as a new nature? To place it in the ranks of virtue, is to misunderstand the role of the radical principle of operation which it must play with regard to the infused virtues, i.e. with regard to the virtues which emanate from it. These have for object the elevation of the activity of the powers. How could there be harmony in the supernatural organism if the very essence of the soul were not transformed and renewed by habitual grace?

The infusion of grace in us corresponds to a *new birth* (cf. Jn. 3:5-8). A thing must be before it acts, it must be supernaturally before it acts supernaturally. The sanctification of the essence of the soul must precede the sanctification of the powers.

It must be admitted that this analogy based on the natural organism leaves the mind dissatisfied. It is necessary to complete it and to compare grace with being itself and with the life of God. As the infused virtues are in us the participated reflection of the attributes of God in the order of operation, so sanctifying grace is the participated reflection of the divine nature itself in the order of being. But then in God this nature and these attributes are only one, because there is not in Him any real distinction between being and acting. In man grace and the infused virtues which emanate from it are distinct as the essence of the soul and the powers which proceed from it are distinct. The *whole man,* in his being and in his acting, is thus sanctified in view of his entering into participation in the very life of God.

In a word, habitual grace is a quality which affects the essence of the soul in virtue of a new nature; it is the fruit of a new birth ("nature" and "birth" have the same etymology and imply each other). Infused virtues destined to make us act in connaturality with our new nature proceed from this grace as the powers of the soul proceed from its essence. Man in the grace of God possesses in his interior self the principle of an operation properly divine in such a way that henceforth, while remaining a creature, he will be able to know and to love God as God knows and loves Himself.

3. THE DIVERS FORMS OF GRACE

Without pausing at the external graces, namely, favorable circumstances susceptible of guiding man toward the good and of restraining him from the path of evil, let us speak of internal graces which imply various varieties.

(a) *Sanctifying and Charismatic Grace*

The first point of view that we take, that of the finality of grace, appears in an expression of Jesus destined to situate in their true place the extraordinary gifts which accompanied the preaching of the 72 disciples: "But do not rejoice in this, that the spirits are subject to you, rejoice rather in this, that your names are written in heaven" (Lk. 10:20); and the same opposition is found in this apostrophe also: "Many will say to me in that day, 'Lord, Lord, did we not prophesy in thy name, and cast out devils in thy name and work many miracles in thy name?' And then I will declare to them, 'I never knew you. Depart from me you workers of iniquity' " (Mt. 7:22-23). There are then certain graces which render man pleasing to God, and others which can be granted to man without necessarily transforming him.

A closer examination of these last graces reveals their social character: these gifts of prophecy, of exorcism, of miracles, and all those which St. Paul calls attention to in the first chapter of the Epistle to the Corinthians (I Cor. 12:8 ff), are ordained to the common utility of the Church, since they lead infidels to believe and facilitate the progress of Christians. Theology calls this type of grace: *gratia gratis data,* gratuitous grace, or often "charism," in contrast with *gratia gratum faciens,* sanctifying grace ordained to the sanctification of him who receives it. Let no one deceive himself in this. Sanctifying grace is not less gratuitous, just as man is not less animal even though opposed to "animal" in the logical classification of living beings capable of sensation. The qualification of genus has been in both cases reserved for certain species. And from another point of view, if gratuitous grace is first ordered to the utility of all, it does not follow that it is never in any way sanctifying for him who possesses it.

The division sketched between sanctifying grace and gratuitous grace is inserted into a providential order which makes them both serve to bring man back to God. Sanctifying grace appears as the fundamental, personal, irreplacable value, while the other type of grace has for its function to aid the birth and the growth of sanctifying grace in others. It is at the service of sanctifying grace.

Which is the better of these two graces? It would seem that it should be charismatic grace. It is ordained to the common good and that should take precedence over individual advantage. Grace of state or permanent grace of function among the first (such as the charism of infallibility attached to the papal office), is among others a marvellous gift which employs a power that God does not generally grant to anyone but the saints. Ecstasies, miracles, which sometimes indicate sanctity of Christians, appear among the common run of mortals as more precious graces than the simple theological life common to all the faithful in the state of grace.

The temptation is subtle, and we allow ourselves to be often drawn by it in our evaluation of sanctity. Yet St. Paul leaves no doubt about the matter. After having enumerated all sorts of "charisms" the apostle adds: "And I point out to you a yet more excellent way" (I Cor. 13:1), and this way is that of charity which presupposes sanctifying grace.

The reason of this primacy is taken from the point of view of finality, i.e. from the point of view in which the two graces are distinguished. Immediately ordained to the sanctification of man, sanctifying grace constitutes a greater testimony of divine friendship than charismatic grace—a simple favor which of itself has only a mediate relation to sanctification. The superiority of sanctifying grace springs from its basic theological character; it alone is capable of realizing in a soul union with God and with the whole order of grace. Even if they favor it, the conjunction of the charisms with sanctity remains accidental. The Blessed Virgin herself does not seem to have performed any miracle.

(b) *Habitual Grace and Actual Grace*

Sanctifying grace is given us under two forms which must be pointed out here in order to situate them in the whole: habitual grace and actual grace.

We often designate habitual grace as "sanctifying grace." That is correct; its primary role is to consecrate man to God, to make him holy. But actual grace is also sanctifying. The division "habitual grace-actual grace" is made from another point of view. The one is possessed by the soul in the form of a habit, a permanent disposition, in the manner of a virtue, but affecting the whole being; the other influences the soul only by transitory movements on the occasion of acts to be performed.

(c) *Operative and Cooperative Grace*

It is St. Augustine and not St. Paul who originated the distinction of sanctifying grace into "operative" and "cooperative." This distinction concerns the concurrence of the will with grace. "God himself," says St. Augustine, *"works* in us the beginning—in order to achieve he *cooperates* with those who wish; this is why the apostle says: "I am convinced of this, that he who has begun a good work in you will bring it to perfection until the day of Christ Jesus" (Phil. 1:6; cf. *De gratis et libero arbitrio,* c. 17). In order that we may begin to will, God takes the initiative, he *works without us* in order to touch our will; but when we will, when our own will passes into act, he cooperates with us. In other words, certain graces precede the deliberate will, and these are operative graces; others sustain it, and these are cooperative graces. Let us be careful not to misunderstand this distinction. Operative grace is not reserved to indeliberate and irrational acts which precede the use of free will. Neither does this division take in that of the action of man in "passion" and in "human acts." Operative and cooperative grace concern free acts. With cooperative grace the human will is capable of taking the initiative for its act, grace sustains and aids it. This attitude of initiative presupposes in fact that one have already the principle of his action, that one be equipped for performing a supernatural act. For acts with respect to which man is not yet equipped supernaturally, not having in him the principle of his action, the grace of God alone can actively operate; the will can only give its consent. This is true of all the initial acts: first movement of conversion toward God under the influence of actual grace, complete justification of the impious, that is, sanctification of the sinner, but also of the acts which surpass the habitual supernatural possibilities of man under the grace which he possesses: a more intense act of charity for example.

Every grace—actual grace and habitual grace—is then operative or cooperative. Actual operative grace intervenes especially during the first movements of the will toward God. Habitual grace is operative in the initial act of "justification," cooperative in the sequel, that is, in all meritorious activities. We shall discover further on, in speaking of its effects, these two aspects of grace.

(d) *Other Divisions*

The theologians of the middle ages recognized a very simple final distinction, that of *prevenient grace* and *subsequent grace.* This distinction refers to the priority or the posteriority of one effect of grace in relation to another in such a way that to do justice to this division the theologian has only to regard the successive effects of grace: the healing of the soul, the fact of willing the good, of effectively realizing it, its perseverance, etc. And as each effect can be considered either with regard to the one which follows it or with regard to the one which precedes it, grace in each will be prevenient or subsequent according to the point of view which one takes. The conversion of the sinner is a prevenient grace in relation to the will of doing the good which follows it. And the latter, which is subsequent grace with respect to the conversion, is prevenient with regard to a given concrete act of charity which the convert makes.

When the theologians who came after St. Thomas employ the term prevenient grace, it is in a totally different sense: instead of referring to the one effect considered in relation to another, the term of the relation becomes simply the free will which the grace *precedes*.

In the language of the Council of Trent, grace is called "excitant" when it draws man away from sin, and "assistant" when it applies the will to the good. *Excitant grace* has for its proper effects spontaneous and indeliberate acts which precede the consent of the free will. *Assistant grace* is applied to free acts. We know the two activities which spring from prevenient grace in the modern sense. In the language of St. Thomas, it is of operative grace that we should speak instead of prevenient grace, which means something else. It is legitimate to say that operative grace implies these two functions of "anticipating" and of "aiding" (the will).

It is evident how careful one must be in using the theological vocabulary in what concerns grace.

But this is not all. The theological quarrels of the 16th century have considerably enriched, and not always in a commendable way, the theological language on grace. We shall simply mention for the record the distinction furnished at this time between sufficient and efficacious grace.

The distinction would take account of a verified fact: there are souls in which grace is increased, others on the contrary which seem to reject it. Whence comes therefore the efficacy of grace? If the efficacy of grace is attributable to God alone, how can man remain free? And how is it that all men are not saved? If it is man who renders grace efficacious, do we not fall into the Pelagian or semi-Pelagian error? Theologians have then coined the concepts of *sufficient* grace, that which furnishes to man only the possibility of doing good, and of efficacious grace which furnishes in addition the realization of the good. Thus they think they have resolved the problem of the universal saving will of God by agreeing that sufficient grace is refused to no one.

We shall not enter into these discussions for we would never get out of them. More than one problem, there is in it a mystery for which it is important to have a religious understanding. To face God it is necessary to stop trying to explain everything rationally in the style of the friends of Job; it is necessary to remember what He is with regard to us and what we are with regard to Him. The saints have an understanding of this mystery which relieves them of every problem of this kind.

We are in fact creatures even while being adoptive sons of God. On the level of nature, as on that of grace, God is necessary for our existence as for our activity. His action in us, in symbiosis with our action does not suppress our liberty, since on the contrary we would not be free without a certain action of God in us which creates, safeguards, and expands our liberty. But this action of God which is constitutive of our very being touches us at a psychologically indiscernible depth. All research which is placed on a psychological level is driven into an impasse and is really menaced with falling into worse errors. The grace of God—like His predestinating providence and like His government in us—is psychologically indiscernible in our own acts. A sane theology owes it to itself to safeguard, on the one hand the liberty of God and the gratuity of His gifts against all Pelagianism and naturalism, and on the other, the liberty and the effort of man against all quietism. Only a metaphysical theology and a theology which keeps close contact with the word of God, especially the major texts of St. Paul on justification—and such we think is the theology of St. Thomas—can do this.

Rather than utilize the second categories, we shall prefer in the *Theology Library* to hold to the fundamental notions of the theology of St. Thomas and to maintain with him—what it is possible to do while remaining on an ontological plane—that the grace which God gives is always efficacious.

The numerous divisions of grace which we have just seen do not make up a multitude of graces. It is one, but its unity includes all the gradations which the complexity of the human-divine symbiosis requires in view of what we may do. The gift of God is as simple as God Himself, but His gift is adapted to our needs which are manifold.

4. WHENCE COMES GRACE?

(a) *God the Sole, Efficient Cause of Grace*

Our point of view here is not to vindicate the divine origin of grace against the claims of free will. Even the fiercest Pelagians have never claimed that man was the efficient cause of grace.

The basic verification which justifies our question is that of the complexity of the organisms of salvation. God is not engaged solely in the distribution of grace: Scripture tells us that all grace comes from Christ; the Church, on the other hand, is aware that the sacraments are not limited to signifying grace, but that they cause it; finally, the transaction of the members of the mystical body entails all sorts of graces. Whence then comes grace? The answer leaves no doubt, however little one may think about what grace is. How could a *formal participation in the divine nature*, which habitual grace is, have any other cause than the divine nature itself? How could the divinization of the soul, according to the beautiful formula of the Greek Fathers, be done by a creature? Every other cause would remain infinitely disproportioned with regard to such an effect. Only fire can render objects incandescent; only God can *deify* creatures, the intermediaries which He uses to communicate grace have only an *instrumental role*; the sacraments and especially the humanity of Christ are instruments in some physical sense; they produce grace necessarily where God applies them. The personal action of the angels and of men is of another order. God makes use of them in order to dispose to grace or the better to prepare for it.

(b) *Role of Free Will in the Reception of Grace*

Is it in inertia that grace seizes us?

We have already raised the problem of the preparation for grace apropos of the necessity of grace. We insisted then on the necessity of actual grace to prepare us for habitual grace, and we emphasized the primacy of the divine initiative. Should we say likewise that an actual grace is necessary to prepare us for an actual grace? If so, are we not falling into a vicious circle? Such a question is not raised. The movement of God does not require of the creature any special aptitude to be moved by God, for every creature possesses, inasmuch as it is a creature, this basic aptitude to be moved by its creator. Everything can be stirred up by Him who moves everything.

If it is true that God gives an actual grace to prepare us for habitual grace, does not man also have a part to play in its acquisition? In fact, habitual grace being a nature, and so a form and not a simple movement, can be inserted in us only according to the laws which govern the action of "matter" and of "form" in every material being. "Form" can be given to "matter" only if the latter is already disposed to receive it. Man must, then, dispose himself for grace. We know already that this preparation is the fruit of a collaboration with actual grace which arouses in us the voluntary movement of consent to grace. The coming of habitual grace does not surprise man in inertia, but in a work, sometimes difficult and austere, of preparation under the influence of grace. We are able to produce certain cases in which the preparation will seem to be non-existent, such as the conversion of St. Paul, although habitually it is not like this. God is patient and ordinarily respects the time of human effort and preparation. But let us not reduce the problem to its psychological aspects. The disposition of which there is question must be understood on the plane of being; it corresponds to a necessity of the metaphysical and not the psychological order, and this is why it can be realized in an instant. It is however quite fitting that an eminent personal gift such as that of divine friendship which is proposed to us in habitual grace should not take place in man without a vital reaction whose rhythm is harmonized with that of our nature in order to dispose us to receive it.

Is grace given with certainty to him who is disposed?

A classical saying whose source can be seen in Origen holds for certain that "God does not refuse grace to him who does whatever lies in his power." A semi-Pelagian interpretation seems at first sight to be required. We have seen that it was inadmissible. How then are we going to interpret the traditional saying? We cannot understand it except in the following way: "God does not refuse grace (habitual) to him who does what lies in his power (but not without the help of actual grace)." Understood in this way, the infallibility of the saying is not based on the effort of man but on divine grace which sustains this effort. It is in the sole measure in which the divine good pleasure gives us to accomplish these acts even to their normal fulfillment with His actual grace, that He undertakes to prolong His benevolence by the gift of habitual grace. At every stage of its infusion, grace is under the sign of the gratuity and the divine good pleasure.

Let a man do what he can do as a man, let him conform himself to the demands of his nature insofar as he is able, and he will not acquire on this ground any right to grace. Just as God can choose the foolish in order to confound the wise (cf. I Cor. 1:27), God can choose to give His grace to a man who would have worked less than another to prepare himself for it.

It is not the same however with the refusal of grace. If such or such a one does not receive a grace, it is because he has not done what lay in his power. We return to the principle: "If there are any who are saved, it is to their savior that they owe it; if there are any who are lost, it is only themselves that they have to blame." Under the pretext of enlarging the goodness of God the theologian would alter it if he made of it a justice of which the good will of man would be the measure, and in some way, the judge.

(c) Corollaries

Is grace equal in everyone?

In a sense, grace places us in possession of the supreme good. There can be no question of more or less apropos of grace. Nevertheless what is impossible on the side of the object which grace enables us to attain, is possible on the side of the subject who participates in the gift. The last word, here again, as in every question of grace, is to be sought in love, the source of the liberalities of God. Love escapes egalitarianism. It is entirely unforeseeable, entirely spontaneous, as the parable of the workmen in the vineyard suggests (Mt. 20:15).

A proper understanding of this inequality demands that we do not forget to consider the social dimensions of the divine economy of salvation. Just as in the natural order the ordered diversity of natures permits a deployment of the eminent perfections contained in the divine simplicity, so the diversity of graces manifest the infinite richness of the gift of God. "But to each one of us was given according to the measure of Christ's bestowal . . . for building up the body of Christ" (Eph. 4:7, 12); this text has directly in view the "charisms," but it is also applied to the distribution of sanctifying grace.

Is it to be said that there is in God a different love for each of His creatures? Certainly not, for the love of God is God Himself; but the manifestations and the effects of this unique love are varied: the cause is unique, the effects are numerous and divers.

Can one know that he has grace?

Heretics and the "illumined" have often made appeal to religious experience to try to justify their position before the legitimate hierarchy. Is it possible to gauge in ourselves the level of supernatural life? Can the presence of grace in the soul be made perceptible to experience?

Let us exclude the extraordinary case of a special revelation of God which can be produced according to the divine good pleasure for reasons of which God is the sole judge; the life of saints furnishes us with certain examples of it. Still, this kind of revelation is rare and incontrovertible.

There remains at least the possibility of a certain inference from the effects of grace which is at work in the soul. A soul which is found to be in the grace of God should normally perform acts which reveal the presence of grace. It is not necessary to deny that a certain continuity in the good, a joy springing from the most humble acts of the spiritual life, those which are least flattering to self love, are favorable indices of the presence in the soul of the grace of God. But the question is to determine the value of these signs. Are they purely conjectural indices, or proofs leading to certitude?

Let us be on our guard not to force expressions of this kind. "God is sensible to the heart." On earth we never grasp more than the effects of God. Now, the supernatural effects and the effects of nature are presented to us under similar and often identical appearances. And we do not possess any means of discerning with certainty these two kinds of effects; the supernatural is not an object of experience. "It is," Pascal would say, "of another order." We do not have then any "proof" of grace. A saint like Joan of Arc answered wonderfully well when she said to her judges who asked her if she were in the grace of God: "If I am, may God keep me in it; if I am not, may He put me in it."

This transcendence of the supernatural with regard to human experience condemns in their principle all the gnoses of the false mystics. Man cannot find in these pretended experiences anything but a fallacious security of which he will perhaps be the victim. Medieval theologians loved to cite here the text, otherwise badly understood, of Ecclesiastes (9:1): "No one knows whether he is worthy of hatred or of love." If the text of the vulgate is here somewhat uncertain, there remains the expression of St. Paul: "For I have nothing on my conscience, yet I am not thereby justified; for he who judges me is the Lord" (I Cor. 4:4).

The filial confidence which we place in the Lord and not in ourselves suffices however to eliminate any morbid anxiety; it presents the advantage of inclining us to place ourselves completely in the hands of the Father and at least to weigh our own value. It can then be a sign which permits us—to ourselves, or rather to those from whom we seek counsel and guidance—to conjecture that we are walking in the way of the Lord and are in His friendship.

5. THE EFFECTS OF GRACE

The effects of grace cannot be studied without taking account in the first place of the state of man who receives this grace. Is he a sinner?—The reception of grace means for him conversion, the rejection of past faults, the return to God; grace makes of him a "new man," it transforms him completely. It is said, and we shall see what it means, that he *justifies* himself. Is he already in the "state of grace"? —Growth in this state signifies for him a *meritorious activity*. Justification and merit are then the two possible effects of grace according as it is given to a sinner or to a just man.

Justification, in its first moment, is an effect of operative grace; and merit, since by definition man freely plays in it his part, is an effect of cooperative grace. Operative grace and cooperative grace are *causes* with regard to justification and merit which are the *effects*.

(a) *Justification*

Definition: "Justification" is a term which theology takes from the Bible. The word is therefore to be understood in its biblical sense, or at least, for us, in its New Testament sense—after the transformation which it undergoes from the fact that the economy of salvation is no longer had through the Law of Moses but through the grace of Jesus Christ. Thus the Christian theology of justification is founded principally on the doctrine of St. Paul who assumed the ancient concept of justification in adopting it, in renewing it even, into the perspective of the new Dispensation. We cite as one example this important text of the Epistle to the Galatians: "And the Scripture, foreseeing that God would justify the Gentiles *by faith* announced to Abraham beforehand, 'in thee shall all the nations be blessed' . . . But that by the Law no man is justified before God is evident, because 'he who is just lives by faith' " (Gal. 3:8, 11).

According to the old Dispensation, the just man could be defined as he who religiously follows and expresses in his life and actions the norm established by God in His law. The just man is he who was found perfect according to the law. Since perfection is measured by an external law, was it not normal to express it by the term "justice"? The just, he who observes *exactly* the law, is the perfect man, today we would even say, the *saint,* but it is necessary to observe that the word has in biblical language another meaning or at least another origin. God is holy par excellence. Things, and persons are holy in the measure in which God appropriates them to himself. In the new Covenant, all Christians are saints from the time that they are baptized in water and the Holy Spirit and thus consecrated to God. St. Paul addresses the larger number of his epistles to the "saints" who are in a given city. Thus we should be attentive to the uses which the Bible makes of certain words and we should not identify too quickly the word *just* with the word *saint.*

According to the New Testament justice does not result from conformity to an external law but from conformity to a gift which God makes to us interiorly, and this conformity is effected actively in the faith. We understand faith, however, in the Paulinian sense of the word which connotes at the same time, adherence, confidence, gift of self, spiritual espousals. "Justice" then establishes in the soul the harmony of our relations with God, it restores to man the primitive likeness which he had with God when he was created "in his image," it makes him a friend of God. *Justification* is the passage from the "state of sin" to the "state of justice." It is normally the fruit of baptism, but it must grow far beyond our baptismal "sanctification" until the grace in us has produced its final effects. Justification can also be the fruit of penitence. In other words, justification is the passage from the state of sin to the state of grace and is always accompanied in our heart by a returning, that is, a conversion.

It is necessary to add that the word justification can be understood in our language in two senses: in the active sense, and it is then the act of God which justifies the sinner; in the passive sense, and then it is the operation by which the sinner is found justified. The passivity of which the sinner is here the subject, let us say once more, is in no way of the psychological order; it coincides on the contrary with an "activity" and certain personal efforts on his part—activity and efforts which do not escape the sovereign causality of God.

The Components of Justification

The part of God: For Luther, who declared himself on this point the authentic interpreter of St. Paul, the state of justice in which justification terminates does not go beyond the juridical order of non-imputation. The "justified" sinner according to Luther is simply provided with a new sentiment of "faith" according to which he is confident that God, in virtue of the merits of Christ, no longer takes account of his sins, that he no longer imputes his sins to him. The justice of justified man is a purely declarative justice. God declares that man is saved but his sins and his misery remain; he is not changed except in this sentiment of faith which causes him to put his confidence in the merits of Christ.

Every interpretation of justification which would not achieve true justice of our sins robs grace of its true foundation; moreover, the Council of Trent rose up against the theory of non-imputation. If God saves us by allowing us to remain in the state of sin, His salvation would do us no good, would not really save us. The sacred texts, so full of realism—which call to mind the "new birth" in St. John, the "new man," the "new creature" in St. Paul and we could multiply these expressions—cannot be interpreted by a simple juridical non-imputation. The Christian life would no longer be anything but a sad comedy or a sham if it were denied all internal value of true justice, i.e. of a justice which excludes sin and adorns life with genuine virtues. We believe therefore that justice really destroys sin. "For those whom he has foreknown he has also predestined, to become conformed to the image of his Son, that he should be the first-born among many brethren; and those whom he has predestined, he has called, and those whom he has called, he has also justified; and those whom he has justified, he has also glorified" (Rom. 8:29-30). All these words: predestination, production in the image of His Son, vocation, justification, glorification—and one might add, adoption, sanctification—do not mean the same thing but are all pregnant with the same reality and indicate the same novelty, the same creation in him to whom they are attributed. For St. Paul, the law is nothing, circumcision is nothing, "imputation," and every other conception of the juridical vocabulary is likewise nothing. "What counts is to be a new creation" (Gal. 6:15). If moreover the doctrine of St. Paul suffers some difficulty here or there, it is due to the fact that he is engaged in controversy. The same cannot be said of St. John or of St. Peter.

It is in all truth that "We are called and are children of God," that we have been made "children of light," that we have become "participants in the divine nature," and it is necessary to understand the phrase of Romans: "Now to him who works, the reward is not credited as a favor but as something due. But to him who does not work but believes in him who justifies the impious, his faith is credited to him as justice" (Rom. 4:4-6), in the strong sense which is that of the overall doctrine of the New Testament. The faith which justifies the impious is not a sentiment capable of co-existing with sin, it is an adherence to God absolutely transforming and converting, which quite naturally fits in with the whole procession of virtues. The Paulinian faith is the movement which harmonizes the soul with God, and, from light to light, renders it more and more similar to the divine model.

It is not therefore necessary to say that if the divine act of justification destroys sin it is because it corresponds to an infusion of grace. To remit sin, let us remember, is for God to remit an offense which has been committed against Him, to make peace, no longer to be offended. In short, it is for God to restore His friendship. But what does that mean in God? We have already said that God does not change and that all the changes of attitude of God with respect to His creatures always mean a change in the creatures and not in the Creator. To remit the offense, to remit the sin, to no longer impute it, to give His peace, to bestow His friendship, means that there is something new in the creature thus restored to the friendship of God, and this new thing is what we call grace. "Grace" understood as a favor of God never goes without "grace" understood as a gift which the creature receives.

A man can pardon another who retains with regard to him certain bad intentions. In reality he pardons by forgetting, by no longer looking, by no longer wishing to look, and the pardon is always painful for him since it changes nothing, it reestablishes no correspondence between him and the offender. The gesture is generous, but it is limited and this limit proceeds from the weakness of man who does not have the power to change the heart of his neighbors. Such is not the pardon of God. God sees everything, considers everything, and if He pardons, it is to reestablish a true peace, a harmonious order that was destroyed; His pardon is creative, He turns the will of the sinner, and makes of his enemy a true friend freely converted.

Let us apply these principles to the Christian sacraments which confer the grace of justification. Whether it be baptism or whether it be penance, these sacraments if they really bring us pardon of our sins cannot leave us in any way in a state of sin. It would be false to think for example that it is enough to avow even a venial sin in order that it be pardoned if one remains formally attached to it and if one has no intention of regretting it. The grace of the sacrament of penance is on the contrary a grace of repentance (of actual repentance for mortal sins; of at least virtual repentance, i.e. such as would imply regret for sin if it were presented, for venial sins). In fact, the sacramental economy changes nothing in the economy of justification as anyone can read throughout the New Testament.

Let no one say now that God could remit sin without giving His grace, by making some sort of neutral creature out of the sinner who would be neither His enemy nor His friend. If he had never sinned, man would have been able—at least we can see no reason for not agreeing to it—to exist in this neutral state without sin and without divine grace. But from the moment that he sins, God can remit his sin only by a special act of benevolence. And to say that God is *benevolent* toward the sinner, means nothing, as we have just shown, if it does not mean that the sinner receives an effect of this benevolence, grace. To be the subject of a favor from God, or of His benevolence, or of His affection, or of His mercy, or of His grace, is always to be personally and interiorly transformed by this favor or this love.

The part of man: We do not need to ask here whether man should prepare himself for grace but simply whether man should supply his active and personal part to the divine act which justifies him. From a certain point of view, this would be to return to the Lutheran error, that is, to imagine a subject which receives grace in a purely passive and inert fashion. God loves beings according to their nature; his moving of free beings does not injure their liberty—quite the contrary. Although justification may be an effect of operative grace, it cannot be produced without a free reaction of man. A liberty moved by God is not a chained liberty but a true liberty. We are never more ourselves than when in the hand of God. And yet this liberty which we manifest in justification does not mean that the latter is a fruit of cooperative grace: the turning of the will, however free it may be, is not attributable to the cooperation of a sinful will, i.e., a bad will, but to God alone.

Let no one imagine himself capable of discovering all these things through any psychological research. The activity of God combines with our own in such a way that it is absolutely psychologically indiscernible by us. Without being pantheistic, it is true to say that God is more ourselves than we are.

Justification then presupposes a free activity of man. In what does this activity consist? We have already made allusion to faith. In fact, justification comprises first of all an act of faith. The just man lives by faith, as St. Paul tirelessly declares. We understand, let it be repeated, the living faith which operates through charity. God does not save us without ourselves. He justifies us in such a way "that what he does in us, we ourselves also do." Grace engages us personally in such a way that when it is given to us it necessarily provokes in us an act of living faith. As the child who comes into the world manifests his life exteriorly by crying, so man reborn to the life of a child of God immediately posits an act of living faith. But while in the first case, there is only a manifestation of life, in the second there is an interior and vital act par excellence. Since God touches our soul by infusing His grace into it, He inclines it toward Himself by making it produce this act of living faith. At the beginning of the divine life of the soul of the adult—for the infant incapable of acts, God gives the *habitus* of faith, i.e. the power of performing acts of faith when its intelligence will have become capable of these acts—there is this act of living faith, the fundamental act which deserves to be called without any play on words "an act of birth." Man cooperates in his divine birth by an act of faith.

The logic of the movement which carries us toward God implies also that we reject sin. Justification implies on our part both an act of adherence to God and an act of voluntary opposition to sin. A living faith that is pregnant with hope and charity is necessarily accompanied by penitence and the fear of God. It is in the nature of faith which is born in the soul of the justified to give little by little growth and maturity to all the virtues which it necessarily brings with it. To say that faith leaves us in our sin, that is, in our opposition to God, in our misery, and that it is content to give us the assurance that God will no longer regard our sin, would be on the one hand to forget what His pardon is; not being able to change Himself, God necessarily changes those with whom He enters into new relations; on the other hand it would be to misunderstand the psychological scope of the loving confidence and of the gift of self which it supposes and which entails the basically good orientation of every creature. We cannot oppose faith and virtues, for where faith "which justifies the impious" takes root, the soul becomes basically good and possesses in germ all of the virtues. Similarly, we cannot oppose faith and works, for true faith manifests itself normally by good works: "Therefore he who knows how to do good, and does not do it, commits a sin (Jas. 4:16). When St. Paul declares: "But to him who does not work but believes in him who justifies the impious, his faith is credited to him as justice," this cannot be understood in the sense that a really living faith might do without the works which normally proceed from it, but in the sense that "justice" according to God is established in us, in our heart, in our faith, and not in the external acts which the law commands. The justice of the new Dispensation is interior; the law is inscribed in our hearts; the kingdom of God is within us. This non-opposition of the faith and of works is moreover declared in a blunt text of St. James: "Thou hast faith, and I have works! Show me thy faith without works, and I from my works will show thee my faith" (2:18).

To sum up, the justification of the sinner comprises four phases: 1) God gives His grace and thus stirs up the soul of the sinner; 2) the latter returns then to God in a movement of living faith; 3) and against his sin in a movement of repentance; 4) finally, God consecrates in some way this double movement inspired by his grace by remitting the sin. Let us be on our guard however against considering these four phases as four temporal stages. It would be more true to consider them rather as *aspects* of one and the same movement which analysis leads us to distinguish in this manner. Moreover we are going to speak of the manner in which the order indicated is to be understood.

Synthetic Grouping

Time in justification: The four components which the analysis of justification permits us to distinguish are not, we have just said, the successive phases of the act by which God makes a just man out of a sinner. Justification is, of itself, instantaneous, since it depends only on one element, the infusion of grace which arouses and contains in some way the three others. That is understood if we recall that the created will is entirely dependent on God who can transform it in an instant without thereby doing any violence. That in such and such a precise case God may wish to prolong the preparation does not mean that justification, i.e. the infusion also of sanctifying grace, is not instantaneous.

The order of nature: At any rate, however instantaneous justification may be, it comprises from one phase to another an order of nature whose interlocking we may try to see.

The infusion of grace is first. God is the author of our justification and nothing can be done without Him. "It is he who has first loved us," declares St. John. The rebellious will has no power to return to God unless God gives it His help.

Then comes—always in the order of natures and not by temporal stages—the part of man. It comes only then because it is entirely under the tenure of justifying (or sanctifying) grace. Man is turned toward God in a movement of living faith and sets himself against sin in a movement of repentance: faith is first, for it is on account of God and in the name of God that sin is detested; there is no reason here for opposing sin without considering God. Finally there comes the end of the movement which is the remission of sin.

Justification Evaluated Among the Works of God

It is always a delicate matter to compare the different works of God with one another in order to determine which is the greatest; it would even be an indiscreet and frivolous exercise if curiosity were the only motive. In fact this evaluation should result in our appreciating the gifts of God.

St. Augustine tries it in his Commentary on St. John: "It is a greater work to make a just man out of a sinner than to create heaven and earth." Because it terminates in making man enter into the friendship of God, justification takes precedence over creation, which remains a stranger to the intimate life of God.

Let no one say that by its dimensions the work of creation is of greater weight than the salvation of an individual. St. Thomas does not hesitate to reply that "The good of grace for a single soul is greater than—*maius est*—the natural good of the entire universe." One thinks of Pascal: "It is of another order. . . ."

Should we not then conclude that the final glorification of the just is also preferable to the justification of the sinner? If we consider the value of the benefit granted, certainly it is the greater good. But if we think of the gratuity of the benefit, we must admit that the justification of the sinner, a work of pure mercy, shows still better the divine liberality than his final glorification when he is already justified. Justification is furthermore a gift.

(b) *Merit*

To speak of merit is to evoke a *right to compensation*. What then can a *right* of man over God mean? To place eternal life at the end of our effort as a reward merited in justice seems to deny the very gratuity of grace. The Pelagians did not escape from this conclusion, and their attitude is found in many deviations of the religious spirit in which one is inclined to treat of the affairs of God as he would treat of banking operations. It is against caricatures of this kind that Protestantism rebelled. The affair of indulgences, so poorly presented by churchmen, was one of the reasons for Luther's revolt.

But we forget for one reason or another that merit is not the cause of grace; it is its *effect*, the effect of cooperative grace. A conception of merit which would not emphasize the principal role of grace in the meritorious act would be monstrous and indefensible.

Nature and basis of all merit before God: Merit and retribution go together. Retribution is what anyone has merited for his work or for his effort; it is in some way the price of the work accomplished or the effort. And just as to pay the just price is an act of justice, so to give the wage "merited" is an act of justice.

But there is justice and justice. Perfect justice exists only between equals, then it is merit in the strictest sense. I agree with an artisan that he should do for me a certain work. He does it; he has perfectly "merited" the price which he in all honesty has determined.

Where there is no equality in the exchange, there is only relative justice. And likewise there is no longer any but a relative merit. Thus a son can acquire a certain merit before his father; the latter, satisfied with the work of his child, will gladly reward him for it. The reward is really a gratuitous act on the part of the father, nevertheless it recognizes the value of the work done and it can be said of the son that he merited it. Thus it is, all due proportions observed, with justice between God and ourselves. Here we are at the maximum of inequality. Everything that man has, he receives from God. If there is still a certain justice in it, it cannot be understood as a justice of equality but only as a justice of proportion, in which each one, proportionally to what he is, does what he is able to do. It must be remarked however that man is not in a position to do anything unless God enables him to do it. Thus the merit of man, even understood proportionally, supposes that God gives him the power to act as he wills. In other words, the merit which man acquires before God by his activity is nothing else than that for which God has given him the power to do; it is nothing else than the terminus of an activity conceived and established for him by God. We can, if we wish, compare the reward due to merit to what natural beings obtain by their own movements or by their natural operations: a given fruit, or flower, which produces a plant; but we must be careful that the rational creature is capable of moving himself by his own free will: it is by himself that he acts and this is why we can speak of merit in his regard. We cannot attribute it to the plant under the pretext that it yields flowers and fruits. And yet, man has as great a need as the plant, even a greater need, of a divine movement in order to produce his spiritual fruit which is the free act.

These considerations show us that we cannot understand the nature of merit without an appeal to two levels of explanation: the more universal one is that of relations with justice; the other, which is a particular application of the first to the case considered, is that of the growth and fructification of the living. It is what we have just done. We began with an analysis of the relations of justice and we finished with a consideration of the fructification of living beings. This does not mean that we refuse to admit a "certain" justice between God and His creature, and so a certain merit of the creature, but we have explained in what sense, and only in what sense, justice and merit are present: "I have chosen you and have appointed you that you should go and bear fruit, and that your fruit should remain" (Jn. 15:16). We are far from the narrow juridicalism of the Pelagians; we are also far from any absolute extrinsicism such as that of the Lutherans or the Calvinists. The design of God is that man should reach eternal life by means of acts *proportionate* to this end. God could have given us the fruit without in any way waiting to go out of us; but he willed, due regard being given to the dignity to which he wished to raise us, that man should merit eternal life by proportionate acts. It is in this divine disposition that we must look for the foundation of merit.

There is here therefore, as in all true merit, real justice. Grace confers on our acts a dignity such that they constitute a title in justice for the attainment of eternal life through which they are by means of it proportioned. It remains true, nevertheless that God is a debtor only to Himself, not toward us, since it is by a free and gratuitous act that He has established this disposition. Gratuity and necessity are not opposed to each other, for they do not play on the same stage. Necessity entirely suspended from a first gratuity can in no way injure it. It manifests on the contrary the magnanimity of the gratuitous disposition of God.

Merit and liberty: Let us develop certain consequences of what we have just presented. In the merit of which we speak there is no mercenary preoccupation with gaining anything. The absolute dependence of man with regard to God is there entirely preserved; but that does not prevent man from being free and it is from this liberty, acting under the movement of grace, that he derives the honor of "meriting." It is liberty and liberty alone which provides the basis for merit. Man, having regard simply for the work done, rewards those to whom he owes something in justice. God, on the contrary, rewards the just not in consideration of the work done but in accordance with the free manner, that is, with the measure of love, with which he has done it. Merit is a kind of physical property of the good moral act, that is, of the free act directed toward its end.

It follows from this that every morally good act, by the very fact that it is free, is meritorious. It makes little difference whether this act be one "of precept," that is, obligatory, or whether it be one "of counsel" and supererogatory. The act of justice by which we render what we owe is not less meritorious than the gracious act by which we give an alms apart from what is necessary if it is done with similar love.

It follows from that also that if we acquire some merit before God, it is not because we bring Him something. God has nothing to receive from us that He does not already possess and which He has not given us the power to give Him. God has nothing to gain even from our worship. That which wins us any merit before God is always a gain for us, not for God.

Thus, by our merit we do not render God strictly obligated in our regard. If God is obligated, it is by virtue of a disposition established by Him in advance, according to which He "rewards" the acts that He gives us to do.

It follows from that finally that all merit comes from our charity. Let us develop this point.

Merit and charity: There are two ways of considering merit, or, if you wish, two aspects of the meritorious work.

On the one hand, merit comes from the disposition established by God. God disposes that man acquire his good by his own activity; this is the reason why the good obtained has value of merit with respect to the act performed.

On the other hand, merit comes from free will. Man, unlike all the other animals, has the privilege of acting by himself, voluntarily. Whence it is that he merits. A free act is worthy of being honored or punished.

Whether we consider merit under one aspect or the other, it is clear that it resides principally in charity.

In the first place, eternal life toward which God directs the movement of the soul consists in the enjoyment of God; but the movement toward the loving possession of God is nothing else than the very act of charity. It is charity which urges us to seize God and it is charity which involves in us all the other virtues—which would have no relation to our last end without it.

In the second place, it is evident that the act which is the most free, i.e. the most voluntary, is the one which is made with the greatest love. Here again, merit springs principally from charity.

Let us then give up the false idea according to which it is the difficulty of the work which constitutes merit. No, the difficulty increases merit only to the degree that it obliges our love to surpass itself in some way to overcome an obstacle. But even then, what has obtained for us merit, is not the difficulty, it is the love which we have put into it. Difficulty is a proof, it constitutes the proof of our love, it obliges us to give it in full measure: "And if I deliver my body to be burned," says St. Paul, "yet do not have charity, it profits me nothing" (I Cor. 13:3). A veritable paradox, but one which emphasizes the irreplacable efficacy of charity.

All acts of virtue have value only through the charity which inspires them. Even faith is meritorious only if it works through charity. If I have to move mountains, says St. Paul again, and have not charity, it profits me nothing.

Merit and eternal life: Can we merit eternal life? The question demands a twofold answer according as we consider man deprived of grace or established in grace.

Man deprived of grace.

The merit of man, we have said, depends on a pre-established order. God has conceived the activity of man in such a way that it is capable of bearing the excellent fruit which is eternal life. Man can then merit eternal life. Had not God disposed the activity of man in view of this end, eternal life could not be attained or merited. "No one can come to me unless the Father who sent me draw him . . ." (Jn. 6:44). Now the germ that God has deposited in our soul in order that it grow into eternal life is grace. Without grace, man cannot "merit" eternal life nor attain it.

A second obstacle moreover prevents man deprived of grace from meriting eternal life, and it is sin. Sin, an offense against God, makes us enemies of God and moves us away from eternal life. Now sin cannot be remitted except by grace.

Man established in grace.

The meritorious activity of man can therefore be considered in two ways. We can consider the act of man simply according to what it is and according to the liberty from which it proceeds. It is thus for example that the father considers the work of his son. The reward which he gives him is not due in strict justice, it is designed simply to honor a good act in which the child has given full measure of service. Likewise, the virtuous activity of man is without proportion to eternal life and has no title in strict justice to merit. Nevertheless it is a free activity in which man gives the best of himself and there is a certain fittingness that God who is good should reward him according to the excellence of His infinite power. We say that man merits *de congruo* eternal life. It is a merit of simple propriety.

But we can consider the act of man insofar as it proceeds from the grace of the Holy Spirit which is in him. Then the value of the merit should be willed according to the power of the Holy Spirit who seizes us interiorly, directs us toward God, and who is in us as "a fountain of water springing up unto life everlasting" (Jn. 4:14). Thus considered in its divine origin and cause, the act of man merits *de condigno,* i.e. in justice, or at least in dignity, eternal life. We can also add that the value of the act should equally be estimated according to the dignity of grace. Now it is through grace that man, become "a participant in the divine nature," is adopted as son of God, and it is because he is son that he has a right to the heritage: "But if we are sons, we are heirs also—heirs indeed of God and joint hears of Christ . . ." (Rom. 8:17).

Extension of merit. What can we merit? We have already seen in what way we could "merit" eternal life. We raise the same question apropos of the first grace, of conversion, of the increase of grace, of final perseverance, of the grace of others, of temporal goods.

Two principles control the reply that we can give to each of these questions.

1. The merit of man depends essentially on the order pre-estab-

lished by God. Man merits and merits only that for which God has disposed human activity. The tree produces determined fruits "each according to its kind." Thus man established in grace conceives God in his own heart.

2. The principle of merit is not itself an object of merit. The tree is not the cause of its own seed from which it has issued. Man cannot merit unless he has the sanctifying grace which is at the beginning of all his merits.

We do not merit the first grace, but we can merit a subsequent grace in view of the grace already received. We can likewise merit *de condigno,* in dignity, the increase of grace or, what practically amounts to the same thing, the increase of charity.

Can we merit in advance the grace to rise again on that day on which we will fall into sin? Let us note well the meaning of this question: it is not a problem of knowing whether a sinner can merit the grace of his conversion for this question has already been solved negatively, but of knowing whether a just man can merit the grace to rise again after he has fallen into sin. There again, the answer is negative. Merit *de condigno,* based on the control of the soul by the Holy Spirit, is in fact arrested as soon as sin intervenes. If certain new graces are given which lead to the rehabilitation of the sinner, they do not spring from this merit, for there is an interruption of the divine assistance. The merit of suitability can no longer make valid its claims: the sinner is not enabled to present even a past merit so long as he remains a sinner, and moreover, his actual sin would place an obstacle to the efficacy of the merit if he could present it. The sinner can only invoke the mercy of God.

Can man merit perseverance? We must note that there are two kinds of perseverance. First, the perseverance of glory (that of the saints in heaven) is that which renders the free will incapable of sinning, not for lack of liberty, but on the contrary, through the "consummated grace" which the blessed in heaven possesses. To merit this kind of perseverance is quite simply to merit eternal life; we have already pronounced on that.

But there is a second kind of perseverance—that of this life, i.e. that of a will continually susceptible to failure since it is not yet confirmed in grace. Now we have said that merit depends essentially on an order pre-established by God. In order that the soul persevere, i.e. in order that the movement of its charity terminate in eternal life, it is necessary that the control of the soul by the Holy Spirit be destined to this end. This depends on the divine "control" which is the principle of all merit and which God accords according to His free love. Man therefore cannot merit final perseverance.

Here is an example. That an apple tree produce apples is, we can say, in its power. But that an apple tree indifferently produce pears, apples, or peaches, is not in its power. It produces only that for which it is made. This is only a comparison and must not be pushed too far. It can however help us to understand that man is able to merit the perseverance of glory for which he is made, since he is established in grace *for that,* and that he cannot "merit" final perseverance in this life, since this perseverance must qualify his entire life. Man can merit all graces, grace after grace, except the first and that of final perseverance.

We must be careful not to consider everything from the angle of merit. Although perseverance cannot be merited, we obtain it by asking God for it for ourselves and for others.

And this leads us to ask precisely in what manner we can merit grace for others.

We have already said that we can consider the meritorious act in two ways which provide the occasion for two types of merit.

If we consider the meritorious act insofar as it is under the control of the Holy Spirit and ordered to a determined end, the merit which qualifies it is a merit *de condigno,* of justice. It is clear that we cannot merit *de condigno* grace for others since the movement of the Holy Spirit in us is not ordained to this term; it is personal for us. Only Christ merits *de condigno* grace for all men since His personal grace is destined to this universal efficacy. Moreover, "For it became him for whom are all things and through whom are all things, who had brought many sons into glory, to perfect through sufferings the author of their salvation" (Heb. 2:10). The grace of Christ is a capital grace.

If we consider the meritorious act simply under its aspect of free act, the merit which qualifies it is a merit of suitability, it is fitting that God should reward according to His omnipotent goodness the man who gives freely and generously his full measure. From this point of view we can merit grace or the salvation of one of our brothers. It is fitting that God, whose will we are accomplishing, consider our friend; that is, our brother, as a bit of ourselves; the laws of friendship demand this. That unfortunately does not prevent the soul from being able to set up an obstacle to it by its sin.

A last question: can we merit temporal goods, such as health, food, success, riches? Here we must consider that the "good" of man is of two kinds: the absolute good is union with God, as the psalmist declares in writing: "My good is to be united with God" (Ps. 71); the relative good is everything that is good for the moment only or which is good only from a certain point of view. Temporal goods are of this kind; we can merit them to the degree and in the measure only in which they are ordained to the absolute good, i.e. in which they are truly goods. Once the first grace has been received we can then "merit" health, joys, successes, comfort on the same grounds as the other helps that lead us to eternal life—on the same grounds for example as growth of charity. So long as our body lives we will have need of a certain number of goods—the exercise of virtue presupposes physical life—and God will dispense them to the just to the degree and in the manner which is suitable or, sometimes, according as they know how to ask for them. But it happens also that what we might consider according to appearances as evils are in reality goods by which God disposes us to become more closely united with Him.

If we consider temporal goods not in relation to eternal life, but in themselves, then they are no longer properly speaking goods. Or at least it is only under certain aspects that they are goods, for "what exists" is a "good." From this restricted point of view man can still merit them on condition of understanding well that he does not merit them for eternal life. Man merits them if for example God takes charge of his will and moves him to acquire these goods. But in acquiring them it is also possible that the intention of man be not what it should be. It is thus that the wise women of *Exodus* I, obtained what they wanted—that the male children might be saved —and yet they were not afraid to tell a lie. Again, certain nations were able to conquer the people of Israel despite their bad intention; but God made use of them to punish His people and to prepare it to receive its salvation.

CONCLUSION

Grace is a "divine seed" (I Jn. 3:9) which God puts in us in order that it may grow and produce fruit even unto eternal life. As God has made plants and trees in order that they might produce fruit "each according to its kind" (Gen. 1:12), so we can say that He places in man this seed of eternal life in order that it produce its proper fruit. It is thus that grace makes us "merit" eternal life, i.e. that it makes us acquire it, at the end of a movement in some way natural, through the divine forces which it disposes in us. The grace which comes to us from God bears us toward God. To be a child of God, "of the race of God" (Acts 17:28-29), is to be able to say to God, and to say it effectively, not from the lips but from the heart, in the Holy Spirit, with the Son: "Abba," that is to say, "Father."

REFLECTIONS AND PERSPECTIVES

On the one hand, man is a creature for whom God is transcendent, even though he is also immanent; between the creature and God there is an unbridgeable distance. On the other hand, man, by grace, is called to be the son of God and to enjoy with Him intimate filial and friendly relations. A sane theology should always respect these two facts, the two terms of this fundamental antinomy. Transcendence does not exclude immanence; creation by God does not exclude the liberty of man; the fear of God does not exclude the love which is due Him; the fact that we are "others" as creatures does not exclude the fact that we are of the race of God and participate in the divine nature as sons of God; the gratuity of the gift of God does not exclude the fact that it is necessary for our salvation.

What is to be thought of the Protestant assertion: "God is subject, never object, man is object, never subject," that is, there is not in man any "ownership" of grace which God alone possesses? Explain and criticize.

Natural and supernatural. History of the word "supernatural"; its different meanings at different periods. How was theology led to coin the word? Can we speak of a "natural" end for man? In what sense?

The "states." Can we speak of a state of "pure nature"? In what sense? What does Revelation teach us on the subject? Can we distinguish other states than those of integral nature, wounded nature, redeemed nature? Define and describe the state of "original justice."

Nature and mind. Can the mind be considered as a "nature" in the same way as other natures? To define it by its four causes, what would be the final cause? Can we say that the mind is the only nature whose end surpasses its natural potentialities? Problem and mystery of the natural desire for God. Can we say that in creating "minds,"

God by that very fact disposed himself to make friends and sons? In other words, can the mind have another end than God in the unitive vision? Answer the question from the different points of view of Revelation, philosophy and theology.

Liberty and sin. What is liberty? Define created liberty. Show that liberty is not the power to commit sin and that it can even exclude it (Christ, the Blessed). Show however that if it is not good that man should sin, it is better that he be capable of sinning. Is the peccability of the angel attributable to its simple nature or to the fact that it is susceptible of receiving or refusing grace? "Would the angel be impeccable if grace had never been offered it"? Has this question any meaning?—Is it true that "voluntariness" always means free, gratuitous, moral, meritorious? Can we distinguish a natural and a necessary voluntary appetite and a free voluntary appetite? In what sense?—How explain the inability to sin of the Blessed? What does the "comprehension" of God mean, term of hope, "confirmation in grace"? Is this "confirmation" possible in this life? Are there examples of saints in the old or the new Testament which might justify such an hypothesis?

Grace and vision of the world. In what sense can it be understood that the supernatural is *added* to nature? Could the nature of man, in right or in fact, be totally self-sufficient? Is the supernatural destiny of man in the line of his nature or is it something foreign to it? Does the invitation to the supernatural life find a certain echo in the nature of man, and a certain correspondence, or does it find him quite unprepared (in right or in fact)?

What is the part of the man who has been touched by sin, and what is the part of the man who is susceptible to being helped by grace? Does sin attack the body also? the material world? Does grace also affect the body (presently and at the Resurrection)? the material world? Comment on and explain Rom. 8:19-22; Phil. 3:20-21; I Jn. 3:2.

The Christian life conceived as a "return to paradise": the exactitude of this conception? Can we see in Gen. 2:5-25 a lesson in part eschatological? And in Adam a type or an antitype of the new man?—Is the resurrection of the body imputable to the same grace as Baptism? Comment on Rom. 8:11 and I Cor. 15:35-38. How can St. Paul attribute to the eucharistic communion received unworthily the power to render the body ill (I Cor. 11:30)?

Can the grace of the Christian be measured? What is its limit?

its measure? How can we say that it is greater in one than in another? Is the habitual grace of Christ which contains them all "finite" or "infinite"? The grace of the Blessed Virgin? What is meant by saying that grace "divinizes" man? Show inasfar as possible the exactitude and the limits of this expression.

Grace and the Sacraments. Is the infusion of grace bound up with the Sacraments? Can a Christian increase in grace or recover grace after it has been lost? outside the Sacraments? Study from this point of view the history of the hermits, beatified or canonized, who for centuries lived without the Sacraments of the Church: Penance, Communion, Mass, Extreme-Unction. Justify this ancient institution of the eremetic life by showing that there is in the Sacraments another aspect than that of the "conferring of grace."—Can there be Christian grace outside the visible Church? (In Protestant sects, in Islam, in Hinduism, etc.) Is it conceivable that God is served by the religious institutions of Protestants, Mussulmans, Hindus or Buddhists in order to give or to increase grace? If these graces exist, should they be assigned any limits? Can the expression "non-Christian grace" have any meaning? What?

Grace, mysticism, state and law. What does the expression "mystical graces" mean? Can we conceive an intermediary state of grace between exile and heaven? between the state of those who being justified are yet capable of sin, and the state of those who are confirmed in grace? A certain "mystical state"—is there any which places the soul outside its present condition? Justify or refute such doctrines, on the basis of facts and of theology.

History of mysticism. Definition. Exact meaning.

Does the expression "state of grace" mean a stability in grace? Of what kind of stability is it a question? A critique of this expression. Gather together all the expressions in the New Testament which are applicable to the soul endowed with grace by God.

What does the expression "grace of state" mean? Distinguish "grace of state" from charism. To what kind of states do these graces apply?

New Law. Show the equivalence of the *New Law* and grace. How can the New Law be defined as grace, and grace as the New Law (opposed to the Old Law)?

BIBLIOGRAPHIE

1. Révélation de la grâce.
On se référera surtout à:
J. Guillet, *Thèmes bibliques,* Études sur l'expression et le développement de la Révélation, Paris, Aubier, 1950. De beaucoup le meilleur pour la partie sémantique.
P. Denis, *La Révélation de la grâce dans saint Paul et dans saint Jean,* Liège, La Pensée cath., 1948.
A. Descamps, *Les justes et la justice dans les évangiles et le christianisme primitif hormis la doctrine proprement paulinienne,* Louvain, Publ. univ., 1950.
L'étude principale est cependant celle de Bonnetain, Art. *Grâce,* dans le *Supplément du dictionnaire de la Bible.* Travail plein de choses utiles quoique broussailleux et d'utilisation laborieuse.

2. Théologie de la grâce.
A. Études historiques:
H. Rondet, *Gratia Christi,* Paris, Beauchesne, 1948. Essai d'histoire du dogme et de théologie dogmatique à l'occasion de cette histoire.
J. Auer, *Die Entwicklung des Gnadenlehre in der Hochscholastik,* t. II, *Das Wirken der Gnade,* Fribourg, 1951.
M. Landgraf, *Dogmengeschichte der Frühscholastik,* Teil I, Regensberg, 1952.
H. Lais, *Die Gnadenlehre des heiligen Thomas in der Summa contra Gentiles und der Kommentar des Franziskus Sylvestris von Ferrare,* Munich, 1951.
B. Théologie:
Saint Thomas d'Aquin, *La grâce,* Trad. et notes de R. Mulard, Paris, Éd. de la Revue des J., 1929.
J.-H. Nicolas, *Le mystère de la grâce,* Liège, Éd. de la Pensée Cath., 1951.
R. Morency, *L'union de grâce selon saint Thomas,* Montréal, Coll. de l'Immaculée Conception, 1950.
C.-M. Lachance, *Le sujet de la grâce et sa guérison selon saint Thomas,* Ottawa, Éd. du Lévrier, 1944.

BIBLIOGRAPHY

BOOKS

Arami, M., *Life Abundant.* New York: F. Pustet Co., 1948.
Garrigou-Lagrange, Reginald, O.P., *Grace.* St. Louis: B. Herder Book Co., 1952.
Jauncey, Ernest, *Doctrine of Grace.* New York: The Macmillan Company, 1925.
Joyce, G. H., *Catholic Doctrine of Grace.* Westminster, Md.: The Newman Bookshop, 1950.
Matthews, J. V., *Actual Grace and the Spiritual Life.* Liverpool: The Mercier Press, 1950.
———, *With the Help of Thy Grace.* Westminster, Md.: The Newman Bookshop, 1944.

Scheeben, Matthias J., *The Glories of Divine Grace*. Cincinnati: Benziger Bros., 1886.
————, *Nature and Grace*. St. Louis: B. Herder Book Co., 1954.

ARTICLES

Bourassa, T., "Adoptive Sonship," *Theological Studies*, 13: 309-355 (Sept., 1952).

De Letter, P., "Sanctifying Grace and Our Union with the Holy Trinity," *Theological Studies*, 13: 33-58 (March, 1952).

Donnelly, Malachi J., "A Reply," *Theological Studies*, 13: 190-204 (June, 1952).

Hughes, D., "Dynamics of Christian Perfection," *Thomist*, 15: 247-288 (April, 1952).

Kennedy, J. P., "Reflections on Human Nature and the Supernatural," *Theological Studies*, 14: 280-287 (June, 1953).

McDonaugh, A., "Partnership: Man's Cooperation with God's Grace," *Sign*, 29: 20 ff (Sept., 1949).

Wheeler, M. C., "Actual Grace According to St. Thomas," *Thomist*, 16: 334-360. (July, 1953).

AUTHOR INDEX

Abraham, 29, 274
Adeney, W. F., 23
Albert the Great, Saint,
xii, xiii, 150
Amand, 140
Ambrose, Saint, xix, 147,
148, 180, 220
Amiot, F., 23
Arami, M., 410
Aristotle, xiv, 49, 74, 77,
98, 101-102, 104, 117,
122, 123, 150, 157,
158, 167, 179, 180,
182, 183, 189, 190,
191, 209, 220
Augustine, Saint, xii, xix,
46, 47, 49, 77, 93,
101, 130, 140, 146,
147, 148, 158, 159,
180, 215, 234, 244,
247, 250, 251, 256,
306, 309, 355, 356,
374, 383, 398

Baius, 263, 357, 358, 368,
369
Baudouin, C., 40, 171
Beauvoir, S. de, 45, 140
Beirnaert, R. P., 171
Berdiaeff, N., 140
Bergson, H., 110, 210
Bernard, Saint, xii
Bernard, R., 181, 182,
187, 201, 202, 226,
268
Biot, R., 129
Bonaventure, Saint, xii,
xiii, 246, 251
Bonsirven, J., 23
Bossuet, 27
Bourassa, T., 411
Boutonier, J., 129
Bouyer, L., 244
Bovon, J., 22

Brown, B. F., 336
Bruno de Jesus Marie,
171
Brunschvicg, L., 250
Buckley, J., 68

Callan, C., 336
Calvin, 357, 358
Carrel, A., 129
Carrouges, M., 267
Cassian, xv, 356
Celestine V, Pope, 355
Chazal, M. de, 38
Chevalier, J., 180, 181,
227
Cicero, xviii, 157, 180,
287, 306, 336
Claudel, P., 74, 268
Clement of Alexandria,
Saint, xix, 147
Clement of Rome, Saint,
xvii
Confucius, 77
Connell, F. J., 68, 174,
227
Councils: Carthage, 251,
353, 356; Florence,
260; Jerusalem, xix,
281; Lyon, 260; Or-
ange, 251, 356; Qui-
ersy, 251; Sens, 251;
Trent, 237, 251, 263,
357, 380, 385, 393

De la Barre, A., 67
De Letter, P., 411
Deman, T., xv, xxix, 67,
260, 268
Denis, P., 410
Descamps, A., 410
Descartes, 146
Dewar, L., 23
De Vaux, 335
Dharme, 143

Dodd, C. H., 23
Donnelly, M. J., 411
Donnelly, P., 68
Dostoievsky, 49
Dubarle, A. M., 265
Dumas, G., 174
Dumas, J. B., 67
Dumont, L., 181
Dupont, J., 23
Durkheim, 61, 109
Dwelshauvers, G., 181,
182, 186

Epictetus, 287
Epicurus, xviii

Farrell, W., 68, 174, 175,
227
Festugière, 35, 140
Foucald, C. de, 60
Francis de Sales, Saint,
xv
Freud, 88, 128, 152, 164,
170, 171

Gardeil, A., 68, 210, 227
Garrigou-Lagrange, R.,
68, 130, 139, 140, 410
Gaudel, 246, 249, 251,
268
Gemelli, P., 171
Gide, A., 38, 45, 108
Gillet, M. S., 67, 138,
174
Gilson, E., xxxix, 67,
68, 173, 174
Ginunez, V., 175
Goguel, M., 22
Grabowski, 269
Green, J., 60
Gregory the Great, Saint,
xix, 149
Guénot, 152

413

ANALYTICAL INDEX